W9-BCL-337

MILTON STUDIES

XXVI

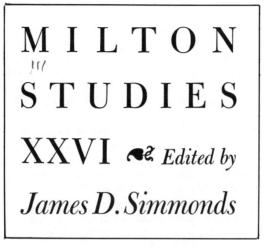

MILTON STUDIES

XXVI *Edited by*

James D. Simmonds

UNIVERSITY OF PITTSBURGH PRESS

MILTON STUDIES

is published annually by the University of Pittsburgh Press as a forum for Milton scholarship and criticism. Articles submitted for publication may be biographical; they may interpret some aspect of Milton's writings; or they may define literary, intellectual, or historical contexts – by studying the work of his contemporaries, the traditions which affected his thought and art, contemporary political and religious movements, his influence on other writers, or the history of critical response to his work.

Manuscripts should be upwards of 3,000 words in length and should conform to the old *MLA Style Sheet*. Manuscripts and editorial correspondence should be addressed to James D. Simmonds, Department of English, University of Western Australia, Nedlands, Perth, W.A. 6009, Australia. Manuscripts and correspondence should be sent via air mail.

Milton Studies does not review books.

Within the United States, *Milton Studies* may be ordered from the University of Pittsburgh Press, Pittsburgh, Pa. 15260.

Overseas orders should be addressed to Baker & Taylor International, 1114 Avenue of the Americas, Fifth Floor, New York N.Y. 10036-7794, U.S.A.

Library of Congress Catalog Card Number 69-12335

ISBN 0-8229-3654-2

US ISSN 0076-8820

Published by the University of Pittsburgh Press, Pittsburgh, Pa. 15260

Baker & Taylor International, London

CONTENTS

MILTON STUDIES

XXVI

THE SOLITARY COMPANIONSHIP OF *L'ALLEGRO* AND *IL PENSEROSO*

Casey Finch and Peter Bowen

SINCE THE ORIGINAL publication of *L'Allegro* and *Il Penseroso* in 1645, readers have treated the poems as companion pieces. This much, rightly enough, has gone unchallenged. There has, however, been little agreement concerning the exact nature of the companionship they form. As Gerard H. Cox has recently said, "it is obvious that 'L'Allegro' and 'Il Penseroso' are companion poems, but precisely how and why they are related remains an open question."[1]

In the commentary that has grown around Milton's paired poems in the last two centuries, a number of critics have emphasized their similarity to one another, as though the companions were in fact identical twins. These willy-nilly find themselves writing in a tradition initiated by Samuel Johnson's laconic complaint that in *L'Allegro* and *Il Penseroso*, though Milton's "images are properly selected and nicely distinguished," nevertheless "the colours of the diction seem not sufficiently discriminated. I know not whether the characters are kept sufficiently apart. No mirth can, indeed, be found in his melancholy; but I am afraid that I always meet some melancholy in his mirth."[2] For such critics, both poems comprise the utterances of a unified speaker concerned to experience the delights of the ideal daily cycle.[3] Whatever its interpretive conclusions, this critical tradition—often quite fruitfully—reads the poems as a kind of unified chain untwisted from what Allegro calls the "hidden soul of harmony."[4] Both *L'Allegro* and *Il Penseroso*, as it were, play the same song in different keys. But other critics—often reading the poems as expressions of Milton's own internal debate over the choice of a poetic career—have emphasized the antithetical nature of the two poems, arguing that, despite superficial similarities, the poems ultimately stand in stark opposition to one another. Insisting that *L'Allegro* and *Il Penseroso* "*are* sharply contrasted," E.M.W. Tillyard states, "from first to last the poems are constructed on the contrasted eulogy of day and night."[5] Still others, comfortable with neither extreme, argue that together the companion poems form a kind of dialectic. Maren-Sofie Røstvig points out that though in *L'Allegro* and *Il Penseroso* the "personalities are directly opposed [and] find happiness in settings and activities which are equally opposed," the poems are nevertheless "complementary and not contradictory."[6] As Norman B. Council has it, "*L'Allegro* and *Il Penseroso* give artful form and harmony to the total experience they have acquired. . . . One vision neither excludes nor includes the other. Two leaves of a diptych, *L'Allegro* and *Il Penseroso* together provide a picture of Milton's 'cycle of universal knowledge.'"[7]

But, meanwhile, almost nothing has been said specifically of the companionship itself; for the majority of critics, it seems simply to go without saying. Exegeses in whatever form invariably locate the poems in one relation or another. But whether *L'Allegro* and *Il Penseroso* are considered insufficiently delineated, sharply contrasted, or operating in a kind of dialectic, their companionship as such is everywhere taken for granted. When they have done so at all, critics have accounted for this companionship by working from the inside out; each has first arrived at separate interpretations of what Mirth and Melancholy mean in their respective poems, and then attempted in one way or another to synthesize the two readings. It is as if the poems were best read separately at first, and only afterwards seen as continua. Few critics have investigated the poems' companionship not simply as a function of their adjacency but as their very condition of possibility.

For the companionship of *L'Allegro* and *Il Penseroso* generates its own rhetorical conditions and calls for interpretive methods quite unlike those that suffice for single or isolated poems.[8] What would be the form of a criticism that attempted to account rigorously for the nature of this companionship? If, for instance, it is true, as Harold Bloom argues, that new texts (ir)rationally revise old, that poems generally mark moments of struggle or, as the case may be, intense companionship with their precursors, what are we to make of a pair of poems that seem more interested in revising one another than (mis)reading earlier poems? What are the critical consequences if texts such as *L'Allegro* and *Il Penseroso* operate not as separate entities that happen to lie side by side, nor even as opposing or complementary panels of a diptych, but as a dynamic structure in which meaning is generated by the poems' interactions? For *L'Allegro* and *Il Penseroso* ask the reader to locate meaning exactly where none can be statically found; what meanings they yield are derived not from either poem but precisely from their relation to one another. What John Guillory calls a "succession of voices" operating in the Miltonic poem in general and creating the effect of an interior dialogue of "poets talking and listening to one another" is literalized in *L'Allegro* and *Il Penseroso*.[9] We cannot therefore treat their companionship simply as a conventional or generic consideration that can be held in abeyance as we read them. Instead, the relationship of *L'Allegro* and *Il Penseroso* creates a unique situation in which the reader confronts neither two separate poems nor a single, two-part poem but rather the companionship of utterances at once separate and fused. Radically dualistic, the companion poems thus register a powerful alternative to the isolationism, self-sufficiency, and integrity that elsewhere Milton champions (in his praise, for instance, for the Lady's chastity in *Comus* and in his insistence on the self-sufficiency of Scripture in *Of Prelatical Episcopacy*). As such, the poems embody what Barbara K. Lewalski sees in *Paradise Lost* as the "basic human predicament" in which one's fundamental autonomy must be reconciled with "the need for the other, the inescapable bonds of human interdependence."[10]

For while the poems urge a unification with one another, they insist on a necessary and inviolable condition of independence. This seeming paradox is both the project and promise of companionship: to be separate and together at once. The subjects/narrators, Allegro and Penseroso, float through the poems comingling with others and deploying a vocabulary of companionship even as they remain ultimately apart, not only from each other, but from everything else around them. Indeed, the two poems—so prominently married by a tradition of publication—seem unavoidably locked in a condition of textual self-consciousness where, no matter how hard each tries to extricate itself from the embrace of the other, neither can stop thinking and dreaming about its companion. And for the reader, correspondingly, all attempts to establish an intimacy with either poem will be distanced by a lingering remembrance and anticipation of his or her liaison with the other; the very double structure of *L'Allegro* and *Il Penseroso* necessitates the reader's infidelity to either poem. At every level, the poems refuse a sentimental representation of perfect union, and attempt instead to establish between themselves a dynamic relation that can never be closed. We will argue that this relation can best be described as a *solitary companionship*, an oxymoronic condition of shared solitude in which the poems are fused and separated in one and the same movement. First, however, it will be useful to explore more generally the function of companionship in Milton's paired poems and in Milton's work as a whole.

This much is certain: Milton's companion poems above all concern companionship. Johnson's apparently sensible claim that "Mirth and Melancholy are solitary" and that in the poems "no mention is therefore made of a philosophical friend or a pleasant companion" is nevertheless misleading;[11] for there is little in the companion poems that is not an instance, in one form or another, of the desire to share and to merge. In

L'Allegro we hear the merry, companionable music of the "Bells" and "jocund rebecs" that "sound / To many a youth, and many a maid, / Dancing in the Checker'd shade" (93, 94–95). We follow the "Cock," in his sexualized desire for companionship, as he struts stoutly and enticingly before his "Dames" (49, 52). We watch, as well, the amiable train of Mirth's companions as it gathers:

> Jest and youthful Jollity,
> Quips and Cranks, and wanton Wiles,
> Nods, and Becks, and Wreathed Smiles,
> Such as hang on *Hebe's* cheek,
> And love to live in dimple sleek;
> Sport that wrinkled Care derides,
> And Laughter holding both his sides. (26–32)

Jest, Jollity, Sport, Laughter—each personification is characterized by flirtatiousness and as such presupposes an immediate and intimate acquaintance with whom it can exchange its playful glances and smiles; like Hebe, cupbearer of the Olympic gods, each encourages good cheer and companionship. Indeed, in *L'Allegro* as a whole the world itself is personified and in this way made companionable. The pastoral "Hamlets" themselves enticingly "invite" us, even as friends might, to join them in their musical frolicking:

> Sometimes with secure delight
> The upland Hamlets will invite,
> When the merry Bells ring round,
> And the jocund rebecs sound
> To many a youth, and many a maid,
> Dancing in the Checker'd shade;
> And young and old come forth to play
> On a Sunshine Holiday. (91–98)

The natural world—indeed, the very order of things—is flirtatious, procreative. Significantly, with Allegro, we see "Mountains on whose barren breast / The laboring clouds do often rest" (73–74). In *L'Allegro* there is no outside to the movement of companionship; the earth and the sky themselves are sexually paired.

Il Penseroso, for its part, discovers Melancholy, its presiding deity, "commercing" companionably "with the skies" (39). Melancholy, of course, is the offspring of an incestuous liaison, a companionship that has broken bounds:

> Thee bright-hair'd *Vesta* long of yore,
> To solitary *Saturn* bore;

His daughter she (in *Saturn's* reign
Such mixture was not held a stain).
Oft in glimmering Bow'rs and glades
He met her, and in secret shades
Of woody *Ida's* inmost grove,
While yet there was no fear of *Jove*. (23–30)

The melancholic deity thus comes from a kind of licentious mirth, an incestuous companionship enacted again and again between Vesta and Vesta's father, Saturn. The originary moment of the goddess of solitude, ironically, is thus emphatically imaged as an intimate meeting, a "mixture," as Milton has it, of familial companions. And what is more, through the course of this supposedly solitary poem, we hear of the marriage of "*Canace*" (112);[12] of Aurora's sensual companionship with Cephalus, "the Attic Boy" (124); and of "such consort as [the waters] keep" (145) with one another. The very "*Daemons*" of the poem, as if guided by the spirit of companionship, have "a true consent / With Planet, or with Element" (95–96). Penseroso's deity, moreover, is graced by her attendant train, her sphere of companions. As the poet implores:

And join with thee calm Peace and Quiet,
Spare Fast, that oft with gods doth diet,
And hears the Muses in a ring
Aye round about *Jove's* Altar sing.
And add to these retired Leisure,
That in grim Gardens takes his pleasure;
But first, and chiefest, with thee bring
Him that yon soars on golden wing,
Guiding the fiery-wheeled throne,
The Cherub Contemplation. (45–54)

Calm "Peace and Quiet," then, are joined garrulously with Melancholy. Fast comes to the festival. And Contemplation—given by definition to solitude, to soaring through the skies—seems, like Leisure, to have quit a customary retirement in order to participate in the solemn but nevertheless festive and companionable occasion.

The very rhetorical postures of the companion poems tell also of companionship; for, as Geoffrey Hartman observes, each speaker "is not petitioning but propositioning his goddess."[13] Each poem thus narrates a kind of companionship or, rather, a courtship in which the supplicant banishes a rival in order exclusively to proposition his desired deity. Each does so, moreover, in a vocabulary, ubiquitous in the twinned poems, of meeting, consorting, commercing, neighboring, linking, and marrying. Each appropriately invokes the presence of companions (Corydon and Thyrsis) and lovers (Vesta and Saturn, Zephyr and Aurora, Orpheus and Eurydice, Venus and Bacchus). And each thus sponsors a kind of marriage. We might indeed regard Hymen, though officially present only in *L'Allegro*, as the presiding deity of the companion poems; everywhere in them marriages (official or otherwise, sanctioned or almost scandalous) are proposed, described, and enacted.

The most significant companionship, however, operates not among the poems' characters or personae but between the poems themselves. For as the history of their readership attests — a history that recognizes how the poems' insistent use of personification invites readers, in turn, to personify the poems themselves — *L'Allegro* and *Il Penseroso* are best read against or, rather, alongside one another, as companions. But what precisely does the companionship between *L'Allegro* and *Il Penseroso* constitute? And what, in general, is the nature of companionship for Milton?

We would do well to look briefly, by way of an answer, to *Paradise Lost*. For, as Jean Hagstrum rightly suggests, "the rich and complex ideal of the divorce tracts — a companionship that is amorous, relaxing, spirited, cheerful, comforting — is fully realized in the Edenic happiness of Adam and Eve." "Men and women are refreshed by 'apt and cheerful conversation' (preface to *Divorce* 1; 2:235), 'conversation' being a term that referred more broadly to total companionship than it does today." Now, for Milton, companionship's "most endearing quality arises from its union of contraries of total individuality and total mutuality."[14] Edenic companionship apparently involves a mysterious admixture of difference and identity of which, in Milton's words, "meet and happy conversation is the chiefest and the noblest end."[15] As God explains in his reply to Adam's unconscious request for a wife, for "conversation with his like to help, / Or solace his defects" (VIII, 418–19):

> I, ere thou spak'st,
> Knew it not good for Man to be alone
> . . . .
> What next I bring shall please thee, be assur'd,
> Thy likeness, thy fit help, thy other self,
> Thy wish, exactly to thy heart's desire. (VIII, 444–45; 449–51)

"Thy likeness"; "thy other self" — companionship marks the strange and delightful intersection of similitude and otherness, identity and difference. As Janet E. Halley has it, "Adam and Eve discover their sameness and equality as well as a structure of differences that makes each the incomplete part of a heterosexual pair that is the only whole."[16] Such a union constitutes what Milton — in an excised song from the Trinity Manuscript "Arcades"—calls a "high misterious holie spousall."[17] And since it requires a harmony of dissonant parts, a *coincidentia oppositorum*, it is perhaps inevitable that everywhere in Milton's oeuvre—as here in *Paradise Lost*—such companionship is most intensely articulated in its loss or absence; it is as though the precarious unity of companionship could be fully realized only in solitude. Recall, for instance, the words of the grieving Thyrsis for his lost companion in "Epitaphium Damonis":

> Pectora cui credam? quis me lenire docebit
> Mordaces curas, quis longam fallere noctem
> Dulcibus alloquiis, grato cum sibilat igni
> Molle pirum, et nucibus strepitat focus, at malus auster
> Miscet cuncta foris, et desuper intonat ulmo?[18] (45–49)

Here, while Milton's tenacious, repetitive syntax conducts a kind of deliberate and extended search for the lost object of desire, the interrogative mood seems correspondingly though futilely to seek a reply from the very companion, Diodati, who has died (prematurely) and who therefore cannot respond. The "sweet conversation" (*dulcibus alloquiis*) that once functioned almost literally as sustenance against hunger and as shelter against the elements is, as in *Lycidas* (an elegy mourning yet another premature death), fully understood only in its loss, as though intensely present, paradoxically, only in its absence.

This same spirit of companionship, this same doubleness, informs *L'Allegro* and *Il Penseroso*. For the companion poems' "conversation"—etymologically rooted both in the Latin *conversari* ("to live with") and in *convertare* ("to turn around or back")—involves both a marriage of opposites, a state of living with and continually inverting the other, and a play of presence and absence. Cox's reminder of Boethius's words from *De arithmetica* is pertinent here: "Non sine causa dictum est, omnia quae ex contrariis, harmonia quadam conjungi atque componi. Est enim harmonia, plurimorum adunatio, et dissentientium consensio."[19] Contextualizing *L'Allegro* and *Il Penseroso* within the hermetic rather than the Neoplatonic tradition, Cox reads the pleasurable variety of the poems as "less an end in itself than the means to realize what was called the coincidence of contraries" (p. 50). It is, we would argue, precisely this paradoxical mutuality of modes—modes that remain nevertheless sharply distinguished—that characterizes the companionship of *L'Allegro* and *Il Penseroso*. Their "conversation" is structured as a play of absence and presence, of identity and difference.

Tropologically, this companionship, this "coincidence of contraries," constructs an oxymoron. Noting the privileged use of oxymora in Milton's poetry, Leland Ryken defines them mystically as "the principle of combining two empirical phenomena to suggest a transcendental realm in which the sum is greater than the parts."[20] And it is useful, certainly, to bear this notion in mind while reading *L'Allegro* and *Il Penseroso*, for together the companion poems suggest a "realm" quite different from what each might inhabit independently. The term *transcendental*, however, is misleading, since the movement between oxymoronic terms is horizontal rather than vertical. Secondly, *sum* implies a finality, an interpretive stasis which would, in effect, dismiss the individual identity of either poem by prematurely erasing the border between them. The paradox of the oxymoron, on the contrary, results precisely from letting the border between its terms stand, even as we are forced continually to shuttle across it. Such has been, from the beginning, the paradoxical nature of *L'Allegro* and *Il Penseroso*.

The oxymoronic condition is articulated by Penseroso as an ecstasy: "Dissolve me into ecstasies, / And bring all Heav'n before mine eyes" (165–66). This utterance constitutes a prayer for the erasure of borders, the dissolution of the body, even as it insists on the distinction between subject and object, between "mine eyes" and "all Heav'n." Poetically, it is each speaker's ecstatic trespassing of one poem's border to enter the other, his precarious crossing of the space between *L'Allegro* and *Il Penseroso*, that constructs the figure of an oxymoron. The trespass additionally transforms the linear progression of the poems into an endless circle or, rather, a kind of Mobius strip, a simultaneously two-sided and one-sided loop on which *L'Allegro* and *Il Penseroso* are continually doubling back on one another. What is banished in the first poem is oxymoronically invoked in the second, only to be banished again in the first. This process, as the criticism of the poems attests, is quite endless.

Indeed, together the two companion poems or, rather, *their companionship itself* constitutes a kind of Derridean double session where the play of their meaning—and the meaning of their play—functions somewhere between them and within them at once. Like the *Paradise Lost* of Herman Rapaport's analysis, *L'Allegro* and *Il Penseroso* form a "text that is cloven, whose terms are . . . in play in the ribbon that at once separates and confuses them." Together they enact a bifurcation, a folding over onto one another of two texts, so that the blank space between them, the fold, the residence of their meaning, lies in a state of perpetual suspension. Each poem functions by referring to a half-absent, half-present text, in Milton's words, its "likeness" and its "other self."[21] We might argue—thinking at once of rabbinical exegeses, of Blake's *Songs of Innocence and Experience*, and of John Ashbery's "Litany"—that

L'Allegro and *Il Penseroso* are best read as a double-columned poem in which each column reveals itself in terms of its other, exists on the threshold of the other, invading it and yet remaining apart.

Together the poems thus constitute a paradigm for the contingencies of intertextual relations; to read them is to experience a bifurcated text neither half of which is separate nor inseparable from its "likeness" and its "other self." Each is to the other a kind of mirror that reflects even as it distorts it. Here we are reminded of the interplay of likeness and difference, of absence and presence, operative in the similes of *Paradise Lost* or, for that matter, of *Paradise Regained*, where the epic narrator compares great things with small or "small things with greatest" (*PR* IV, 564). What Rapaport says of the Miltonic epic is equally true for *L'Allegro* and *Il Penseroso:* "A present moment can be understood as the effect of moments which are strictly speaking not present or there at all. The scene of the now is, therefore, always an effect of scenes elsewhere" (pp. 81–82). The conversation between *L'Allegro* and *Il Penseroso* is played out in the oscillations of a double structure: the meaning of the one resides ultimately in the other, is both replaced by and mimed by the other. Readers find themselves continually shuttling back and forth across the precarious space between the poems, a space that simultaneously separates and joins them.

But while Milton's companion poems indeed enact such bifurcated intertextuality, at the same time we must remain alert to a certain movement by which they refuse the deconstructive condition of indeterminacy. For the Derridean doubling exposes merely the familiar and rather inconsequential "law of indecision," the empty and politically uncommitted notion of undecidability inherent in the fold of a doubled text that ultimately escapes any exhaustive treatment. But if the larger meanings of *L'Allegro* and *Il Penseroso* are finally inexhaustible, there is at the same time no moment within them that resists interpretation, that sets up deliberate barriers to reading. The trouble with deconstruction—in its vulgar form at any rate—is that it habitually confuses the inexhaustible with the undecidable.[22] Whatever indeterminacy is operative in *L'Allegro* and *Il Penseroso* functions as a means to an end and not an end in itself. The poems' double structure leads not to the immobilized condition of undecidability but rather to a movement of endless expansion, a plurality of meanings and not a state of meaninglessness. Nowhere in *L'Allegro* and *Il Penseroso* do we confront what Rapaport discovers in *Paradise Lost*—a "Miltonic economy of strategic twisting or torsion, what amounts to a violent skidding movement in which fallen and unfallen [or mirthful and melancholic] columns of language are put into relation" (p. 72).

The Miltonic economy at play in the companion poems, rather, is a movement of oscillation, a wafting to and fro, a modulation, a caress and not a torsion. The difference is crucial; it involves the distinction between a Derridean language of violence and a Miltonic language of pleasure and companionship. For if the blank space between *L'Allegro* and *Il Penseroso* forms an abyss, a moment of pure suspension, the result is nevertheless as immeasurably meaningful as it is delightful.

The result, indeed, is an immensely pleasurable abundance of meanings. From our experience of the poems themselves we know that whatever aporia they create through their doubleness generates not discomfort and undecidability but rather an expansive pleasure, Miltonic delight, and specifically the suspended, timeless enjoyment of companionship. This must be stressed; the play of absence and presence, of identity and difference, that constitutes the contingent and oxymoronic companionship of the two poems, does not undermine their structure with an entropic or deconstructive force. Readers are neither immobilized nor excluded from the play of doubleness; instead, they are flirtatiously courted by the poems, individually and as companions. What is more, just as the abundance offered by the poems' landscapes and situations brings their personae not to a condition of stolid immobility but to an almost childish excitement about new experience, so as readers we discover ourselves neither frozen in the face of textual indeterminacy nor lost in a netherworld of meaninglessness; rather, we are caught up, like the poems, in the joy of unfolding, exploring, and seeing new things. Allegro exclaims, "Straight mine eye hath caught new pleasures / Whilst the Landscape round it measures" (69–70), and Penseroso thrills "to unfold / What Worlds, or what vast Regions hold / The immortal mind that hath forsook / Her mansion in this fleshly nook" (89–92). Each speaker takes an almost imperialistic pleasure in annexing new discoveries into his poem's domain; and readers have shared the exuberant delight of such expansiveness.

To be sure, though, the effect of the continuous loop the poems form is to defer forever the stasis of resolution. Each poem "closes" not on a final but on a conditional note. Allegro says to the deity, "These delights if thou canst give, / Mirth, with thee I mean to live" (151–52); and Penseroso, for his part, concludes, "These pleasures *Melancholy* give, / And I with thee will choose to live" (175–76). Stanley Fish's comment that "these conditionals are false because the conditions they specify have already been met" is only partially true.[23] For the pleasures are simultaneously enjoyed *and* deferred. Much of the poems' satisfied tone results precisely from the deferral of pleasure, as is indicated both by the prevalent use of the conditional and by the implied conditional of imagined situations. This is significantly also the pleasure of the Miltonic oxymoron, a pleasure that perpetuates itself by continually deferring resolution. In either poem, the speaker must logically dismiss a previous desire in order to pursue its opposite. In the larger conversation between the poems, however, each banishment is in turn converted into an invocation, each invocation into a banishment. This loop produces an almost dizzying effect in which the banishment of each deity coincides with its invocation, and the propositions at the end of the poems never exclude the possibility that something better might come along. There can thus be no ideal reader of *L'Allegro* and *Il Penseroso*, for no oscillation of comparison can swing back and forth fast enough to place the reader in both poems at once.

The poems' companionship resolves this problem, nevertheless, by locating pleasure not in fixing borders or making clear distinctions but in imagining seemingly endless possibilities. By offering an ostensibly infinite field of new options, the poems articulate the oxymoron of solitary companionship not as an indissoluble marriage but as a continually reconfiguring series of partnerships. In this respect, *L'Allegro* and *Il Penseroso* anticipate Milton's conviction in *The Doctrine and Discipline of Divorce* that marriages are formed and broken according to spouses' inward sense, at one moment, of absolute union with one another and, at the next, of irrevocable incompatibility: "for as the glory of God & [spouses'] esteemed fitnes one for the other, was the motive which led them both at first to think without other revelation that God had joyn'd them together: So when it shall be found by their apparent unfitnes, that their continuing to be man and wife is against the glory of God and their mutuall happines, it may assure them that God never joyn'd them" (YP, II, 276–77). There is no sense of continuity here, no allegiance that binds one moment to the next; rather, life is articulated as a discrete series of paratactic moments, each divided sharply from the other. One minute, God has *already* joined these companions; the next, God has *already* divorced them or, rather, they were never joined in the first place. Any sense of an identity stable enough to survive these moments of transition is altogether elided; and we are left with a (non)succession of moments, each frozen in time, each absorbing into itself all of the past and all of the future. Phenomenologically, *L'Allegro* and *Il Penseroso* seek to transcend the ultimately confining laws of time and space, moving here and there in their pursuit of infinite pleasure, encouraging a dreamlike atmosphere, a sort of polymorphous perversity that continually discovers pleasure everywhere, and feels no obligation to linger. While the speakers, as many critics have noted, are acutely alert to their surroundings, they are at the same time almost completely unaware of just how drastically the landscape is shifting under them. Allegro moves within a matter of lines from "Russet Lawns and Fallows Gray" (71) to "Mountains" (73) to "Meadows" (75) and "Tow'red Cities" (117). Hartman locates this free spirit in the apparent democracy operative among the poems' mythic elements, in the admixture of "established divinities (Venus, Mab, Aurora); personified abstractions (Melancholy, Tragedy, Mirth); and spirits of the place (the 'Mountain Nymph, sweet Liberty'). [Milton] does not encourage us to discriminate the kindred spirits; in fact, by mixing them with a fine promiscuity, he produces the sense of a middle region in which everything is numinous and semidivine" (*Beyond Formalism*, p. 286). This "fine promiscuity" extends to the poems' movements, which shift with almost no differentiation between stories and dreaming and physical description. This mood, moreover, is "semidivine" because, being neither absolutely human nor absolutely divine, it plays delightfully at the very borders of difference.

Each poem, we would argue, is a dreamscape of sorts, and as such can be read profitably (though certainly not definitively) as the other's unconscious, as a dream lying beneath its companion. Each dreams (and is the dream of) its other, even as Eve in *Paradise Lost* had been wont—before Satan's insinuations—to dream of Adam, her companion and her other self (*PL* V, 30–32). It is helpful to conceive of the relation between the two poems as a dynamic in which each performs on its companion a series of tropes and reversals not unlike the Freudian dream-work.

John Via, for instance, notices that the nightingale of *Il Penseroso* finds its inverted image in the lark *L'Allegro*. Tillyard points out that whereas in *L'Allegro* the "great Sun" (60) shines brightly and triumphantly, in *Il Penseroso* "the sun is futile, serving merely to show the foolish motes that hover in its beams."[24] In *L'Allegro* the deity is implored to "Come, and trip it as ye go / On the light fantastic toe" (33–34); in *Il Penseroso*, by contrast, the speaker asks, "Come pensive Nun, devout and pure, / Sober, steadfast, and demure" (31–32), "Come, but keep thy wonted state, / With ev'n step, and musing gait" (37–38). Mirth, in the second of her genealogies, was conceived sociably and frolicsomely in a brightly lit bed of flowers:

The frolic Wind that breathes the Spring,
Zephyr with *Aurora* playing,
As he met her once a-Maying,
There on beds of Violets blue,
And fresh-blown Roses washt in dew,
Fill'd her with a daughter fair,
So buxom, blithe, and debonair. (18–24)

Melancholy, on the contrary, is conceived in "Bow'rs and Glades" (27) and in the "secret shades / Of woody *Ida's* inmost grove" (28–29), that is, in the green darkness of the forest. Or again, the "not unseen" (57) of *L'Allegro* directly reverses the "unseen" (65) of *Il Penseroso*. One poem continually discovers a dreamy, troped version of itself in the other.

Consider, for instance, the poems' much-discussed towers. Cleanth Brooks and Don Cameron Allen have analyzed the different occurrences of the tower in the poems, contrasting the studious Platonist in the tower of *Il Penseroso* with the more social towers of *L'Allegro*. It is said of Allegro's eye that "Towers and Battlements it sees / Bosom'd high in tufted Trees, / Where perhaps some beauty lies, / The Cynosure of neighboring eyes" (77–80). And Penseroso implores:

> let my Lamp at midnight hour,
> Be seen in some high lonely Tow'r,
> Where I may oft outwatch the *Bear*,
> With thrice-great *Hermes*, or unsphere
> The spirit of *Plato* to unfold
> What Worlds, or what vast Regions hold
> The immortal mind that hath forsook
> Her mansion in this fleshly nook. (85–92)

Thus, while Allegro *sees* a tower, Penseroro *is seen* in a tower. But whereas the tower in *L'Allegro* houses a "beauty" watched by "neighboring eyes," the tower in *Il Penseroso* houses a Neoplatonic enthusiast who "outwatch[es] the *Bear*." The active locates its other in the passive; but equally, the passive, the seen, in *L'Allegro* is relocated in the studious, vigilant, and active seer of *Il Penseroso*. There is, moreover, no reason to doubt that the tower Allegro discovers "high in tufted Trees" is the selfsame tower from which Penseroso ponders the dawn of day. *L'Allegro* dreams *Il Penseroso* by imagining a figure in the tower conscious of the attention it draws. One poem, as it were, "sees" the other, if only as a distant, dreamlike vision.[25]

Each poem inverts the other and is, in its turn, transformed through a dreamlike mechanism into the other. It is helpful to think of these displacements as the operations of Fancy, which Adam describes to Eve in his strikingly Freudian theory of dreams:

> But know that in the Soul
> Are many lesser Faculties that serve
> Reason as chief; among these Fancy next
> Her office holds; of all external things,
> Which the five watchful senses represent,

She forms Imaginations, Aery shapes,
Which reason joining or disjoining, frames
All what we affirm or what deny, and call
Our knowledge or opinion; then retires
Into her private Cell when Nature rests.
Oft in her absence mimic Fancy wakes
To imitate her; but misjoining shapes,
Wild work produces oft, and most in dreams,
Ill matching words and deeds long past or late. (*PL* V, 100–13)

In Eve's ominous dream, "Mimic Fancy" has translated Reason's thoughts by a distorted mimesis, "Ill matching words and deeds" to produce its "Wild work" of "Imaginations" and "Aery shapes." But, as we have seen, the structure of *L'Allegro* and *Il Penseroso* complicates matters since both dream and are dreamed by the other. In effect, the companion poems constitute a system continually and delightfully at play, recycling itself again and again through a perpetually renewed series of displacements, what Thomas M. Greene calls a pattern of "retrospective internalization."[26]

This operation is seen most clearly in the banishments that function as prologues to both poems. These banishments, of course, work first of all to clear a space for the propositioned deity; but at the same time, this space is necessarily occupied by the opposing deity. In each case, that is, the banishment simultaneously invokes and exorcises the deity, if simply because the offending deity must be invoked *in order* to be exorcised. In addition, the banishments belong properly by their subject matter to the other poem. Their incursions into the companion poems—the presence of mirth in the prologue of *Il Penseroso*, of melancholy in the prologue of *L'Allegro*—mark the most obvious mechanism by which each poem finds its way into the other. Banishment paradoxically proves the surest means by which one poem invades the other; for if each poem desires to banish from within itself the other, it can do so only by uttering its name, by conjuring up its antagonistic presence. Mirth must call on Melancholy to be mirthful; and Melancholy must invoke Mirth in order to be alone. The poems unravel the very distortions they produce even as they cannot stop raveling new strands together; in a loop that is delightfully endless, what one poem twists the other untwists.

Indeed, Miltonic companionship problematizes the very distinction between twisting and untwisting, between, as it were, *L'Allegro* and *Il Penseroso*. For in the companion poems there are always *two* operations, what we might call a simultaneous dreaming and undreaming. And it is at this threshold, the threshold of the Miltonic oxymoron, that the poems turn on one another in a strange and delightful double movement, a kind of endless conversation in which each poem remains inviolably itself *and* grounded by the other. Together they enact a solitary companionship.

Consider, for example, Allegro's penultimate prayer:

> And ever against eating Cares,
> Lap me in soft *Lydian* Airs,
> Married to immortal verse,
> Such as the meeting soul may pierce
> In notes, with many a winding bout
> Of linked sweetness long drawn out,
> With wanton heed, and giddy cunning,
> The melting voice through mazes running;
> Untwisting all the chains that tie
> The hidden soul of harmony. (135–44)

This constitutes a frantic race which is both an entangling and an untwisting. The passage unfolds in a play of oppositions, a vocabulary of companionship (marrying, meeting, linking, tying) placed oxymoronically alongside a vocabulary of separation (piercing, melting, untwisting). Indeed, the two oxymorons embedded at the passage's center ("wanton heed, and giddy cunning") are emblematic of its general oxymoronic nature. Transitory "*Lydian* Airs" are married to "immortal verse." The soul meets, and nevertheless pierces (or is pierced). Music links and untwists.

And while Allegro longs for a music that will breach an epiphany, "Untwisting all the chains that tie / The hidden soul of harmony," Penseroso, for his part, longs "to unsphere / The spirit of *Plato* to unfold" the immortal soul (88–89). Cox's analysis is worth quoting at length:

> In both cases, the prefix *un-* expresses the opposite and complementary reaction to some antecedent action, for harmony clearly has to be chained before it can be unchained just as the spirit of Plato has to be ensphered before it can be unsphered. As the optative mood of the passages suggests, the preceding action is potentially reversible by someone who has learned enough to know what he as yet does not know: if one knows that the soul of harmony is hidden, it potentially can be manifest; if one knows that the spirit of Plato has been ensphered, it can be unsphered. (P. 46)

Twisting and untwisting, ensphering and unsphering—such is the Miltonic vocabulary of the twin operations of dreaming and undreaming. What is finally untwisted or unsphered, however, is always the other poem.

For, meanwhile, *Il Penseroso* provides a kind of critique of the prayer in *L'Allegro*. From the melancholic poem we know that the prayer to pierce (or be pierced by) immortal verse, to untwist "the chains that tie / The hidden soul of harmony," constitutes an empty dream. As Penseroso well knows, a frantic race, a giddy oscillation between opposing terms will never manage a true transcendence. Rather, a kind of quiescence is required, a pious solitude in which the votary, far from violently piercing (or being pierced by) immortal verse in an abrupt and startling epiphany, is instead quietly dissolved ("Dissolve me into ecstasies, / And bring all Heav'n before mine eyes" [165–66]). Indeed, what is finally available is not a fully prophetic strain, but rather "something *like* Prophetic strain" (174, emphasis added).

At the same time, *L'Allegro*, for its part, does not hesitate to comment on *Il Penseroso*. Penseroso, for example, imagines that the power of Melancholy might

> bid the soul of *Orpheus* sing
> Such notes as, warbled to the string,
> Drew Iron tears down *Pluto's* cheek,
> And made Hell grant what Love did seek. (105–08)

But as *L'Allegro* reminds us—or tells us in advance—this constitutes a distorted or censored version of the myth, indeed an empty dream. One day, to be sure,

> *Orpheus'* self may heave his head
> From golden slumber on a bed
> Of heapt *Elysian* flow'rs, and hear
> Such strains as would have won the ear
> Of *Pluto*, to have quite set free
> His half-regained *Eurydice*. (145–50)

But it will be in Elysium, and the dream will occupy the space of the conditional. Whatever resurrective power Orpheus's song might have had will be dissipated by death. In *L'Allegro*'s more melancholic version of the myth, the dead Orpheus is able to reminisce only on what success the song he hears *might* have had. In the meantime, of course, Eurydice remains only "half-regained." *L'Allegro* unravels the dream of *Il Penseroso* and exposes the oneiric wish that compelled the supposedly melancholic poem. What one poem twists, the other untwists.

Ultimately, this process in the companion poems can never end. For whatever is unraveled in one poem, whatever is unmasked, is simultaneously modulated, troped, and raveled again in the other. A complete account of the poems' oxymoronic and solitary companionship, of their conversation, would therefore be impossible, if simply because their double structure never allows this conversation to fall into silence, into a finality or immediacy. Thus Fish's application of reader-response theory in his witty essay, "What It's Like To Read *L'Allegro* and *Il Penseroso*," demonstrates the ineffectuality of reading either of Milton's companion poems as an immediate experience. Fish claims that whereas *L'Allegro* frees us from the burden of interpretation "because its parts are arranged in such a way as to exert no interpretive pressures," *Il Penseroso*, by contrast, "operates to *enjoin* the responsibility" of interpreting (pp. 123, 125). So while in *L'Allegro* we are never asked to choose one reading over another (who or what, for instance, comes to the window in line 46?), in *Il Penseroso* we are forever forced into just such interpretive choices.

But Fish's conclusion—that in *L'Allegro* this "absence of choice is a function of the absence of interpretive pressure"—is possible only through the *exertions* of an interpretive pressure, only by pitting the poems against one another, indeed, by choosing. For to recognize, as Fish has it, that between the poems "every point of contact is a point of contrast" (pp. 125, 126), the reader must continually read either poem *through* the other; he or she must—as Fish's own comparison amply demonstrates—continually compare the companion poems. What it's *really* like to read *L'Allegro* and *Il Penseroso* is to be forever half-consciously aware of the other poem, vaguely to understand that your reading is controlled by what you have read already, and will read anew as you continue along the endless loop the poems form. Such is the nature of the solitary companionship of Milton's companion poems; each poem is radically contingent upon the other, even as it struggles to repress the other.

By wrestling vigorously not (immediately at any rate) with the history of the literature but instead with one another, by forming a continuous loop that doubles back on itself infinitely, by simultaneously dreaming and undreaming one another, Milton's companion poems appear to hover or, rather, to orbit one another in a kind of solar system they themselves inaugurate and complete, if only by spinning about in an endless, expansive circle. Nothing other than the brooding *Il Penseroso* lies behind the skipping, light-hearted *L'Allegro*. And behind *L'Allegro*, in turn, there is only that dark, corrective, and melancholic poem, forever misreading it, forever waiting in the wings for a chance either aggressively to supplant or benignly to join hands with its companion. But Melancholy as a modality (as the eighteenth century understood and as the various romanticisms so skillfully forgot) is impossible without Mirth.[27] Like Adam and Eve at the end of *Paradise Lost*, the companion poems are at once solitary and joined hand in hand.

For each poem presents just beneath its surface a faintly recognizable depth which, when penetrated, turns out to be the surface of the other poem. Finally extracting one companion from the other would be, indeed, a Psychean task; for *L'Allegro* and *Il Penseroso,* like mirth and melancholy, are as inextricable as Milton's good and evil in the famous passage from *Areopagitica:*

> Good and evill we know in the field of this World grow up together almost inseparably; and the knowledge of good is so involv'd and interwoven with the knowledge of evill, and in so many cunning resemblances hardly to be discern'd, that those confused seeds which were impos'd on *Psyche* as an incessant labor to cull out, and sort asunder, were not more intermixt. It was from out the rinde of one apple tasted, that the knowledge of good and evill, as two twins cleaving together, leapt forth into the World. And perhaps this is that doom which *Adam* fell into of knowing good and evill, that is to say of knowing good by evill. (YP II, 514)

It is precisely this kind of *involution*, this kind of radical contingency, that articulates the relation of Milton's companion poems "as two twins cleaving together." It is also *our* doom—or, rather, our pleasure—to know *L'Allegro* by *Il Penseroso, Il Penseroso* by *L'Allegro.*

Fish's apology for the linguistic entrapments of *Paradise Lost* offers a more appropriate model: "Only by forcing upon his reader an awareness of his limited perspective can Milton provide even a negative intuition of what another world would be like."[28] By participating oxymoronically in a solitary companionship, each of Milton's twinned poems not only provides a "negative intuition of what another world would be like," but attempts in fact to include that other world within itself. It is this structure, always opening itself to the imagination of other possibilities, that inaugurates a system of continuous play, a system that bridges the distance between desire and satisfaction. In *L'Allegro* and *Il Penseroso,* indeed, desire functions *as* satisfaction. Thus, these poems, forever performing the strange oscillations of dreaming and undreaming, of twisting and untwisting, at once defer satisfaction and grant it; for what each companion dreams, what each desires, will always be the other. And it is precisely this desire for the other that makes it impossible for us ever to read either poem absolutely in isolation or to read them simultaneously; instead, the reader, like the poems themselves, takes an unending pleasure in this solitary companionship.

New York University
Rutgers University

NOTES

For the advice they proffered upon scrupulous readings of early drafts, we are grateful to Ernest B. Gilman, John Rogers, James Schamus, and Arnold Stein.

1. Gerard H. Cox, "Unbinding 'The Hidden Soul of Harmony': *L'Allegro* and *Il Penseroso*, and the Hermetic Tradition," *Milton Studies*, XVIII, ed. James D. Simmonds (Pittsburgh, 1983), p. 45.

2. Samuel Johnson, *Lives of the English Poets*, ed. George Birkbeck Hill (Oxford, 1905), vol. I, p. 167.

3. For an excellent reading of the poems as visions of an ideal day, see Sara R. Watson, "Milton's Ideal Day: Its Development as a Pastoral Theme," *PMLA* LVII (1942), 404–20. Cleanth Brooks, *The Well Wrought Urn* (New York, 1947), pp. 53, 84, calling *L'Allegro* and *Il Penseroso* "twin halves of *one* poem," analyzes how the cool half-lights filtering through the poems symbolically illuminate them as modulated "choices which can appeal to the same mind." In a similar spirit, Rosemond Tuve, *Images and Themes in Five Poems by Milton* (Cambridge, Mass., 1962), p. 35, argues that both poems, for all their apparent differences, finally constitute a single "'praise', the form of 'demonstrative oration' called *encomium.*" The poems' relation to encomia is also noted by A.S.P. Woodhouse and Douglas Bush, eds., *A Variorum Commentary on The Poems of John Milton: The Minor English Poems*, gen. ed. Merritt Y. Hughes (New York, 1972), II, i, 228.

4. John Milton, *L'Allegro*, in *Complete Poems and Major Prose*, ed. Merritt Y. Hughes (New York, 1957), 144, hereafter cited parenthetically in the text.

5. E.M.W. Tillyard, *The Miltonic Setting: Past and Present* (London, 1957), pp. 20, 21. A.S.P. Woodhouse, "Notes on Milton's Early Development," *UTQ* XIII (1943–44), 85, discovers not companionship but competition, suggesting that the poems set forth "rival conceptions of a life of pleasure, the one active and social, the other contemplative and solitary." These critics, accordingly, locate the poems within one or another of several Renaissance generic traditions. Some, with Tillyard, discover as a paradigm the tradition of the debate (academic, burlesque, or otherwise) of which especially Milton's own First and Sixth Prolusions are illustrative. Others, perhaps most notably J. B. Leishman, "*L'Allegro* and *Il Penseroso* in Their Relation to Seventeenth-Century Poetry," in *Milton's Minor Poems* (London, 1969), pp. 120–159, point to the tradition of companion poems, outstanding examples of which include the pair formed by Marlowe's "The Passionate Shepherd to His Love" and Ralegh's "If All the World and Love Were Young" as well as Fletcher's song in praise of melancholy, "Hence, All You Vaine Delights," and the reply of William Strode, "Returne My Joys." See also *John Milton: "L'Allegro" and "Il Penseroso,"* ed. Elaine B. Safer and Thomas L. Erskine (Columbus, Ohio, 1970), p. 3, hereafter called Safer and Erskine.

6. Maren-Sofie Røstvig, *The Happy Man: Studies in the Metamorphoses of a Classical Ideal* (Oslo, Norway, 1962), p. 100, rpt. in Safer and Erskine, p. 28.

7. Norman B. Council, "*L'Allegro, Il Penseroso,* and 'the Cycle of Universal Knowledge,'" in *Milton Studies*, IX, ed. James D. Simmonds (Pittsburgh, 1976), pp. 216, 203. For these critics—and today their opinion prevails—*Il Penseroso* invariably constitutes the transcending moment of the twin poems. As Don Cameron Allen argues in *The Harmonious Vision: Studies in Milton's Poetry* (Baltimore, 1970), enlarged ed., p. 21, "The dream of 'L'Allegro' is slighter in substance, common in poetic experience, and it leads to the sham reality of the theater and the 'wanton heed' and 'giddy cunning' of Lydian

music. The dream of 'Il Penseroso' is of a far higher order, a 'strange mysterious dream' which is succeeded by a mysterious music, 'above, about, or underneath,'" In the words of David Miller, "From Delusion to Illumination: A Larger Structure for *L'Allegro – Il Penseroso*," *PMLA* LXXXVI (1971), 37, "the delights of L'Allegro are real and valued, but like the glories of Greece they cannot stand against the ecstasy of Christian contemplation." As such, the poems mark a steady ascent from delusion to illumination. And for Cox, "Unbinding," 50, 51, whereas in *L'Allegro* the "persona has experienced the pleasing satisfaction of natural harmony," in *Il Penseroso*, by contrast, "Milton extends the possibility of pleasure from the natural to the celestial world"; in the second poem, then, the persona is "prepared for hermetic revelation of a yet higher harmony." But, as we shall see, the poems form an endless loop and not an ascent that leads from *L'Allegro* to *Il Penseroso*.

8. Insisting that *L'Allegro* and *Il Penseroso* "cannot be thought of as one long poem," Herbert J. Phelan, "What Is the Persona Doing in *L'Allegro* and *Il Penseroso?*," in *Milton Studies*, XXII, ed. James D. Simmonds (Pittsburgh, 1987), p. 18, goes so far as to argue that indeed "they ought to be read as separate poems." But Phelan's very thesis depends, of course, on ignoring his own advice; his conclusion that *Il Penseroso* is "the better of the two poems because it exhibits a higher degree of verbal sophistication" (p. 12) is based not on separate readings of the companion poems but on a single reading that juxtaposes one with the other.

9. John Guillory, *Poetic Authority: Spenser, Milton, and Literary History* (New York, 1983), p. 63.

10. Barbara K. Lewalski, "Milton on Women – Yet Once More," *Milton Studies*, VI, ed. James D. Simmonds (Pittsburgh, 1974), p. 5.

11. Johnson, *Lives of the English Poets*, vol. I, p. 166.

12. Interestingly in this respect, Milton here refers to the fourth book of the *Faerie Queene* as, in part, a companion poem to the *Squire's Tale* that completes Chaucer's "half told" tale by marrying Triamond and Canace.

13. Geoffrey Hartman, *Beyond Formalism* (New Haven, Conn., 1970), p. 288.

14. Jean H. Hagstrum, *Sex and Sensibility: Ideal and Erotic Love from Milton to Mozart* (Chicago, 1980), p. 28. In the seventeenth century, of course, the term *conversation* carried within it the same sexual register that *intercourse* carries today.

15. *The Doctrine and Discipline of Divorce*, in *The Complete Prose Works of John Milton*, ed. Don M. Wolfe et al. (New Haven, 1959), II, p. 246, hereafter cited in the text as YP. Milton seems to be responding directly to Augustine's words – to be eerily echoed in Adam's speech in *PL* X, 889–95 – in *De Genesi ad litteram imperfectus liber*, where the Church Father states: "If Adam needed company and good conversation [when God created Eve], it would have been far better managed to have [created] two men as companions and not a man and a woman" (IX, v, 9 [our translation]).

16. Janet E. Halley, "Female Autonomy in Milton's Sexual Poetics," in *Milton and the Idea of Woman*, ed. Julia M. Walker (Chicago, 1988), p. 232. Halley's remark raises the issue of gender relations which is crucial to Milton's notion of companionship but which space limitations will not allow us to explore here. Though much needs to be written on the gendered nature of Miltonic companionship – which is as often homoerotic (consider Milton's friendship with Diodati) as it is heterosexual. Worthwhile efforts, besides Halley's fine essay, include Marcia Landy, "Kinship and the Role of Women in *Paradise Lost*," in *Milton Studies*, IV, ed. James D. Simmonds (Pittsburgh, 1972), pp. 3–18, Lawrence Stone, *The Family, Sex, and Marriage in England, 1500–1800* (New York, 1977); Edward Le Comte, *Milton and Sex* (New York, 1978); Cheryl H. Fresch, "'And brought her unto

the man': The Wedding in *Paradise Lost*," in *Milton Studies*, XVI, ed. James D. Simmonds (Pittsburgh, 1982), pp. 21–33; William Kerrigan, *The Sacred Complex: On the Psychogenesis of "Paradise Lost"* (Cambridge, Mass., 1983); and Diane Kelsey McColley, *Milton's Eve* (Urbana, Ill., 1983).

17. John Milton, *Poems Reproduced in Facsimile from the Manuscript in Trinity College, Cambridge* (London, 1970), p. 4.

18. "To whom shall I confide my heart? Who will teach me to alleviate my mordant cares and shorten the long night with delightful conversation while the ripe pear simmers before the grateful fire and nuts burn on the hearth, when the wicked southwind makes a general confusion outside and thunders in the peak of the elm?" (Hughes's translation.)

19. Boethius, *De arithmetica*, II, p. 32, cited in Cox, p. 50. "Not without reason is it said that everything made up of contraries is organized and connected by certain harmonies. Harmony, after all, is a fusion of pluralities and a unity of dissimilitudes" (our translation).

20. Leland Ryken, *The Apocalyptic Vision in "Paradise Lost"* (Ithaca, N.Y., 1970), p. 91.

21. Herman Rapaport, *Milton and the Postmodern* (Lincoln, Neb., 1983), pp. 71, 177.

22. We should emphasize here that we take issue only with the vulgar forms of deconstruction whose leitmotif is the misguided notion that whatever indeterminacy texts display is somehow crucial to their cultural deployment. We have no complaint with the forms of deconstruction that are concerned with the way that meaning itself (and not meaninglessness) is generated, secured, and put to use.

23. Stanley Fish, "What It's Like To Read *L'Allegro* and *Il Penseroso*," in *Is There a Text in This Class?* (Cambridge, Mass., 1980), p. 132.

24. John A. Via, "The Rhythm of Regenerate Experience: *L'Allegro* and *Il Penseroso*," *Renaissance Papers* (1969), 53 (many others, of course, have noticed this as well); Tillyard, *Miltonic Setting*, pp. 20–21.

25. Moreover, while the "beauty" that "lies" in the tower of *L'Allegro*, which is called specifically "the Cynosure of neighboring eyes," refers to the constellation of Ursa Minor by which Phoenician mariners navigated in antiquity (Woodhouse and Bush, p. 291) and which is now watched by the eager, "neighboring eyes" of the poem's pastoral landscape; in *Il Penseroso*, the persona envisions outwatching "the *Bear*," that is, Ursa Major. Thus, whereas *L'Allegro* figures Ursa Minor, the cynosure watched as a guiding light, *Il Penseroso* imagines outwatching Ursa Major. One poem reverses and circumscribes the other, even as Ursa Major literally surrounds Ursa Minor in the northern sky. "Cynosure," that is, in *L'Allegro* marks simply the condensed center of attraction; but hovering just "around" it, as its wide periphery and its latent meaning, is the bear of Ursa Major, its starry and metonymic companion. For Allen, Penseroso imagines a tower which "has no existence outside the mind of the poet" (*Harmonious Vision*, p. 17). But this is true only if "the mind of the poet" does not include the imaginative world of *L'Allegro*. For, as we have seen, the tower in the darkness of *Il Penseroso* finds its other situated precisely in the unrolling, brightly lit landscape of *L'Allegro;* the expansive vision that imagines "what Worlds, or what vast Regions hold / The immortal mind that hath forsook / Her mansion in this fleshly nook" is condensed into the sheer perception of a figure very much delighted with the "fleshly nook" of this world.

26. Thomas M. Greene, "The Meeting Soul in Milton's Companion Poems," *ELR* XIV (1984), 164. It is interesting to note that the poems thus do not operate as Adam—who assures Eve that "Evil into the mind of God or Man / May come and go, so unapprov'd, and leave / No spot or blame behind" (*PL* V, 117–19)—imagines dreams to oper-

ate. For in their incursions into one another, the companion poems always leave behind a residue of themselves.

27. We might argue that to the extent that English Romanticism, at any rate, sets up *Il Penseroso* as its great model text — ignoring both the corrective measures upon which *L'Allegro* insists and the necessity of reading the mirthful poem alongside and against the melancholic poem — the movement as a whole represses the balanced variety at the very heart of Milton's enterprise.

28. Stanley Fish, *Surprised by Sin: The Reader in "Paradise Lost"* (New York, 1967), p. 4.

MILTON'S EARLY POEMS ON DEATH

Clay Daniel

Readers usually agree that Milton's Latin epicedia, written in the autumn and winter of 1626, are indistinguishable, undistinguished poetical exercises that tell us something about the young poet's literary development but reveal little of significance about his thought.[1] However, there is considerable significance in Milton's treatment in these poems of a theme to which he would continue to turn as long as he would continue to write poetry: death. The problem of death, which will again and again leave its mark on Milton's poetry, here leaves its first visible etchings. In these poems Milton does not so much lament as question and ultimately explain the nature of death in light of his belief in God. Of course through the centuries scholars from Augustine to Calvin already had elaborated a standard Christian position that, broadly stated, sees death as the punishment that a just God inflicts upon guilty man for his link with original sin, together with all the other sins he has added to his individual account. Milton for the most part accepts this position, and upon this cornerstone will erect an epic poem that will seek to "justify the ways of God to men" as it examines "Man's First Disobedience, and the Fruit / Of that Forbidden Tree, whose mortal taste / Brought Death into the World, and all our woe."[2] *Paradise Lost* takes great pains to show us that God is the omnipotent and infallible architect of death, using death to punish the wicked and to reward the virtuous. However, these early poems do not so much illustrate this Christian paradigm as seek to explain deaths that would seem to violate the position that death is the punishment of sin. How can we explain the deaths of the pious and learned amidst a rabble that is left untouched? Why does God allow a Christian infant to be born and then seemingly obliterated? How can we explain God's allowing a devout and skilled young clergyman to die while a corrupt and ignorant clergy continues to creep and intrude and climb over the face of the earth?

I

The Latin epicedia do not anticipate *Paradise Lost*. Instead, together with "On the Death of a Fair Infant Dying of a Cough," they form a pattern that culminates in *Lycidas*. We can see this pattern most clearly by understanding the relationship between Christianity and classicism in the poems. Milton does not, as is usually argued, simply use classicism to complement Christianity in the Latin poems or merely subordinate classicism to Christianity in "Fair Infant" and *Lycidas.*[3] Though Milton sometimes, as in the epicedia on the bishops, uses classical imagery to represent a Christian truth, for the most part he uses classical imagery to represent the anomaly of his paradigm and Christian imagery to resolve that anomaly (when he does resolve it). When representing the problem of death as an apparent random killer, he makes it the classical agent of inscrutable fate or the subordinate of the gods of the underworld or even, as in the infant ode, the consequence of chance, and the other gods cannot interfere with death's operation. However, though benevolent gods cannot prevent death, malevolent ones can inflict it at the behest of one of the aforementioned classical agencies. The consequence of this divine mayhem is indiscriminate or malicious slaughter. These Fates and meddlesome, malevolent, circumscribed deities are particularly disagreeable to a strongly Protestant Milton who insists on the freedom of the will in God and man. This insistence is especially evident in *De Doctrina Christiana*, Book I, chapter ii, where Milton delineates a concept of deity that repudiates the separation of God and fate and that contradicts "the nonsense poets write about Jove" (YP VI, p. 134). So, when explaining apparently senseless deaths, the poems use Christian imagery to reveal a benevolent, omnipotent deity who uses death to chastise the wicked, exalt the pious, and enforce a benign order in the world.

I cannot overemphasize that I will not present *the* classical view of the relationship between the classical gods and fate. I will look at *Milton's* view of this relationship as it is given to us in these early poems; and in these poems, Milton opposes his classical and Christian concepts of death. We can discern Milton's intention to undermine classicism in relation to Christianity and paganism by examining Milton's selection of materials from classical myth and from the logoi and topoi of classical rhetoric. Milton had ample precedent for asserting everlasting life and, to a lesser extent, providence in the classical world.[4] He does at times avail himself of these classical precedents to represent a Christian truth (*Elegia Tertia* and *In Obitum Praesulis Eliensis*) or even a genuine pagan truth (*Epitaphium Damonis*). But, except in *Epitaphium Damonis*, which would require another essay to examine, Milton takes up the darkest strands of classicism to represent the pagan tradition.

With regard to the gods' relationship with death, Milton adopts, with the modifications already noted, the classical tradition that death supersedes them. In classical mythology, the gods' control of death often is determined by their control of fate, which—whether as *moira, aisa,* the *daimon,* or some other entity—classical mythology frequently designates as the arbiter of death. The relationship between the classical gods and fate is complicated and sometimes contradictory. In the Homeric tradition, "frequently Fate and gods seem to be interchangeable in their functions. If Fate spins men's lots, so also do the gods."[5] In some places where the gods appear to be subject to fate, as in the *Odyssey* (III, 269; IX, 52) and the *Iliad* (XVII, 322), they "are constrained, not indeed by Fate as a higher power, but by their own *moirai.*"[6] However, in other places, Homer sometimes actually represents the gods as subject to fate, as in the *Odyssey* (IX, 528–35), where Poseidon permits Odysseus to escape Polyphemus, or as in *Iliad* (XVI, 433–61), where Zeus is unable to preserve his son Sarpedon, an event that Milton alludes to in *In Obitum Procancellarii Medici* (13–16). This tradition was expanded in post-Homeric poetry, where "Fate was at times definitely separated from the gods and sometimes even set above them" (Greene, *Moira,* p. 16). Hesiod expresses this view in his *Theogony,* which tells of the Fates,

> who at their birth
> bestow upon mortals their portion
> of good and evil,
> and these control the transgressions
> of both men and divinities. (218–20)[7]

In his poetry, Milton consistently adopts this tradition. It is not the only classical tradition, but it is Milton's, though with the qualifications noted above.

Milton extends his opposition between classicism and Christianity to the consolations. Since Milton believed that eternal life is the providential reward for those who choose to obey God's laws, it is only within a Christian context that the poems offer genuine consolation. In poems that maintain the classical position that the world is overrun by malicious and/or impotent deities who act at the whim of a Fate that renders freedom of the will almost meaningless, death cannot be the providential door to immortal life for those who choose wisely. Consequently, when portraying his classical view of the afterlife, Milton avoids the consoling precedents of classical myth and rhetoric. Though generally "the classical elegist lacked the optimistic faith in immortality which is an article of Christian dogma,"[8] there was a Latin literary tradition that did offer the consolation of a blissful afterlife. As early as Menander of Laodicea, this rhetorical topos allowed the poet to "remind the sorrowers that the one for whom they weep is in Elyzium." This logoi is evident, among many other places, in poems by Ovid and Statius that speculate on the deceased's enjoyment of the Elysian Fields.[9] Another kind of immortality is evident in Virgil's *Eclogue V*, which celebrates the deification of Daphnis (probably Julius Caesar), and this divine prerogative would be extended to all deceased emperors. More mundane forms of immortality become a common consolation in epitaphs of less exalted Latins.[10] Milton, on the whole, excludes this tradition from the pagan consolation in the poems that we will examine. Instead, he adopts the Homeric tradition that the afterlife, even for a hero like Achilles, is bleak indeed.

A clear pattern of the Miltonic *consolatio* emerges in the epicedia, "Fair Infant," and *Lycidas*. The epicedia examine the deaths of the pious custodians of Cambridge. The deaths of these men, who had lived long and useful Christian lives, do not exactly violate Milton's paradigm, for they merely have discharged their debt, if not to nature, at least to God. However, Milton does not use the occasion of the deaths of these pious and prominent Cantabrigians to expound on the wages of sin and thus the inevitability of death. Instead, the poet dwells on the disquieting fact that death claims the learned and pious with the same stroke as it gathers in the ignorant and useless or, worse, that passes over the rabble altogether. This latter point leads Milton in these poems to posit the frightening possibility that the virtuous are sometimes killed because of their virtue.

In the first of the epicedia, *In Obitum Procancellarii Medici*, unfathomable Fate sends a vengeful Persephone to eliminate the vice-chancellor because he was overly successful as a physician. The poem's consolation is highly conditional, even ironic. Milton's next epicidium, *Elegia Secunda*, asserts that Death, or "Mors" (4), acts in compliance with Avernus (17) or Hades. This mystifying killer passes over the rabble to sate herself on the learned. The poem makes no effort to console. *Elegia Tertia* once again views Death, "Mors fera" ("fell Death"), as an agent of the underworld, "Tartareo diva secunda lovi" ("goddess second to Tartarean Jove") (16). Death is as incomprehensible here as in the previous poems, killing with indiscriminate ease, an ease embodied in the plague that Milton highlights in the poem's beginning. However, this poem attempts to console, and Milton mixes classical and Christian imagery to give us a vision of the deceased in heaven. The consolation fails, however, and evidence suggests that Milton intentionally undermined its effectiveness because genuine consolation is out of place in a world where death is not a providential instrument for punishing those who violate God's immutable laws and rewarding those who abide by them.

The last of the epicedia, *In Obitum Praesulis Eliensis*, prepares for a convincing representation of the Christian afterlife by repudiating the classical view of death in the previous elegies. The assertion of God's eternal providence invests the deceased's ascent into heaven with a validity lacking in *Elegia Tertia*. Consequently, only *In Obitum Praesulis Eliensis* successfully synthesizes Christianity and classicism. However, this synthesis does not represent Milton's concept of classical providence but rather a genuine example of classical imagery representing Christian truth. In these poems, it is the only example of Milton using classical imagery to portray a Christianlike Providence.

"On the Death of a Fair Infant Dying of a Cough" examines another perplexing side of the problem of death: how do we explain the premature death of the pious, in this case a Christian infant? The poem uses Christian imagery to establish the beneficence of death in a world supervised by God's providence and opposes this view to the meaninglessness of death within the context of classical "chance," here abetted by divine bumbling rather than malevolence. In its explanation, the poem expands the consolation provided in *In Obitum Praesulis Eliensis*. It adopts that poem's position that death is actually a boon to the virtuous, who now experience joys incomparable to any to be had on earth. However, the question remains of why God did not permit this worthy infant her allotted threescore years and ten and *then* reward her with heavenly glories. Specifically, there remained a problem that was of particular interest to Milton, who seems to have despised an unearned and self-centered bliss as much as he did a cloistered and unexercised virtue: how does God compensate for the loss of the good the deceased might have wrought on earth? To assert eternal providence, "Fair Infant" expands the consolation to assure us that the infant has been transformed into a celestial advocate that will help mankind much more as this entity than she possibly could as flesh and blood, as she will now be able to "stand 'twixt us and our deserved smart" (69). Additionally, the death prepares the way for the birth of someone who will work such wondrous goodness that the family name will be enshrined "till the world's last end" (77), a prophecy also intended to console the bereaved mother.

The themes developed in the earlier poems reach their complex climax in *Lycidas*. Milton's masterpiece combines the problems examined in the epicedia and "Fair Infant": the death of Edward King afforded Milton the opportunity to explain the questions raised by the enigma of learned, pious clergymen who die amidst an ignorant, useless, and thriving rabble. Additionally, young King's death highlighted the prematurity that provided the puzzling aspect of the infant's death. How can we reconcile this kind of death to a belief in providence? In its explanation, *Lycidas* will take the pattern set forth in "Fair Infant" and parlay it into a masterpiece. It will use classical imagery to weave the mystery of fate, the malice of the underworld, and the blindness of chance into the single horror of "the blind *Fury* with th'abhorred shears" (75), the ultimate embodiment of death in Milton's ancient world; and it will also include the divine blundering of "Fair Infant" in a comic procession of gods who confess their complete inability to prevent Lycidas's death. It then will reject this view as an accurate assessment of the cosmos, using Christian imagery to reveal that providence guides death to bless the virtuous with heaven and to endow the earth with an active and wayfaring Miltonic saint who benefits the world as a supernatural guardian. Additionally, death in this poem marks out for destruction the ignorant who shove, neglect, and glut themselves to their bellies' content, a stark contrast to the epicedia, in which death in its classical guise favored the learned, useful, and pious, who died meaninglessly amidst a prosperous rabble.

II

In Obitum Procancellarii Medici is the first of Milton's epicedia, and it forcefully elaborates the problem of death but leaves the resolution to be worked out in the later poems. And what is the problem concerning death? It is the age-old problem that death often appears to be a force unto itself, randomly striking where it will, without regard to justice or reason, defying the idea that it is subject to Providence. Milton, as he will do in all of these early poems, uses classical imagery to portray this desperate landscape. As the poem opens, it claims that death is an irresistible force ruled by "Parca," "the Goddess of Fate" (2). This assertion establishes that death, controlled by a Fate that supersedes the gods, is an event that the gods cannot forestall. Milton hammers in this point with numerous citations of the untimely and often violent deaths of the gods' mortal offspring. The poem cites the violent deaths of Apollo's children, Aesculapius and Chiron (whom innate immortality cannot preserve from death), and his lovers, Coronis and Hyacinthus. Milton also reminds us that not even Zeus, father of gods, can save his children Hercules and Sarpedon from horrific deaths (8–16). Milton's treatment of Sarpedon's death especially reveals his undermining of the classical tradition. Relating Sarpedon's death, Homer precedes it with a debate between Zeus and Hera (*Iliad* XVI, 431–61).[11] Zeus wants to thwart fate and thus save his son and asks Hera's advice. She warns that such an action "will waken grim resentment" in the rest of the gods, who will also want to rescue a mortal "son from the strong encounter" (447–49).

Such interference would set "the laws of the universe at naught."[12] Milton reduces this philosophical debate, which provides a position resembling Milton's position in *De Doctrina Christiana,* that though God is utterly free he chooses to act according to universal laws (VI, 146), to a scene in which a prostrate deity helplessly weeps over the fate of a favorite.[13]

As the poem concludes we learn that Persephone has killed the physician (37–40). Is Milton modifying his position that Parca is the supreme arbiter of death, making death also the subordinate of the underworld deities? Though classical mythology does not grant the gods of the underworld any special control over death, this position appears in the other two Latin funeral poems that adopt Milton's classical view of death, *Elegia Secunda* and *Elegia Tertia,* which omit references to a Fate. Here, however, it is more probable that Milton cites Persephone to highlight one of the more unhappy aspects of Milton's pagan landscape: though gods cannot prevent death, they, as the executioners of Fate, can inflict it. Hector's death was procured by "fraude turpi Palladis invidae" ("the shameful deceit of vengeful Athene") (13); Aesculapius was the victim of Zeus's thunderbolts (26–28); Apollo, for one reason or another, dispatches Chiron, Coronis, and Hyacinthus; and here Persephone plunges the good doctor into the "horribiles barathri recessus" ("frightful depths of hell") (36).

Milton skillfully uses a traditional part of the elegy, exaggerated praise of the deceased, to render this problem even more bleak. The poem tells us that Apollo himself came to Gostlin for his medical lectures (29–32) and that his ability to thwart death incurred Persephone's ire (37–40). This is not merely Milton's use of standard Renaissance hyberbole. This praise accentuates the argument that death jealously preys upon the learned and useful, killing them because they are exceptional. To support this point, the poem repeatedly cites the deaths of wise healers—Chiron, Macheon, and Aesculapius, whom Zeus killed for the same reason that Persephone killed Gostlin: he proved too great a benefactor to mankind by saving too many lives. Persephone has fatefully reasserted her dominion by showing that this medical savior, who tutored Apollo himself in the art of medicine, lacked the skills to save himself. But in doing so, she has revealed the lack of providence in a pagan world that sees its best men marked out for destruction.

This dismal situation casts an interesting shadow across the speaker's consolation:

> Sit mite de te iudicium Aeaci,
> Subrideatque Aetnaea Proserpina,
> Interque felices perennis
> Elysio spatiere campo. (45–48)

[May the judgement of Aeacus upon you be gentle, and may Sicilian Proserpina smile! May you walk forever among the blessed in Elysium!]

The hope that Persephone, the same deity who slew the medical *Wunderkind*, will smile on the judgment meted out to her new conquest, whom we last saw making his way to her realm through "horribiles barathri recessus," makes the consolation desperate indeed. This desperation is heightened by the poet's wish that "purpureoque hyacinthus" ("the purple-lipped hyacinth") (44) should adorn the grave. This flower in a cemetery does not represent eternal life; in these poems, the deceased in heaven represents eternal life. Instead, Milton cites this myth to highlight once again the limits of the gods, for the flower sprang from the blood of yet another of Apollo's luckless favorites, Hyacinthus, whom this divinity *accidentally* killed through the subterfuge of yet another jealous deity, Zephyrus (who envied Apollo his relationship with the boy). Clearly, Milton intentionally left uncertain whether the doctor makes his way to Elysium. From first to last, the poem remains entrenched in the classical landscape where human life counts for very little. Death is a whim of fate, executed by the ire or accident of the gods; and since heaven belongs to those who responsibly exercise their free will in a world created by a benign, omnipotent, and wise providence, the poem leaves the doctor in the hands of an angry god who deprives the world of healers, while mankind is compensated, if at all, with a grave turned flower bed.

Elegia Secunda, like *In Obitum Procancellarii Medici*, uses exclusively classical imagery, as it represents death as a mystifying, unrelenting killer. This brief poem—its twenty-four lines make it the shortest epicedium—omits references to Parca. Instead it assigns control of death to the deities of the underworld:

Magna sepulchrorum regina, satelles Averni
Saeva nimis Musis, Palladi saeva nimis,
Quin illos rapias qui pondus inutile terrae? (17–19)

[Great queen of sepulchers, accomplice of Avernus—too terrible to the Muses and too terrible to Pallas—why do you not make your prey of those who are useless burdens of the earth?]

Death, "Mors" (4), clearly is subordinate to "Avernus," or Hades, being its "satelles," an attendant or "accomplice" as it is rendered here. But Hades does not stand in relation to Ridding's death in the same way that Persephone stood to Gostlin's death in the previous elegy. Rather, this god of the underworld displaces Parca as the supreme arbiter of death, while Mors has taken on Persephone's vacated position as "magna sepulchrorum regina." Mors kills at the bidding of Hades, just as Persephone, queen of the underworld, under the auspices of Parca, killed Gostlin in *In Obitum Procancellarii Medici.*

Whatever Death's subordination to Hades, she once again supersedes the other deities: "Saeva nimis Musis, Palladi saeva nimis" ("too terrible to the Muses and too terrible to Pallas") (18). In *In Obitum Procancellarii Medici* the gods were unable to intercede for their progeny, and here the poem makes that point with references to the dead beadle's connection with Athene (1–2, 18) and to the deaths of Hippolytus and Aesculapius (9–10), great favorites with Diana and Apollo respectively. But the poem makes this point most emphatically by personifying death as a beadle, an official crier. Death personified as a beadle adds a new twist to the position in the previous elegy that the gods are unable to protect their mortal favorites. That theme darkens, as the beadle Death, unlike Apollo in his slaying of Hyacinthus, *intentionally* eliminates one of her own followers, the beadle Ridding.

Finally, *Elegia Secunda* reinforces the previous poem's contention that death is as perversely senseless as it is autonomous. In *In Obitum Procancellarii Medici* malicious deities, at the behest of unfathomable Parca, specialize in dispatching gifted physicians; and here Queen Death incomprehensibly deprives the world of the useful Ridding while permitting the rabble to linger into ripe and useless old age. The poet wails to Death, "Quin illos rapias qui pondus inutile terrae?" ("Why do you not make your prey of those who are useless burdens of the earth?") (19). "Saeva nimis Musis, Palladi saeva nimis," indeed.

This poem, like *In Obitum Procancellarii Medici,* fails to dispel the terrors of random, meaningless death. In fact, *Elegia Secunda* even lacks the desperate consolation of its predecessor; it provides no consolation at all. Rather, this gloomy poem, echoing several Latin analogues, can only counsel a nigh hopeless lamentation as it bids, "Fundat et ipsa modos querebunda Elegeia tristes, / Personet et totis naenia moesta scholis" ("Let wailing Elegy herself pour out her sad dirge and fill all the schools with its sound") (23–24).[14]

Though all four of the epicedia were written at about the same time, *Elegia Tertia* usually is coupled with Milton's other funeral elegy for a bishop, *In Obitum Praesulis Eliensis,* to contrast with his slighter, more strictly classical efforts commemorating the deaths of Gostlin and Ridding. *Elegia Tertia,* unlike the previous poems, does attempt to provide genuine consolation, and in this effort the poem, like the later lines on Ely, avails itself of Christian imagery. However, the consolation fails, and in this respect *Elegia Tertia* should be grouped with the first two funeral elegies as developing the problem of how death can be reconciled with providence, a problem resolved in *In Obitum Praesulis Eliensis.*

As *Elegia Tertia* opens, we once again encounter death as an indiscriminate killer. Milton first cites the example *par excellence* of random and almighty death: the plague. The plague at this time was busily erasing one-sixth of the souls of greater London, some thirty-five thousand human beings. The speaker harps on the random terror of the plague in the poem's first eight lines:

> Moestus eram, et tacitus nullo comitante, sedebam.
> Haerebantque animo tristia plura meo,
> Protinus en subiit funestae cladis imago
> Fecit in Angliaco quam Libitina solo;
> Dum procerum ingressa est splendentes marmore turres
> Dira sepulchrali mors metuenda face;
> Pulsavitque auro gravidos et iaspide muros,
> Nec metuit satrapum sternere falce greges.

[I was grief-stricken, and without any companion I was sitting in silence. Many sorrows were besetting my spirit, when, lo, suddenly there arose a vision of the baneful destruction which Libitina wrought upon English soil when dire death—terrible with his sepulchral torch—entered the bright, marble palaces of the patricians, attacked the walls that are weighted with jasper and gold, and presumed to mow down hosts of princes with his scythe.]

Here again we see death delighting in snuffing the exceptional, as the plague ravages patricians in their palaces. How can we reconcile this indiscriminate slaughter with a belief in the Christian God? The poet makes no effort to explain here and instead neatly evades this issue by shoving it into the classical past, deciding that Death acts under orders from Libitina, the ancient Italian goddess of corpses. Then the speaker refocuses from pestilence to another kind of plague—war. In lines 9–12, Milton yet once more bewails Death's fine taste for the superior, as he laments the "intempestivis" ("untimely") (10) deaths of Protestant heroes in the Thirty Years War.

How can we account for so much senseless death? The poem tells us in line 16. This is the first line of the formal lament for Bishop Andrewes, and it adopts the rather complicated stance that we have examined in the previous poems, especially *Elegia Secunda:* "Mors fera" ("fell Death") is "Tartareo diva secunda Iovi" ("goddess second to Tartarean Jove"). Death once more is the lethal subordinate to a god of the underworld. But clearly Death here, as in the other two elegies, cannot be contravened by the other gods. Divine intercession is futile, for Death ravages "pulchrae Cypridi sacra rosa" (20) ("the rose, that is sacred to the beautiful Cypris") and "quod alunt mutum Proteos antra pecus" ("the dumb herd which the caves of Proteus nourish") (26).

As the first two epicedia make abundantly clear, in a world where death serves either fate or the gods of the underworld, it can only amount to a random slaughter whose only pattern is that death often singles out the extraordinary. This theme, introduced with references to plague and war in the prologue to the lament, is taken up almost immediately in the lament itself with references to prophetic birds dying with ordinary ones (23–25) and to the destruction of so many of the striking beauties of nature by Death's "fluvio contermina" ("poisonous breath") (21). And, like the previous poems, it laments that Death is particularly fond of the exceptional, here dwelling on the "nobileque" ("noble") (29) victim, using this exaggerated praise to heighten Death's perversity. But, instead of contrasting the nobility of the dead with the surviving rabble, the poem becomes a little more egalitarian by turning to vegetable and brute nature as a foil. With all of plant and animal life to decimate (16–26)—which it does with relish—the poet mourns that Death also hunts down a noble and excellent human.

> Invida, tanta tibi cum sit concessa potestas,
> Quid iuvat humana tingere caede manus?
> Nobileque in pectus certas acuisse sagittas,
> Semideamque animam sede fugasse sua? (27–30)

[Envious one, when such vast power has been granted you, what pleasure is there in staining your hands with human slaughter, in sharpening your unerring darts against a noble breast, and driving a spirit that is half-divine from its habitation?]

In the consolation of *Elegia Tertia* (51–67), Milton for the first time in the epicedia mingles Christian and classical imagery. Replete with various biblical echoes, especially of the Book of Revelation (as in *Lycidas*), the poem tells us how ravaged nature is bathed in a radiant light and the deceased, saluted with divine noises, is taken up to heaven. The consolation also frequently echoes and/or alludes to Lucretius, Catullus, Martial, Virgil, Ovid, Horace, Tibullus, and Apuleius among many others; and Andrewes's ascent into heaven echoes the entrance into Olympus of Hercules—who makes a famous choice that is impossible in Milton's classical cosmos—in the Hellenic tradition, and of various emperors and heroes in the Latin tradition.[15] The consolation, however, is unconvincing, as the fusion of classical and Christian imagery fails. The consolation "does little to suggest a heaven appropriate to the refined spirituality of Lancelot Andrewes." A consolation in which "the gratification of every sense is deftly suggested" is, however, "exactly appropriate to the earthbound *ingenium* of the Latin elegiac poet" whose persona the speaker assumes. Thus, "the young Milton was perfectly aware of a discrepancy between his Christian and classical materials and indeed used it to circumscribe firmly any grandeur on which his *consolatio* might seem to verge."[16] Indeed, nowhere is this discrepancy more clear than in Milton's adaptation of Ovid's *Amores*, I, v, 26. This adaptation in itself would seem to prevent us from seriously regarding the splendors of the ornate consolation (so different from the severe beauty of *Lycidas*). As the celestial vision concludes, the poet declares in the poem's last line, "Talia contingant somnia saepe mihi" (68) ("May dreams like these often befall me!"). The poet here echoes Ovid's glowing account of his "golden day" of sex with Corinna.[17]

Why does Milton use the discrepancy between his classical and Christian materials to circumscribe and even to undermine the consolation? In addition to the reasons cited above, we should note also that *Elegia Tertia* gives only Milton's version of the classical view of what impels death—that it is a random, unpredictable killer that serves the whim of the underworld. This view of death in no way prepares us for the glories of the lengthy consolation. Since heaven is the reward for making proper and free use of the will in a providential universe, it is totally inappropriate in a chaotic universe where death serves no divine purpose except for perhaps divine vengeance on the all too virtuous. In order to include a convincing, and thus for Milton a Christian, consolation, Milton must reveal in the poem that death, far from being an instrument of random or vengeful havoc, is actually guided by the deft hand of a benevolent providence. And this is what he does in *In Obitum Praesulis Eliensis*, which he quickly began after *Elegia Tertia*, and which is the only one of the epicedia to synthesize successfully his classical and Christian imagery.

In Obitum Praesulis Eliensis, Milton's poem on the passing of Nicholas Felton, is composed in a classical meter that identifies it as an invective against death rather than as a eulogy for the deceased.[18] To this effect, Milton reshuffles the gods for yet a new hierarchy of death. It follows *In Obitum Procancellarii Medici* in designating Fate as the supreme arbiter of death. The prior poem had presented Fate as a single goddess, Parca, and here it is reintroduced in its plural form as "ferreis sororibus" (11) ("the implacable sisters" or the Fates—*Parcis*). However, it deviates from that poem by subordinating to Fate(s) not Persephone, but the executioner of the other two epicedia, Death (11, 32) (Mors), or as the poem also calls her, "Tumulis potentem saepe . . . deam" (17) ("the goddess who is powerful in the grave").[19] At this point, death is the chaotic, often malicious force that we have seen in the other three funeral elegies. And once again this force has cut down one of the excellent, "generis humani decus, / Qui rex sacrorum illa fuisti in insula / Quae nomen Anguillae tenet" ("the ornament of mankind, who were the prince of the saints in that island called Ely") (12–14).

However, the poem does not use praise here, as in the other epicedia, as a launching point to lament that death is incomprehensible and perversely vengeful, and then give us a catalogue of deaths from classical myth to support this contention. Instead, Felton's voice from beyond the grave reveals the true nature of death. The bishop assures us that death is not the chaotic, dark subordinate (*filia*) of the autonomous Fates, the underworld (Erebus), or the Furies (Erynis—as also will be suggested in *Lycidas*). Instead, in a complex echo of Hesiod's *Theogony*, lines 904–06, the bishop reveals that death (Mors) serves a providential God and so has the providential qualities associated with it in Milton's Christian cosmos:

> Non est, ut arbitraris elusus miser,
> Mors atra Noctis filia,
> Erebove patre creta, sive Erinnye,
> Vastove nata sub Chao:
> Ast illa, caelo missa stellato, Dei
> Messes ubique colligit;
> Animasque mole carnea reconditas
> In lucem et auras evocat,
> Ut cum fugaces excitant Horae diem,
> Themidos Iovisque filiae;
> Et sempiterni ducit ad vultus patris;
> At iusta raptat impios
> Sub regna furvi luctuosa Tartari,
> Sedesque subterraneas. (31–44)

[Contrary to your notion, O deluded wretch, Death is not the dark daughter of night, nor of Erebus nor of Erynis; nor was she born in the gulf of Chaos. But she is sent from the starry sky to reap God's harvest everywhere. As the flying Hours, the daughters of Justice and Jove, arouse the day, so she summons into the light and air the spirits which are buried under the weight of flesh, and she leads them into the presence of the eternal Father; but because she is just she sweeps the wicked away to the realms of grief in dark Tartarus, to the infernal abodes.]

Hesiod in the *Theogony* (904–06), in a major departure from mainstream classicism, reverses his previous assertion that the Fates are the daughters of Night (217–18) to maintain that they are the daughters of

Jove and Justice. Here Milton's poem repudiates its previous assertion that "implacable" Fates ("ferreis sororibus") control death and then echoes the providential view of this Hesiodic position. Just as "Themidos Iovisque filiae" ("the daughters of Justice and Jove") (40) bring light out of darkness, so death providentially liberates the good souls from the sordid prison of the flesh so that they may enjoy the bliss of heaven, while the "impios" ("wicked") are sent to "luctuosa Tartari, / Sedesque subterraneas" ("dark Tartarus, / . . . the infernal abodes") (42–44). Providence, not inscrutable Fates that negate free will, nor malicious underworld – or any other – deities who interfere with man's exercise of free will, controls death to enforce God's eternal decrees concerning death and sin. Now choice becomes all-important. Here, at last, those who, like Nicholas Felton, choose to exert themselves in pursuit of learning, piety, and usefulness – like Milton – gain the upper hand, while those who choose to remain wicked – something that Milton at this time often took to denote ignorant and useless – are condemned to the dismal misery of the underworld. Within this context, for the pious at least, death is one of the greatest of blessings. Felton claims:

> Hanc ut vocantem laetus audivi, cito
> Foedum reliqui carcerem,
> Volatilesque faustus inter milites,
> Ad astra sublimis feror,
> Vates ut olim raptus ad caelum senex,
> Auriga currus ignei. (45–50)

[I was glad when I heard her calling and eagerly I left my sordid prison. Among the winged warriors I was carried aloft, clear to the stars, like the venerable prophet of old, charioteer of a fiery chariot, who was caught up to heaven.]

In this poem, the fusion of Christian and classical elements works. Amidst references to "deam . . . triformem" ("the triform goddess") (56–57) and the "nitentes . . . fores . . . Olympi" ("the shining portals of Olympus") (62–63), we hear of "vates ut olim" (49) and God's providential rescue of Elijah. The traditional classical arbiters of life and death – the Fates – are denounced as "deities which cannot be harmed and are swift to anger" (29–30) but who are subordinate to a providential Jove, who takes on Christ's function of judging the dead, a task performed in classical mythology by Aeacus, Minos, and Rhadamanthus. Milton transforms the underworld into a fit hell for the wicked; and Felton, like the Roman emperors and heroes, ascends into a heavenly Olympus, which Milton, following Ovid among others, locates somewhere beyond the Milky Way.[20] This fusion, however, does not indicate that Christianity and classical mythology complement one another in the poem. Jove's judgment of mankind is not supposed to represent a genuine classical position; rather, Milton fuses classical with Christian imagery to provide a Christian resolution to the problem of death that the other three elegies had developed with classical imagery.

III

"On the Death of a Fair Infant Dying of a Cough," probably written in 1628, addresses another particularly troublesome instance of death: the death of an infant.[21] The poem seeks to explain "why from us so quickly" the infant departed (42). Why does God allow an infant "no sooner blown" to be "blasted" (1)? If providence did not intend for the infant to live, why all this waste of suffering and grief? In answering these questions, "Fair Infant," the first of Milton's original English poems, begins where *In Obitum Praesulis Eliensis* ends. In its explanation the poem adopts that epicedium's vision of heavenly glory bestowed upon the worthy by Christian providence. However, "Fair Infant" includes three critical modifications of the pattern. First, it does not fuse but rather opposes Christian and classical imagery. Second, it does not explicitly reject classical entities before it designates providence as the arbiter of death. Rather, it implicitly reveals providence—and the lack of it in Milton's classical landscape—by presenting opposing classical and Christian consolations. And last, it expands the consolation to explain how God compensates humanity for any earthly good that the early death precludes.

Before revealing that the wisdom of providence has arranged the infant's death (stanzas IX–XI), Milton uses classical imagery to represent the problem of death as we have seen it in the epicedia: it is a senseless killer in a world without providence and thus a world with a bleak prospect for an afterlife. In this poem, chance, the province of the whimsical Fortuna, replaces the Fates or underworld deities as the ultimate arbiter of death.[22] The poem's first four stanzas introduce this theme, as we get a comic variation of the fatal gods in the Latin poems; there death was often inflicted by a malicious god, but here it is the result of a vain god's accident. It seems that bumbling old man Winter, fretting over his dismal reputation for romantic conquests, "unawares" (20) slew the infant: he "thought to kiss / But kill'd alas" (5–6). Not only are the gods unable to preserve the humans they love, but their love (here perhaps more appropriately called self-love) causes them to become the accidental executioner of the beloved. Stanza IV reinforces this theme of chance, of ungodly clumsy carnage, as it harkens back to the one instance of this in the epicedia (*In Obitum Procancellarii Medici*, 41–44), relating how

Apollo "with unweeting hand" struck down "his dearly-loved mate," Hyacinthus (23–24).

The theme of chance appears again in stanza VII. This stanza posits the possibility that it was "by mischance" (44) that the girl was born, that she was a star shaken from the roof of Olympus by the clamor caused by the gods' war with the Titans. Since the infant's birth was a "mischance," she took the first opportunity to return to her proper abode. Milton's citing of the clash between the gods and the Titans seems uninformed, since the war preceded the infant's birth by many centuries. But actually the myth masterfully supports the assertion that the world is subject to chance rather than providence, as it echoes another aspect of the gods in the epicedia: their decidedly circumscribed power. True, the gods win their wars, but not with the divine ease that the Father and Son manage their victory in *Paradise Lost*, Books V–VI. Here, in an echo of Hesiod's *Theogony*, we hear talk of "the ruin'd roof / Of shak't Olympus" (43–44). Milton reinforces this point by also citing the possibility that the war between the gods and the gaints ("earth's Sons") (47) forces a "goddess" to "hide" her "nectar'd head" in less exalted quarters (48–49). Within the fiction, the victim is a goddess; but within the facts, the victim is all too human, and the fiction causes us to ask, "In a cosmos where gods must strive to preserve their own unjust destruction, how can they protect mortals from a similar mischance?"

The classical stanzas offer only a highly qualified hope for an afterlife. Stanza IV relates Hyacinthus's transformation into a flower but laments Winter's inability to duplicate that feat with the infant. And even if Winter were equal to the task, this classical form of immortality offers no solace in a poem that begins with a comparison of the dead infant to a blighted flower. Stanza V relates the speaker's struggle to believe in any form of afterlife for the infant:

> Yet can I not persuade me thou are dead
> Or that thy corse corrupts in earth's dark womb,
> Or that thy beauties lie in wormy bed,
> Hid from the world in a low delved tomb;
> Could Heav'n for pity thee so strictly doom?
> Oh no! for something in thy face did shine
> Above mortality that show'd thou wast divine. (29–35)

This stanza dwells on the corpse rotting in the grave. The hope for a happier situation is suggested most forcefully by the memory of the infant's shining face, which related after the grim lines on the corpse heightens rather than alleviates the mood of despair. This despair continues in stanza VI, which consistently hedges its bets on the existence of an afterlife, as the speaker implores the spirit of the infant to "resolve" his doubt:

> Resolve me then oh Soul most surely blest
> (If so it be that thou these plaints dost hear)
> Tell me bright Spirit where'er thou hoverest
> Whether above that high first-moving Sphere
> Or in the Elysian fields (if such there were). (36–40)

These flickering hopes of an afterlife do little to dispel the powerful images of death conjured in the previous stanza. Those horrible images dominate the poem until the Christian stanzas persuade us that providence has installed the infant in heaven where she exerts herself on behalf of sinners below.

Here we should note that just as the poem provides classical counterpoints to Christian providence and afterlife, it also includes a counterpoint to the good purpose for which God turns death in the Christian stanzas. Though strictly speaking, stanzas VII and VIII give the classical explanation of why the babe was born, we should interpret the divine identities ascribed to the babe in connection with the explanation in stanzas IX–XI of why the infant died. Then we see the contrast between the uselessness to humanity of the babe's classical guises and the divine boon to humanity of the infant's Christian transformation into an angelic intercessory. Stanza VII first identifies the infant as a star whose fall to earth was caused by the war between the gods and the Titans, and then it sees her as a goddess imperiled by the war of the giants on the gods. Here reigns divine enmity between this world and heaven, with no respite in that war. Stanza VIII highlights this divine enmity by suggesting a variety of identities for the departed infant, all positive—Justice, Truth, Mercy (or Virtue or Peace)—but all, the poem implies, useless to mankind because they have deserted "the hated earth" (51), not to intercede on its behalf but to effect a total separation. Milton emphasizes this point with his citation of the "just Maid" (50) or Astraea. Astraea was not the only but the last deity that fled the wicked world in disgust. Justice—and Truth and Mercy—were driven from the earth by the accumulation of evil that explodes in the wars mentioned in Stanza VII. Furthermore, this estrangement is accentuated by another connotation of the "just Maid": her virginity. The virgin Astraea flees the earth when she is endangered in an impious world, similar to the infant soul's departure from the menaces of Winter in stanzas I–II. But the poem's Christian explanation says that the infant left the earth to serve as our Christlike advocate in heaven. Astraea removes herself from the earth because she despises it. Even in the unlikely case that Astraea here has returned to "the hated earth" to do it "some good" (56), she remains only for a brief "visit" (52). This world and the next are in eternal disharmony, and the death of this classical "Christlike" divinity fails to produce any benefits.[23]

After stanzas I–VIII use classical imagery to give us the problem of death much as it was elaborated in the epicedia, the last three stanzas use Christian imagery to solve that problem. First, we learn of the babe's immortality. But the consolation avoids creating the kind of baroque visions that conclude *Elegia Tertia* and more successfully *In Obitum Praesulis Eliensis.* Rather, it anticipates *Lycidas* in the austerity of its celestial vision. We are told simply and directly that the corpse was not so much a "blasted" flower (1) as a "human weed"—with its inevitable punning connotations—that has been liberated of its "golden-winged host" who will fly up to the bliss of heaven (57–58). There the babe enjoys from the heavenly fount the joys radiated on all those "creatures Heav'n doth breed" (61).

This assertion of eternal life, though a happy contrast to the graveyard imagery of stanza V, is not sufficient to establish eternal providence. Milton, unlike the classical authors of such consolations or their Christian imitators, seems to be more interested in this world than the next. Despite his intense Platonism, Milton does not see this world as a shadow; he sees it as a battlefield or, as he says later in *Areopagitica,* a "race, where that immortall garland is to be run for, not without dust and heat" (II, 515). And when someone appears to have attained that garland by not merely slinking out of that race but never even having begun it, we must search for the hand of providence in the matter. Specifically, we must look further to discover how the death benefits those of us who remain amidst the struggle below. The poem provides three answers. First, the brief appearance of this little messenger was sufficient to have "set the hearts of men on fire / To scorn the sordid world, and unto Heav'n aspire" (62–63). But if the infant was capable of such feats, why did she not linger into maturity and, like the mighty infant of the Nativity ode, produce even greater benefits for humanity? As stanza X laments,

> But oh! why didst thou not stay here below
> To bless us with thy heav'n-lov'd innocence,
> To slake his wrath whom sin hath made our foe
> To turn Swift-rushing black perdition hence,
> Or drive away the slaughtering pestilence,
> To stand 'twixt us and our deserved smart? (64–69)

Whatever glimpses of heaven the infant has provided to us, we remain in a world of woe, menaced by the death that we deserve for our first parents' foul revolt ("his wrath whom sin hath made our foe"). But we cannot help crying out for the divine assistance of one who might have proved the solution to the lingering problem of "the slaughtering pestilence" (68), already touched on—and abandoned—in *Elegia Tertia*. Yet, instead of lending a light to a death-darkened world, the mighty spirit of the infant itself has melted back into the next world, giving us no more than a glimpse of a heaven we burn to attain. At this point stanza X appears on the verge of repeating the classical predicament of stanzas VII–VIII: humanity is in conflict with divinity, and so we suffer without respite. But then, at last, we receive the Christian explanation in the last line of the stanza. Since providence created the infant "to stand 'twixt us and our deserved smart," the infant departed the earth to act as our advocate in heaven, where it "canst best perform that office" (70). The infant's death, then, is a positive event. Since death, even in the form of a plague (and Milton had ample biblical precedents here), is God's punishment for sin, the infant can best "stand 'twixt us and our deserved smart" as a Christlike mediator in heaven. So far as the Christlike infant reconciles God and sinners, sin, and thus death, becomes less and less.

Despite the speaker's assurances that the infant can best benefit humanity in heaven, there remains the fact that if heavenly intercession were enough, Christ would never have had to incarnate, mature, preach, and die. Milton tidies up this apparently unhappy aspect of the infant's death in his address to the bereaved mother—Milton's sister Ann—for "her false imagin'd loss" (72). Milton asserts that God only "lent" (75) the baby to her; if the mother endures her grief with the great Christian—and Miltonic—virtue of "patience" (75), then God will recompense her with a child "that till the world's last end shall make thy name to live" (77). This statement, which is not simply Renaissance rhetoric aimed at consoling his again pregnant sister, provides the final rebuttal of the classicism of stanzas VII–VIII. The infant's arrival on the earth was the result of neither divine mischief, impotence, nor fear. It was an instrument of God's purpose; God has "lent" the babe to the mother to provide her with a trial that if successfully endured will compensate her—and mankind—with the eternal blessing of a babe who will mature into a Christlike hero. Thus Milton's much-commented on elevation of the babe into an angelic intercessory is essential to establishing that providence uses death to bring tremendous good from the apparent evil of death. The world benefits from an exhortation to virtue, a heavenly intermediary, and the expectation of the birth of a Christlike benefactor; and the deprived mother can look forward to a glorious offspring that will linger on earth long enough to establish a maternal fame that will remain until "the world's last end."

IV

In Milton's September 23, 1637, letter to Charles Diodati, written just two months before the composition of *Lycidas*, the poet reveals his state of mind: "You ask what I am thinking of? So may the good Deity help me, of immortality! And what I am doing? Growing my wings and meditating flight; but as yet our Pegasus raises himself on very tender pinions. Let us be lowly wise!"[24] Are we to believe that Milton really was unaware that at *anno aetatis 29* he already had composed some verses that the world would not willingly let die, among them the Nativity ode, *L'Allegro* and *Il Penseroso*, and his *Mask?* What then is Milton thinking of here? I suggest that when Milton considers his previous efforts inadequate he is not thinking of his more successful, more secular efforts; he is thinking of his religious poems, specifically his poems on death. The epicedia and "On the Death of a Fair Infant" are much more complex than usually acknowledged, but they hardly qualify as great religious poetry. Milton seems to have viewed the poem on his niece as a failure, as it was the only one of his English poems to be excluded from the 1645 volume of his poems. Milton is more explicit about his dissatisfaction with another poem on death, *The Passion*. This poem's "roving verse" attempts to confine itself to "the stroke of death he (Jesus) must abide" (20–22). The passion provided the poet with a potentially ideal subject in relation to his earlier poems on death, for it incorporates the themes developed in the early poems on death: the untimely death of a pious and learned man, a "son of god" even, in a world where the wicked apparently are left to sin on unimpeded. Milton abandons the poem, declaring that he was "nothing satisfied with what was begun." Milton attributes this failure to his inadequate preparation, saying that the subject was "above the years he had, when he wrote it." During his studious retirement at Hammersmith and Horton, the goal of Milton's intense, arduous studies was to prepare himself to serve God as man and poet, acquiring the skills that he lacked when he composed the early poems on death or attempted to write *The Passion* in 1630. And, significantly, Milton would be serving God and man in writing a great poem on death, for such poems in explaining the ways of God to men are in the truest sense religious poems. Indeed, *The Passion* in stanza I announces itself as a companion poem to Milton's only successful religious poem until *Lycidas,* the Nativity ode (which, significantly, celebrates death's opposite—birth). But, in the autumn of 1637, Milton meditated a major flight on a sacred rather than a secular Pegasus that would enable him to explain in verse the enigma of untimely death. This religious aspect, especially as it appears in the early poems on death, is the "tender pinion" of the ambitious Pegasus that takes flight in *Lycidas.* We usually date Milton's debut as an immortal religious poet as 1667. I suggest that Milton did not meditate five or twenty-five years on his flight but engaged on his new course in *Lycidas,* riding a sacred Pegasus that soars high above the pastoral hills as it justifies the ways of God to men.

It is clear from the letter to Diodati that Milton, after a nearly three-year silence, was ready to write poetry again, putting to poetic use the preparation he had undergone at Hammersmith and Horton. When he was asked to contribute to *Justa Eduardo King* in the autumn of 1637, Milton seized this occasion as a splendid opportunity to restate the themes of the early poems on death in a way that would gain the author "immortality." King's death combined the issues raised in the epicedia and "Fair Infant"—and *The Passion*—for here was the death of someone who was certainly young and, perhaps with a little poetic license, wonderfully pious and learned as well. As for his learning, King, because of his "present sufficiency and future hopes," received a fellowship at Cambridge.[25] As for his piety, there is also solid evidence on King's behalf. When King's ship struck a rock and disappeared beneath the calm, deep waters of the Irish Sea, the young pastor reputedly knelt upon the deck for a serene moment of final prayer. King, whom Milton did not know that well, was no John Keats, nor even an Arthur Clough, but apparently he was possessed of enough piety and learning so that Milton could use him to suit his own poetic purpose. Milton transforms King, as he tends to do with the Cantabrigians of his earlier poems, into an incarnation of learning and piety: Lycidas. The death of Lycidas becomes the great example of the early, senseless death of a potential benefactor of mankind. History steps in here to help Milton invest this occasion with another theme from the epicedia: while the good die, the worthless thrive. A case could be made that the clergy were neither as wicked nor as stupid as Milton paints them. But the poet exaggerates their negative qualities, just as he exaggerates Edward King's positive ones, to serve his thematic purpose. The Anglican clergy becomes an embodiment of thriving ignorance and corruption, the wretchedness represented in the epicedia by the rabble: they become "blind mouths" (119)—the poem itself provides no more specific epithet. So we have the learned and pious Lycidas drowning senselessly at sea while ignorant and corrupt "blind mouths" eat, drink, and make merry.

In asserting eternal providence, Milton uses the pattern apparent in "Fair Infant." He retains the two-part consolation of that poem; however, where "Fair Infant" implicitly established providence, and the lack of it, in its consolations, *Lycidas* follows *In Obitum Praesulis Eliensis* in explicitly addressing the issue of providence. In the classical world, Milton fuses fate (from *In Obitum Procancellarii, In Obitum Praesulis Eliensis*), accident or chance (*In Obitum Procancellarii*, "Fair Infant"), and malevolent deities (all of the early poems on death) into the menacing figure of "the blind *Fury* with th' abhorred shears" (75). Milton, or more properly the swain, does not mistake the Fate Atropos for a Fury; he avails himself of a classical tradition that combined fate and vengeance into a single force, which he identifies as a Fury. Adding blindness to the Fury, "not a recognized attribute of either Fate or Fury," infuses the image with connotations of chance, of Fortuna.[26] This tightly compressed image, echoing the prior poems on death, suggests that destiny is shaped by an incomprehensible, maleficent Fate.

The "blind *Fury*" appears in a context that emphasizes a theme prominent in the earlier poems: the good die while the bad thrive. Developing this theme, Milton elaborates an equation implicit in the early poems: to be good is to exert oneself in the pursuit of learning while to be bad is to allow oneself to remain mired in ignorance. Yet, in a world without providence, the sacrifices and hard-earned fruits of learning that make one good are nigh meaningless, except in a negative way, in relation to death. *Elegia Secunda* heightens the shock of Ridding's death by pointing out that the learned gentleman died while the ignorant rabble prosper, and *Elegia Tertia* bemoans that death, with all of a soulless nature at its disposal, sates itself on erudite Bishop Andrewes. Worse, in this classical landscape, usefulness and learning often invite death, as in *In Obitum Procancellarii Medici.* King's death allows Milton to restate this problem superbly. The swain meditates the death of the learned Lycidas amidst hedonistic "Blind mouths! that scarce themselves know how to hold / A Sheephook, or have learn'd aught else the least / That to the faithful Herdman's art belongs" (119–21). Voicing the dilemma of the learned, the swain asks,

> Alas! What boots it with uncessant care
> To tend the homely slighted Shepherd's trade,
> And strictly meditate the thankless Muse?

Were it not better done as others use,
To sport with *Amaryllis* in the shade,
Or with the tangles of *Neaera's* hair? (64–69)

Since death is the whim of "the blind *Fury* with th' abhorred shears," the apprehensions raised by the death of Lycidas are confirmed rather than dispelled. The learned swain is dead, and there is no good brought forth from this evil in the classical landscape. In the climactic conclusion to the first of the poem's three movements, Phoebus reveals that the afterlife is the same for those who choose to endure the rigors of learned asceticism ("to scorn delights, and live laborious days" [72]) and for those who bury themselves and their art in a hedonist's oblivion. The god offers only possible "heavenly" fame, not life, for the very limited few who are willing and able to master the god's ideal (76–84). If Milton intended this consolation to complement rather than to oppose the Christian consolation of heavenly glory, he could have drawn on a classical tradition such as the Elysian Fields or deification. Instead, Phoebus's offer of heavenly fame reflects a fatalism embodied in a "blind *Fury*" that minimizes freedom of the will. Following the lead of the earlier poems on death, this classical consolation assigns the same annihilation to all men and women, whether they choose to live the rare life of a pure poet or the hedonistic life of "blind mouths."

Despite Phoebus's consignment of all humanity to anihilation, readers have persisted in seeing Phoebus's offer of "heavenly" fame as an adumbration of the Christian consolation of eternal life.[27] But three facts in particular undermine this position. First, Phoebus here does not prefigure Christ; allusions to the unhappy fates of his "beloved"—Daphne, Hyacinthus, and his son and priest Orpheus—establish a Phoebus hinted at in *In Obitum Procancellarii* and "Fair Infant": he is a pagan deity who must acquiesce to the furious onslaughts of fate rather than a Son of a Deity whose providence is fate. His consolation, then, can no more prefigure Christianity's consolation than paganism's "blind *Fury*" can anticipate God's providential justice.

Second, the swain is admonished that if he finds favor with "all-judging *Jove*," then "of so much fame in Heav'n expect thy meed" (82–84). But the swain, in the grandest of classical traditions, clearly is contemplating an earthly fame. As Milton's fit reader would have recognized, the god's offer of celestial fame is nigh worthless without a concomitant offer of eternal life. In a world "to good malignant, to bad men benign" (*PL* XII, 538), celestial fame befits a wayfaring Job who looks anxiously to God's gift of heaven after the obloquy of earth. This Christian position is expounded forcefully in Matthew, v, 11–12, in which Jesus admonishes his hearers to spurn worldly fame and to court a corrupt world's disapproval: "Blessed are ye, when men shall revile you, and persecute you, and shall say all manner of evil against you falsely, for my sake. Rejoice and be exceeding glad: for great *is* your reward in heaven: for so persecuted they the prophets which were before you" (King James Version). Milton adopts this position as early as his *Seventh Prolusion*, which states,

How little pleasure could the empty praise of men give to those dead and departed worthies whom no pleasure and no sensation from it could reach! But we may look forward to eternal life which will never erase the memory of our good deeds on earth. Whatever lovely thing we may have done here we shall be present to hear praised there. And there — as many men have seriously thought — those who have lived temperately and dedicated all their time to worthy studies and thereby helped mankind, will be enriched above all others with knowledge that is peerless and supreme. (Hughes, p. 628)

As his September 23, 1637 letter to Diodati indicates, for the Christian Milton an "immortality" of earthly and/or celestial fame that he wins through writing great religious poetry would be a fitting complement to the eternal life provided by that religion. But for the pagan who thinks he is destined to annihilation, without the prospect of heaven or hell, heavenly fame loses its celestial appeal, and a comfortable, worldly fame would seem far more agreeable. Phoebus's fame does not prefigure the Christian God's approval but rather demonstrates that the two religions are so incompatible that the positive element in one becomes the negative element in the other.

Finally, the poem suggests that Phoebus's consolation, unsatisfactory as it is, is not even afforded to the pastoralist Lycidas. Phoebus responds not only to the swain's despair over Lycidas's death but to his musings on his poetic vocation. Milton crafts Phoebus's consolation to address both of the swain's perplexities simultaneously. Reading for the god's response to the swain's speculations on his poetic vocation, we find it in his twitching of the swain's ears, which indicates, as it does in Virgil's *Eclogue VI*, 1–5, the god's disdain for the poetry of "mortal soil" (78), the pastoral. According to Phoebus, Lycidas can achieve fame as neither the singer nor the subject of the pastoral, an inferior genre with a strictly limited, "earth-bound" appeal. The poet can obtain "immortal" fame only by winning the approval of the immortal "all-judging *Jove*," who is an avid admirer of the Apollonian tradition. As Marjorie Hope Nicolson has pointed out, "Milton was too good a classicist to give the epithet 'all-judging' to the wrong deity. Jove was not the judge of Hades; Rhadamanthus was."[28] Milton assigns the epithet to Jove because Jove is judging poetry and the deeds it celebrates, not shades, nor even immortal souls, which the poem's paganism does not allow humanity. The poem alludes to Hesiod's *Theogony*, which also is echoed "undoubtedly" in the swain's appeal to the "Sisters of the sacred well, / That from beneath the seat of *Jove* doth spring" (15–16).[29] Hesiod relates, at considerable length, how the Muses "by their singing / delight the great mind of Zeus, their father, who lives on Olympos" (36–37). Hesiod's Muses instructed him "to sing the race of the blessed gods everlasting" (33), and Phoebus indicates that the ways and deeds of the gods and their favorites is the only subject worthy of immortal song. Though the swain initially champions the pastoral as "lofty rhyme" (11) and begins the poem by invoking Apollo's laurel and the "Sisters of the sacred well," the god refutes the swain's florid claims by pronouncing that "*Fame* is no plant that grows on mortal soil" (78) and withholding immortal honors from the lowly pastoralist. The swain seems to kiss the rod when he designates the portion of his pastoral that relates the Olympian's appearance as its "higher mood" (87). Apollo's consolation would exclude the pastoralist Lycidas from immortal honors, and since the god never mentions the dead shepherd, we must assume that Lycidas has been relegated to oblivion. The choice, then, that Phoebus allows is not between the hedonism that ends in annihilation and the purity that brings immortal life, but between pastoralism and profound religious poetry. But this is a predetermined choice within the context of the "lowly wise" Milton's masterpiece, which transforms the lowly pastoral into profound religious poetry that exalts the "low" wisdom of Christianity.[30]

Before the poem gives the second part of the classical consolation (100–02), the swain in the poem's second movement (85–131) seeks answers from a procession of mourning gods. In this movement, Milton invests the gods with another characteristic given them in the earlier poems: they are at best the hapless, limited classical divinities of all the earlier poems on death, and at worst they are the comic bunglers of "Fair Infant." Milton transforms the traditional procession of mourners into a catalogue of failed gods who neither mourn nor console nor know. The impression created by Milton's modifications is apparent in Johnson's contemptuous summary of "how one god asks another god what is become of Lycidas, and how neither god can tell."[31] First, as Johnson perceived, in *Lycidas* none of the classical gods mourns as they do in classical pastorals where even the young Olympians Apollo and Aphrodite sometimes mourn.[32] That Milton purposely represented the gods as not mourning is indicated later in the poem when the speaker, introducing the poem's Christian consolation, addresses not the gods of the procession but shepherds who do not even appear in the poem: "Weep no more, woeful Shepherds weep no more, / For *Lycidas* your sorrow is not dead" (165–66); and this point is reiterated in line 182. The deities do not mourn nor do they account for why Lycidas has died. Insted they play or, perhaps more significantly, they themselves fruitlessly search for answers to explain the cause of Lycidas's death. The gods' baffled, bland groping for how and why the deceased perished is Milton's invention—perhaps his echo of "Fair Infant"—for it has no precedent in either his classical or Renaissance analogues.[33] Milton's third innovation reinforces the preceding two. In Theocritus's *Idyll I* and Virgil's *Eclogue X*, deities put mostly probing, wise questions to the languishing victim; but in *Lycidas*, god futilely asks god to explain why the dead has died. This Olympian ineptitude is enacted with a fine, grim humor that has not been remarked, except by Johnson, who thinks the humor his and not Milton's. Neptune, apparently too preoccupied to appear himself, sends son Triton ("that came in *Neptune's* plea") to ask the winds and the waves ("and sage *Hippotades* their answer brings") "what hard mishap hath doom'd this gentle swain?" (87–99). The winds, never a very reliable source, "knew not of his story" and can only say that "the Air was calm" while "sleek *Panope* with all her sisters play'd" on the tranquil sea under which Lycidas disappeared (97–99). Hippotades, god of wind, could impress only an exceptionally ardent, uncouth swain as "sage," as his report, again spotlighting sporting deities, provides us with a declaration of ungodly ignorance. These proceedings represent perhaps a ghastly parody of the Holy Trinity: Neptune the Father sends Triton the Son to consult with "sage" Hippotades, god of wind, counterpart to the Holy Spirit, the Hebrew word for which can mean "wind" or "breeze," and which in a well-known passage in Genesis takes to the water. Certainly, there has not been such divine bumbling since old man Winter tried to lay hands on the infant. Unable to explain or to console, this divine comedy of errors—of frolicking nymphs, hapless gods, and corpses—forces the swain himself to explain why Lycidas died.

The swain, at almost exactly the midpoint of the poem's three movements, gives the second part of the classical consolation. As in "Fair Infant," this poem attempts to explain why the lamented died and how that death benefits the survivors. Its classical response follows in the pattern of hopelessness that characterizes the classicism of Milton's previous poems on death. The swain concludes that Lycidas's death was caused by "that fatal and perfidious Bark / Built in th'eclipse, and rigg'd with curses dark" (100–01). Absolving the gods from causing Lycidas's death, this consolation emphasizes the inevitability of death. But it also establishes that death is the meaningless consequence of the blind, inscrutable necessity of the sinister stars. This bleak assessment of the lightless ways of fate echoes the swain's previous despair that the lack of providence leaves his "destin'd Urn" to be filled at the whim of a "blind *Fury*." In fact, since, with Phoebus's acquiescence, the swain has asserted the absence of a providence that could order the course of pagan events, the question of whether there is any significance to death has already been negatively answered, and the rustic swain here simply recasts his prior assertion in the quasi religious form of astrology.[34] In this part of the consolation, as in "Fair Infant" and Phoebus's response, Milton excludes a classical tradition that would anticipate rather than oppose its Christian counterpart. Again, Virgil's *Eclogue V* is the outstanding example, as it includes the apotheosis of Daphnis, who, as a star, sheds his beneficent influence over the earth. And this classical consolation of transformation into a star was not restricted to heroes but accorded, though not in pastorals, to more pedestrian mortals as well.[35] Rejecting this tradition for his poem, Milton transforms the stars from symbols of eternal life into the enigmas of eternal malice. Together, Phoebus's and the swain's answers, echoing the earlier poems on death, represent the comprehensive failure of pagan religion to console humanity in the face of death.

After presenting its classical consolation, the poem then prepares for its Christian consolation by introducing "the Pilot of the *Galilean* lake" (109). St. Peter's prophecy, as M. H. Abrams argues, is "nothing less than the climax and turning point of the lyric meditation."[36] In this "turning point," the poem refocuses from paganism's "blind *Fury*," fate and random malice, to God's providential justice. St. Peter's prophecy establishes this providence by revealing that, as in *In Obitum Praesulis Eliensis*, Providence supervises death, using it to punish the wicked, for "that two-handed engine at the door / Stands ready to smite once, and smite no more" (130–31). This shining example of providence reverses the gloomy predicament of the good in the poem's classical section—which simply restated the predicament given in the epicedia. St. Peter shows us that death prefers not the ascetic in pursuit of learning but rather those driven "for their bellies' sake" (114), who choose to remain ignorant of God's truth as they "sport with *Amaryllis* in the shade, / Or with the tangles of *Neaera's* hair." Later, the poem's Christian consolation will reveal that God raises the pure and learned into the perfect bliss of heaven while blessing the earth with a supernatural guardian.

This emphasis on the saving power of learning exalts freedom of the will. In Milton's pagan landscape, this freedom is worthless, for reasons that we already have seen in this poem as well as the epicedia. But if providence rewards the pure and punishes the corrupt, then the ability to choose wisely assumes enormous importance. The corrupt clergy chose their corruption, just as the "faithful" herdman chose to apply himself to the upright and pure. Milton emphasizes this freedom to choose by equating corruption with ignorance and holiness with knowledge of God's ways, an equation that reflects Milton's belief that "the end then of learning is to repair the ruins of our first parents by regaining to know God aright" (*Of Education*, II, 366–67), a position presaged in the *Seventh Prolusion*. Christian priests could either pursue their own wicked fancies, "and when they list, their lean and flashy songs / Grate on their scrannel Pipes of wretched straw" (123–24): or, like John Milton at Horton-Hammersmith, they could apply themselves "to know God aright." They were free to choose, and their choice is a matter of eternal life and death.

After firmly establishing the Christian context of the poem, Milton finally confronts the ineluctable fact that Edward King died, as did his infant niece, an apparently useless death. Yet the poem tells us that God brings forth good from apparent evil both in heaven and on earth. The poem reveals that Providence ordains that the apparent evil of the setting sun will end in the splendors of the dawn and that Edward King will be raised from his watery bier into heaven "through the dear might of him that walk'd the waves" (173). The poem shuns the elaborate classicism of the heavenly visions of *Elegia Tertia* and *In Obitum Praesulis Eliensis*, instead relying on the Book of Revelation for a simplicity that characterized his description of his infant niece in heaven. In *Lycidas*, the poet neither embroiders scripture nor tortures the reader's understanding, as he does with the poem's classical imagery, through a maze of entangling allusion, type, antitype, and echo. While the "two-handed engine" hovers over the sensual and ignorant on earth, we see the deceased in heaven enjoying a bliss reserved for those who have chosen the hard liberty of asceticism and, Milton suggests, its consort learning: Lycidas, as only virgins can, comprehends "the unexpressive nuptial Song" (176), the Christian pastorals of the "sweet Societies / That sing, and singing in their glory move, / And wipe the tears for ever from his eyes" (179–81).

The Christian consolation's explanation of why Lycidas has drowned confirms the providential wisdom asserted in the Pilot's prophecy. In this explanation, the poem once again parallels "Fair Infant." Milton transforms his niece into a heavenly intermediary, and here God works "large recompense" (184) for the apparent loss of a promising clergyman by enthroning the deceased as "the Genius of the shore" (183), a shore perhaps abandoned by the poem's playful nymphs. This guardian spirit "shalt be good / To all that wander in that perilous flood" (184–85). As with the death of the archetypal good shepherd, from the apparent evil of death issues great, if not infinite, good.

Milton's early poems on death are complex. The poems are neither the simple mingling of Christianity and classicism nor the literary exercises of a talented student. The Latin epicedia contain a tension between their Christian and classical elements that is resolved only in *In Obitum Praesulis Eliensis,* which adopts classical imagery to represent death in Christian terms. Milton refines this resolution in "On the Death of a Fair Infant," using classical imagery to give a bleak classical view of death as the source of great evil and then opposing this view to the Christian concept of death as the source of great good, which he relates in Christian imagery. This pattern provides the basis for Milton's masterpiece, *Lycidas.*

University of New Orleans

NOTES

1. I will use William Riley Parker's ordering of the Latin poems, "Notes on the Chronology of Milton's Latin Poems," *A Tribute to George Coffin Taylor*, ed. Arnold Williams (Chapel Hill, 1952), pp. 113–31, which is based on Milton's dating and placing of them in the 1645 edition of his poems. In that edition, Milton grouped the poems chronologically into two sections according to their meter, "Elegiarum Liber" and "Sylvarum Liber." *Elegia Secunda* and *Elegia Tertia* appear under the former heading, while *In Obitum Procancellarii Medici* precedes *In Obitum Praesulis Eliensis* in the latter. Since *In Obitum Praesulis Eliensis* clearly refers to *Elegia Tertia*, it must have been written after that poem; and *In Obitum Procancellarii Medici*, though misdated by Milton, from his assigning it an earlier date than the others "we may infer that it was written *first* of the four poems commemorating persons who died in the autumn of 1626" (p. 121). That leaves only *Elegia Secunda*'s placement in question, and I accept Parker's assertion that it was composed second in the group, after *In Obitum Procancellarii Medici* and before *Elegia Tertia.*

For other datings of the Latin poems, see the entries for the individual poems in *A Variorum Commentary on the Poems of John Milton*, vol. I, pt. i, ed. Douglas Bush (New York, 1970).

For an assessment of Milton's thought in the Latin epicedia, see A.S.P. Woodhouse, "Notes on Milton's Early Development." *UTQ* XIII (1943–44), 70; and R. W. Condee,

"The Latin Poetry of John Milton," in *The Latin Poetry of English Poets*, ed. J. W. Binns (Boston, 1974), pp. 58–92. Condee says that "most of these poems are badly overfreighted with classical learning and, unlike the clever manipulation of Ovid in 'Elegia Prima', the learning serves no purpose" (p. 63).

2. Though Milton wrote *De Doctrina Christiana* nearly twenty years after writing the early poems, there is no reason to believe that the younger Milton did not on the whole adhere to the book's in many ways orthodox explanation that death is the punishment for sin. In fact, these early verses indicate that he did adhere to it. *De Doctrina Christiana*, I, xi, "Of the Fall of Our First Parents, and of Sin" emphasizes that the Greek word for sin, ἀνομία (1 John iii, 4), means "breaking of the law" (VI, p. 382). Milton then analyzes the two ways in which we transgress God's law. The first kind of sin is "common" sin. We all are guilty of "common" sin because our first parents broke faith with God and thus incurred the penalty for that breach—death. Even if it were possible to lead perfect lives we still would be punished for common sin in the same way that the innocent children of those convicted of high treason must also suffer. The second type of sin is "individual" sin, and "all men commit sin of this kind" as well. Individual sin is "the sin which each man commits on his own account." It, like common sin, can be divided into two subdivisions, "evil desire, or the will to do evil, and the evil deed itself" (p. 388). Individual sin also can be traced to the original disobedience of our first parents: "Our first parents implanted" in us the desire to sin, or "evil desire." This desire, in itself a sin, impels us to "actual" sins, or crimes (p. 388–90).

According to *De Doctrina Christiana*, I, xii, "Of the Punishment of Sin," "After sin came death, as its affliction or punishment" (p. 393). For our common sin, we must die, eventually. However, we are sped along this common course by individual sin. Milton explains that "in scripture every evil, and everything which seems to lead to destruction, is indeed under the name of *death*. For physical death, as it is called, did not follow *on the same day* as Adam's sin, as God had threatened" (p. 393). In other words, to sin is to die, though a little at a time. So central is this fact to Milton's thinking that, in Milton's view, an act is real only if it accords with divine law. An act that contravenes God's law—in a word, *sin*—is really no act at all. In *De Doctrina Christiana*, I, xi, "Of the Death which is Called the Death of the Body," Milton elaborates:

> the evil action or crime itself . . . is commonly called "actual sin." . . . Not because sin is really an action, on the contrary it is a deficiency, but because it usually exists in some action. For every action is intrinsically good; it is only its misdirection or deviation from the set course of law which can properly be called evil. So action is not the material out of which sin is made, but only the ὑποκείμενον, the essence or element in which it exists. (P. 391).

Parenthetical citations of Milton's prose, unless otherwise stated, refer to *The Complete Prose Works of John Milton*, ed. Don M. Wolfe et al. (New Haven, 1953–82), cited as YP. Citations of Milton's poetry refer to *John Milton: Complete Poems and Major Prose*, ed. Merritt Y. Hughes (New York, 1957).

3. For a standard account of the relationship between Christianity and classicism in the Latin epicedia, see Don Cameron Allen, *The Harmonious Vision: Studies in Milton's Poetry* (1951; rpt. Baltimore, 1970) pp. 41–47; and John M. Steadman, *Milton's Biblical and Classical Imagery* (Pittsburgh, 1984), p. 3. For the relationship of classicism and Christianity in "On the Death of a Fair Infant Dying of a Cough," see Allen as well as Hugh MacLean, "Milton's *Fair Infant*," ELH XXIV (1957), 296–305.

This study of death in Milton's early poetry omits his lines on Shakespeare, Hobson the carrier, and the Marchioness of Winchester. "On Shakespeare" deals only tangentially with death, and the lines on Hobson provide a merely comic look at death. The poem on the marchioness is written in a Jonsonian style that clashes with the classicism of the poems that we will study. Though the epitaph refers to the Fates (15, 28) and chance (27) and celebrates the heavenly elevation of the marchioness into a queen (74), the poem lacks the pattern that emerges in Milton's other early poems on death.

4. See Allen, *Harmonious Vision*, pp. 41–47; and Richmond Lattimore, *Themes in Greek and Roman Epitaphs* (Urbana, Ill., 1962), pp. 55–65, 215–16.

5. William Chase Greene, *Moira: Fate, Good, and Evil in Greek Thought* (New York, 1944), p. 15.

6. "Fate," *The Oxford Classical Dictionary*, 1970 ed., p. 431.

7. Milton refers to this tradition in his *Arcades*, which refers to the Fates as "the daughters of *Necessity*" (p. 69). Later, however, Milton will make Satan advocate this position in *Paradise Regained* and in *Paradise Lost* (I, 116–17; II, 392–94 [through Beelzebub]). See Barbara Lewalski, "Time and History in *Paradise Regained*," in *The Prison and the Pinnacle*, ed. Balachandra Rajan (Toronto, 1973), p. 57.

Citations of Hesiod, placed in the text, refer to *Hesiod*, trans. Richmond Lattimore (Ann Arbor, Mich., 1959, 1965).

8. O. B. Hardison, Jr., *The Enduring Monument: A Study of the Idea of Praise in Renaissance Literary Theory and Practice* (Chapel Hill, 1962), p. 127.

9. Allen, *Harmonious Vision*, pp. 43, 49–50, citing Ovid's *Amores III.* (X, 59–66) and Statius' *Silvae II.* (VI, 98–102). Allen comments that Seneca's *Ad Marciam* offers a heavenly consolation that complements Christianity's to the degree that "we are not surprised that after the Renaissance had read it the fiction of Seneca's conversion to Christianity got abroad" (pp. 49–50).

10. See Lattimore, *Greek and Roman Epitaphs*, pp. 55–65, 215–16.

11. Citations of the *Iliad* refer to *The Iliad of Homer*, trans. Richmond Lattimore (Chicago, 1951).

12. "Fate," *The Oxford Classical Dictionary*, 1949 ed.

13. In Homer, Zeus weeps "tears of blood" (*Iliad* XVI, 459).

14. For the analogues, which include Ovid, Martial, and Statius, see *Variorum Commentary*, I, i, 64.

15. For the echoes of classical verse in the consolation, see *Variorum Commentary*, I, i, 73–76.

16. Michael West, "The *Consolatio* in Milton's Funeral Elegies," *Huntington Library Quarterly* XXXIV (1971), 236. G. W. Pigman, *Grief and English Renaissance Elegy* (New York, 1985), p. 105, also notes the unconvincing consolation, saying of the speaker, "Strictly speaking, one cannot even say whether he has understood the Christian significance of the dream. It is important to see that the complaint against death goes unrebuked. . . . Grief and the questioning of death's place in the universe are allowed to remain even after a vision of heaven."

For the versification in the epicedia, also see Steven M. Oberhelman and John Mulryan, "Milton's Use of Classical Meters in the *Sylvarum liber*," *MP* LXXXI (1983–84), 131–45.

17. *Variorum Commentary*, I, i, 14.

18. West, "The *Consolatio*," 236–37.

19. The *Variorum Commentary* states that the goddess could be Mors or Persephone or Libitina (I, i, 203). I suggest, in view of Milton's other poems on death, that the goddess probably is Mors.

20. *Variorum Commentary*, I, i, 207.

21. For the poem's date, see William Riley Parker, *Milton: A Biography*, 2 vols. (Oxford, 1968), vol. II, p. 738 n 46; and *Variorum Commentary*, II, i, 119–20.

22. Fortuna was "an Italian goddess identified in classical times with Tyche" ("Fortuna," *The Oxford Classical Dictionary*, 1970 ed.) In classical times, "*Tyche* works obscurely, lifting up one man and pushing down another (Soph. *Ant.* 1158f.), and is finally heard as 'chance', a principle ruling all of human life (Demetrius of Phaleron *apud* Polybium 29.21; cf. Plato, *Leg.* 709 b); such *tyche* is 'a blind and wretched thing' (Menander *apud* Stobaeum I, 7. 3)." ("Tyche," *The Oxford Classical Dictionary*, 1970 ed.). It is also "jealous," and "punitive" (ibid). The "blind fortune" of the Renaissance and Shakespeare (*Merchant of Venice*, II, i, 36; *Coriolanus*, V, vi, 117) is the descendant of this *tyche*.

23. For Astraea's identification with Christ, see Jackson Cope, "Fortunate Falls as Form in Milton's Fair Infant," *JEGP* LXIII (1964) 660–74.

24. *The Works of John Milton*, 18 vols., ed. Frank Allen Patterson et al. (New York, 1931–42), vol. XII, p. 27.

25. Qtd. from "Edward King," *A Milton Encyclopedia*, vol. IV, p. 183.

26. *Variorum Commentary*, II, ii, 664. For a more extensive relation of the present argument, see my "The 'blind *Fury*,' Providence, and the Consolations of *Lycidas*," *Explorations in Renaissance Culture* XIII (1987), 101–25.

27. For the dissenting view, see J. Martin Evans, *The Road from Horton: Looking Backwards in "Lycidas"* (Victoria, B. C., 1983), p. 48, who observes that "Phoebus Apollo's response to the crisis is generally agreed to be inadequate, either because it is couched in pagan rather than in Christian terms, or because it sounds too pat and aphoristic"; David Daiches, *A Study of Literature for Readers and Critics* (1948; rpt. New York, 1964), pp. 82–83; and *Poems of Mr. John Milton: The 1645 Edition with Essays in Analysis*, ed. Cleanth Brooks and John E. Hardy (New York, 1951), p. 179*n*.

28. Marjorie Hope Nicolson, *John Milton: A Reader's Guide to his Poetry* (New York, 1963), p. 96*n*.

29. *Variorum Commentary*, II, ii, 644–45.

30. For Milton's endeavor to create a Christian pastoral in *Lycidas*, see Jon S. Lawry, "'Eager Thought': Dialectics in *Lycidas*," *PMLA* LXXVI (1962), 27–32; rpt. in *Milton: Modern Essays in Criticism*, ed. Arthur E. Barker (New York, 1965), pp. 112–24; and Isabel MacCaffrey, "*Lycidas:* The Poet in the Landscape," in *The Lyric and Dramatic Milton*, ed. Joseph H. Summers (New York, 1965), pp. 65–92. Also, Phoebus's citation of Hesiod as the paragon of religious poets reenforces the classical consolation's deemphasis of the distinction between purity and hedonism. Plutarch relates that the aging Hesiod was guilty of a sexual indiscretion that cost him his life, as the violated girl's brothers murdered the poet and flung his body into the sea. It was wafted to shore by dolphins, and Phoebus, deciding that the poet merited immortal fame, ordered his tomb to be built at Orchomenos (*The New Century Classical Handbook*, ed. Catherine B. Avery [New York, 1962], p. 561). Milton later alludes to this myth in line 164 (J. Martin Evans, "*Lycidas* and the Dolphins," *N&Q* [1978], 15–17).

31. "Milton," *Lives of the English Poets*, ed. G. B. Hill (New York, 1967), vol. I, p. 164.

32. Bion's *Lament for Adonis* lingers over the grief of Aphrodite (98–104), and both Apollo and Aphrodite are indicated as mourning in Virgil's *Eclogue V* (112–13). See Watson Kirkconnell, *Awake the Courteous Echo: The Themes and Prosody of "Comus," "Lycidas," and "Paradise Regained" in World Literature with Translations of the Major Analogues* (Toronto, 1973).

33. In classical elegies, the gods, though not treated as inept or indifferent, are some-

times portrayed as the malevolent entities that we have encountered in Milton's epicedia. See Aphrodite in Theocritus's *Idyll* I (Kirkconnell 86) and Hades in Bion's *Lament for Adonis* (Kirkconnell 100).

34. For the relationship between astrology and religion in the classical world, see Franz Cumont, lecture IV in *Astrology and Religion among the Greeks and Romans* (1912; rpt. New York, 1960). For Milton's knowledge of astrology, see Lawrence Babb, *The Moral Cosmos of "Paradise Lost"* (East Lansing, Mich., 1970), pp. 30–31. Also see *Arcades*, line 52, and *Epitaphium Damonis*, lines 79–80, which complain of Saturn's maleficent influence.

35. Lattimore, *Themes in Greek and Roman Epitaphs*, pp. 311–13. Lattimore observes that this consolation "seems to represent a real strand of pagan thought worked into the Christian doctrine" (p. 312).

36. M. H. Abrams, "Five Types of *Lycidas*," in *Milton's "Lycidas": The Tradition and the Poem*, ed. C. A. Patrides (New York, 1961), p. 228. He adds that the Pilot's invective prepares us for the poem's Christian resolution because "without it the resolution, inadequately grounded, would seem to have been contrived through Christ as a *Deus ex machina.*"

LYCIDAS: HURLED BONES AND THE NOBLE MIND OF REFORMED CONGREGATIONS

George H. McLoone

IN HIS DISCUSSION of *Lycidas,* Jon Lawry emphasizes that the poem's agon is caused by "the apparent distance between the stance of earth and Heaven," a distance resolved by the transcending power of "eager thought" in the speaker's mind, one able to retain "incomplete propositions" even as it moves conclusively toward a sense of heavenly union.[1] In the course of this struggle, pastoral imagery of the classical kind and its "Olympian stance" appear "less potent and therefore less real than the oceanic tempests of loss," although, ironically, these same pastoral images hint at renovation and faith and make "Multiple contacts with consolatory immortality" (pp. 101–05). The very "impotence" provokes the speaker's eventually right judgment, that of Jove's heavenly perspective. From this perspective, nature and man can be reconciled as well, since death, in the doctrine underlying the poem, derives from original sin and not from nature itself. The forces of nature do not kill Lycidas, but rather the "contrivance" of the faithless bark, implicitly linked to Satan and to sin (p. 111). By the end of the poem, "a circle has joined Heaven and earth, first in consolation, then in forms of salvation, and finally in divine celebration." The poem's shepherds are not only comforted but also related to heaven along with Lycidas, signifying the renovation of society through the agency of Christ. For the speaker, too, "the isolation of death is revoked." Hence, even though *Lycidas* is metaphorical, it is also doctrinal (pp. 118–19).

Lawrence Hyman, on the other hand, argues that restoration in *Lycidas* is not a doctrinal effect, and that, in our response to the poem, doctrine and aesthetics remain opposed: "It is the pastoral tradition, particularly as this tradition is given renewed power by Milton's deliberate and highly conscious control over his form, not our twentieth-century scepticism, that makes us see the resurrection in *Lycidas* as an aesthetic experience rather than as a religious belief."[2] The "feelings within the poem and the feelings that exist outside of the poem" are distinct. The allusion to Christian resurrection in the poem "is simply another metaphor" for a general, imagined sense of renovation: "It is not poetry that is brought into the higher syntheses of Christianity, but rather the Christian *consolatio* that is brought into the imaginative experience of the poem" (pp. 29, 32).

Perhaps somewhere between reading *Lycidas* as a celebration of aestheticism and as a celebration of doctrine are a number of analyses of the speaker's identity, his maturing sense of self as both poet and priest. Stanley Fish, for example, believes that "the suppressing of the personal voice is the poem's achievement, and that, eventually, "the determined anonymity of *Lycidas* should remind us that the poet's fierce egoism is but one half of his story."[3] Peter M. Sacks relates the theme of loss to the elegist's maturing ego in more specifically Freudian terms: "The work of mourning involves a castrative moment of submission to death and to a necessary deflection of desire." Milton's text moves from an emphasis on mother and female figures to images of authoritative fathers, implying the speaker's discovery of "a trope for procreative force that outlasts individual mortality." The "crux in the mourning" is the allusion to Orpheus's death and to his mother's failure to protect him, "a recapitulated loss of the mother together with a scenario of castration." Here, the youth's immature "economy of sacrifice and reward" collapses, and "the notion of reward must be revised, a revision somehow earned more fully" by the submission to death on the part of the poet. Consolation is therefore found by the poet in "a resurgent yet displaced and spiritualized sexual energy" which will "triumph" over the images of castration in the text.[4]

To be sure, parts of the criticism are mutually exclusive. Nonetheless, a synthesis of doctrine, aesthetic effect, and psychological affect is possible in interpreting the poem, I believe, when we attend to the resonance of its recurrent symbol, the body of Lycidas. As the criticism repeatedly implies, Lycidas is a metaphorical and aesthetic figure of some kind and, of course, a saintly identity in the mind of the elegist. I would like to discuss not only the elegist's developing attitudes toward the metaphor as signifying his maturing identity but also his implicit concern for the right relationship between this identity and the ecclesiastical body—the congregation of both the visible and the invisible church experiencing the crisis of reformation. I hope to explain both the affectively reforming and Reformation psychology of Milton's pastoral voice by considering the Pauline concept of the mystical body of the church as an important antecedent of *Lycidas*, one linking the crisis of mind and personality to that of ecclesiastical discipline and doctrine in ways that illuminate the meaning of the poem.[5]

We might first consider that the headnote added to *Lycidas* in the

1645 edition of Milton's *Poems* is itself a developmental kind of statement, one suggesting the maturing identity of a congregational poet—i.e., a pastoral elegist who will demonstrate both personal and ecclesiastical reformation: "*In this Monody the Author bewails a learned Friend, unfortunately drown'd in his passage from* Chester *on the* Irish *Seas*, 1637. *And by occasion foretells the ruine of our corrupted Clergie then in their height*" (CM, I, p. 76). *Monody* is of course a song by one voice, and the term connotes the solitariness and introspection of the singer perhaps more than would *eclogue* or *elegy*. The second sentence, however, if indignant in tone, is more spiritually nurturing and congregational in its underlying attitude and significance. The image of the drowned friend will be balanced, perhaps outweighed, by that of corruption in the visible church, a prophecy embracing "our" clergy. This harsh but productive witnessing is in turn comparable to a communal ministry and its exhortative liturgy.[6]

Elements of a lyric psychology of ruin leading to reform in the poetic text derive from the author's historical sense of the church discipline of threatened and actual excommunication in the course of pastoral nurture. In the historical context regarded by Milton as helping to explain the structure of the poem, pastoral discipline and nurture have been wrongly and selfishly practiced by the established hierarchy of pastors and prelates. One implied promise of the poem, however, is that church discipline can be rightly understood and practiced by a congregation purged of hierarchic influence, and by the individual Christian accepting his mature identity as minister, or shepherd, by virtue of his membership in the mystical body of the invisible church. In the poetic text, the pilot's foretelling of ruin and his witness against "corrupted," morally dead clergy can also be understood as a psychologically displaced prophecy against the swain's own self-protecting, immature aestheticism, his hierarchic stage of artistic development demonstrating a "Noble" (71) but also infirm elegiac practice and persona. Hence, the polemical ramifications of the "occasion" afforded by personal grief are continuous with the lyric's expressive celebration of a maturing, congregational personality, the mind of a rightly shepherding poet.

The monodistic voice in the text first would preserve the ego's precedence and supposed authority. Its self-centered aestheticism, work associated with some future inscription, and the elegist's own "destin'd Urn" (20), mounts a defense against an authentic obligation—one implied by the omniscient and prophetic tone of the headnote—to apply personal grief ecclesiastically and beyond the self. The monodist's bewailing "a learned Friend," unlike the eventual application of learning and grief, begins as a centripetal kind of mythography, an "Inwrought" (105) exercise by a fearful and perhaps somewhat tyrannical ego, to borrow the term from its later context describing Camus's aesthetic vestments ("Inwrought with figures dim"). The "uncouth Swain" (186), however, a term implying a less egoistic yet more mature identity for the elegist, will denigrate or abandon the aesthetic, cultic structures such as the "fondly" dreamt wish for mythic significance and protection (56), or the evoked appearance of a flower-strewn body, the work of a "Sicilian muse" (133). These have displaced an ego threatened by the consequence of sin and by the actual, "dread voice" of reform (132). The pilot's "dread voice" is also a consequence of sin and therefore in keeping with the harsh reality of death. However, unlike the monodist's previous, mythographic image of "the blind *Fury*" (75), that of the pilot's voice and threatening suggests the potential rewards of authorized, inspired instruction. His presence nearly reforms the procession of mourners and is a more useful and rightly reasoned liturgy, one reifying the transcendent integrity of the mystical body of the church even as it castigates the selfishness of established clerics, figured as merely appetitive bodies.

In his monodistic state of mind, mythographic (rather than piloting) pastoralism is a tempting, purgatorial kind of contract, a covenant of works between the elegist and his sources, "Sisters of the sacred well" (15). This covenant derives from a youthful ego's supposed dominion over death as well as life. It is a structuring reaction to the threat of losing control over the efficacy of works—here, textual or poetic works circumscribing death and expressing ambition. The pilot's speech implicitly demeans this covenant and the cultic, prescribed tradition of aesthetic limits with which the monodistic ego has become invested. In the more fully authorized context introduced by the pilot's speech, aesthetic works are better related to deeds as expressions of mature faith, a faith admitting the sinful causes of mortality and acknowledging that salvation is ultimately unaffected by works in themselves. The supposed authority of expressive lyricism in the opening lines of the poem will be subsumed by prophetic lyricism, because mythographic pastoralism, like the mistaken discipline and disciplining of the traditional clergy, is too often work without faith, mere extension of an ego protecting itself. Piloting pastoralism, on the other hand, lyrically expresses faith even as it promises true discipline by means of deeds. Eventually, another authorial, or omniscient and authorized voice will declare that the "uncouth Swain" sang expressively—"Thus sang . . . to th' Okes and rills," (186)—yet the swain who is now identified as such and authoritatively fixed in the pastoral setting is also imagined entering future, uncircumscribed contexts: "Tomorrow to fresh Woods, and Pastures new" (193). His expressiveness here seems to transcend both a monodistic self obsessed with egoistic grief and the authorial self drawn to a historical crisis, although both aspects of the elegist's personality can serve the mystical body. The last line of the poem, accordingly, is expressively figurative and historically prophetic. The ending implies that a new authorial voice is quoting or somehow paraphrasing the swain, a lyric laborer; yet this last expressive effect, ambiguously assigned to swain or narrator, may also seem to generate a voice that is simultaneously subjective and objective, one singing in the mystical body of the church rather than in the confines of prescriptive pastoralism.

"My destin'd Urn" had been a safe but sad boundary for the elegist's identity, and its terminal imagery is metonymous with supposedly safe pastoral vehicles ensuring self-preservation.[7] In the end, however, this artifact is like that vehicle conveying the elegist's alter ego, Lycidas — the "perfidious Bark" (100), a work failing to sustain him. The monodist's fear of dissolution, however, is contravened by the pilot's authorized predictions of the necessary kind of dissolution that precedes reform. This voice, also part of the swain's labor but one not limited by the "Bitter constraint" (6) of subjective grieving, breaks down the ego's artifacts and its protective boundaries in the course of its authorized and more productive ministry of witness. Without a reforming kind of dissolution or its prospect, Lycidas might have developed that "Inwrought" identity of his mentors — "old *Damaetas*" (36) and the "reverend Sire" (103), Camus, the antecedents of an established, unproductive clergy. Instead, he is claimed by the pilot as a "young swain" anticipating future reformation, and he exists viably in the pilot's mind as a paradigm for what ought to be the reformed church ("How well could I have spar'd for thee young swain, / Anow of such as for their bellies sake" (113–14). The pilot displays the keys of more fruitful instruction and liturgy than Camus can provide. His keys instruct sinners, opening their minds to the importance of forgiveness. Although it is "dread," his voice significantly reforms the pastoral liturgy of grief; it incorporates the reality of mortal dissolution with the mystical body of the church as a whole, the invisible church that exists simultaneously in heaven, in the congregation, and in the mind.

The fresh woods and pastures of the Swain's own genius may attend to the "dread" voice of authorized, reformed pastoralism again, and here we might compare the mature, pastoral voice of Milton's later sonnet, "On the Late Massacher in Piemont" (1655):

Avenge O Lord, thy slaughter'd Saints, whose bones
Lie scatter'd on the Alpine mountains cold,
Ev'n them who kept thy truth so pure of old
When all our Fathers worship't Stocks and Stones,
Forget not: in thy book record their groanes
Who were thy Sheep and in their antient Fold
Slayn by the bloody *Piemontese* that roll'd
Mother with Infant down the Rocks. Their moans
The Vales redoubl'd to the Hills, and they
To Heav'n. Their martyr'd blood and ashes sow
O'er all th' *Italian* fields where still doth sway
The Triple Tyrant: that from these may grow
A hunder'd-fold, who having learnt thy way
Early may fly the *Babylonian* woe.

In this context, "thy book" (5) is not merely funereal inscription invalidating anger and indignation. Rather, by recording affective sounds ("groanes") and not dicta or names and statements, the Lord's text generates reformation transcendentally. Spatial boundaries seem to collapse when the sounds of suffering are heard simultaneously by vales, hills, and heaven. Eventually, the image of mortal dissolution, the "scatter'd" bones (2) of these true Christians, may engender a Christian liberty of consciousness as well as of national circumstance. Instruction in "thy way / Early" motivates escape from "*Babylonian* woe" (13–14), the depressing cultural limitation and psychology caused by seemingly secure but actually uninspired worship of "Stocks and Stones" (4), iconic structures established superstitiously or perfidiously.

The image of Lycidas's hurled bones also engenders an eventually liberated, ministerial consciousness. In a sense, like the bones, Lycidas has fled early from the "pledge" asserted by debilitated authority and its aesthetic "edge" or limit (103–07), but the uncertain location of the bones encourages a better kind of liturgy than that of the "Laureat Herse" (151). The escape or direction of the elegist as well as his alter ego is toward the heavenly kingdom of "unexpressive nuptial Song" (176), an aesthetic liturgy beyond the margins of prescribed texts and egoistic structures. The hurled bones rest in a dynamic kind of peace, one comparable to the sanctified ubiquity of the mystical body of the invisible church and its expressive, unbound liturgy.

Exclusion as an edifying threat, the discipline symbolized by the pilot's keys and by the "two-handed engine" (130), is of course part of the literature of the ongoing Reformation encouraged by Milton. The lyric process of grieving in the poem and the reformation of "bodies" in variously cultic and institutional senses are comparable to Milton's antiprelatical exhortations to reform the Christian community through improved understandings and applications of church discipline in clerical administration as well as in liturgics. In *Of Reformation*, "Pure Religion" necessarily requires:

to cashier, and cut away from the publick body the noysom, and diseased tumor of Prelacie, and come from Schisme to *unity* with our neighbour Reformed sister Churches, which with the blessing of *peace* and *pure doctrine* have now long time flourish'd; and doubtles with all hearty *joy*, and *gratulation*, will meet, and welcome our Christian *union* with them, as they have bin all this while griev'd at our strangenes and little better than separation from them. (CM, III, p. 62)

One justification for so dismembering the ministerial hierarchy in order to reform it is that the bishops themselves have misunderstood or misapplied the discipline of excommunication, using it "peremptorily" and as a "peece of pure *Primitive Divinity*." "This most mild, though withall dredfull, and inviolable Prerogative of *Christs* diadem excommunication servs for nothing with them, but to prog, and pandar for fees, or to display their pride." Valid excommunication, on the other hand, does not seek "to bereave or destroy the body," if properly applied; "it seekes to save the Soule by humbling the body," and "by Fatherly admonishment, and Christian rebuke, to cast it into godly sorrow, whose end is joy, and ingenuous bashfulnesse to sin." Excommunication is therefore not a seemingly commercial act but rather a form of Christian education. If the godly sorrow

can not be wrought, then as a tender Mother takes her Child and holds it over the pit with scarring words, that it may learne to feare, where danger is, so doth excommunication as deerly, and as freely without money, use her wholsome and saving terrors, she is instant, she beseeches, by all the deere, and sweet promises of Salvation she entices and woos, by all the threatnings, and thunders of the *Law*, and rejected *Gosspel* she charges, and adjures; this is all her Armory, her munition, her Artillery, then she awaites with long-sufferance, and yet ardent zeale. In briefe, there is no act in all the errand of *Gods Ministers* to man-kind, wherein passes more loverlike contestation between Christ and the Soule of a regenerate man lapsing, then before, and in, and after the sentence of Excommunication. (CM, III, pp. 71–72)

In the *Institutes*, Calvin discusses this teaching authority and ministry by first citing Ephesians iv, 10–13, that, in the work of ministry, Christ assigned some as apostles, others as prophets, evangelists, pastors, and teachers, "'for the building up of the body of Christ, until we all reach the unity of the faith and of the knowledge of the Son of God, to perfect manhood, to the measure of the fully mature age of Christ.'" Those rejecting the spiritual food of these nurturing offices, in Calvin's view, "deserve to perish in famine and hunger." He continues, "the face of God shines upon us in teaching"; one sought the face of God in the temple sanctuary because there "the teaching of the law and the exhortations of the prophets were a living image of God, just as Paul asserts that in his preaching the glory of God shines in the face of Christ [2 Corinthians iv, 6]."[8] The authority of the keys conferred on the apostles to forgive sins is a similarly hortatory, educative office, a duty to preach and counsel reconciliation to God through Christ: "Therefore, in the communion of saints, our sins are continually forgiven us by the ministry of the church itself when the presbyters or bishops to whom this office has been committed strengthen godly consciences by the gospel promises in the hope of pardon and forgiveness. This they do publicly and privately as need requires" (Calvin, *Institutes*, p. 1035). In a rightly reformed church, "the keys have an indissoluble bond with the Word." Paradoxically, however, the Word is preached "through men like us." We can therefore "best evidence our piety and obedience toward God if we show ourselves teachable toward his minister, although he excels us in nothing." God hid wisdom "in weak and earthen vessels in order to prove more surely how much we should esteem it." Moreover, "this human ministry which God uses to govern the church is the chief sinew by which believers are held together in one body" (Calvin, pp. 1051, 1054–55).

Milton refers to the keys of disciplinary authority in *The Reason of Church Government*, where he attacks the secular reliance of bishops in enforcing the ministry of censure:

> surely much rather might the heavenly ministry of the Evangel bind her self about with farre more pearcing beams of Majesty and aw, by wanting the beggarly help of halings and amercements in the use of her powerful Keies. For when the Church without temporal support is able to doe her great works upon the unforc't obedience of men, it argues a divinity about her. But when she thinks to credit and better her spirituall efficacy, and to win herself respect and dread by strutting in the fals visard of worldly autority, tis evident that God is not there; but that her apostolick vertu is departed from her, and hath left her *Key-cold.* (CM, III, pp. 251–52)

Self-esteem and the fear of shame should be motives enough for godly behavior, attitudes instilled by the laity as well as by ministers in part from the threat of holy discipline by the congregation as a whole.[9] This manner of closing the door is instructional and therapeutic for the sinner, a "vehement cleansing medicin" that is also "a mortifying to life, a kind of saving by undoing"; "as the mercies of wicked men are cruelties, so the cruelties of the Church are mercies" (CM, III, p. 266).

In *Lycidas*, the pilot's foretelling of ruin for a corrupt clergy is also nurturing. It is within the mood of instructed repentance informing the mortal, and therefore sinful, elegist, bringing him closer to the author's position of relating grief to prophetic witness. The pilot's voice asserts the continuity between pastoral mourning and pastoral discipline. His is also the discriminating office of the mature minister and preacher, the overseer who guides sternly, the pilot with "Miter'd locks" who "stern bespake" (112). His guidance and the ministerial leadership of the entire church body urge the sinner to overcome his alienation through their disciplinary projections. Such is the right use of the keys of authorized forgiveness by means of instruction from those who do know how to hold a sheep hook. Whatever its specific tenor, the "two-handed engine at the door" that "Stands ready to smite once, and smite no more" (130–31) is generally the application of mortifying discipline through exhortation and image. Like the rhetorical "engines of terror" Milton recommends for preachers searching the hearts of sinners (CM, III, p. 265), it mainly "Stands ready," its force exercised in forbidding prospect, it is hoped, rather than in actual use by the communion of saints.

The mature, authorized aesthetic that develops by means of the ritualistic processes of mourning giving way to affective, prophetic assertions of educative love and faith invests the pastoral artist with a more productive consciousness of his own membership in the communion of saints: "At last he rose, and twitch'd his Mantle blew: / To morrow to fresh Woods, and Pastures new" (192–93). Putting on his mantle against the night concedes the elegist's heritage of sin and mortality, but his earthbound existence in time is also the occasion for his incorporating with "him that walk'd the waves" (173). The Christian paradox of death as consummation and consequent engendering of timeless life within the mystical body influences the elegist's projection of his alter ego, Lycidas, in heaven, entertained by "all the Saints" singing "In solemn troops, and sweet Societies" (178–79), the dead singer and builder of lofty rhymes (11) now hearing a song that is "unexpressive" and "nuptial" (176). The image of the alter ego who is also "Genius" and "good / To all that wander" (184–85) conveys a similarly mystical incorporation, one also necessitated by mortal peril and the errors of fallen, wandering humanity. Paradoxically, the "unexpressive" song is framed within the describable song, a "*Dorick* lay," yet seems to transcend the frame as well in a way that is analogous to the reforming of the elegist's understanding of mortality and of the function of pastoral aesthetic. The elegist is therefore objectified in the third person, finally, to indicate the self's nearing the completion of identity, even if the terms of maturity, "the uncouth Swain" (186), are humble and limited in tone. The swain sings in time, history, and convention, first discovering that his self-conscious exercise in mourning commemorates the self-absorption, the alienation, of the artist displacing the crisis of sin with the crisis of technique, then later discovering that his capacity for faith and love is greater than the sum of these parts. The dread voice is loving, declaring the integrity of the communion of saints on earth as it relates death to an ecclesiastical significance taking shape in the swain's song. All these voices, however seemingly disparate, are counterpointed parts of the elegist's identity as a mortal sinner who will nonetheless experience sanctification and its eventual peace of conscience. The shift to omniscience at the close authorizes this complex yet "uncouth" identity.

The dread, witnessing voice is also the earthly counterpart of the loving choir of saints in heaven. It cooperates with the peace of conscience and ecclesiastical integrity experienced by the sanctified, individually and as member of the church. The "dread voice" and the "unexpressive" song are paradoxically the rightly harmonized vocal framework and sounds for accommodating not only the corrupt and the saved but also the variously insecure moods of the elegist. They imply a truly harmonious and firm identity of the whole human being, a mature structure of mind in which the dissolving, juvenile self is not just an alarming prospect but one that can be rightly celebrated. In this reformed context, work is not futile aestheticism but rather more like "works" in the theological sense, an act of worship. By the end of the poem, a context of reformed worship has been constructed and expressed, one supplanting the unreliable context of worship—the unloving, exclusionary rite or merely negative utterance, forms like the "perfidious Bark / Built in th' eclipse, and rigg'd with curses dark, / That sunk so low that sacred head of thine" (100–02).

Perfidy, of course, is the foreseeable outcome of superstition and the misapplied pronouncements of hierarchy. It can result from the dicta or works of "Blind mouthes!" in the pilot's speech (118), the works of those excluding out of narrow selfishness rather than out of love, not having "learn'd ought els the least / That to the faithfull Herdmans art belongs!" (120–21), and producing, "when they list, their lean and flashy songs" (123). The exclusionary pastorate of privilege and sinecure, unlike the reformed pastorate of loving discipline and faith, cannot manage a worthwhile liturgy, one that is a work of the people. Instead, such pastors "scramble" at the congregational "feast" and "shove away the worthy bidden guest" (116–17). What may seem song at first is really a perfidious kind of discipline in their case, a liturgical aesthetic merely "flashy" or, again, one actually "rigg'd with curses dark," to cite the associated context.

Unreformed liturgy not only works to protect a sinfully greedy ego and its boundaries, but is also relatable to the elegist's mood of "Bitter constraint," his sense of unhappy duty compelling him to "pluck" and "shatter" laurel, myrtle, and ivy out of season (1–7). His bitterness at beginning the labor of lyric grieving complicates mere convention by introducing the youthfulness of the elegist as well as Lycidas, and by implying an at least vague sense of longing for a more mature kind of aesthetic. The mature aesthetic, we can gather later, would not be prompted strictly by occasion but by a ripening inspiration, an edifying muse that would develop the speaker as well as his text into states more closely approximating "the unexpressive nuptial Song" of a sanctified community of singers. The mood of constraint, however, first leads him toward delineated works, the inscribed urn as compensation, he imagines, for his monody. This aesthetic covenant of works is apparently justified by the elegist's prospect of the unpreserved, unsung body exposed to an unshaped nature, to the water and wind, without "som melodious tear" as "meed" or due reward for inspired labor (14). Lycidas "knew / Himself to sing, and build the lofty rhyme," and therefore an obligation exists: "Who would not sing for *Lycidas?*" (10–11). But, the conventional, dictated trope of immortality produced by aesthetic commemoration is ironically unsettling. The "fair peace" (22) the elegist would project as a compensation addressed by "some Gentle Muse" (19) in the mortal future is not a worshipful or sanctified context, and the image of aesthetic ("fair") calm is already compromised by the disappointing resonance of "With lucky words favour my destin'd Urn" (20). Such tribute, perhaps one associated with superstitious pronouncements, would not involve the inscriber as pastoral artist in the ministerial sense developing in the poem's later contexts, nor would it consider the dead builder of rhymes to be a nurturing genius and guide, a ubiquitous presence whose new works are sufficiently expressive of glory. The pretended involvement of this first alter ego, the urn inscriber and favorer, is more a power display than a communion. Having announced his possessive seduction of the sisters by admonishing them—"Hence with denial vain, and coy excuse" (18)—the elegist imagines, or aesthetically begets, a favored urn in order to limit and therefore control the boundaries of his self-portrait. The "sad occasion," when so treated as one of covenanted works by the inscriber ego fulfilling the elegist's wish, anticipates the appetitive dicta of the "Blind mouthes" feeding selfish hierarchy. "Lucky" and "as he passes"

(20–21) imply the latent perfidiousness and future indifference of such unreformed, clerical singers as well.

The tribute to pastoral kinship in youth is similarly more contractual than creatively inspired, relatable by "For" to the "need" and "favour" of compensation, even if the setting is rationalized as nurturing places of labor: "For we were nurst upon the self-same hill, / Fed the same flock; by fountain, shade, and rill" (23–24). Here the grieving elegist would shape the past not only to establish mutuality but also to make memory conform to his craving for artifact uncomplicated by a creator's sinfulness, and for a world seemingly without the necessity of atonement. Sin is accordingly nearly excluded, and the foresight of losing innocence is subordinated to "our song" (36). The hints of disorder and mortality in "Rough *Satyrs*," and "Fauns with clov'n heel," and "old *Damaetas*," consequences of the heritage of sin, are factitiously contained, or nearly so, safely enshrined within the aestheticism of pastoral temporality and the margins of Cambridge allegory:

> Together both, ere the high Lawns appear'd
> Under the opening eye-lids of the morn,
> We drove a field, and both together heard
> What time the Gray-fly winds her sultry horn,
> Batt'ning our flocks with the fresh dews of night,
> Oft till the Star that rose, at Ev'ning, bright,
> Toward Heav'ns descent had slop'd his westering wheel.
> Mean while the Rural ditties were not mute,
> Temper'd to th' Oaten Flute;
> Rough *Satyrs* danc'd, and *Fauns* with clov'n heel,
> From the glad sound would not be absent long,
> And old *Damaetas* lov'd to hear our song. (25–36)

The scene, while moving peacefully, beautifully toward a tuneful night, repressively manages fear and desire by melodious effort—the satyrs dance; the fauns are charmed; aged authority is pleased. The tableau, however, does not reform or relate infirmity to atonement, but rather preserves it. Music here does not open the mind to the possibilities of "fresh Woods" anticipated at the poem's second close of day, but instead accompanies the making of centripetal exercise, the song heard by three figures, its allegorical references having no real significance, as Samuel Johnson partially observed, because it has no "real passion," only aesthetic images supporting each other.[10] Loving "to hear" but without sufficient attention to sin is ultimately uncharitable, not nurturing. The young shepherds' attachment to Damaetas is established by pleasure in song, pleasure that is harmless enough but a love subordinating a better charity of aged authority—nurturing admonition. A past in which the consciousness of sin is repressed influences the present to be similarly redundant and unregenerating in its artistry. The "heavy change" noticed next because of Lycidas's absence (37) is also evaluated aesthetically, its significance subordinated to lyricism: "Such, *Lycidas*, thy loss to Shepherds ear" (49). Even though the green landscape is gone (the "Copses green / Shall now no more be seen, / Fanning their joyous Leaves to thy soft layes," 42–44), nature still resembles or reciprocates the mood of the singer as monodist not minister: "Thee Shepherd, thee the Woods, and desert Caves / With wilde Thyme and the gadding Vine o'regrown, / And all their echoes mourn" (39–41). While there is a certain order in this prescribed, mythographic effect in nature, the mourning echoes enclose or preserve grief and, correlatively, the alienated elegist and his mood of "heavy change." The burden of loss and the insecurity of actual nature, the Irish Sea or "the stormy *Hebrides*" (156), the world rightly witnessing mortality as the consequence of sin, are shut out by echo and repetition. Mutability may succumb to the artistic ego's intentional design, but its burden will not be delivered.

In this circumscribed context, one cultivated to ease or mask the necessity of witness and loving discipline, accusation is also redundant, expressing the monodist's alienation. The complaint against the nymphs, absent "when the remorseless deep / Clos'd o're the head of your lov'd *Lycidas*" (50–51), again limits or contains the obligations of love by mythography rather than energizes them. "Love" relegated to the nymphs as unsustaining affection serves to limit the significance of the word; although, as the mythographic context begins its inexorable elaboration, the monodist's self-denigration intensifies, finding its correlative in mythic geographies of resentment:

> Where were ye Nymphs when the remorseless deep
> Clos'd o're the head of your lov'd *Lycidas*?
> For neither were ye playing on the steep,
> Where your old *Bards*, the famous *Druids*, ly,
> Nor on the shaggy top of *Mona* high,
> Nor yet where *Deva* spreads her wisard stream;
> Ay me, I fondly dream!
> Had ye bin there—for what could that have don?
> What could the Muse her self that *Orpheus* bore
> The Muse her self, for her inchanting son
> Whom Universal nature did lament,
> When by the rout that made the hideous roar,
> His goary visage down the stream was sent,
> Down the swift *Hebrus* to the *Lesbian* shore? (50–63)

In Milton's draft of the passage, the Muse had been described as looking ahead, beyond herself, and golden, implicitly generous:

> What could the golden-haired Calliope
> For her enchanting son
> When she beheld (the gods far-sighted be)
> His gory scalp roll down the Thracian lea.[11] (58–63)

The revision, however, returns us to "The Muse her self" as a contextual framing of Orpheus's birth, a redundancy that contains or confines the clause, "that Orpheus bore." Implicitly, the delivery or letting go through pain of prior identity is impeded by "her self," and the song of "her enchanting son" is drowned out by "the hideous roar" of envy. This singer's dismemberment is in turn contained spatially by "the swift *Hebrus*" and "the *Lesbian* shore." His body's mythographically limited boundaries can then be contrasted, albeit again implicitly, with a more Reformation-minded geography of Spain, Scotland, home, and the stormy, wild ocean separating the tyrannical past yet occasioning a reformed future (155–64).

Orpheus, of course, was also a doomed celebrant and pastoral minister. In the *Metamorphoses* to which Milton alludes, he is the son and priestly singer of Phoebus ("vatis Apollinei"),[12] and the protector and teacher of the proper rites of Bacchus ("orgia tradiderat," XI, 93), the god also grieving at the Maenads' savagery and the singer's loss (XI, 68). Similar to Lycidas's scattered yet eventually harmonious presence, Orpheus is dismembered physically but fulfilled spiritually, consummately when his shade finds Eurydice a second, final time ("membra iacent diversa locis," ["The poet's limbs lay scattered all around"], XI, 50; "invenit Eurydicen cupidisque amplectitur ulnis; / hic modo coniunctis spatiantur passibus ambo," ["(He) found Eurydice and caught her in his eager arms. Here now side by side they walk"], XI, 63–64). The wondrous event ("mirum," 51) of the singing, severed head is also both dead and alive ("flebile lingua / murmurat exanimis," ["mournfully the lifeless tongue murmured"], XI, 53), and it evokes an echoing response from the river's banks ("respondent flebile ripae," ["mournfully the banks replied"], XI, 53). The grotesque fragmentation of the poet has not stopped his song, and his dripping head still receives the protection of Apollo (XI, 56–60). Bacchus, here called Lyaeus (XI, 67), "deliverer from care" in turn avenges his celebrant by transforming the Maenads into oaks, and then by deserting their fields for other vineyards, accompanied by a better group of devotees (XI, 67–86). The Maenads had been angry at Orpheus for his indifference to them, his implicit contempt for their improper celebrations and appetites (XI, 7). They accordingly extended their sacrilegious behavior into disrupting the hard work of field laborers, then into murder using the abandoned implements of tillage (XI, 29–43). Unmoved by supplicating gesture as well as by his song, they demonstrated their impiety by killing the poet: "ad vatis fata recurrunt / tendentemque manus et in illo tempore primum / inrita dicentem nec quicquam voce moventem / sacrilegae perimunt (XI, 38–41).

["They rushed back to slay the bard; and, as he stretched out his suppliant hands, uttering words then, but never before, unheeded, and moving them not a whit by his voice, the impious women struck him down."]

Despite the important similarities with the fate of Lycidas, however, the narrative mode and the narrator's attitude in the contexts implied by the allusion are significantly different. Ovid's text, like the relationships it depicts, is inwrought, its changings promiscuously breeding myth after myth of various impieties and retributions, a text in perpetual motion reflecting the narrator's first inclination: "In nova fert animus mutatas dicere formas / corpora" ("My mind is bent to tell of bodies changed into new forms"), (I, 1–2). To be sure, there are moral possibilities in the narrative, but they are bound or impeded by the apparently endless, insatiable demands of mythographic appetite. On the other hand, the Orphic allusion in Milton's text becomes a terminal case, its ornateness cracking under the onslaught of the elegist's questioning, and its moral significance, even if arrived at negatively, surviving as the mythography fades into the speaker's discontent. Hence, the questions simultaneously emphasize and undermine the elegist's mythographic tendency, the aestheticism protecting his ego. The dialogue with this aesthetic self is in turn undermined by the affective reaction, "Alas! What boots it with uncessant care," implying the alienation of a self caught up in bargaining. Disturbingly, the mythographic kind of context becomes increasingly untenable, yet also what the ego seems to crave most, the event continuous with fame, "the spur that the clear spirit doth raise / (That last infirmity of Noble mind) / To scorn delights, and live laborious dayes" (70–72). The covenant of works, here a kind of purgatorial aesthetic, displaces appetite with egoism; it does not develop a mature, moral psychology. Even if the aim is heavenly, a covenant so compromised is infirm, wrongly preserving the juvenile identity yet remaining in "Noble mind."

Phoebus's reply to the prospect of the "*Fury* with th' abhorred shears" (75) cutting off the poet's life suggests an overcompensating ego, the ego here displaced as the Apollonian, protective father of the poet. The reply is a reversion to the authority of external, hierarchic dicta after his looking into the abyss — the panic at dissolution and annihilation prosodically emphasized by the line's severe, medial pause: "And slits the thin-spun life. But not the praise, / *Phoebus* repli'd, and touch'd my trembling ears" (76–77). The "praise," "perfet witnes" of Jove (82), and his pronouncement on works ("each deed," 83) further magnify the craving for authoritative verbal designs against the unpredictable, wild act of "the blind *Fury*" and against the "broad rumour" that "lies" in an equally dark abyss of language (80). A more comforting reply, we can assume, should include the covenant of faith and grace, even though this Jovian witness can serve as an expedient distraction.

A more principled kind of heavenly justification by faith rather than by works is of course the traditional, reformed view Milton argues in the *De Doctrina*, even though he does emphasize "the works of faith."[13] He distinguishes between the merely formulaic works of the old law (perhaps implicitly as well of the remnants of the old law in Anglican practice) and the works of "a true, living, saving faith." In his reading of St. Paul (Romans iii, 28), "Faith has its own works, which may be different from the works of the law. We are justified therefore by faith, but by a living, not a dead faith; and that faith alone which acts is counted living" (CM, XVI, pp. 37–39). He develops the cultural ramifications of the gospel's better covenant and more heartfelt textualism in his discussion of "the Gospel and Christian Liberty":

> The gospel is the new dispensation of the covenant of grace, far more excellent and perfect than the law, announced first obscurely by Moses and the prophets, afterwards in the clearest terms by Christ himself, and his apostles and evangelists, written since by the Holy Spirit in the hearts of believers, and ordained to continue even to the end of the world, containing a promise of eternal life to all in every nation who shall believe in Christ when revealed to them, and a threat of eternal death to such as shall not believe. (CM, XVI, p. 113)

The new dispensation also affects the pastorate: "'The priesthood being changed, there is made of necessity a change also in the law. . . . There ariseth another priest, who is made not after the law of carnal commandment'" (Hebrews vii, CM, XVI, p. 129).

Further, legalistic discipline in the church, "that law," which is a vestige of the old law, impedes the present life and development of Christians:

> To these considerations we may add, that that law which not only cannot justify, but is the source of trouble and subversion to believers; which even tempts God if we endeavor to perform its requisitions; which has no promise attached to it, or, to speak more properly, which takes away and frustrates all promises, whether

of inheritance, or adoption, or grace, or of the Spirit itself; nay, which even subjects us to a curse; must necessarily have been abolished. (CM, XVI, p. 137)

The supposed utility of the law and its works in teaching us the doctrine of sin can also be misleading. Moreover, "the performance" of the law's works can alienate the Christian rather than incorporate him with Christ:

Besides, if the law be the means of leading us to a conviction of sin and an acceptance of the grace of Christ, this is effected by a knowledge of the law itself, not by the performance of its works; inasmuch as through the works of the law, instead of drawing nearer to Christ, we depart farther from him; as Scripture is perpetually inculcating. (CM, XVI, p. 149)

Christian liberty, on the other hand, develops a mature identity for the believer. As "men instead of children," we can work freely, expressively ("in love"), without institutional constraints:

Christian liberty is that whereby we are loosed as it were by enfranchisement, through Christ our deliverer, from the bondage of sin, and consequently from the rule of the law and of man; to the intent that being made sons instead of servants, and perfect men instead of children, we may serve God in love through the guidance of the Spirit of truth. (CM, XVI, pp. 153–55)

Accordingly, there is not "a sufficient warrant for those edicts of the magistrate which constrain believers, or deprive them in any respect of their religious liberty." Milton then extends the disciplinary benefits of enfranchisement to the "sealing of the covenant of grace," the sacraments of baptism and the Lord's supper. He contrasts them to the rituals of the old law, circumcision and Passover, and regards them as also liberated from the practice of the established church and of the Roman church (CM, XVI, pp. 163, 165).

In *Lycidas*, the "perfidious Bark" is comparable to the institutional structures that ostensibly carry a pastor and Christian but that actually betray him, if paradoxically sending him toward salvation and the role of "Genius" in this instance. The full exercise of Christian liberty, then, is achieved by Lycidas within the invisible church's mystical body and not in the visible institution. This Christian liberty and laboring manhood is also about to be approached by the "uncouth Swain" contemplating the "fresh Woods and Pastures new" inviting tomorrow's works of faith. The disciplinary impediments relatable to an unreformed egoism and its contractual, mythographic defenses, the works of an infirm if noble mind, are similarly perfidious structures. Ironically, on this occasion, they carry the elegist toward disillusionment, his "false surmise" (153). The "Bitter constraint" (6) of the sad occasion expresses a problematic mood of grief and artistry laboring defensively, not yet expressively. The pilot, however, dissonant and iconoclastic in his "dread voice," seems utterly free from the mythographic context, unresponsive to its processional characters, yet somehow relatable to them in time and space: "Last came, and last did go, / The Pilot of the *Galilean* lake" (108–09). Like the pilot's attitude, if unlike his tone, a reformed consciousness of ministry suggests that "eager thought" (189) rather than "Bitter constraint" should be prior to work, just as faith is prior to loving works. Like the pilot in time and timelessly, the reformed consciousness approaches the same pastures and woods as the unreformed. The swain's attitude of "enfranchisement" at the poem's close, however, is a significant difference from his initial mood of alienation. Such is the lyric inheritance of the pilot's keys. Hence, the pastures are new and the woods fresh, cleansed, as the sinner is "absolved from sin and death" in the better covenant rightly conveyed (*De Doctrina*, CM, XVI, p. 29).

Earlier, sin, work, and death were topics challenging the ego's supposed dominion over the reality of time, but they were relegated to an unenlightened sense of gratification, their theological significance repressed by the mind's last infirmity. The elegist's considering release from the "Shepherds trade" and its seemingly closed, perhaps profitless economy ("What boots it with uncessant care / To tend the homely slighted Shepherds trade," 64–65) was not the edifying, piloting complaint of the mature Christian. Escaping from a covenant of "laborious dayes" (72) when he thought to "strictly meditate the thankless Muse" (66) anticipates Christian liberty, but here the desire for freedom is subordinated to a rhetorical justification of the compulsion for fame: "Were it not better don as others use, / To sport with *Amaryllis* in the shade, / Or with the tangles of *Neaera's* hair? / *Fame* is the spur" (67–70). Hence, the shift from fame as rumor to fame as Jovian reward merely reconstructs the covenant of works preserving the juvenile ego. Imagining the dissolved body as a static icon signifying reward and fame and not as ministering in the work of faith preserves a similarly embalmed egoism. "To strew the Laureat Herse where *Lycid* lies" (151) is aesthetic work expressing fear but ironically deadening the occasion for a ministry of faith.

Rejecting the iconographic body and fame as worthwhile objects of aesthetic labor, therefore, liberates the ego previously displaced by the imagined corpse. The affective lament, "Ay me!" admits both hope and fear, echoing yet repudiating the mythographic "AI" decorating Camus's vestments, their "edge / Like to that sanguine flower inscrib'd with woe" (105–06), in his guise as celebrant of an outworn, contractual covenant: "Ah; Who hath reft (quoth he) my dearest pledge?" (107). The affective utterance of the Christian elegist, however, opens his mind to the gospel's authoritative, informal, and paradoxical definitions of fame. The lament expressing the unreformed mind's lack of authenticity or authority in the two preceding lines ("For so to interpose a little ease, / Let our frail thoughts dally with false surmise," 152–53) now occasions the elegist's mature ministry of witness. It is as though the elegist, fatigued and disillusioned by his contextual artistry of floral cataloguing, hears and heeds the voice of the real, a grace not given to Camus, who remains wrapped up in the aesthetics of grief, infirmly, at least slowly, searching for forensic rather than prophetic answers. For the reformed elegist, Lycidas is better regarded as unavailable for ritualistic and perhaps reductive pledges. He is "to our moist vows deny'd" and indefinitely present. "Under the whelming tide," he "Visit'st" or "Sleep'st" (157–60) in the liberated imagination of the elegist and in the indefinitely located but nonetheless certain presence of the mystical body. Here, the alter ego suggests the elegist's ego as Christologically contingent rather than mythographically and liturgically masterful, and therefore free, enfranchised: "So *Lycidas* sunk low, but mounted high" (172) hears "the unexpressive nuptial Song" (176); he hears a consummate text without the boundaries of prescribed articulation and does so "Through the dear might of him that walk'd the waves" (173).

The reforming of a covenant of works into a subordinate context implying the ascent of the covenant of grace, where works express faith worshipfully, resolves the elegist's grief. The presence of Lycidas in heaven is nonetheless sensuously aesthetic, and the ministry of angels to him is somehow corporal, affective and sanctified healing or nurture. "With *Nectar* pure his oozy Lock's he laves, / And hears the unexpressive nuptial Song" (175–76); "all the Saints above" (178) "entertain him"; "In solemn troops, and sweet Societies" they sing "And wipe the tears for ever from his eyes" (177–81). The elegist then assigns Lycidas a task of physical, cognitive, and perhaps psychological ministry that is coterminous with the completion of identity: "Hence forth thou art the Genius of the shore, / In thy large recompense, and shalt be good / To all that wander in that perilous flood" (183–85). Both the work of the future and the baptismal naming of the developed personality in terms of Christian work rather than pastoral ease are expressive of faith and adoration. The saints "singing in their glory move" as they minister to Lycidas (180); Lycidas "In thy large recompense . . . shalt be good." His ministry will be to pilot or guide the erroneous, a task that is simultaneously a reward, an atonement, and also glorification. This admirable labor, like the saints' singing, does not cause salvation or fame, but rather expresses a prior condition of transferred merit from "him that walk'd the waves."

The elegist in turn is assigned a laborer's title, "the uncouth Swain" (186), by a second authorial or authorized voice, similarly omniscient. The unknown, unsophisticated servant has accomplished a day's work by means of "Quills" and thought, and now we know who he is under the eye of eternity, a humble worker who exalts the sanctified and prophesies against the unreformed. That "He touch'd the tender stops of various Quills, / With eager thought warbling his *Dorick* lay" (188–89) reveals his willingness to hazard various modes of lyric witnessing within a larger frame of harmony; his task was to shift from mode to mode (or "mood" in line 87), yet at the same time maintain the integrity of the whole song. Hence, the swain's work is both glorification and atonement by means of the expressed rather than the unexpressive song. On earth, his presence and labor will demonstrate both mortal necessity and immortal possibility. He too can sink in the course of his ministry, but he is still meant for the task.

The sometimes sweet, sometimes dread voice of an ultimately nurturing church, the ministry of the communion of saints, is the elegist's paradigmatic lyric, one eventually absorbing the mythographic voices disguising the ego's fear of dissolution. Johnson's famous complaint against the aesthetic pastoralism of *Lycidas*, that "where there is leisure for fiction there is little grief," merely confusing and unmoving poetry, "irreverent combinations" of pastoral identities, is correct in part (*Lives*, p. 96). The monodist's searching for significance in the mode of mythographic pastoral does necessitate, however, his mature self-accusation of disillusionment. This enlightened condition of mind regards the real as a divine love that addresses sin and its consequent mortality rather than relegating our heritage to hierarchic displacements of egoism. The youth's fear of death, the elegist reveals, is really a fear of the ego's loss of dominion, his identity previously continuous with a fame threatened with interruption by the "blind *Fury*," then reiterated mythographically as "so much fame in Heav'n." Such stylized, displaced fear of death is a kind of "fiction," an expression not of theologically based grief but one closer to vain anger at discovering the reality of a complex self needing to experience the authority of educated forgiveness. The "sad embroidery" (147) of mythographic pastoralism ironically preserves this anger and seems to validate an undeveloped ego. This is a certain identity, but one in which sorrow, unlike the saved Lycidas, is dead. The dread voice, however, the pilot authorized to cooperate with Christ and with the Spirit, reanimates sorrow as a promise for "eager thought." Such occasional grace transforms monody into a lyric work of the communion of saints singing in heaven and in the mature, laboring mind.

Northern Virginia Community College

NOTES

1. Jon S. Lawry, *The Shadow of Heaven: Matter and Stance in Milton's Poetry* (Ithaca, 1968), pp. 96–99.

2. Lawrence W. Hyman, *The Quarrel Within: Art and Morality in Milton's Poetry* (Port Washington, N.Y., 1972), p. 23.

3. Stanley Fish, "*Lycidas:* A Poem Finally Anonymous," in *Milton's Lycidas: The Tradition and the Poem*, ed. C. A. Patrides (Columbia, Mo., 1983), pp. 322, 340.

4. Peter M. Sacks, "*Lycidas,*" in *John Milton: Modern Critical Views*, ed. Harold Bloom (New York, 1986), pp. 272–74, 279, 281. See also Donald M. Friedman, "*Lycidas:* The Swain's Paideia" on the developing roles of poet and priest, in Patrides, *Milton's Lycidas*, p. 20.

Stewart A. Baker, "Milton's Uncouth Swain," in *Milton Studies* III ed. James D. Simmonds (Pittsburgh, 1971), pp. 38–43, in his discussion of stylistic levels in the poem, points out that the Orpheus reference "serves as the mythological synthesis for the figures of priest and prophet," and that "the poem itself is ritual," recapturing "the Dionysiac rites of youthful friendship and loss." The poem therefore "celebrates" an "Orphic sensibility." Eventually, the swain undergoes a kind of "transfiguration" when he moves from "the role of poet to prophet."

5. In *De Doctrina*, I, 24, "Of Union and Fellowship With Christ and His Members, Wherein Is Considered the Mystical or Invisible Church," Milton cites Romans xii and 1 Corinthians xii on the fellowship "through the Spirit" of the regenerate with the Father and the Son and with each other, "The Communion of Saints." Also citing Romans ii, 29, he observes that the fellowship is "mystical," and therefore "not confined to place or time." In *The Works of John Milton*, ed. Frank Allen Patterson et al. (New York, 1931–38), XVI, pp. 57–63. Unless otherwise indicated, quotations from Milton's poetry and prose are from this edition, cited as CM.

For a discussion of the doctrine as it is echoed here and in Milton's other prose works, see Timothy J. O'Keeffe, *Milton and the Pauline Tradition* (Lanham, Md., 1982), pp. 203–54. See also Michael Lieb, "Milton and the Organicist Polemic," *Milton Studies*, IV, ed. James D. Simmonds (Pittsburgh, 1972), pp. 79–99, and his recent book, *The Sinews of Ulysses: Form and Convention in Milton's Works* (Pittsburgh, Pa.: Duquesne University Press, 1989), pp. 21–37.

6. The informal liturgy of Independent and Separatist congregations would allow for including prophecy as part of the ministry of the word. The famous divine, John Cotton, for example, regards prophetic exhortation as an important part of regular worship services and, therefore, as part of the life of the congregation. See *The Doctrine of the Church* (London, 1644), p. 6. This is consistent with Baillie's observation, *The Westminster Directory*, ed. Thomas Leishman (Edinburgh, 1901), p. 117, that the Independents

would share the ministry of the word with different members of the congregation contributing to the service, "'one to pray, and another to preach, a third to prophecy, and a fourth to dismiss with a blessing.'"

On the significance of the prophetic attitude in *Lycidas*, see William Kerrigan, *The Prophetic Milton* (Charlottesville, Va., 1974), pp. 261–62, 161–63; Joseph Wittreich, *Visionary Poetics: Milton's Tradition and his Legacy* (San Marino, Calif., 1979), pp. 135–36; and John C. Ulreich, "'And By Occasion Foretells': The Prophetic Voice in *Lycidas*," in *Milton Studies* XVIII, ed. James D. Simmonds (Pittsburgh, 1983), pp. 3–23.

7. Friedman, "*Lycidas*," in Patrides, *Milton's Lycidas*, p. 3, observes, "the swain tries to shield himself against the pain of reality by . . . pastoral convention." Similarly, Balachandra Rajan, "Lycidas," in Patrides, *Milton's Lycidas*, p. 275, "The false surmise is not only that there is no laureate hearse; it is also the assumption that absorption in a ritual, however ardent, can serve to protect one against the assault of reality."

8. John Calvin, *Institutes of the Christian Religion*, trans. F. L. Battles, ed. John T. McNeill, Library of Christian Classics XXI (Philadelphia, 1960), pp. 1016–19.

9. CM III, pp. 265–66. Cf. the *De Doctrina*, I, 32: "The administration of discipline is called "the power of the keys"; a power not committed to Peter and his successors exclusively, or to any individual pastor specifically, but to the whole particular church collectively" (CM XVI, p. 327).

10. The "inherent improbability" of Milton's pastoral fiction, Johnson, *Lives of the English Poets* (London, 1968), I, 96, argues, "always forces dissatisfaction on the mind." The dissatisfaction, however, is felt by the monodist as well, especially after the pilot's speech implies an alternative mode of pastoral as nurturing admonishment, as I discuss above.

11. Cited in *The Poems of John Milton*, ed. John Carey and Alastair Fowler (New York, 1972).

12. Ovid, *Metamorphoses*, XI, 8, The Loeb Classical Library (Cambridge, 1964), vol. II. Further references and their translations in the Loeb edition are cited parenthetically by book and line.

13. William C. Riggs, "The Plant of Fame in *Lycidas*," in *Milton Studies*, IV, ed. James D. Simmonds (Pittsburgh, 1972), pp. 151–62, also cites Milton's interpretation of the "works of faith" in the *De Doctrina*. Riggs sees the Christian regeneration of the singer in the poem as "creative action, a work of faith emanating from a regenerate spirit ingrafted in Christ." By the end of the poem, the singer "has, finally, accomplished an active, 'eager' work of faith, which in turn anticipates new action" (pp. 159–60).

We might compare Milton's view of the old covenant as one of works, the new as one of grace in his later poetry. John T. Shawcross, "Milton and Covenant: The Christian View of Old Testament Theology," in *Milton and the Scriptural Tradition: The Bible Into Poetry*, ed. James H. Sims and Leland Ryken (Columbia, 1984), pp. 160–91, summarizes Samson's agon in these terms:

> Samson consistently argues for his fulfilling God's purposes by works . . . but it is not until inward spirit has wiped away pride that he can achieve one great act of deliverance (line 1389), which represents faith and obedience. . . . In complement to *Paradise Regain'd*, where the New Covenant is developed and contrasted with the Old, *Samson Agonistes* shows how the concept of the covenant as one of works is false. (P. 186)

ANALOGY IN THE SCIENTIFIC IMAGERY OF *PARADISE LOST*

Harinder Singh Marjara

SCIENCE ALWAYS ASPIRES to be an objective and rational quest for the truth of nature. However, there has been an increasing awareness in recent reassessments of the nature of science that science frequently falls short of this ideal and that scientific knowledge does not always consist of the truth of nature which has been proven or validated with experiments but is occasionally founded on no more than educated guesses and conjectures.[1] In the seventeenth century, the sense of this shortfall was even more acute than it is now. As a result of the protracted Copernican controversy, epistemological certainty gave place to positivism, probabilism, and a realization that on many occasions scientists have to be content with uncertainty. There was, in addition, the idea of forbidden knowledge, which humbled and restrained many natural philosophers in their ambition to know the truth about God or nature, particularly since God "th' invisible King, / Onely Omniscient, hath suppresst in Night" many facts about "Heav'n," which is "too high / To know what passes there." Milton reflects these trends when he makes his Raphael admit that to describe "what surmounts the reach / Of human sense" is a "Sad task and hard" and perhaps "Not lawful to reveal".[2]

The crumbling of the Aristotelian system, in particular, resurrected several alternative philosophical schools, and the resulting diversity of philosophical approaches to science heightened the sense that the truth of nature may never be known for sure. Science is seen, by Bacon, as contaminated by "the various dogmas of philosophy," so that he considers the beliefs of ancient and modern natural philosophers as "All these invented systems of the universe, each according to his own fancy, like so many arguments of plays." Bacon names this "false notion" as "the Idols of the Theatre."[3] He also attributes the limitations of science to what he calls the "Idols of the Caves," which refer to the preconceptions and prejudices that trammel human reason: "although our persons live in the view of heaven, yet our spirits are included in the caves of our own complexions and customs, which minister unto us infinite errors and vain opinions." The limitations of science are also attributed to the inadequacy of verbal communication, named by Bacon as the "Idols of the Marketplace," according to which "Words are but the current tokens or marks of Popular Notions of things." Hobbes considers these limitations as "equivocation of names," which "maketh it difficult to recover the conceptions from which the name was ordained."[4]

These inadequacies of human reason and communication, and especially the inherent proclivity of the human mind toward preconception and even fancifulness, often oblige scientists to resort to imaginative speculation in their descriptions of nature. Scientists who break new ground do so not only with their observations but also with the help of their imagination and intuition, as well as their faith in nature's unity and consistency, even though they are reluctant to acknowledge it. "Scientists," according to Peter Medawar, "are usually too proud or too shy to speak about creativity and 'creative imagination'; they feel it to be incompatible with their conception of themselves as 'men of facts' and rigorous deductive judgments."[5]

Many philosophers have recognized the inevitability of the use of imagination in rational thinking. Gianfrancesco Pico della Mirandola notes that imagination is "placed on the border between intellect and sense" and that the superior faculties "would fail in that function which nature has bestowed upon each of them unless imagination support and assist them." Bacon, following Pico, considers imagination as "an agent or *nuncius*" between the "provinces" of "Understanding and Reason" on the one hand and "Will, Appetite and Affection" on the other. According to Henry More, "*Reason* is so involved together with *Imagination*, that we need say nothing of it apart by itself."[6] Reason is so dependent on the lower faculties that it can easily lead the scientist into fantasies, chimeras, and deception. In Aristotelian epistemology, imagination is considered not only indispensable to rational activity but also untrustworthy.[7] Many Renaissance philosophers made imagination the scapegoat for the shortcomings of science. Pico attributes the "differences in opinion that have come down even to our time from those great philosophers" to their "imagination." In natural philosophy, according to Bacon, we ought to pursue the goal of rationality, but this goal is extremely difficult to achieve because "there is seducement that worketh by the strength of the impression . . . not so much perplexing the reason as overruling it by power of the imagination." Henry More rejects the Cartesian ideas concerning the soul since they are "polluted with the impure Dregs of *Imagination*." In Glanvill's opinion, "we *erre* and come short of *science*, because we are so frequently misled by the evil conduct of our *Imaginations*."[8]

Imagination is indispensable to Milton as a poet of the unseen in order to build up a concrete vision of the reality that is outside ordinary human experience. Milton, who is narrating the war in heaven "with the tongue / Of Angels," wonders with what on earth to "Liken" the events in heaven "That may lift / Human imagination to such highth / Of Godlike Power" (*PL* VI, 300–03). Nevertheless, it is the same "Godlike Power" and "proud imaginations" that lead Satan into self-delusion, deception, and to the use of rhetoric in order to abuse the minds of a third part of the angels with the fiction of liberty and equality with God. It is not surprising, therefore, that the attitude of Renaissance philosophers toward imagination is ambiguous.

One of the results of the use of imagination and speculation in scientific discovery is the tendency in scientists to depend on rhetoric and emotive language, especially when they are giving shape to a new theory, or are in the thick of a controversy. Scientists sometimes use rhetoric to dress up the products of pure speculation to give them the appearance of scientific truth. Copernicus in *De revolutionibus,* Galileo in his *Dialogue* on the two world systems, and Harvey in his *Exercitationes* addressed to the Younger Riolan, are obliged by the controversial nature of their hypotheses to rely on rhetoric. Harvey mounts a spirited and even virulent attack against his critics, who, as he says, "cavill" and "bark" and "shew their own vanity and folly, and their baseness and want of arguments. . . . Just as when the raging wind advancing the waves in the Sicilian Sea dashes them in pieces against the rocks with *charybdis,* they make a hideous noise, and being broken and reverberated, hisse and foam."[9]

However, the more important consequence of scientists' dependence on imagination is the inevitability of the use of analogies in scientific discourse. The ideal way to pronounce a truth of nature is "from the things themselves" and, failing that, "through the medium of names," which "are the likeness or images of the things which they name," as Plato expresses it. However, "There are no names given to anything by nature; all is conventional and habit of the users,"[10] and consequently names prove inadequate and sometimes even misleading, as Bacon and Hobbes also point out. "The light of humane minds," says Hobbes, "is Perspicuous Words, but by exact definition first snuffed, and purged from ambiguity," a desirable endeavor but often extremely difficult. "Metaphors, and senseless and ambiguous words," according to Hobbes, "are like *ignes fatui;* and reasoning upon them, is wandering amongst innumerable absurdities," and therefore, in demonstration, they must be "utterly excluded." However, he recognizes that the "understanding" has now and then the "need to be opened by some apt similitude."[11]

The basic role of analogies is to point out an inherent and implied correspondence between two phenomena in order to make the explanation clearer and more graphic to the understanding. For Bruno, analogies have the force of hieroglyphics, or speaking pictures, that embody ideas and make them memorable.[12] Most Renaissance natural philosophers made use of graphic analogies, including Galileo, who compares the comet's tail to the light reflected through a caraf streaked by an oily finger, and Descartes, who represents the planets and the stars rolling in the sky by comparing them to things floating in a river. Boyle uses the analogy of the mechanical compatibility of lock and key to represent the manner in which tiny particles of matter fit each other.[13]

When building a new hypothesis, scientists find it convenient, and sometimes even necessary, to interpret a new and unfamiliar phenomenon by comparing it to one with which we are already familiar. The unknown, the unknowable and the obscure, is explained in terms of the known. Bacon points out that analogies or "*Instances Conformable*," are extremely useful in instances "when the senses entirely fail us" because of the remoteness or minuteness of the observed phenomenon. Such analogies are "employed, when things not directly perceptible are brought within reach of the sense, not by perceptible operations of the imperceptible body itself, but by observation of some cognate body which is perceptible."[14] Milton, in *De Doctrina Christiana*, Book I, chapter 4, expressly recommends this method with regard to obscure biblical passages which can often be explained better "from analogy . . . for what is obscure must be illustrated by what is clear" (CM XIV, p. 119).

Analogies are sometimes used to overcome other limitations, for example, the inadequacy of a flat diagram to represent a complex three-dimensional reality, which can be described more suitably by a metaphoric analogy. Kepler notes that Copernicus used the metaphor of "*nucleum*" or "kernel" because he was "truly caught in perplexity over the point, which could not be relieved by flat diagrams, though it could be by solid models."[15] This tendency inspired Copernicus, as well as Tycho and Milton, to represent the motions of the planets, which were generally expounded by flat and abstract geometrical diagrams, by the concrete image of the starry dance.[16]

The most striking use of analogies in scientific writings occurs in the form of what may be described as "reduction" analogies, which compare one scientific phenomenon to another or use an image from one field of science to describe a phenomenon from another in order to link them into a more unified view of nature. Analogies of this sort provide a clue to the essential unity of nature, and as such they conform to Platonic heuristic, which depends less on the Aristotelian logical method of disjunctive analysis and more on perceiving likenesses. The comparisons go beyond the Platonic notion of the world being created in imitation of the ideal types in heaven to another Platonic notion that the world emanated from the unity of God and diversified into many. When divine unity gives way to diversity, things "which come to partake of likeness come to be like in that respect and in just so far as they do come to partake of it," while they remain unlike in other respects. By this process "all things are one by having a share in unity and at the same time many by sharing the plurality" (*Parmenides*, 128e–129a). The perception of likenesses in natural phonomena yields analogies that link them to other phenomena with which they partake of the unity.

Bacon considers "Analogy," which he also calls "*Parallels, or Physical Resemblances,*" as "the first and lowest steps towards the union of nature." He goes on to give various "Conformable Instances," including the "similitude or conformity which has been remarked between man and plant inverted," and concludes that instead of "over-curious diligence in observing the variety of things, and explaining the exact specific differences of animals, herbs, and fossils," men's labor should "be turned to the investigation and observation of the resemblances and analogies of things, as well in wholes as in parts" since "these it is that detect the unity of nature, and lay a foundation for the constitution of sciences" (*Works*, IV, 164–67). However, Bacon is also aware of the dangers of overdoing it, since representations of nature often become falsified by the excessive zeal of scientists to yoke diverse phenomena together. He notes in his *Advancement of Learning* that "whereas there are many things in nature as it were *monodica, sui juris* [singular, and like nothing but themselves;] yet the cogitations of man do feign into them relatives, parallels, and conjugates" (*Works*, III, 395).

Analogies can be viewed as Milton's solution to the basic problem of how to "unfould / The secrets of another world" and to accommodate the unseen, spiritual world to the human sense and understanding. In *Paradise Lost*, Milton takes into consideration the possibility that the earth is "but the shaddow of Heav'n," and "By lik'ning spiritual to corporeal forms" (V, 573–75) and by "measuring things in Heav'n by things on Earth" (VI, 893), he describes a plausible and convincing celestial world. He depicts his physical universe with an emphasis on similarities and analogical interrelationships between the various levels and parts of it, beginning with the lower "corporeal forms" and rising up to the "spiritual" forms in heaven. The tangible world of sense experience is used as a metaphor for the unseen and unknowable world of spirit since at the earthly level the forms are manifested in their most concrete shapes.

Basing himself on the faith in nature's unity and uniformity, Milton extends the relative certainties of the sensory and concrete physical phenomena to apply to the higher and invisible spiritual forms, the reality of which can at best be speculated and conjectured. The analogical comparisons move up the scale from matter to spirit, from the earth to the moon and the sun and from human beings to angels. In most descriptions, the emphasis is on concrete scientific imagery rather than on abstract statements of typological similarities. Analogies are used frequently with an emphasis on explicit scientific imagery, indicating very clearly that the similarities hold the key to the essential unity of nature.

Analogies are the scientists' way of implying and often highlighting the unity of nature. Aristotelian scientists compared the phenomena of thunder and lightning to those of comets and meteors in an attempt to ascribe a fundamental unity to the various underground and aboveground phenomena: from volcanoes, earthquakes, and the generation of metals inside the earth to *ignis fatuus*, storms, hail, thunder, meteors, and comets in the atmosphere. All these phenomena were linked together by the concept of vapors or "exhalations," which were supposed to be produced by the evaporation of water and other materials such as sulphurous, mercurial, and other salts, particularly during the processes of generation. In Milton's time, most of these phenomena became analogically linked to the explosion of gunpowder through sulphur and niter, the main ingredients of gunpowder, with which the exhalations were supposed to be charged. The similarities between the report of the explosion of gunpowder and the peal of thunder led to the possibility that there were particles of sulphur and niter in the air, which produced the loud explosion of thunder and the bright flash of lightning.

Thunder and gunpowder are expressly associated with each other by Milton in the metaphors of "chaind Thunderbolts and Hail" used in relation to the assault by the satanic forces with their cannons and gunpowder (VI, 589). They are even more explicitly related to each other in the images of "two black Clouds" which are with "Heav'ns Artillery fraught" and which come "rattling on" (II, 714–15). In the speech by Moloch, who counsels "open war" against heaven, and who recommends that they turn their "tortures," meaning "*Tartarean* sulphur," into "horrid Arms / Against the Torturer," Milton is evidently highlighting the analogical link between the two natural phenomena: in answer to "his Almighty Engin," God "shall hear / Infernal Thunder, and for Lightning see / Black fire and horror shot with equal rage" (II, 64–69).

The tendency among scientists to use analogies is of immense value to Milton in depicting nature. To make his universe convincing, Milton moves analogically from the familiar to the unfamiliar, from the human to the suprahuman, and creates such powerful and vivid images that the reader recognizes it as real. There is imaginative pleasure in perceiving similarities between two apparently unrelated things, but scientific analogies also play the much more important role of linking natural phenomena into a complex, intermeshed, and unified system. The perception of nature in Milton's time, as at all times, was pervaded by several abstract metaphysical assumptions, which are tacitly acknowledged by Milton and sometimes explicitly emphasized. Even though the images are sufficiently visual and concrete, the undercurrent of scientific abstraction—which relates the images to other images, to the underlying scientific ideas, and to the basic first principles of nature—forms an essential element in the poetic presentation of nature in Milton's epic. When, for example, Milton uses the image of "the great Mother" (VII, 281) for the formation of the earth and the oceans at the time of Creation, he is doing so with the obvious intention of emphasizing that the Creation was a process akin to the generation of animals, and that all generation involves a *matrix* principle. Milton's emphasis on the vitalism of the processes of generation, or the harmony of heavenly motions as a dance, is dictated not by his conviction of their literal truth, but by the susceptibility of these ideas to fit into his idea of the universe. Analogies are sometimes taken by Milton to a poetic extreme in order to build up a complex structure of parallels at various levels of the universe, a process that results in a vision of the universe that is endowed with unity as well as hierarchy, leading up from the lowest forms on earth to the highest in heaven in a continuous and unified chain of being.

Milton uses the power of poetry and imagination to make structured and analogical images, together with the assumptions of nature's unity, harmony, teleology and beauty, the means of building up a much more unified and aesthetically satisfying vision of nature than is possible for a scientist, who must always keep his eye on facts. A poet finds it much easier to reconcile inconsistencies, improbabilities, far-fetched notions, and conjectures by the use of imagination and rhetoric than a scientist using prose, since a prose treatise must maintain a certain degree of logical decorum. In Milton's epic, the various aspects and levels of ontology are interlinked in such a way as to make the entire created universe manifest universal characteristics. There are a number of unifying ideas, for example, "grosser feeds the purer" or "time measures motion." Most of these ideas that Milton uses in his scientific imagery have been taken from the basic postulates of contemporary science.

Of all the philosophical tenets that enable Milton to unify nature and knit his world into a network of analogies, the most basic is his belief in the material nature of the universe, a belief that corresponds to the Plotinian Neoplatonic notion of matter emanating from God.[17] Milton postulates that all matter is derived from God as "one first matter all" and diversified into corporeal substances, all of which are endowed with similar physical traits, and that this matter rises up in the scale of being and is transformed through a gradual process of refinement into substances that are superior in nature but not so very different in their fundamental characteristics. Milton works out a picture of the universe in which the earth, the moon, the planets, the sun, and heaven form the various steps in a hierarchical ladder, each step made of the same matter but existing in a superior essence.

The plurality of worlds is an idea that is crucial in this regard. The Galilean observations suggested the possibility of the moon being like the earth in its physical properties and Venus being the image of both the earth and the moon. Milton emphasizes the similarities by endowing the moon with rivers, mountains, valleys, and clouds. These similarities are ultimately based on the scientific faith in the universality of nature and confirm for Milton the possibility that the universe manifests similarities at the physical as well as spiritual levels. Milton would not have gone as far as he does in his comparison between the earth and the moon had it not been for his metaphysical faith in the unity of matter, which leads him directly to view this similarity as a part of the general unity of nature. What is important to note is that Milton begins at the lower end and moves up. The "new Lands, / Rivers or Mountains" observed in the "spotty Globe" of the moon enable Milton to focus on the similarities of physical features between the two bodies. From there, Milton goes on to speculate about other similarities. The spots that Adam can see "As clouds" may rain, and rain may produce "Fruits in her soft'nd Soile, for some to eat / Allotted there" (VIII, 145–48). The analogies could not have been more thorough.

It must be pointed out that not all scientists reacted to Galileo's observations in the same way. Galileo himself focused on the unchanging lunar landscape which indicated to him that the moon had no clouds, and that it was different from the earth in this and perhaps other particulars. In addition, he was more impressed by the idea of variety in the universe than by that of the unity of matter. Galileo's Salviati is prompted by "natural reason" and by his imagination ("not from sure observation but mere possibility") that the things on the moon were "'Very different and entirely unimaginable by us'; for this seems to me to fit with the richness of nature and the omnipotence of the Creator and Ruler."[18] For Milton, nature, as created by God, is characterized by essential unity rather than by rich variety, and he emphasizes it by accentuating the similarities between the earth and the moon and between the moon and Venus. The idea of nature's unity, which Milton prefers, is no less scientifically tenable than that of the richness and variety of nature, which Galileo postulates, and both are equally appealing to the imagination.

Milton envisages a universe in which the various levels are similar even to the extent that they share in continuous interaction. The basic idea that enables Milton to endow his nature with unity and demonstrate this unity in the various analogies is that of "nourishment." For Milton, whatever is created must be nourished; moreover, nourishment is provided by the lower to the higher, an idea that is expressed by him in the postulate "grosser feeds the purer." Bacon also voices this postulate when he says: "Nourishment should be of an inferior nature and a simpler substance than the body nourished. Plants are nourished by earth and water, animals by plants, men by animals" (*Works*, V, 241). Milton goes beyond plants, animals, and human beings and makes this principle universal for all of nature. In Milton's universe, the images of feeding interrelate the earth with the heavens: "Earth and the sea feed Air, the Air those Fires / Ethereal, and as lowest first the Moon." The spots on the moon are said to be "unpurg'd / Vapours not yet into her substance turnd." The earth's exhalations feed the moon and the moon in its turn exhales nourishment "From her moist Continent to higher Orbes" (V, 407–26). That the heavenly bodies need nourishment was a Stoic idea, which was revived by Lipsius and Mersenne, among others, and was also expressed as an esoteric Hermetic idea by Paracelsus. Henry More refers to it by citing Paracelsus: "That the stars eat and are nourished, and therefore must ease themselves; and that those falling stars . . . are their excrements."[19] For Milton, these links of nourishment between the earth, the moon, and the sun form merely one aspect of the unity prevailing in the whole range of natural processes in all of God's creations, including the sun, heaven, and hell.

The analogical comparisons begin with physical features such as the hill of Paradise, which is compared to the sacred hill in heaven. There is a hill even in hell, whose "griesly top / Belch'd fire and rowling smoak." Hell has lakes like the earth, though they are "fiery," in keeping with the nature of hell. There are rivers on the sun, not unlike those of Paradise, with the difference that instead of water they run "Elixir" and "potable gold." The stars, and even heaven and hell, are referred to as "continents" separated from each other either by the "illimitible Ocean" of Chaos or the pure liquid "air" of interstellar space, referred to at other times as "the Glassie Sea," in response to various traditions. Chaos is described as "the wilde expanse . . . Of fighting Elements" or as "the emptier waste, resembling Air," metaphors that emphasize their similarity with the atmosphere of the earth. In Chaos, there is a "tumultuous cloud / Instinct with Fire and Nitre," the constituents of gunpowder, just as there are sulphur and niter present in the atmosphere of the earth, sent up by the generation of metals and other animate and inanimate objects in the form of exhalations, which occasionally explode into thunder and lightning. These references highlight the similarity between Chaos and the atmosphere surrounding the earth, related in both cases to sulphurous and nitrous exhalations and to the potential for the creation and generation of natural objects.

The sun resembles the earth in both the processes of generation that take place there and the presence of the objects found on its surface as a result of those processes. The sun is infinitely brighter and made up largely of precious metals and stones: "If mettal, part seemd Gold, part Silver cleer" and "If stone, Carbuncle most or Chrysolite, / Rubie or Topaz" (III, 591–98). Milton's sun is obviously solid like the earth with waterlike fluids flowing in its rivers. The fields and regions on the sun "Breathe forth *Elixir* pure, and Rivers run / Potable Gold" (III, 607–08). The alchemical metaphor is conspicuous and is obviously intended to make the analogical link between the processes of generation on the sun and those practiced by alchemists.

The same is true of Milton's heaven, where "the Trees / Of life ambrosial frutage bear," and vines "Yield Nectar" in a manner that reminds one of the garden in earthly Paradise. From their boughs each morning the angels "brush mellifluous Dewes, and find the ground / Cover'd with pearly grain." On earth, God has "Varied his bounty so with new delights, / As may compare with Heaven" (V, 426–32). There is little doubt that these "Trees / Of life" which bear "ambrosial frutage" are generated by the same natural process as they are on earth. The clue to this analogy lies in the images of ambrosia and nectar, which Henry More also exploits: "the *Nectar* and *Ambrosia* of the Poets may not be mere fable. For the *Spirit of Nature*, which is the immediate instrument of God, may enrich the fruits of these *Aerial Paradises* with such liquors, as being received into the bodies of pure *Daemons*, and diffusing it self through their vehicles, may cause such grateful motions analogical to our *tast*."[20] However, it is not only the poet's nectar and ambrosia that prompts Milton to paint heaven in the image of the earth but also the scientific faith that heaven must partake of the unity of nature, which is based on "one first matter" that lies at the origin of all natural phenomena. Heaven, which is described by Satan as a "continent," is "adornd," like the earth, with "Plant, Fruit, Flour Ambrosial," and even "Gemms & Gold." Satan goes on to expound "from whence they grow": there are present "Deep under ground, materials dark and crude, / Of spiritous and fierie spume" materials that are also present in the earth in the form of sulphur and niter, which when "toucht / With Heav'ns ray . . . shoot forth / So beauteous, op'ning to the ambient light" (VI, 473–81). The presence of ambrosial fruits, nectar, gems, and gold in heaven, as well as of precious metals and rivers running potable gold on the sun, indicates very clearly that not only are all ontological levels beyond the sphere of the moon subject to change, like the earth, but these changes are also analogical to those on the earth.

However, the analogical similarities between the various phenomena do not preclude differences of degrees and levels. As matter rises higher, it becomes more refined and spirituous. This Neoplatonist idea is attributed to Philo Judaeus by John Wilkins, and to Cusanus, who speculated on the beings inhabiting the sun and the moon as "more intellectual and spirituall" than those on the earth. Wilkins also speculates on the moon as well as the stars being "Heavens and Elysian fields" or "an inferiour kind of heaven or paradise,"[21] ideas that are not only echoed by Milton but made to fit neatly into his hierarchical scheme of things.

In Milton's cosmos, the most enigmatic phenomenon that defies all description is that of Chaos since it resembles nothing within human experience. Milton is obliged to resort to counteranalogies, and he constantly describes Chaos in terms of contrast with created nature. Chaos is "boundless," as opposed to "Heav'n and Earth," which the Creator sets "within appointed bounds." The character of Chaos as "matter unform'd and void" makes sense only in contrast to nature, which is endowed with both definite forms and plenitude. Created nature is characterized by the regularity of time measured by the motions of the heavenly bodies and by dimensions in terms of length, breadth, and height, which are equally definite and measurable, whereas Chaos is without dimensions, "where length, breadth, & highth, / And time and place are lost" (II, 893–94). The images of darkness and of anarchy, war, and confusion in relation to Chaos contrast with the images of light and harmony used for created nature. However, since darkness, confusion, and war are not uncommon on the earth, these also provide suitable analogical images to describe the "vast immeasurable Abyss" of Chaos as "Night" and as "dark illimitable Ocean without bound." The exterior of the sphere of the created universe becomes analogous to the surface of the earth and the surrounding Chaos becomes "a Sea, dark, wasteful, wilde" where "furious windes" and "surging waves" rise like mountains and "assault / Heav'ns highth, and with the Center mix the Pole" (VII, 211–15).

The tendency to see similarities between the phenomena of nature arises out of the universality of natural processes involved in the transformation of the primary matter into a diversity of natural objects. This is obvious in the similarities between inanimate and animate nature with regard to the processes of generation. Milton exploits the tendency among scientists to universalize the processes of generation on vitalistic principles and equates the changes in inanimate nature with animal birth, growth, and decay. The poet uses the images of seed, copulation, and womb to describe, among others, the generation of precious stones and metals inside the earth. The earth is described as the "great Mother," which "Op'ning her fertil Woomb teem'd at a Birth / Innumerous living Creatures, perfet formes" (VII, 454–55). The image corresponds to the mythological images of Gaia and Tellus, which also emphasize the notion that all generation in the universe involves a female principle as matter and a male principle as form. The use of the obvious procreative metaphor in Milton's reference to the "mounted Sun" that "Shot down direct his fervid Raies to warme / Earths inmost womb" (V, 300–02) bears testimony to the process of the generation of metals and plants on the earth as being analogical to animal reproduction. The process of creation is also described as a procreative act: "the Spirit of God" sat on the "vast Abyss" like a dove "with mighty wings outspread," his "vital vertue infus'd" into it and made it "pregnant" (I, 20–22; VII, 234–36).

A fundamental idea was the role of heat in all generative processes, and especially the analogical relationship between the heat of the stars and that from other sources, such as the generative and "concoctive heate" of the human body (V, 437). This idea goes back to Plato, who speaks of "the similar principle circulating in each and all of them; for example, that should be called 'fire' which is of such a nature always, and so of everything that has generation" (*Timaeus*, 49e). Aristotle explicitly points out the kinship between the heat of the sun and the heat of animal bodies with regard to their generative power.[22] In the chapter "De calido innato" of his *De generatione animalium*, Harvey points out the role of bodily heat in the processes of animal generation and its kinship to the stellar influences. The same idea is expressed by Henry More with regard to semen: "there is a spirit contained in the spumeous seed, and in this spirit a nature analogous to the Elements of the Stars."[23]

Milton emphasizes the analogical role of heat in processes of generation by the use of the image of "concoctive heate." Concoction was understood primarily as a process involved in digestion, but was analogically applied to other processes of change as remote from each other as cooking, healing, manufacture of medicines, ripening of fruits, growth of embryos, and generation of metals, all of which required heat in one form or another. Tycho uses the analogy of the "concoction" of metals in the bowels of the earth to explain the "generation" of the nova of 1572.[24]

The process of concoction was at best vaguely understood. It was described by analogy, according to Harvey, as a process of "liquifaction," "separation," "fermentation," "putridity," or "distillation." But it was universally believed to be "a work of Nature or of something which is innately hot," and perceived as "the alteration of the whole of a substance which occurs in the process of generation and corruption."[25] Most natural processes in which the end result was a more refined, more concentrated, and more effective substance were described analogically as concoction.

Milton refers to this process in relation to a variety of phenomena, such as the digestion and assimilation of food by the angels; the process used by alchemists to convert dross substances to gold, elixir, and the philosophers' stone; and the making of gunpowder from the crude materials of nature. The rebellious angels found "Sulphurous and Nitrous Foame" in the soil of heaven and "with suttle Art" they "Concocted," "adusted," and "reduc'd" these ingredients "To blackest grain" (VI, 510–15) to be used as gunpowder. That the process is viewed as being similar to the process of digestion is indicated by the use of the metaphor "Concocted."

The process of concoction enables Milton to highlight the similarity between human beings and angels, both of whom need to be nourished by the food that is tasted, concocted, digested, and assimilated in their respective bodies in the same way. Having spoken about the transubstantiation that occurs in angelic bodies as a result of concoction, Milton goes on to illustrate the process by comparing it to the work of "the Empiric Alchimist" who "Can turn, or holds it possible to turn / Metals of drossiest Ore to perfect Gold" (V, 439–43). It is essentially the same process that occurs on the sun, as described in Book III. Heat is an essential ingredient in this process, whether it is the "concoctive heate" of the human or the angelic body, the "fire / Of sooty coal," or the heat of the sun, all of which become analogically similar.

Milton moves from one aspect of reality to another and metaphorically fuses the two into a larger perception of the unity of natural phenomena. The substance of angelic spirits is specified as that of "purest light" (VI, 660). The analogy between spirits, light, and fire is appropriate because, in the Renaissance, light was commonly considered a refined substance like spirit. According to Bacon, the vital spirits are "more akin to the substance of flame."[26] Milton, however, takes this analogy a logical step further by attributing infinitely fast speeds to angels, who are presumed to be made of a pure substance akin to light. Raphael mentions, in this connection, the "Speed almost spiritual" at which planets are capable of moving, even though they have visible and tangible bodies. Others, such as Henry More, also made a similar analogical link between spirits and light with regard to their fast motion: "The nature of the *swiftness of motion* in these spirits is much like that of *Light*, which is a body as well as they."[27] This same analogical imagination leads Milton to refer to the heavenly spirits as "Ethereal Vertues" (II, 311) or as "Ethereal Powers" (III, 100), since the spiritual substance that the angels are made of is akin to light and ether.

The simile contained in the reference to "Th' animal Spirits that from pure blood arise / Like gentle breaths from Rivers pure" (IV, 805–06) is based on the perceived analogy between the process by which exhalations rise into the air and the manner in which spirits are formed out of blood, an analogy that is pointed out by Harvey when he refers to the bodily spirits as "exhalation, or vapours of the blood."[28] However, the analogy goes beyond that to highlight the similarity between the nature and operation of exhalations and bodily spirits, as it does in Harvey, who compares the circular "motion" of the vapors rising from the wet earth and falling back to the earth with the circular motion of the blood and its spirits in the body.[29]

Similarly, the angels, standing "in Orbes / Of circuit inexpressible . . . / Orb within Orb" (V, 594–96), are evidently described using the metaphor of planetary motions, with an obvious emphasis on the similarity between the two phenomena in terms of the purity and perfection of their substance, which is symbolized by the harmony of their motions. The motions of the angels are repeatedly represented by analogy with those of the stars. Besides the "Mystical dance" of the angels, which "Resembles nearest" the motions of "yonder starrie Spheare / Of Planets and of fixt in all her Wheeles" (V, 620–22), Milton also represents the travel of Uriel to the earth as taking place on a beam of sunlight and the flight of Satan to the earth along "th' Ecliptic" in "many an Aerie wheele" (III, 740–41). The metaphors of planetary motions are meant to point up the similarity between the nature and role of the angels and those of the planets. In the description of "Th'Arch-Angel *Uriel*, one of the seav'n" who "are his [God's] Eyes / That run through all the Heav'ns, or down to th' Earth" (III, 648–51), the metaphor focuses the reader's attention on the similarity between the angels and the planets as agents and ministers of God's rule over the universe, expressed also by the image of "ministring light," a similarity that is made explicit by the number "seav'n" and by using the image of "Eyes," which Milton also uses when he refers to the sun as the "Eye and Soule" of the world.

These analogies have important implications for Milton's epic, among which the most important is the unified texture given to the poem by the network of metaphors that link Milton's world into a unity. The earth is typologically linked to the starry world and the stars are related to angels. The angels in their turn are closely linked in natural unity to human beings. The result is that the universe of *Paradise Lost*, in spite of the infinite spaces and eternal time, becomes unified by the application of universal natural laws. The phenomena that take place in these vast spaces and unending time remain recognizable. Much of the action takes place far away in heaven, in Chaos, or in hell, but it is related with a much greater sense of relevance and recognition to human experience than it would have been if heaven or hell were depicted as places that had no analogical kinship with the earth.

Milton's analogies in *Paradise Lost* sometimes oblige him to stray into regions that were forbidden as unorthodox and even heretical. The most obvious one is the lowering of the status of angels to bring them closer to human beings by the attribution of the need for food and love to angels. Milton emphasizes the close ontological link between human beings and angels by the similarity of the process of eating and the concoction of food. This link is further elaborated by insisting that the angels are subject to all sensitive functions, such as enjoying love and feeling all kinds of happy and sad emotions. Raphael enlightens Adam regarding the need that angels have for love to be happy, since there is no happiness without love. The comparison with human beings, even in the prelapsarian state, is explicit: "Whatever pure thou in the body enjoy'st / (And pure thou wert created) we enjoy," with a difference, of course, arising out of their being essentially incorporeal, so that "Easier then Air with Air, if Spirits embrace, / Total they mix, Union of Pure with Pure" (VIII, 620–29). The bodily functions of angels are of the same kind as those of human beings but not of the same degree.

Milton might be implying in these references the Platonic distinction between the higher love of angels and the lower carnal love of human beings,[30] as Cowley is supposed to be doing in his poem "Answer to the Platonick." Cowley avows that his love shall be like "*Angels love*" "When I'm all Soule." Until then, he prefers to express his love carnally, similar in kind to that of beasts but of a higher degree, as is man's taste for culinary delights in relation to gorging by beasts. Milton, on the other hand, describes angelic love in scientific terms as a "sensitive" bodily function and expresses it with the human analogy.

An important aspect of the man-angel analogy is that the theme of the fall of the angels is made more relevant to the human experience and destiny. *Paradise Lost* begins with the fall of the angels, which is duplicated later on in the poem by the fall of Eve and Adam. When Raphael tells Adam and Eve about the fall of the angels and the war in heaven, he does it with the obvious understanding that man can learn from it. There are parallels as well as obvious differences between the experiences of man and angels. Just as the apostate angels are expelled from the heavenly Paradise, so is the human pair from the earthly Paradise. The difference is that whereas the fallen angels are bound with adamantine chains in hell and damned eternally, human beings are allowed to roam the earth in hope of salvation. The fall of Satan, his anguish, desperation, and enormous effort to escape his destiny can be seen as relevant to human experience.

Milton makes the experience of the angels carry a lesson for man by depicting the angels as recognizably human, as much as is permitted by the differences in their essences. If the nature of the angels had been totally different and the angelic fall had been inspired by an entirely different set of circumstances and motivation, the reader would not have seen the relevance of the angelic fall to his own experience. But by the similarities between human beings and angels, emphasized as much as they are, the reader is able to relate to and understand the fall of the angels.

The basic idea that underlies the analogies between human beings and angels is that all nature tends to rise in the scale from corporeal to spiritual forms. This belief, which is based on both the alchemical belief in the transformation of dross materials into perfect forms, and the Pauline faith that the corruptible will be transformed into incorruptible (1 Cor. xv, 54) is fundamental to Milton's eschatology. Raphael assures Adam that "time may come when men / With Angels may participate" and "from these corporal nutriments perhaps" bodies of human beings may at last turn all to spirit "Improv'd by tract of time, and wingd ascend / Ethereal" like angels (V, 492–501). The same idea is expressed by Henry More, who believes that "the soul of man is capable of very high refinements, even to a condition *purely Angelical,*" so that the "Souls of men arrived to such a due pitch of purification must at last obtain *Celestial* Vehicles."[31]

It is evident that Milton lowers the status of angels and brings them closer to human beings in order to render more plausible the possibility of man rising to the status of angels. If the rise of man's body and spirit to the state of angelic spirits is to be a credible idea, it must be based on a universal natural process of the refinement of matter from material to spiritual forms. Milton notes the transformation of matter into spirit in various contexts, above all in Raphael's exposition of how all matter is descended from God and must rise up to him. He gives concrete scientific analogies for this process. First, there is the process by which from the root "Springs lighter the green stalk," then the leaves "More aerie," and "the bright consummate floure" which "Spirits odorous breathes." Second, there is the process of the refinement of food into spirits, which continues in human bodies, where the food eaten as "nourishment" is "by gradual scale sublim'd / To vital Spirits" and to animal and intellectual spirits (V, 479–85). An analogical process of concoction and refinement occurs in angels whose "Intelligential substances" require food in the same manner as man's "Rational" substances, so that they become capable of performing the whole range of functions from tasting, concocting, digesting, and assimilating food to intuitive reasoning, which is specific to their nature (V, 407–13).

It is obvious that these analogical processes, which take place in plants and in human and angelic bodies, are extremely important for human destiny since Milton's faith in the rise of man to the status of angels and to God is based on the scientific possibility, in fact certainty, that matter can be refined and transubstantiated until it reaches the state of spirit. The process of refinement would have enabled Adam and Eve, and their progeny, to rise to heaven and dwell there for eternity as angels and Gods if they had not disobeyed God's only command. Following their transgression, the physical transformation of their bodies into incorporeal substances that would enable them to rise to heaven is still possible, but only as a result of the miracle of resurrection, which is the result of God's grace and the Son's sacrifice to atone for man's transgression. In order to ensure that man could rise to the spiritual and incorruptible state of angels, whether naturally or as a result of resurrection, which would overcome the corruption of death, Milton needed his nature to provide for this possibility at the scientific level. He endows nature with both unity and continuity, whereby all substances and beings in his universe are allotted their places in nature's hierarchy, depending on the state of refinement and purity of their essences, and yet are able to move up the scale of being from corporeal to incorporeal forms. Milton makes this universe plausible by weaving a pattern of analogies into its fabric.

Université du Québec à Trois-Rivières

NOTES

1. J. H. Lesher, "On the Role of Guesswork in Science," *Studies in History and Philosophy of Science* IX (1978), 19–33, contradicts Jonathan L. Cohen, "Guessing," *Proceedings of the Aristotelian Society* LXXIV (1973–74), 189–210, to affirm the legitimate role of guesswork in science. See Peter Medawar, *Limits of Science* (New York, 1984), p. 33. Galileo also says that "science will always remain approximate"; *Sidereus nuncius: Telescopes, Tides, and Tactics*, trans. Stillman Drake (Chicago, 1983), p. 120.

2. Paradise Lost V, 564–77; VIII, 172–73, in *The Works of John Milton*, 18 vols., ed. Frank Allen Patterson et al. (New York, 1931–38), the edition cited throughout.

3. *The Works of Francis Bacon*, 14 vols., ed. J. Spedding, R. L. Ellis, and D. D. Heath (1857–74; rpt. New York, 1968), IV, 55, cited hereafter as *Works*. The importance of the "Idols" to Bacon's philosophy is discussed by Paolo Rossi, *Francis Bacon: From Magic to Science*, trans. Sacha Rabinovitch (Chicago, 1968), pp. 160–72.

4. Hobbes, *Human Nature: Or, The Fundamental Elements of Policie* (London, 1649), p. 51; Bacon, *Advancement of Learning*, in *Works*, III, 396, 388.

5. Peter Medawar, *Induction and Intuition in Scientific Thought* (London, 1969), p. 55. He considers the scientists' account of their intellectual procedures as "untrustworthy," pp. 10–11. See also Gerald Holton, *The Scientific Imagination: Case Studies* (New York, 1978), and Arthur I. Miller, *Imagery in Scientific Thought: Creating Twentieth-Century Physics* (Cambridge, Mass., 1984), for an emphasis on imagination and visualization in scientific discovery.

6. Pico, *De imaginatione*, trans. Harry Caplan (Westport, Conn., 1971), pp. 31–33. Bacon, *Works*, III, 382; More, "Immortality of the Soul," in *A Collection of Several Philosophical Writings*, 2nd ed. (London, 1662), p. 106, cited hereafter as *Philosophical Writings*.

7. Aristotle, *De anima*, in *The Basic Works of Aristotle*, ed. Richard McKeon (New York, 1941), III, iii, 428a9–12, III, vii, 431a16, notes that to "the thinking soul" images serve as "contents of perception" and "that is why the soul never thinks without an image." See also Alexander of Aphrodisias, *De anima*, II, lviii, 4–6, trans. Athanasios P. Fotinis (Washington, D.C., 1979), p. 82.

8. Pico, *De imaginatione*, p. 47; Bacon, *Works*, III, 382, 392; More, *The True Notion of a Spirit*, appended to Joseph Glanvill, *Saducismus triumphatus or, Full and Plaine Evidence Concerning Witches and Apparitions*, 2nd ed. (London, 1682), p. 159; Glanvill, *Vanity of Dogmatizing: "Three Versions,"* ed. Stephen Medcalf (Hove, Sussex, 1970), p. 95.

9. *De motu cordis* (1628), *De circulatione sanguinis* (1649), in *Anatomical Exercises: The First Text of 1653*, ed. Geoffrey Keynes (London, 1928), p. 177. For Galileo's use of "Emotion, Aesthetic and Persuasion," see Maurice Finocchiaro, *Galileo and the Art of Reasoning: Rhetorical Foundations of Logic and Scientific Method* (Dordrecht, Netherlands, 1980), pp. 46–66.

10. *Cratylus*, in *The Collected Dialogues of Plato*, ed. Edith Hamilton and Huntington Cairns (Princeton, 1961), 439a, 384d.

11. Hobbes, *Leviathan, or the Matter, Forme, and Power of a Commonwealth* (London, 1651), pp. 21–22, 34.

12. L. A. Breiner, "Analogical Argument in Bruno's *De l'infinito*," *MLN* XCIII (1978), 23.

13. *Le monde ou Traité de la lumière*, XI, 57–60, in *Oeuvres de Descartes*, 11 vols., ed. Charles Adam and Paul Tannery (Paris, 1967); Galileo, *Il Saggiatore*, VI, 290–91,

in *Opere*, 20 vols. (Firenze, 1968); Boyle, *Works*, 6 vols., ed. Thomas Birch (Hildesheim, 1966), III, 18.

14. Bacon, *Novum Organum*, in *Works*, IV, 164, 203.

15. Kepler, *Mysterium cosmographicum: The Secret of the Universe*, trans. A. M. Duncan (New York, 1981), p. 91.

16. Copernicus, *Commentariolus*, in *Three Copernican Treatises*, 3rd ed., trans. Edward Rosen (New York, 1971), p. 90. For Tycho, see *Nature and Nature's Laws*, ed. Marie Boas Hall (New York, 1970), p. 61.

17. See J. H. Adamson, "Milton and the Creation," *JEGP* LXI (1962), 758–67, for the relationship of this notion to that of *creatio ex Deo*.

18. Galileo, *Dialogue Concerning the Two Chief World Systems*, 2nd ed., trans. Stillman Drake (Berkeley, 1967), p. 101.

19. "Enthusiasmus triumphatus," in *Philosophical Writings*, p. 32.

20. "Immortality of the Soul," in *Philosophical Writings*, p. 184.

21. Wilkins, *Discovery of a World in the Moone or Discourse Tending to Prove, that 'tis probable there may be another habitable World in that Planet* (1638; rpt. Delmar, N.Y., 1973), pp. 101, 193–99.

22. *De generatione animalium*, II, iii, 737a3–4.

23. Harvey, *Exercitationes de generatione animalium* (London, 1651), p. 474; More, "Immortality of the Soul," in *Philosophical Writings*, p. 118.

24. Aristotle, *De generatione animalium*, I, i, 715b20. Agricola uses the image of "cookery" in *De re metallica*, trans. Herbert C. Hoover and Lou H. Hoover (London, 1912), p. 51*n*. According to Tycho, "all [substances] are not concocted and brought to the same sublimity, and maturity by the powerful working of nature"; *Astronomicall Coniectur of the new and much Admired * [star] which Appered in the year 1572* (London, 1632), p. 10.

25. Harvey, *Praelectiones anatomiae universalis: Anatomical Lectures*, ed. G. Whitteridge (London, 1964), p. 117.

26. Bacon, "Historia vitae et mortis," in *Works*, V, 324.

27. More, "Immortality of the Soul," in *Philosophical Writings*, p. 100.

28. Harvey, *Anatomical Exercises*, pp. 158, 159.

29. Harvey, *De motu cordis*, in *Anatomical Exercises*, p. 59.

30. E. L. Marilla, "Milton on Conjugal Love Among the Heavenly Angels," *MLN* LXVIII (1953), 485–86, and D. C. Allen, "Milton and the Love of Angels," *MLN* LXXVI (1961), 489–90.

31. More, "Immortality of the Soul," in *Philosophical Writings*, p. 147.

ALLEGORY IN *PARADISE LOST*: SATAN'S COSMIC JOURNEY

Kenneth Borris

I

By including the allegories of Sin and Death in *Paradise Lost*, Addison judged, Milton violated standards of heroic propriety; and Johnson condemned it as one of the poem's greatest faults. The allegorical aspect of *Paradise Lost* has embarrassed many subsequent Miltonists who have ignored or sought to restrict or deny it. However, since allegory has now been critically rehabilitated, former biases toward depreciating or minimizing it in Milton's work have lost their literary animus. Fostered by increasingly sophisticated understanding and appreciation of allegory, much attention has recently focused on its role in *Paradise Lost*.[1] Yet, although Milton clearly entrusts the vital tasks of treating the problem of evil and much of Satan's experience to the allegories of Sin and Death, even the minimum claim that *Paradise Lost* involves allegory still remains controversially subject to anxious circumventions or outright denials. Walter B. Davis's important recent article, "The Languages of Accommodation and the Styles of *Paradise Lost*," demonstrates Milton's use of full-scale allegorical techniques and points out that previous critics dodgily interpret the heavenly war "in all of the traditional [fourfold] senses . . . without labeling them as such," and yet obscurely concludes that Milton is "not an allegorist" but an erector of "serial scaffolding."[2] Davis's evidence really shows that Milton's commitment to allegory in *Paradise Lost* is both serious and extensive.

Yet more indicative of the extent of controversy about allegory in Milton studies is Gordon Teskey's likewise outstanding "From Allegory to Dialectic: Imagining Error in Spenser and Milton," which claims that "Milton refuses allegory" entirely in *Paradise Lost*. Contrary to Spenser, that indefatigable fabricator of allegorical complications, Teskey's Milton aims to enforce absolutely clear-cut distinctions in *Paradise Lost* between good and evil, and truth and error. From the very inception of the poem, this special Miltonic purpose jointly precluded serious use of allegory, exploitation of the digressive strayings of narrative romance, and complex analytic presentation of error. Milton practices such an "exclusion of complexity," we are told, that characters are to be judged by "tidy antinomies." In short, "Milton intends his epic to stand on the right side of an abyss he has himself opened between error and truth." This abyss has devoured and negated all possibilities for narrative divagations and for the figurative circumlocutions of allegory itself, which seeks to avoid direct, positive statement. Whereas the action of *The Faerie Queene* signally begins by confronting the reader with an allegorical Error which must be interpreted, and spins out its infinite reticulations from there, Milton simply forecloses on all that at the beginning.[3]

While Teskey's study is admirable and revealing in many ways, especially on Spenser, its conclusions about allegory in *Paradise Lost* are very problematic. Even if his theory of what Milton epistemologically "intends" in *Paradise Lost* were correct, the poem could still subvert it. But if Milton sought to present absolute rather than accommodated truth in *Paradise Lost,* he would have to discount the rhetorical needs of Adam's, Eve's, and his readers' variously limited human perspectives, besides abandoning any vestigial humility. Though Teskey scants the whole issue of poetic accommodation in *Paradise Lost,* where there is any scope for that approach there is potential for allegory, as in Raphael's account of the war in heaven. And if Milton banishes allegory from the poem for supposed opposition to Truth, why not all tropes involving indirection, and ironies in general? Quintilian himself had authoritatively observed their relations to allegory.[4] Moreover, in *Areopagitica* Milton profoundly recognizes that

> the knowledge of good is so involv'd and interwoven with the knowledge of evill, and in so many cunning resemblances hardly to be discern'd. . . . Since therefore the knowledge and survay of vice is in this world so necessary to the constituting of human vertue, and the scanning of error to the confirmation of truth, how can we more safely, and with less danger scout into the regions of sin and falsity then by reading all manner of tractats, and hearing all manner of reason?[5]

By renouncing allegory and representation of error's complexity for the reasons Teskey outlines, Milton would cloister his readers, precluding their scanning of error to the confirmation of Truth, and their active forays into the regions of sin. They would always confront strict, simple, readily resolved moral dichotomies. But if such distinctions are as "tidy" in *Paradise Lost* as Teskey assumes, how could anyone ever have taken Satan for its hero?

Whatever the merits or demerits of Teskey's theory of Miltonic epistemology in *Paradise Lost*, the text itself shows that his conclusions about the impact of that theory on Milton's poetics need substantial modification. Teskey ignores the allegories of Sin and Death, and so we never learn how to reconcile their important, elaborately developed roles in the poem with Milton's supposed rejection of allegory from the start. Moreover, *Paradise Lost* does not sustain the absolute technical and thematic contrasts with Spenser that provide the foundations of Teskey's argument: if Milton's poetics shade even somewhat into Spenser's, then Teskey's strict antitheses between them break down. In Teskey's view Milton seeks to exclude the meanderings of romantic quest-narrative just as he sweepingly rejects allegory and elaborate depiction of error; but the deliberately invented narrative of Satan's journey conforms to romantic and Odyssean paradigms of erratic adventure, as Miltonists have long recognized, and that motif reappears symbolically later, as in the satanic serpent's marvelously labyrinthine approach to Eve, or the bizarre reptilian maze of the demonic wood. In fact, Milton goes to great lengths to acknowledge and portray the complexity of error from the viewpoint of those it seeks to seduce or implicates in misperception—especially his readers. If Milton had totally rejected complex Spenserian representation of error, why is Sin's form so unstable, and pointedly reminiscent of Spenser's Error herself? Milton's practice in *Paradise Lost* appropriates and reinterprets Spenserian motifs and devices; while there are major differences between these writers, their techniques and concerns are not flatly opposed.

Since Milton shares with Spenser a certain community of interest in the development, possibilities, and propagation of heroic poetry, their common recourse to romantic motifs and allegory—however different in application and effect—is only to be expected. Despite Teskey's claim that "After the recovery of Aristotle's *Poetics*, Renaissance critical theorists generally regarded allegory as an empty and tedious game" (p. 16), there was no such consensus. Indeed, endorsements of allegory were common and influential, especially for pastoral and heroic poetry; in his *Discorsi del poema eroica*, for example, Torquato Tasso assumes that allegory is proper to epic as an advantageous means of amplifying its grandeur and profundity.[6] From the commentators' Homer to their Ariosto and beyond, both genuine and assumed precedents of deeply allegorical epic writing had powerfully shaped generic expectations and production, as Tasso's account of his allegory in the *Gerusalemme liberata* and Spenser's poetic practice establish. *Paradise Lost* would reasonably include allegory somehow in its comprehensive recapitulation, reassessment, and redeployment of traditions and conventions attached to the heroic poem.

Satan's cosmic journey involves a hitherto unnoticed yet expansive allegory that shows how thoroughly *Paradise Lost* appropriates and redevelops heroico-romantic allegory for its own purposes. The itinerary shows incidentally that, like Spenser, Milton uses romantic wandering seriously in *Paradise Lost* as a vehicle for elaborate figurative investigation of tendencies to err and their implication in sin and evil. Of course many critics at least accept that Milton uses allegory restrictively in the limited contexts of Sin and Death, Chaos's court, and the Paradise of Fools. But the applications of allegory in *Paradise Lost* are far more important and wide-ranging. These particular allegories are not just anomalies within an otherwise quite literalistic narrative of travel, as previously assumed, but the more simple, readily apparent elements of a sweeping figurative strategy. Allegory comprises a range of techniques that writers can draw upon and mix as suits their artistic purposes; combinations of simple and complex allegorical modes were very common.[7] At its simplest, allegory consists of apparently clear-cut figurative equivalences and straightforward personifications; but, approaching myth and symbolism, complex allegory involves subtly resonant images, language, and structural analogies, and considerable potential for more thoroughly developed characters. Satan's flight is an extensive, complex allegory involving interludes of simpler, more obvious allegory. Rather than somehow becoming simpler or flatter for being allegorical, then, Satan's characterization assumes added dimensions and complexity. The way in which Milton presents Satan's cosmic tour invites allegorical interpretation: the passages of relatively overt allegory encourage figurative reading of the surrounding material, and allegory is unquestionably part of Milton's poetic practice in this section of *Paradise Lost.*

Allegorists had long favored a journey or quest as a narrative medium, of course, and there is no compelling reason in the overall plot itself for Milton to report Satan's journey to earth so thoroughly. The action just requires that Satan obtain knowledge of earth's whereabouts, and get there.[8] Often this kind of apparent irrelevance or straying from the direct purposes of plot helps identify an allegorical narrative because it must express a more or less hidden agenda of considerations beyond the ordinary requirements of its story, and tends to do so through features not strictly relevant to the main action.[9] Beyond the elementary literal function, Satan's progress has "mysteriously . . . meant" thematic relevance to the whole poem, like the heavenly stairs he reaches *en route* (III, 516).[10]

Just as what links together all the plainly figurative elements of Satan's itinerary is his flight itself, that is the governing metaphor of the allegory and the primary means by which the various generic paradigms involved are allegorically transfigured. Of course flight has various roles in *Paradise Lost.* Milton himself imaginatively soars in poetic rapture. While most obviously reflecting the self-exaltation of pride, wrongful ascents like Satan's partly travesty and to some extent criticize motifs of heroic apotheosis celebrating the high merits of human virtue; poets had already freely combined motifs of ascent.[11] In a mostly implicit, figurative way, Satan's exploratory initiative further conforms to the age-old topos of cosmic mental flight, explicitly used elsewhere in Milton's works, so that his flight constitutes a vehicle for complex allegory about prideful intellect and the relation of its aims and powers to evil. The passages of simpler allegory are parts of this comprehensive allegorical whole; from a generic viewpoint its subject is obviously apt for such special attention in *Paradise Lost* because *sapientia* was a standard epic subject, and sometimes treated through allegory.[12] Milton's interpretive synthesis of the heroic quest or journey motif with the flight topos enables a further, epistemological assessment of a fundamental declaration attributed to Satan: "I will ascend above the heights of the clouds, I will be like the most High" (Isa. xiv, 14).[13] Satan himself readily typifies intellectual overreaching because, in an Augustinian tradition, the origin of his pride was intellective: "*There was no other way for angels to sin, but by reflex of their understanding upon themselves;* when being held with admiration of their own sublimity and honour, the memory of their subordination unto God and their dependency on him was drowned in this *conceit.*"[14] Whether or not Milton accepted this view as doctrine, it would have provided a precedent for treating Satan as an archetype of intellectual perversity for at least the purposes of poetic economy. *Paradise Lost* revolves around the problematic relation of evil to the pursuit of knowledge and spiritual attainments; that problem is likewise the focus of even this early part of the poem, allegorically, as it endeavors to frame an appropriate standard of heroism.

In this sense Milton's account of Satan's progress to earth is a further proleptic means of grappling with the implications of human transgression. Milton deals with epistemological aspects of the Fall in general partly by means of terms and imagery drawn from Satan's flight, so that, while anticipating and amplifying many later developments, the allegory constitutes a structural component of *Paradise Lost.* Having crossed Sin's threshold, as it were, by devouring the fallacious fruit, Adam and Eve feel "Divinity within them breeding wings" to attain godlike perspectives and powers, yet must also contend with a perilous inner "abyss" of chaotic impulses (IX, 1010; X, 842), much as Satan finds when soaring heavenward. Rather than just situating his epic on the right side of an abyss he opens between error and truth, then, Milton enters the Stygian pool to track satanic movements (III, 3–21), and thus brings himself and his readers to a higher self-knowledge allegorically won, in part, from the very experience of the dark descent. Attention to the allegory further reveals much acerbic wit. Satan's inadequacies as a cosmonaut satirize intellectual excesses in general;[15] but this allegorized satire generates no simple-minded laughter because its vehicle, Satan's journey, may appear so dynamic, audacious, and threatening from a human viewpoint. In various ways, then, the allegory constitutes a further embedded "commentary" richly supplementing the poem's narrational asides, invocations, and biographical passages. Though confirming the now common assumption that Milton associates allegory with Satan and fallen perspectives in *Paradise Lost*,[16] Milton's treatment of the journey is so extensively and significantly allegorical that the role of allegory in the poem appears much more intriguing and comprehensive than most commentators allow. *Paradise Lost* profoundly reflects the psychologizing tendencies of epic development, in which properties of the heroic poem become vehicles for figurative explorations of the mind.[17]

II

Human ascent through the heavens on the wings of intellectual acuity and enlightenment had long been metaphorically envisioned by writers endeavoring to extol mental powers and potential.[18] As the young Milton confidently exhorts in his Third Prolusion, the wise man was thus to devote his live to achieving a cosmic ascendancy:

> fly even up to the skies, there to behold . . . the source of those tears of early morn; next to peer into the caskets of the hail and to survey the arsenals of the thunderbolts. Nor let what Jupiter or Nature veils from you be concealed. . . . Yea, follow as companion the wandering sun, and subject time itself to a reckoning and demand the order of its everlasting journey. Nay, let not your mind suffer itself to be hemmed in and bounded by the same limits as the earth, but let it wander also outside the boundaries of the world. Finally . . . let it learn thoroughly to know itself and at the same time those holy minds and intelligences, with whom hereafter it will enter into everlasting companionship.[19]

Opening up intoxicating prospects of divine potential breeding wings within, the topos encourages optimistic assumptions that mental powers enable transcendence of earthly conditions. Renaissance writers with strong hermetico-Neoplatonic allegiances such as Giordano Bruno, Cornelius Agrippa, and Pico della Mirandola enthusiastically deploy the topos to emphasize human potential. The *Corpus Hermeticum* itself encouraged them by acclaiming human spiritual power to fly contemplatively through and beyond the heavens, and thus attain a divine likeness in which nothing remains impossible, including comprehension of God.[20] Bruno confidently spreads intellectual wings to soar beyond the skies to the infinite, leaving all others behind as he glides through ineffable cosmic mysteries with utter aplomb.[21] John Dee assures us that, through knowledge of mathematics, which confers magical power, we can "arise, clime, ascend, and mount vp (with Speculatiue winges) in spirit, to behold in the Glas of Creation, the *Forme* of *Formes*, the *Exemplar Number* of all thinges *Numerable:* both visible and inuisible, mortall and immortall, Corporall and Spirituall."[22]

However, as a means of defining human abilities, the topos could serve other purposes through qualification of its fundamental optimism. The mind does not self-sufficiently fly through the heavenly spheres to God's realm, Boethius emphasizes, but depends on Dame Philosophy for wings, flight path, and guidance *en route.* Some Protestant poets who substantially influenced Milton also cautiously temper their enthusiasm. While using the topos for heady exhortation, Spenser insists that humility and divine grace are essential: when we "Mount vp aloft through heauenly contemplation," using "wings" of the "high flying mind," we should not "dare looke vp . . . / On the dred face of that great *Deity,*" "But lowly fall before his mercie seate, / Close couered with the Lambes integrity."[23]

Whereas youthful Milton uses the topos without any reservations, his treatment of it changes as his thought increasingly emphasizes biblical Protestant perspectives. In *De Doctrina Christiana,* written long after the *Prolusions,* Milton mocks intellectual overreachers in a way that ironically deflates attitudes like those implied by the topos when used without strong qualifications:

> we ought to entertain such a conception of him [i.e. God], as he, in condescending to accommodate himself to our capacities, has shown that he desires we should conceive. For it is on this very account that he has lowered himself to our level, lest in our flights [*nos elati*] above the reach of human understanding, and beyond the written word of Scripture, we should be tempted to engage in vague cogitations and subtleties.[24]

We only have any meaningful conception of God, Milton affirms, insofar as he lowers himself to us, not because we can intellectually engage him on his own level.

This passage helps clarify Milton's complex and extended use of the topos in *Paradise Lost.* The narrator's own insistently enlightened imaginative flight through the cosmos evokes the topos yet qualifies it through emphatic dependence on divine aid.[25] However, the account of Satan's flight incorporates the topos into the narrative in an implicit way that allegorically satirizes presumptions of fallen intellect and provides a means of evaluating responses to questions of knowledge.

At the outset of Satan's journey Milton's wording immediately establishes its figurative relation to exploratory intellectual flight: "Satan *with thoughts inflamed* of *highest* design, / *Puts on swift wings*, and towards the gates of hell / *Explores* his *solitary Flight*" (II, 630–32; emphasis mine). Furthering Satan's designs, his wings and flight are in one sense extensions of satanic thinking, put on "along with" his thoughts, and also perhaps "by way of" them, in an added figurative sense. Even apart from the topos wings had long symbolized thought, prescience, or intellectual acuity.[26] Figurative wings and flight appear throughout Milton's writings, so that Satan's wings can well have more than literal meaning. The conventionality of angelic and demonic wings does not in the least discourage interpretation of Satan's wings in *Paradise Lost:* these attributes of spirits are figurative anyway, basically to express transcendence of time and place as humanly known.[27] In Satan's case, this standard meaning combines with the further compatible one of cosmic intellectual flight.

After his departure Satan's course broadly reflects the topos. Winging audaciously heavenward Satan explores "secrets of the hoary deep" and surveys with wonder "the sudden view / . . . at once" of the firmament in its starry dance, from the universal outer shell (II, 891; III, 540–61). He visits the sun, confers with its guiding angelic intelligence, beholds empyreal heaven, and stands on its mysterious stairs. This is the sort of exploratory cosmic grand tour that writers like the hermetic Neoplatonists claimed to take intellectually with their own winged thoughts of highest design, and that Milton himself recommends in his Third Prolusion: taking mental flight we should wander far beyond mere earthly limits, closely follow the sun, and at last attain the pinnacles of wisdom in knowledge of the heavenly intelligences. The widely influential Boethian itinerary for the mind's cosmic flight is reasonably normative for the topos; the intellectual aviator follows "bright Phoebus waies," tracing "the circles of the starres," and finally sits "vpon the highest orbe," returning to the lost homeland of God's rule.[28] But when Satan flies back to his original "native seat," his frame of mind makes him *persona non grata* (II, 1050).

Of course there is a crucial difference between ordinary uses of the topos and Milton's here, for its application to Satan's journey is wholly ironic. As anticipated in *De Doctrina Christiana,* Milton inverts the usual function of the topos: praise of the mind's great potential, to exhort attainment of the ultimate intellectual and spiritual heights. Various features of Satan's journey rebuke such confidence. The satanically proud ascent affords at best just a teasing glimpse of heaven and precludes access (III, 523–25). Moreover, users of the topos like Bruno or even Du Bartas and Boethius never seem to anticipate, at least in context, that intellectual flight through the cosmos could be anything other than a splendid triumphal progress heavenward. But Milton often describes Satan's flight reductively, and these deflations have purposes more entertaining and profound than just mockery of Satan and his presumed heroic status. The relation of Satan's flight to the topos satirizes proud intellectual ascents in general. As Satan's swift wings are put on with thoughts inflamed, so the highest design he can frame is just the overhasty product of a mental inflammation.

III

In dealing figuratively with the bounds of intellectual powers, Satan's flight provides an allegorical framework for the incidents of his journey; Milton thus reorganizes and reconstitutes the relevant heroic models of adventurous quest for allegory appropriate to his own agenda. Satan's ungodly flight plan almost immediately brings him to Sin and Death, and this allegorical efflorescence of his mental state expresses its origins, conditions, and consequences. Though Satan as putative renewer of lost dominions broadly travesties Aeneas, Satan's main heroic counterpart as a quester is Odysseus, and he wanders also like heroes of romantic epic; Sin recalls Spenser's Error and Duessa, and the Paradise of Fools Ariosto's Limbo.[29] Such wandering could readily express psychological conditions of sin because it had already been associated with human tendencies to err by various writers such as Spenser. Error and wandering etymologically coincide in the Latin *errare;* knightly errantry in *The Faerie Queene* must first confront the Error endemic in the wandering wood of fallen human experience. Tortuous routes and going astray are indeed basic biblical metaphors for sin and wrongdoing, and "err" itself comprised the meanings "to go wrong in judgement" and "to sin" as well as "to wander."[30] Milton explores the relation of Satan's intellectual characteristics to his general deviancy, as it were, by using flight patterned on the topos for Satan's main means of travel. While still serving the broader allusive functions noted by previous commentators, the heroic models are allegorically redeveloped so that Satan's erratic career through the cosmos, overgoing all heroic precedents for divagation, expresses a paradigmatic aberrancy of the mind.

In view of the allegory about violation of intellectual values, Odysseus's journey is especially apt as primary heroic analogue, for the Odyssean model is intellectually pointed. Heroic exemplar of virtues of the mind for Sidney, Tasso, Minturno, and many others, he was protégé of Athena, goddess of wisdom, whom Satan's cerebrally misconceived Sin travesties. And Odysseus's journey had been interpreted as an allegory of the contemplative life. Yet, as Cicero, Dante, and Paolo Beni caution, Odysseus could exemplify dangerous excess in quests for knowledge, or prudence and wisdom lapsed merely into guile.[31]

Though many have studied Satan's encounter with Sin and Death as an incident, assessing it in the figurative context of Satan's flight yields much further insight. Satan confronts what has malignly existed within him since the first instant of his turning from God; later, Adam and Eve experience their own inner genesis of sin and death. Sin opens the way for Satan to proceed with his sinful design. And, in doing so, the arch-sinner passes over the threshold of the Sin that his mind has conceived: an allegorical prototype for commitment to sin or sinful action. "To transgress" indeed means "to step across," etymologically, and Milton appears to have used that here as his allegorical point of departure. The daunting potentialities and disorders of Chaos, which Satan must then reckon with, reflect the impact of sin on the mind. The family reunion at hell's gate is an obviously allegorical introduction to the journey's broader, subtle allegory about the mind as it is compromised by conditions of fallen awareness.

As such, that initial encounter aptly emphasizes the power of evil to transform the mind, just as Milton's Sin is very much an agent of transformation. The biblical text underlying the incident warrants such an emphasis, for it describes involvement with sin as a degenerative process progressively deforming a creature's affinities: "Then when lust hath *conceived*, it *bringeth forth* sin; and sin, when it is finished, *bringeth forth* death" (James i, 15; emphasis mine). Having conceived Sin, Satan strikingly changes when she erupts painfully from his forehead, and he visibly degenerates thereafter until his final metamorphosis reveals him at a reptilian nadir on the scale of creaturely beings. Satan's monstrous misconception vitiates the intellect: in rupturing his head, it travesties Zeus's generation of Athena and the Father's of the Son as his Word fraught with divine wisdom.

After undergoing various repulsive mutations herself, Sin becomes a troublesome flux of hounds and coiling tail; but her most important attribute is the key for hell's gate. It expresses the power of sin to effect momentous change: to open the door of perverse opportunity, so to speak, through which personal options become malignantly transformed.[32] Like hell and Sin herself, her symbolic threshold exists in a sense within all fallen creatures, the poem implies, insofar as sin discloses dark and disordered realms of mental errancy. "Sad instrument of all our woe" (II, 872), Sin's key is a symbolic extension of her transforming power that emphasizes how much sin can alter perspectives and change personal horizons; the revolution in satanic alternatives that the key effects is an archetypal disclosure of sinful possibilities.[33] In Milton's cosmos, turning the key is Sin's pivotal, most momentous act. Such gates affording free passage to ideas and intentions participating in the nature of Sin open too, as it were, when the Fall decisively changes the structure and perceptions of the human mind in *Paradise Lost.*

Indeed, the transformation of the gates when they burst open, with a significantly portentous crash that shakes hell's depths, may well symbolize that which sin effects on the mind. In epic tradition gates had long been used and interpreted as symbols of mental states, powers, or functions. Besides the Homeric gates of dreams there are gates of sleep and passion in heroic poems, and Aeneas's descent through the cave-mouth of Avernus is clearly in part an excursion into the self.[34] In any case Milton's hell is a place that is also an inner reality. Though crafted with infinite care and apparently inviolable (II, 645–48), these gates suffer drastic change when the potent device of Sin works upon them:

> in the key-hole turns
> The intricate wards, and every bolt and bar
> Of massy iron or solid rock with ease
> Unfastens. (II, 876–79)

Adam too has intricate inner bolts, bars, and "wards" in a sense, like God-given conscience, so that he is "Sufficient to have stood," like the gates themselves (III, 194–95, 99); but under the persuasive ministrations of sin how changed he becomes. A door of sinful perception opens in his and Eve's minds, in effect, when their original sin withdraws the "veil" of "innocence, that . . . / Had shadowed them from knowing ill" (IX, 1054–55). To shut Sin's gates, or restore them to their original condition, excels her power; sin cannot be redemptive or reverse the mental effects of the Fall. Those are the Son's prerogatives, who will "obstruct the mouth of hell / For ever" so that Satan's and Sin's degenerate offspring Death must become himself "the gate of life" for humanity (X, 636–37; XII, 571).

Whether or not the opening of the gates themselves is a psychological symbol, Satan's passage over Sin's threshold emphatically expresses involvement with sin. While detailing a cosmic adventure broadly analogous to storm-tossed Odysseus's wanderings at sea, characteristics of Satan's journey point to effects of sin on created intellects so as to mock and censure intellectual overreaching. The cosmic context enables explosive effects of satiric hyperbole: over against the mystic immensities of Milton's universe, satanic efforts to overmaster them come to seem absurdly impertinent.

The gates of Sin open up a dark, abysmal prospect of intractable confusions. Much as "the sacred influence / Of light" and the beauties of creation imply God's active presence in *Paradise Lost* (II, 1034–35; V, 153–59), this domain from which God withholds his full creative benevolence manifests what absence or rejection of God implies, like hell itself. The physical features of Milton's cosmos broadly reflect spiritual conditions. Hell, existing within Satan and all fallen creatures, is an enclave of Chaos (I, arg.; VI, 50–55), and both have related psychological meaning. In this sense, what Satan sees beyond Sin's threshold is a spectacular Miltonic analogue of an ungodly mental state—inane and vacuous, so to speak, and chaotically forbidding.[35] Sin itself is without measure, and "alwaies an excesse," Milton comparably declares in *Tetrachordon;* and so "The least sinne that is, . . . is as boundlesse as that vacuity beyond the world [i.e., ordered universe]."[36] A stringent irony heightening the satiric effect is that Satan himself is dismayed and hesitates before becoming involved in this ur-aporia that in one sense figures forth his own inner state. Likewise, the rebel angels' "monstrous" vision of the wild abyss beyond God-given heavenly bounds horrifies them; yet, ironically, what they perceive in part reflects what they have become, and they plummet to the level of their own abysmal way of thinking (VI, 856–66).

While there are many precedents for Milton's expressive analogy between Chaos and the fallen condition, *Paradise Lost* itself delineates the analogy clearly enough.[37] Milton explicitly relates Chaos to human social, moral, and intellectual failings. Social disorders like armed conflicts provide means to describe Chaos; and Rumour, Tumult, Confusion, and Discord are Chaos's attendants (II, 959–67). After the Fall, Chaos's influence extends to produce earthly disorders. Moreover, after conceiving Sin, Satan experiences "Confusion worse confounded" and grievous inner disorder (II, 996, 752–58); later, "horror and doubt distract / His troubled thoughts, and from the bottom stir / The hell within him," so that "in the lowest deep" of his mind "a lower deep / Still threatening to devour . . . opens wide" (IV, 18–20, 76–77). Such a state, "Alien from heaven, with passions foul obscured," marked by "So deep a malice," reproduces the vertiginous depths of Milton's cosmos as an inner reality; it exists in fallen Adam and Eve as it does archetypally in "the author of all ill" (IV, 571; II, 381–82). Their original sin causes "high winds . . . within / . . . to rise, high passions," which shake "Their inward state of mind, calm region once / And full of peace, now tossed and turbulent," a "troubled sea of passion" (IX, 1122–26; X, 718). Like Satan tormented within "as from the hateful siege / Of contraries," Adam finds himself in an inner "abyss of fears / And horrors," "from deep to deeper plunged" (IX, 121–22; X, 842–44).

For Satan, Adam, and Eve, Sin introduces them to an inner chaos, and Satan's journey allegorically amplifies that psychic event. The Sin Satan has conceived ushers him directly into Chaos, just as Discord is her "first / Daughter" (X, 707–08). Various similarities further reflect the close relationship between Sin and Chaos. Milton links Sin, her son Death, and Chaos with darkness, restless turmoil, and instability of form, which had often been associated with evil: Satan conceives Sin "In darkness," for instance, while Death appears "black . . . as night" and Chaos dwells with "eldest Night" (II, 754, 670, 894). Satan's progress after the encounter at hell's gate sets the flight-of-the-mind topos over against a figuratively psychic chaos resulting from commitment to sin. This satiric juxtaposition demolishes the pretentious tendencies of the topos by stressing the destructive impact of sin on created intellects.

The environment of the mind averse to God, the allegory implies, is a bewildering morass of confusion, meaningless vacuity, and overwhelming, unorganized potential; a boundless hoary deep where the creature, having banished God as prime authority of the mental universe, becomes beset by internal disorders and caprices of chance. When the powerful symmetries of the gates, with their demarcation of just limits and bounds that should not be transgressed, yield to Sin's promptings, ceaseless competition of "Hot, Cold, Moist, and Dry" ensues, with Chaos as "umpire" further embroiling the fray, and Chance governing all as in the atheistic conception of the cosmos attributed to Epicurus in the Renaissance (II, 891–910). While this conflict could relate to humoral disorder from a psychological viewpoint,[38] the allegory need not be so specific: the general analogy between Chaos and inner turmoil as a function of sin is broadly relevant here anyway. Within Chaos, self-control for the creature is at best illusory, just as Satan's mission becomes wholly subject to "chance" (II, 934–38). Likewise, when the Fall abysmally disorders Adam and Eve's "inward state of mind," understanding and will become subjected "To sensual appetite," making their minds "turbulent," or a "hateful siege / Of contraries," and human resolutions at least to some extent arbitrary (IX, 1121–31, 121–22).

In Milton's cosmos, where God is the foundation of being, order, and good, a creature that has turned from God is cosmically at a loss, and Satan's difficulties in Chaos figuratively dramatize this state of jeopardy. It brings a burden of knowledge and choice, Milton implies, impossible for any creature to sustain without crippling distortions. *Paradise Lost* hinges on Adam and Eve's violation of a single divine prohibition, through which they commit themselves to sin, in opposition to God, and throw themselves upon their own resources. Once they transgress the limit to their action implied by obedience to divine authority, a bewildering plethora of possibilities manifests itself. The original sin quickly ramifies, just as Sin herself ends in convoluted folds, undergoes various permutations, and generates all manner of disturbing progeny. To *trans*gress is to pass beyond some limit and be confronted with the manifold implications of its absence, such as possibilities for further, related transgressions, or new ones that may then suggest themselves, which in turn diversify. Crossing Sin's threshold introduces a Chaos that, through its sheer potentiality, expresses the overwhelming potential of transgression; and the archtransgressor's confrontation with that is archetypal.[39]

Milton further develops this figurative dimension of Chaos, where time and place are lost and distinctions confounded, through the ubiquitous marine imagery. The sea had long been associated with bewildering, intractable flux and the manifold contingencies of creaturely existence. Dealing with that condition requires innumerable choices involving individual preference as well as ethical consideration, and yet some shift in events may thwart or subvert them, or be supplanted in turn by some very different development. However much like Scylla, Sin passes into a swirling Charybdis of polymorphous possibilities and unforeseeable consequences, so that in this sense, too, "the wicked *are* like the troubled sea, when it cannot rest, whose waters cast up mire and dirt. *There is* no peace . . . to the wicked" (Isa. lvii, 20).[40] The allegory shows that all Satan's own powers of self-determination are soon overwhelmed under the full impact of the inchoate (II, 934–38). In Milton's universe only the supreme being can cope alone with such a vast threat to the personal organization necessary for the possession of any identity beyond the pressure of chance and circumstance. Likewise only he can master the confusing potentialities of Chaos to produce the beauteous creation that to some extent manifests his identity, and only he can cope with full knowledge of evil.[41]

Hence Satan's cosmic journey is fundamentally absurd, like his whole opposition to God; and his passage through Chaos, where he is especially at risk, affords much scope for satire and black comedy that allegorically relate to hubristic flights of the mind. Over against the enigmatic expanses of Chaos and the universe God can create from it, Satan finally appears a puny, deluded figure in willful, pointless jeopardy, for all his titanic audacity. Of course in *Paradise Lost* as a whole Satan is a complex character eliciting a range of responses from us, as when he addresses the sun on Mount Niphates. But Satan's gyrations in Chaos, which are sometimes completely hapless, far exceed storm-driven Odysseus's wanderings, or those of romantic heroes, including even Ruggiero astride the wayward Hippogriff, so that Satan travesties heroic roles in his extremity of error. Moreover, though so much at a loss, Satan is ironically in his own element to the extent that Chaos expresses his inner state.

Absurdly soaring heavenward by means of Sin, Satan at first "rides / Audacious" as Bruno could wish on his "sail-broad vans," yet soon meets a "vacuity" more than "vast" enough to swallow and regurgitate all he has in mind:

> all unawares
> Fluttering his pennons vain plumb down he drops
> Ten thousand fathom deep, and to this hour
> Down had been falling, had not by ill chance
> The strong rebuff of some tumultuous cloud
> Instinct with fire and nitre hurried him
> As many miles aloft. (II, 927–33)

In a striking comeuppance, so to speak, mere "chance" saves the creature who valorizes "unconquerable will . . . / And courage never to submit or yield" (I, 106–08). Clearly his powers are finite and conditional, so that Milton deflates Satan's distended notions of self-reliance from the outset of his high endeavor: the grand latitude of his self-acclaimed will is necessarily and aptly limited by his own contingent being. Satan's helpless commitment to vacuity, punning on the sense "vacancy of mind or thought," satirizes the fundamental emptiness of his pretensions and of all fallen minds with exalted estimations of their own capabilities. They are as vain, Milton implies, as the pennons with which Satan seeks to surmount the vacuity attending his endeavor; that external void figuratively manifests the spiritual effects of the inner void generated by his aversion to God. However, while satirically reducing Satan's heroic grandeur in one way, Milton's complex allegory may still increase it in another by deepening our awareness of the odds Satan surmounts in proceeding at all, and thus also of the energy and persistence with which he pursues his misdirected, fateful purpose.

Having exploded Satan's lofty self-conceptions many miles, Milton administers a further satiric rebuff by drenching them in the muck of a "boggy Syrtis," where this bedraggled cosmic aviator "swims or sinks, or wades, or creeps, or flies," "With head, hands, wings, or feet" (II, 939–50). Despite Satan's pursuit of self-sufficiency through the overdriven energies of his will, he is finally reduced to using all his Odyssean wiles to obtain guidance from the addled anarch Chaos; the high-flown satanic scheme takes direction, then, from confusion. In pointed contrast, storm-tossed Odysseus finds respite and guidance in the glorious palace of the Phaeacian ruler "Alci-nous," meaning "strength of mind," whom the gods "made wise in counsel."[42] The possibility of such a humiliation as serpentine creeping, even with the head, did not occur to writers like Bruno and the youthful Milton when using the topos of mental flight. Only when "the sacred influence / Of light appears" can Satan proceed with any surety, so that his high presumption ironically comes to manifest an indispensable reliance on God (II, 1034–35). The chaotic phase of Satan's journey and Book II conclude with the manifestation of the golden chain symbolizing God's harmonious cosmic order, a decisively simple rebuke to all Satan's errancies. Milton's blackly comic mockery of Satan's benighted predicament in Chaos allegorically applies to aspiring minds disordered and "darkened" by sin, like fallen Adam and Eve's (IX, 1054), that "wander beyond all limit and satiety" (*Areopagitica*, CM IV, p. 320).

That the Paradise of Fools manifests itself from the satanic experience of Chaos, in effect, makes the epistemological implications of Milton's Chaos clear indeed. This chaotic annex modeled on Ariosto's Limbo of Vanities or realm of lost wits satirizes human errors and confusions, especially false philosophical and religious beliefs. Proceeding from Sin on pennons vain, Satan is blown about by chance in chaotic confusions and vacuities; likewise, "when sin / With vanity had filled the works of men," "all things . . . vain" and those with erroneous or empty ideas similarly fly heavenward only to be blown "ten thousand leagues awry" in the purlieus of Chaos (III, 444–97). In a parody of the mental flight topos, these intellectual lightweights ascend like ephemeral "vapours" to become the mere "sport of winds," which frustrate their entry into heaven just as that comes to seem tantalizingly possible.

As fools are teased and excluded at the "foot / Of heaven's ascent," so is Satan, progenitor of all their vanities and misconceptions, when he reaches heaven's "lower stair" (III, 523–25, 540). In the topos of intellectual ascent, arrival at heaven's doorstep would normally lead to the glorious visions of heaven and God. Instead, this moment becomes the absolute upper limit of Satan's arduous flight through the cosmos: the stair leads up to bliss that eludes and thus reproves him. Here at its apex Satan's mode of flight incurs its consummate rebuke, for Milton relates the stairs to Jacob's ladder, which commonly symbolized right contemplative ascent and Christ as the way to heaven.[43] Decisive in the allegory of the journey, then, these stairs are indeed mysteriously meant. Heaven's gate to which they lead, and from which creation proceeded, symbolically opposes Sin's baneful one, which initiates Satan's destructive procedure; the ladderlike flight of stairs likewise opposes Satan's hubristic self-transports with an effectively pedestrian alternative.

While Satan's ascent does not at last yield any beatific vision, Milton further modifies the contemplative view of the cosmos common in applications of the mental flight topos so that it exposes further satanic failings. Satan's apt initial "wonder" at the heavens merely produces narrow-minded, self-centered "envy" (III, 542–54). And Milton severely qualifies Satan's perspective on the universe by displaying God's first. God's perception of Satan's "wearied" flight, so diminished as to seem rather punily mock-heroic, like the devils dwarfed in Pandaemonium, opens to us "from his prospect high, / Wherein past, present, future he beholds," thus apprehending all Satan's devices and their ultimate consequences (III, 69–79). God's view from the heavenly summit is itself part of an epistemological motif complementing that of flight in *Paradise Lost,* for Milton often uses the Boethian paradigm of knowledge as far-reaching vision to express differences in apprehension and awareness, as characters attempt or experience various kinds of ascent. But compared with God's absolute preeminence, Satan and other aspirants appear unworthily deficient. Likewise, over against marvels of creation like heaven, the sacred light, the golden chain, the astral dance, the glassy sea, and the sun, Satan at last appears infinitesimally small-minded as he passes through it all blind and averse to the splendidly revealed creativity of divine love. Of course Milton's mockery of Satan has a very complex effect throughout *Paradise Lost* because we also recognize Satan's fearsome power, relative to human abilities, and his persistent dedication to propagating evil. Nevertheless, Milton handles the flight topos so as to satirize creaturely pretensions and emphasize an insurmountable gap between the most audacious flights of the created mind and divine accomplishments.

To Satan posing as a cherub inspired with "Unspeakable desire to see, and know" all of God's "wondrous works" (III, 662–63), Uriel directly explains God's creative omnipotence and creatures' apt bounds of knowledge. Such desire "leads to no excess" when knowing God's works is a means "to glorify the great work-master"; "But what created mind can comprehend / Their number, or the wisdom infinite / That brought them forth, but hid their causes deep" (III, 694–707). The solar setting, a marvelous realm of especial perceptual clarity (III, 613–21), implicitly rebukes the satanic enterprise. The sun had long commonly symbolized enlightenment, and also Christ or Christian truth, essential for Miltonic wisdom. Here Satan's epistemological perversity stands most brightly revealed because he undertakes his demonic "re-connaissance" of the poem's cosmos only for destructive vengeance against its proper ultimate object for created intellect, God. Satan's Odyssean mastery of disguises and persuasive strategies, which he uses to promote his perceptions throughout his mission, is not only another index of heroic travesty, but also a vehicle for satiric depiction of the state of intellectual powers when debased, overextended, or wrongly oriented. Satanic ingenuity is merely the product of desperately extreme alienation from the supreme good in *Paradise Lost;* so the shifts and apparent attractions of Satan's acumen become themselves symbolic of profound falsity, in a subtilization within narrative of the speciously engaging front of Spenser's Error and of the Sin she spawned in Milton's imagination.

Various supplementary and more direct attacks on high-flown and otherwise vain thoughts just prior to and during Satan's flight further evince its broad epistemological applications. Belial favors thoughts wandering through eternity, nearly Satan's fate in Chaos. Likewise, devils reasoning "high" find "no end," lost in "wandering mazes" of "Vain wisdom . . . and false philosophy"; and those exploring hell find "No rest" either, in a clear travesty of romantic errantry (II, 558–65, 616–28). These exorbitant strayings, especially Satan's, express the rebel angels' absolute commitment to error, but implicitly denigrate human errancies as well. As God indicts human blindness (III, 92–99, 198–210), so Milton criticizes secular literature and philosophy through the devil's speeches and entertainments, human confusions through his accounts of the infernal council, Chaos, and the Paradise of Fools. The "vain" search by "Philosophers" for the philosopher's stone seems paradigmatic for much human intellectual endeavor in Milton's view (III, 600–05), like astronomical theorization later.

Satan's cosmic flight to earth deals allegorically with the conditions and difficulties of intellect compromised by sin, when pursuing thoughts of highest design depends, the poem assumes, on pennons vain. Milton evaluates these aspects of satanic psychology mainly through parody of the mental flight topos. Inverting the broad pattern of the topos and reversing Jacob's ladder too, in effect, Satan's flight just brings him down to earth, where his "mad demeanour" evinces some mental breakdown

(IV, 129). Though spiritually strong in this remorseful moment of felt weakness, Satan turns instead to his own resources; yet the cosmic context of his itinerary has just revealed the absurdity of doing so. Beelzebub's rhetorical question heralding Satan's acceptance of the mission, "What strength, what art can then / Suffice," is unwittingly to the point (II, 410–11). As Milton's God has his enemies in derision (V, 736; cf. Ps. ii, 4), so does the created universe reflecting that divinity. When Satan returns to hell and proudly announces that he has overcome the "vast, unbounded deep / Of horrible confusion" (X, 469–80), for instance, an "allegorical irony" is that this setting Satan finds so repugnant is an analogue of his own horrific and persisting confusion that generated his enterprise.[44] However far he ascends, even to heaven's gate, Satan carries depths opening upon depths within, as he himself recognizes and as fallen Adam likewise inwardly perceives later. The fundamental irony of Satan's journey is that the mental state of which it is an expression cannot get anyone anywhere in the cosmos of the poem. In sharp contrast to heroic quests like those of Aeneas, Odysseus, and the romantic knights, Satan's movements are very much illusory, despite their vast scope, in that he remains within intensely experienced, hellish abysses of the mind to which he accommodates all that he encounters: "Which way I fly is hell; my self am hell" (IV, 75). His wretched "homecoming" in hell travesties Odysseus's at Ithaca partly because the narrative situation constitutes an outward sign of what has been Satan's continuing inner reality. Satan's flight so far subverts the heroic quest-model in that it paradoxically comes to display a psychic commitment to sin more horrifically absolute in the subtlety of fixation than the physical immobility of Dante's Satan, vainly beating his wings while frozen to the infernal depths.

IV

Paradise Lost as a whole ties into the allegory of Satan's flight thematically, and imagistic correspondences reinforce these connections. The journey gathers many images with epistemological significance into a highly charged configuration, and Milton exploits that repertoire of imagery throughout the poem to coordinate expression of its concerns about knowledge. He associates such images not only with Satan's, Adam's, and Eve's temptations and transgressions, but also with the initiatives of Raphael and the epic narrator, and with the couple's regeneration. *Paradise Lost* favors enterprises of the mind if the creature's relation to God is appropriate, just as Milton is not antiintellectual or antiscientific. His position on knowledge, we find, approximates Ralph Cudworth's:

> We think it a gallant thing to be fluttering up to Heaven with our wings of Knowledge and Speculation: whereas the highest mystery of a Divine Life here, and of perfect Happinesse hereafter, consisteth in nothing but mere Obedience to the Divine Will. . . . There is nothing contrary to God in the whole world, nothing that fights against him but *Self-will*. . . . It was by reason of this *Self-will*, that Adam fell in Paradise; that those glorious Angels, . . . dropt down from heaven. . . . They all intangled themselves with the length of their own wings. . . . Now our onely way to recover God and happines again, is not to soar up with our understandings, but to destroy this *Self-will* of ours: and then we shall find our wings to grow again.[45]

Satan aims to corrupt Adam and Eve by playing upon their natural and proper "desire to know" so that they will perversely challenge divine prerogatives (IV, 514–27). While their fall reflects the allegory of Satan's plunge into Chaos, as we have seen, significant analogies extend much further. Eve dreams that eating the fruit of "interdicted knowledge" results in flight heavenward to godlike "high exaltation," where she envisions all earth at once (V, 50–90), much as Satan ascends to a cosmic viewpoint ironically analogous to God's. When inspired by Satan the serpent claims that the fruit similarly rendered its mind so "capacious" that its "speculations high" embraced "all things visible in heaven, / Or earth, or middle" (IX, 603–05). Eve devours the fruit with "expectation high / Of knowledge, nor was godhead from her thought" (IX, 789–90); Adam's motives for eating also involve desire for such supposedly divine "ascent" (IX, 932–37). After eating, both fancy "As with new wine intoxicated" "Divinity within them breeding wings / Wherewith to scorn the earth" (IX, 1008–11). In one figurative sense Satan's own flight explores the implications of a corrupted desire for knowledge like Adam and Eve's, and Milton's satire of Satan's endeavor applies allegorically to that whole state of mind. With inflamed thoughts Satan "spurns the ground" to ascend (II, 929); thus intoxicated, Adam and Eve scorn it likewise.

But, at the very moment of Satan's Odyssean return and prospective epic triumph celebrating how, as Sin thinks, his "*wisdom* gained / With odds what war . . . lost" (X, 373–74; emphasis mine), Satan's high-flown notions reduce him and his cohorts to abject, earthbound serpents, which partly symbolize intellectual perversion. They compulsively eat fruit seeming to be like that of the tree of knowledge, but that turns at once into ashes when bitten (X, 504–77). Their predicament alludes to, yet significantly contrasts with, that of Tantalus. Whereas the gods condemned him to desire fruit and water that would forever remain elusive, Milton's God punitively allows the devils to attain what they desire, but only to savor its bitter insufficiency. Rather than just being tantalized, they must intensely experience a symbolic confrontation with their own deluded commitment to error, or the fruits of satanic fallacy.[46] In this interminably reconstituted annual ritual they can ruminate only on the profound extent of their self-deception just when they think they have secured some fulfilment: "so oft they fell / Into the same illusion" (X, 570–71). While the reptilian forms wreathed in the trees compose a forbidding labyrinth "thicker than the snaky locks / That curled Megaera" (X, 559–60), the orchard of delusive fruit constitutes an infernal wood of error more dire than the obscure woods where Dante and the heroes of romantic epic tracked the limits of human cognition. This arboreal symbol of confounded epistemology epitomizes Satan's whole journey, just as the journey leads here; he has erratically wandered in hellish desolations of the mind ever since first conceiving Sin. But wisdom biblically provides "a tree of life to them who lay hold upon her" (Prov. iii, 18). Though the devils anticipate a triumphal "glorious march" to renewed dominions by way of Sin and Death (X, 472–74), Christ will lead the redeemed from earth, "triumphing through the air" to their new, paradisal realm, wholly transcending heroic models of Odysseus's homecoming and Aeneas's renewal of his civilization in a bettered form (XII, 451–62).

Despite Adam and Eve's desire to ascend to an independently divine state of knowledge, their own deluded consumption of fruit brings them "grosser sleep," pointedly contrasting with the supercharged awareness implied in cosmic flight, and dusty dissolution (IX, 1049; X, 208). Their heavy sleep carries the biblical significances of spiritual and cognitive obtuseness and subjection to death. More ironically still, while they fall partly because of such desire, they cause Sin to grow the "Wings" of power. Travestying God's creatively winged mastery of the cosmos, she flies with Death to subjugate humankind; in their great causeway that perversely overgoes all the megaprojects of epic, the confusions of Chaos are merely compounded (X, 243–324; I, 19–22).[47]

With yet deeper irony the poem assumes that divinity does breed wings within those who remain lowly wise, for "whosoever shall exalt himself shall be abased; and he that shall humble himself shall be exalted" (Matt. xxiii, 12). Lofty satanic presumptions preclude such ascent, and yet Milton's God extends himself to creation and even fallen humanity. When descending to help lesser beings at God's behest, Raphael has the most glorious wings in the poem (V, 247–87). This symbolic celebration of Raphael's exalted lowliness helps account for Milton's marked departure here from the norms of celestial descent in classical epic, where the descent and wings themselves receive relatively perfunctory treatment.[48] Prelapsarian humanity likewise has high potential through lowly obedience: "bodies may at last turn all to spirit, / . . . and winged ascend / Ethereal," Raphael declares, while warning that vain desire for forbidden knowledge would jeopardize present bliss and future exaltations (V, 497–503; VII, 115–30; VIII, 167–78). In Raphael's teaching, Adam discerns, the human pursuit of knowledge properly follows the divinely ordered scale of nature so that, like intellectual pilgrims humbly committed to a creational Jacob's ladder, "In contemplation of created things / *By steps* we may ascend to God," rather than by satanic soarings (V, 508–12; emphasis mine). The faints and slumber induced by Adam's divine and angelic contacts indicate human limitations warranting God's assigned boundaries for knowledge. The restorative sleep following a legitimate form of higher vision contrasts sharply with the insensate one following effacement of God-given delineations of the mind through Adam and Eve's transgression. That psychological catastrophe, to which Satan's breach of hell's gates is allegorically analogous, causes a kind of mental collapse as the mind is left in search of some effective standard to regulate the complexities of experience.

The poem further provides models for positive ascent overcoming effects of the Fall. Though the narrator "intends to soar" "with no middle flight" and compares himself implicitly to the spirit "with mighty wings outspread," he defers to tutelage of his heavenly muse, sister of wisdom (I, 1–26; VII, 1–20). Hence he can safely follow Satan's progress through "Stygian pool" and "utter and . . . middle darkness," perhaps figuratively undergoing and surmounting the perils and temptations of evil, as with many interpretations of Orpheus's passage through the underworld. Milton's declared difference from Orpheus, then, reflects assumed Christian fulfillment of the Orphic mythological type (III, 13–21). Milton founds his epic survey of knowledge on humble recognition of human limits, so that, while soaring even "Above the flight of Pegasean wing" as Urania beckons, he need not fall like Bellerophon from Pegasus through divine disfavor, henceforth "Erroneous . . . to wander and forlorn" (VII, 1–20).

Likewise, when Adam and Eve, filled with prevenient grace, humble themselves before God, their prayers take "flight" to heaven without being "Blown vagabond or frustrate," pass through the "heavenly doors," and appear "Before the Father's throne" (X, 1097–XI, 21). Vain fools and Satan contrarily find themselves blown astray and excluded. This contrast emphasizes how essential indeed is lowliness for Miltonic wisdom: only in that state can the high objectives of the topos be humanly attained.

Divine mercy then provides the couple a further, directly enlightening ascent in the visions of God. While Eve enjoys revelatory dreams,

Michael guides Adam to the sweeping prospect of the paradisal summit and divulges prophetic knowledge of human destiny. By contrast with unqualified versions of the mental flight topos, with Satan's perspective from the heavenly stairs and his Mount of the Congregation, and with Eve's panoramic view of the earth in her satanic dream, Adam attains this perceptual eminence through divinely ordained guidance, and ascends modestly step by step as Jacob's ladder, heaven's stairs, and Raphael's scale of nature, figuratively speaking, would require. The epistemological motif of cleared and clouded eyes, which complements those of ascent, flight, and encompassing vision, further stresses the untraversable gulf between any creature's apprehension and God's.[49] But the reward awaiting the good, Adam finds, is like Enoch's apotheosis "with winged steeds" (XI, 704–11), and the Son's example fulfills this prospect for humanity: "to the heaven of heavens he shall ascend / With victory, triumphing through the air," "reward / His faithful, and receive them into bliss" (XII, 451–62). This ultimate defeat ironically confronts Satan at the peak of his flight, where he perches tantalized on heaven's lower stair, insofar as the stairs are like Jacob's ladder, a symbol of Christ as the salvific way.

From his paradisal top of speculation, Adam can at last define how desire for knowledge properly advances human development. Like a "vessel" he can contain only a limited "fill / Of knowledge," much as Raphael recommended intellectual temperance; beyond that is "folly to aspire" (XII, 553–60; VII, 126–30). Having "sought / Forbidden knowledge by forbidden means," Adam finds that "the sum of wisdom" is instead to obey, love, and depend solely on God with "suffering for truth's sake," as "Taught" by the Son. When supplemented with certain virtues and commensurate deeds, Michael adds, Adam's program recreates paradise within, or secures a homecoming exceeding the fondest dreams of Odysseus, for all his acuity (XII, 278–79, 561–87).

The more lofty and self-centered the pursuits of knowledge are, the more such doctrine humiliates them. Satan's difficulties in flight do so figuratively, with blackly comic effect, as does his series of metamorphic descents on the scale of being. Regarding the body like many human devotees of mental transcendence, Satan deplores that an essence aspiring "to the highth of deity" should find itself committed to corporeal form, even like the animals—"O foul descent!" He realizes that "Who aspires must down as low / As high he soared," only to lament it bitterly (IX, 163–71). However, even Milton's own poetic endeavor seems somewhat qualified, just as the poem often warns that its matter actually "*surmounts* the reach / Of human sense" (V, 571–72; emphasis mine), a choice of words activating the whole accumulated resonance of figurative intellectual ascent in *Paradise Lost.* Though "To ask or search" is not in itself blameworthy, Raphael explains, hidden matters should be left as God's preserve: "heaven is . . . too high / To know what passes there; be lowly wise: / Think only what concerns thee and thy being" (VIII, 66, 167–74). There is no wisdom "higher" for humankind, Michael likewise affirms, than Adam's finally humble kind: not the works of nature, nor the astral names, nor "All secrets of the deep" (XII, 576–79). In a striking parallel, Satan venturing beyond Sin actually perceives "The secrets of the hoary deep" in another cosmic prospect that travesties God's (II, 890–91). Satan's erratic experience of these enigmas typifies the consequences of prying into God's hidden matters, while showing how "wisely" Milton's God concealed rather than divulged them, to protect his creatures from matters dangerously exceeding their intellectual and other capacities (VIII, 71–75). When unfallen Adam declares that "unchecked" roving of "mind or fancy" too readily brings "anxious cares," he ironically anticipates the experiential learning of his fallen self: it is best to "descend / A lower flight and speak of things at hand / Useful" (VIII, 185–200).

Reflecting the Christian paradox of exalted humility, the concluding books of *Paradise Lost* redefine the ascent of enlightenment in terms of lowly acceptance of metaphysical mystery as an enduring condition of life, so that knowledge of self and of serving God, as directed by revelation and providence, become the complementary aims of epistemological endeavor. In this radical reconstruction of the flight topos to avoid satanic possibilities satirized through the allegory of the journey, Milton holds with Cudworth, in effect, that "We must . . . *ascend downward, and descend upward,* if we would indeed come to heaven":

> divine purposes, whatsoever they be are altogether unsearchable and unknowable by us, they lie wrapt up in everlasting darknesse, and covered in a deep Abysse; who is able to fathom the bottome of them? . . . [I]f at our first flight we aime so high, we shall happily [i.e., haply] but scorch our wings, and be struck back with lightning, as those *Giants* of old were, that would needs attempt to invade and assault heaven. (*Sermon . . . at Westminster*, pp. 9–11)

V

Milton's extensive recourse to the repertoire of allegorically charged imagery in Satan's journey shows that, many critics to the contrary, he does not reject, devalue, or marginalize allegory in *Paradise Lost*, but instead appropriates the potential of allegorical epic as a further medium for expressive innovation. In assimilating the heroic *sapientia* theme to the special concerns about knowledge in *Paradise Lost,* he probes epistemological issues in part by way of an allegory based on precedents of adventurous heroic quests. The wanderings of Odysseus, seminal for that theme in epic tradition, become the focus of a new interpretive strategy. The topos of cosmic mental flight projects the heroic quest into new dimensions of space and psychic significance, where questing comes to situate intellectual tendencies to err within the humbling, awesome vastness of the heavens. At the same time, the accumulated resonances of the quest-model furnish a rich basis for evaluating the exorbitant errancies conceived, enacted, and propagated by Satan. These various effects are not merely local, for Milton extends the analogical and symbolic networks of the flight allegory to create yet broader patterns of structural connections and expressive detail. Through reechoing motifs of diction and imagery that evoke aspects of the allegory, widely separated incidents and features of the poem illuminate and amplify each other's significance in mutual relation to Satan's allegorical journey. Not content with any single estimate of the mysterious implications of evil for intellectually capable creatures and their desire to know, this poet of theological commitment engages that problem from various complementary standpoints in *Paradise Lost.* The allegory of the journey provides a means of addressing the problem of evil in an especially challenging, exploratory way, just as the configurations of complex allegory, which impinge upon myth and symbolism, constitute a "dark" and inherently speculative mode of thought.

Of course the invented journey would have attracted Milton as a focus for such exploration because the content of scripturally based parts of the poem would have been far more prescribed for him. But the presence of extensive allegory in this portion of *Paradise Lost* also reflects the widespread theoretical acceptance of allegorically mediated truth as a main justification for including invented and even improbable situations in historically founded epics, as Milton assumed this poem is.[50] However, since much of the poem is self-consciously provisional in attempting to render intelligible impressions of matters beyond human comprehension, this principle of allegorical justification could well apply beyond wholly invented parts like Satan's journey. As that allegory has not previously been noticed, so the allegorical potential of other parts of the poem, including even those with some scriptural basis, deserves serious consideration.

Since epic aims at comprehensiveness, and allegory was often considered a generically apt technical resource for achieving that end, capacious-minded Milton would likely have found complex allegory, with its capacity for producing subtle, comprehensive effects of broadly developed multiple meaning, an attractive means of promoting his ambitions for *Paradise Lost*.[51] The heroic poet could thus address considerations of doctrine in a full yet discreetly implicit way, while also attending to narrative needs; and the capacity of allegory to convey high matter in a conceitful, stimulating manner befits the heightened epic style. Although Milton expelled from his Eden the allegorical abstractions included in his much earlier plan for dramatic treatment of the Fall, it only shows that his estimate of straightforward kinds of personification allegory changed. Avoiding simple allegory does not necessarily imply any aversion to more complex kinds. The long-standing association of allegory with the most ambitious and acclaimed heroic poems would reasonably have encouraged its use in *Paradise Lost*, where the presence of even Sin and Death alone shows that Milton's concept of epic was in some sense allegorical.

In any case, it is not surprising that the incidents of Satan's cosmic journey are parts of an overarching allegory. Since journeys or quests had often involved allegories about heroism, or at least been thought to, Milton naturally reassesses and redeploys the allegorical journey in *Paradise Lost* as part of his program of revaluing heroic precedents in general. Satan's venture has both etiological and parodic relations to its heroic counterparts: it originates and thus points to the flaws of human heroes; yet, insofar as their accomplishments are to any extent estimable or legitimate, Satan's endeavor travesties theirs. Allegorically, his flight pertains to heroic *sapientia* in particular, and the false heroics of presumptuous mental ascent especially generate satire and black comedy when examined over against the awesome setting of Milton's universe. Moreover, the prelapsarian cosmos of *Paradise Lost* itself fosters and propagates allegory, for all things signify truly there, by means of hidden affinities or correspondences involving manifold implications for life.[52] Not just a casual remnant of an older world view, this setting for much of the action, especially prominent during Satan's flight, is a fully functional part of a poem in which allegory has considerable importance. By treating conventions of cosmic mental flight ironically in association with Satan, Milton provides an implicit critique not only of certain aspects of satanic psychology, but also of whole schools of thought and writing, for the topos had long been interpreted to express differing conceptions of human intellectual abilities and prospects.

Such ingeniously sweeping effects are what we have come to expect from *Paradise Lost*, as understanding of its implied critiques of myths and genres, for example, has deepened. The allegory enables Milton to measure the mind and previous estimations of it against the enigmatic depths of the cosmos, while also exploring the psychic cosmos with its own luminous secrets, precipitous heights, and inchoate realms of darkness. Spenser had already far overgone previous models in his figurative transpositions of heroic and romantic conventions of exterior action into simultaneous, mutually reflective spheres of topical, psychological, and other kinds of reference. But Milton pushes this line of heroic development to its ultimate term. The outward parameters of heroic analysis dissolve so completely, at least in Satan's flight sequence, that *Paradise Lost* assimilates all expanses of space into the inward, psychological phase of its program for generic revaluation.

McGill University

NOTES

This study was facilitated by a Canada Research Fellowship at McGill University and a Senior Fellowship at the Centre for Reformation and Renaissance Studies at Victoria University in the University of Toronto. Any contractions within quotations have been silently expanded.

1. See *Critical Essays from the Spectator by Joseph Addison*, ed. Donald F. Bond (Oxford, 1970), pp. 68, 85; and *Johnson as Critic*, ed. John Wain (London, 1973), pp. 293–94. Aside from Davis's and Teskey's articles discussed subsequently, recent studies bearing on this issue include Stephen M. Fallon, "Milton's Sin and Death: The Ontology of Allegory in *Paradise Lost*," *ELR* XVII (1987), 329–50; Kenneth J. Knoespel, "The Limits of Allegory: Textual Expansion of Narcissus in *Paradise Lost*," in *Milton Studies*, XXII, ed. James D. Simmonds (Pittsburgh, 1986), pp. 79–99; Thomas F. Merrill, "Milton's Satanic Parable," *ELH* L (1983), 279–95; Stella Purce Revard, *The War in Heaven: "Paradise Lost" and the Tradition of Satan's Rebellion* (Ithaca, 1980), pp. 111–12, 174–75, 268–71, 287–91; and Samuel S. Stollman, "Satan, Sin, and Death: A Mosaic Trio in *Paradise Lost*," in *Milton Studies*, XXII, ed. James D. Simmonds (Pittsburgh, 1986), pp. 101–20.

2. Walter B. Davis, "The Languages of Accommodation and the Styles of *Paradise Lost*," in *Milton Studies*, XVIII, ed. James D. Simmonds (Pittsburgh, 1983), pp. 103–27; quoting pp. 121, 118.

3. Gordon Teskey, "From Allegory to Dialectic: Imagining Error in Spenser and Milton," *PMLA* CI (1986), 9–23; quoting 10, 15–16.

4. Quintilian, *Institutio Oratoria*, VIII, vi, 44–59; all citations of classical texts refer to the Loeb Classical Library series, unless attributed otherwise.

5. John Milton, *Areopagitica*, in *The Works of John Milton*, ed. Frank Allen Patterson et al. (New York, 1931–40), IV, pp. 310–12; subsequently cited as CM.

6. Torquato Tasso, *Discourses on the Heroic Poem*, trans. Mariella Cavalchini and Irene Samuel (Oxford, 1973), pp. 150–52.

7. Spenser, e.g., sometimes mixes simple and complex allegorical techniques within an episode, as when personifications interact with groups of altogether more full and com-

plicated characters; and the role of a character can even significantly shift from complex to simple, as when Malbecco's transformation into jealousy expresses its dehumanizing effect. On the simple-complex distinction, see Northrop Frye, "Allegory," in *The Princeton Encyclopedia of Poetry and Poetics*, enl. ed. (Princeton, 1974), pp. 12–15; Angus Fletcher, *Allegory: The Theory of a Symbolic Mode* (Ithaca, 1964), and Carolynn Van Dyke, *The Fiction of Truth: Structures of Meaning in Narrative and Dramatic Allegory* (Ithaca, 1985).

8. See Isabel Gamble MacCaffrey, *"Paradise Lost" as "Myth"* (Cambridge, 1959), p. 197. However, though she ascribes Milton's protracted account of Satan's flight to his "intention of including the great archetype of the journey in his poem," Milton presumably considered more than fitting in archetypes, if such an "intention" is attributable to a seventeenth-century writer.

9. Modifying Harry Berger, Jr., on "conspicuous irrelevance" and allegorical interpretation in *The Allegorical Temper: Vision and Reality in Book II of Spenser's "Faerie Queene"* (New Haven, 1957), chaps. 5–7.

10. John Milton, *Paradise Lost*, in *The Poems of John Milton*, ed. John Carey and Alastair Fowler (London, 1968); used for Milton's poetry throughout, and cited hereafter as *Poems*.

11. See John M. Steadman, *Milton's Biblical and Classical Imagery* (Pittsburgh, 1984), chap. 11. Since he focuses on the apotheosis tradition, our purposes and findings differ though they are complementary. See further Steadman's *Disembodied Laughter: "Troilus" and the Apotheosis Tradition* (Berkeley and Los Angeles, 1972), chap. 3.

12. See Ernst Robert Curtius, *European Literature and the Latin Middle Ages*, trans. Willard R. Trask (London, 1953), pp. 170–79; James Nohrnberg, *The Analogy of "The Faerie Queene"* (Princeton, 1976), pp. 58–63; and John M. Steadman, *Milton and the Renaissance Hero* (Oxford, 1967), chaps. 1, 3.

13. Authorized version, cited throughout.

14. Richard Hooker, *Of the Laws of Ecclesiastical Polity*, in *Works*, 6th ed., ed. Rev. John Keble (Oxford, 1874), I, 214 (I, iv, 3); playing on "conceit" in the senses of "ingenious thought" and "pride." Cf. St. Augustine, *De Genesi ad Litteram*, vol. XXXIV of *Patrologia Series Latina*, ed. Jacques-Paul Migne (Paris, 1861), IV, 24, col. 313. See further, Edward J. Montano, *The Sin of the Angels: Some Aspects of the Teaching of St. Thomas* (Washington, 1955); and on the satanic implications, see Knoespel, "Limits of Allegory," pp. 80–81.

15. On Miltonic satire, see John Wooten, "Satan, Satire, and Burlesque Fables in *Paradise Lost*," *MQ* XII (1978), 51–58.

16. Apparently originated by Anne Davidson Ferry, *Milton's Epic Voice: The Narrator in "Paradise Lost"* (Cambridge, 1963), pp. 128–40.

17. See Richard J. DuRocher, *Milton and Ovid* (Ithaca, 1985), pp. 154–62, 205; Alastair Fowler, *Kinds of Literature: An Introduction to the Theory of Genres and Modes* (Cambridge, 1982), pp. 160–64; and Joan Malory Webber, *Milton and His Epic Tradition* (Seattle, 1979).

18. For classical examples, see, e.g., Cicero, *Tusculanae Disputationes*, I, xix–xxi; *Somnium Scipionis*, in *De Republica*, VI, xv–xxvi; *De Natura Deorum*, II, lxi; Lucretius, *De Rerum Natura*, I, 62–79; II, 1044–47; III, 14–30; V, 1198–1217; and Seneca, *Ad Helviam de Consolatione*, VI, 6–8; VIII, 4–6; *De Otio*, V, 3–6; *Epistulae Morales*, LXV, 18–24; LXXIX, 11–13; XCII, 30–33; CII, 21–24, 28–29; and *Quaestiones Naturales*, I, pref., 7–17. Cf. Plato on the wings of the soul, *Phaedrus*, 246, 251, 255c. The myth of Ganymede, e.g., was often held to allegorize contemplative ascent to God in the Renaissance. Lucian anticipates Milton in using winged ascent to satirize high intellectual claims to knowledge

in *Icaromenippus*, passim, *The Ship*, 46, and *Astrology*, 13–15. See, further, Franz Cumont, "Le Mysticisme astral dans l'antiquité," Académie Royale des Sciences de Belgique, *Bulletin de la Classe des Lettres et Sciences Morales et Politiques*, no. 5 (1909), 256–86; and Roger Miller Jones, "Posidonius and the Flight of the Mind through the Universe," *Classical Philology*, XXI (1926), 97–113.

19. Trans. Bromley Smith, CM, XII, p. 171. Cf. "At a Vacation Exercise," 29–52; see also the elegy on the Bishop of Ely, 45–68, The Fifth Elegy, 1–24, *Il Penseroso*, 51–54, and *Comus*, 374–79. For discussion of young Milton's flight motifs and cosmos, see Christopher Collins, "Milton's Early Cosmos and the Fall of Mulciber," in *Milton Studies*, XIX, ed. James D. Simmonds (Pittsburgh, 1984), pp. 37–52.

20. V, pp. 5–6; XI, pp. 19–21; in *Corpus Hermeticum*, ed. A. D. Nock, trans. A.-J. Festugière (Paris, 1945), I, pp. 62–63, 154–56.

21. See *On the Infinite Universe and Worlds*, in Dorothea Waley Singer, *Giordano Bruno: His Life and Thought with Annotated Translation of His Work on the Infinite Universe and Worlds* (New York, 1950), pp. 248–49. See further *The Ash Wednesday Supper*, ed. and trans. Edward A. Gosselin and Lawrence S. Lerner (Hamden, 1977), pp. 88–91; *The Heroic Frenzies*, trans. Paul Eugene Memmo, Jr. (Chapel Hill, 1966), pp. 118–22, 201–04; and *De Immenso*, I, i, in *Opera Latine Conscripta*, ed. F. Fiorentino et al., I, pt. i (Naples, 1879), pp. 201–06. For Pico, see *On the Dignity of Man* and *Heptaplus*, in *On the Dignity of Man*, trans. Charles Glenn Wallis, Douglas Carmichael, and Paul J. W. Miller (Indianapolis, 1965), pp. 7, 13, 106.

22. John Dee, "Preface," in Euclid, *The Elements of Geometrie*, trans. Sir Henry Billingsley (London, 1570), sig. $*1^a$–$*1^b$. Cf. Thomas Digges, *Alae seu Scalae Mathematicae* (London, 1573), sigs. $A1^a$–$B1^a$, $K4^b$–$L3^b$.

23. Boethius, *De Consolatione Philosophiae*, IV, prose i–metre i; Spenser, "An Hymne of Heauenly Beautie," 134–49, in *The Works of Edmund Spenser: A Variorum Edition*, 11 vols., ed. Edwin Greenlaw et al. (Baltimore, 1932–57), VII, 226; subsequent Spenser citations refer to this edition. Du Bartas inconsistently veers between discreet avoidance of Icarian presumptions and, when extolling the powers of the soul, unbounded enthusiasm for the topos: "sometimes leaving these base slymie heapes, / With cheerefull spring above the Clouds she leapes"; flying through the cosmos she lands on God's doorstep, and beholds him "face to face"—"What can be hard to a sloath-shunning Spirit?" *The Divine Weeks and Works*, 2 vols., trans. Josuah Sylvester, ed. Susan Snyder (Oxford, 1979), I, i, 127–50, vi, 831–38.

24. Trans. Charles R. Sumner, CM, XIV, pp. 31–33. His rendering of Milton's jibe at presumptuous intellect seems better than John Carey's in *Complete Prose Works of John Milton*, ed. Don M. Wolfe et al. (New Haven, 1973), VI, pp. 133–34; Maurice Kelley's note indeed acknowledges the relevance of this passage to the whole issue of ascent beyond creaturely capacities in *Paradise Lost*.

25. The most penetrating recent study of Milton's muse is Stevie Davies and William B. Hunter, "Milton's Urania: 'The meaning, not the name I call,'" *SEL* XXVIII (1988), 95–111.

26. See Andrea Alciati, *Emblemata cum Commentariis* (1621; rpt. New York, 1976), embl. 121, pp. 520–21; Valeriano Bolzani, *Hieroglyphica* (1602; rpt. New York, 1976), "De Aquila," pp. 194–95, "De Accipitre," pp. 210, 212; Vincenzo Cartari, *Le Imagini . . . degli Dei* (1571; rpt. New York, 1976), "Saturno," p. 44; and Cesare Ripa, *Iconologia* (1611; rpt. New York, 1976), s.v. "Pensiero," pp. 414–15.

27. See Louis Réau, *Ancien Testament*, pt. 1 of *Iconographie de la Bible*, vol. II of *Iconographie de l'Art Chrétien* (Paris, 1956), pp. 34–37.

28. *Five Bookes of Philosophicall Comfort*, trans. "I.T." [M. Walpole] (London, 1609), IV, metre i (fol. 90[a]).

29. For the heroic filiations of Satan's journey, see Barbara Kiefer Lewalski, *"Paradise Lost" and the Rhetoric of Literary Forms* (Princeton, 1985), chap. 3. On Satan's Odyssean aspect see further Don Cameron Allen, *Mysteriously Meant: The Rediscovery of Pagan Symbolism and Allegorical Interpretation in the Renaissance* (Baltimore, 1970), pp. 294–99; Manoocher Aryanpur, "Paradise Lost and *The Odyssey*," *TSLL* IX (1967), 151–66; and John M. Steadman, *Milton's Epic Characters: Image and Idol* (Chapel Hill, 1959), chap. 13. However, whereas these discussions assume that Milton simply denigrates classical heroes through their correspondences with Satan, the classical heroes, for all their faults, also provide some standards for measuring satanic depravity, as shown by Lewalski and Francis C. Blessington, *"Paradise Lost" and the Classical Epic* (London, 1979).

30. *OED* s.v. "err" v.[1] 1, 3, 4. See Paul Ricoeur, *The Symbolism of Evil*, trans. Emerson Buchanan (New York, 1967), pp. 72–73.

31. Cicero, *De Finibus*, V, xviii, 48–49; Dante, *Inferno*, XXVI, 55–142. For the range of Odyssean assessments, see Allen, *Mysteriously Meant*, pp. 296–97, Curtius, *European Literature*, pp. 170–73, and Steadman, *Renaissance Hero*, pp. 9–10, 18–19.

32. Though seemingly unnoticed by previous commentators, this aspect of Milton's gate symbolism is based on a standard figurative application whereby an opening door or gate signifies provision or initiation of some opportunity, condition, or course of action. See *OED* s.v. "Door" 3, "Gate" sb.[1] 5, and "Threshold" sb. 2a, b. Biblical instances of "door" in this sense are 2 Cor. ii, 12, and Rev. iii, 20.

33. Although again seemingly unnoticed before, this key symbolism applies a figurative commonplace in which a key signifies power to transform some situation or opportunities. See *OED* s.v. "Key" sb.[1] II 3 (figurative). In *The Doctrine and Discipline of Divorce*, Milton particularizes this symbolism in relation to charity: "they shall *recover the misattended words* of Christ to the sincerity of their *true sense* from manifold contradictions, and *open them* with the key of charity" (CM, III, pt. 2, p. 510; emphasis mine). In *Paradise Lost* Milton particularizes it in relation to sin. A biblical context involving such symbolism is Luke xi, 52; Ignaro's keys in *The Faerie Queene* wittily combine this kind of application with symbolically expressed antipapal satire (I, viii, 30–34).

34. The gates of dreams, for which *Odyssey* XIX, 560–67, is the *locus classicus*, appear, e.g., in Virgil, *Aeneid*, VI, 893–98, and *The Faerie Queene*, I, i, 40; see further John Barker Stearns, *Studies of the Dream as a Technical Device in Latin Epic and Drama* (Lancaster, 1927), pp. 56–58. Gates in *The Faerie Queene*, such as Acrasia's, Busirane's, Honour's, Caelia's, or Alma's, frequently mark potential access to states of mind or ways of life implying certain mental conditions. When Aeneas passes through the entrance of Avernus, the psychic aspect of his journey, noticed and extravagantly explored by commentators such as Fulgentius, Bernard Silvester, and Cristoforo Landino, is confirmed by the attendance of personifications like Grief, Want, and Guilty Joys (*Aeneid*, VI, 273–84). Hell's gates conventionally had psychological associations in many later works like *The Faerie Queene*, II, vii, 21–23. See further Merritt Y. Hughes, "'Myself Am Hell,'" *MP* LIV (1956–57), 80–94.

35. On the spiritually expressive aspect of Milton's cosmos, see Lawrence Babb, *The Moral Cosmos of "Paradise Lost"* (East Lansing, Mich., 1977); Balachandra Rajan, *The Lofty Rhyme: A Study of Milton's Major Poetry* (Coral Gables, Fla., 1970), pp. 58–64, 93; and Kester Svendsen, *Milton and Science* (Cambridge, Mass., 1956), pp. 84–85, 231–32, 242. On cosmic moral symbolism and Satan's journey, see H. F. Robins, "Satan's Journey: Direction in *Paradise Lost*," *JEGP* LX (1961), 699–711.

On Milton's Chaos and its psychologically symbolic role, see Robert M. Adams, "A Little Look Into Chaos," in *Illustrious Evidence: Approaches to English Literature in the Seventeenth Century*, ed. Earl Miner (Berkeley, 1975), pp. 71–89; A. B. Chambers, "Chaos in *Paradise Lost*," *JHI* XXIV (1963), 82–84; Dennis Richard Danielson, *Milton's Good God: A Study in Literary Theodicy* (Cambridge, 1982), chap. 2; and Regina Schwartz, "Milton's Hostile Chaos: '. . . And the Sea Was No More,'" *ELH* LII (1985), 337–74. (Discussion of Chaos in Milton's cosmology and metaphysics exceeds our present scope. But, whereas the close affinities of Chaos with evil in *Paradise Lost* have puzzled many because of Milton's good Chaos in *De Doctrina Christiana*, provision of "symbolic" or "allegorical truth," offering insight through provocative connections and surprising analogies, can well take poetic precedence over the requirements of doctrine as it would be expressed in plain prose.)

Chaos is employed as a figure for sin by, e.g., Robert Burton, *The Anatomy of Melancholy*, vol. I, ed. A. R. Shilleto (1893; rpt. London, 1926), pt. 1, sect. ii, mem. 3, subs. 8, pp. 310–11: "But being that we are so peevish and perverse, insolent and proud, . . . we . . . *precipitate ourselves into that gulf of woes and cares*, . . . heap upon us hell and eternal damnation" (emphasis mine). Cf. also Benjamin Whichcote, *Select Sermons* (London, 1698), pp. 71–72: "*The Mind diverted from God wanders in Darkness and Confusion:* But being directed to him, soon finds its way. . . . God only is absent to them that are indisposed, and disaffected. . . . God doth not withdraw himself from us, unless we first leave him" (emphasis mine). Satan's wanderings in the black gulf of Chaos, into which his Sin introduces him, express such perspectives through allegorical narrative. Cf. the Augustinian doctrine that evil is the privation of good, and virtual nothingness; on its Miltonic relevance, see Fallon, "Milton's Sin," 330–32, 348–49; and Stanley Eugene Fish, *Surprised by Sin: The Reader in "Paradise Lost"* (London, 1967), pp. 144, 337–39.

36. CM IV, p. 159; *OED* s.v. "World" sb. II 9, a common meaning in seventeenth-century cosmological contexts.

37. For theological precedent, see, e.g., Schwartz, "Milton's Hostile Chaos," 369; but the concept of the "inner chaos" (a condition ultimately attributed to the Fall) was a commonplace, for which see *OED* s.v. "Chaos" sb. 3a, b. Since sin involved transgression or law-breaking of sorts, it was similarly treated as anomy, or a condition of psychic and social anarchy, for which Chaos is an effective analogy. Cf. *Tetrachordon*, CM IV, pp. 159–61; see further C. A. Patrides, *Milton and the Christian Tradition* (Oxford, 1966), pp. 111–12.

38. This psycho-physiological *allegoria* would be based on the standard analogies between the four humors and the four elements, and between the conflicts and confusions of Chaos and those of contending forces within. Du Bartas, for example, explicitly relates the four conflicting elements within Chaos to humoral and other inner conflicts (*Divine Weeks* I, ii, 47–152). Such analogies are allegorically fundamental in *The Faerie Queene;* opposed to social and psychic concord, Ate, for example, incites hellish and chaotic conflicts between knights who partly relate to psychological impulses or attitudes (IV, i, 19–30, ii, 1, ix, 23; cf. II, v, 22–23).

39. The unruly pack of hounds that Sin spawns and the proliferating runners of the banyan tree in Book IX reflect this symbolism, as Fowler observes in *Poems*, pp. 539*n*, 920*n*. In *Tetrachordon* Milton anticipates the expressive relation between Chaos and the unruly, confused potentials of sin in *Paradise Lost:* attempting to limit or control sin is like trying to put "a girdle about . . . *Chaos*" (CM IV, p. 160).

40. On sea symbolism and Chaos, see Jackson I. Cope, *The Metaphoric Structure*

of "Paradise Lost" (Baltimore, 1962), pp. 52–57, 71. On life as affected by everchanging chance in Renaissance thought and iconography, see Kenneth Borris, "Fortune, Occasion, and the Allegory of the Quest in Book VI of *The Faerie Queene*," in *Spenser Studies* VII (1986), ed. Patrick Cullen and Thomas P. Roche, Jr. (New York, 1987), pp. 123–45, 301–09. Cf. St. Augustine, *Confessions*, VII, iii: endeavoring to comprehend the ultimate implications of transgression, he comparably finds the eye of his mind plunged in an overwhelming abyss of perplexities.

41. On the inclusion of evil in God's omniscience, see *John Milton: Complete Poems and Major Prose*, ed. Merritt Y. Hughes (Indianapolis, 1957), p. 305*n*. Cf. Fish, *Surprised by Sin*, pp. 336–39.

42. *The Odyssey*, trans. A. T. Murray (Cambridge, Mass., 1949), VI, 12.

43. Gen. xxviii, 12, John i, 51. See C. A. Patrides, "Renaissance Interpretations of Jacob's Ladder," *Theologische Zeitschrift* XVIII, (1962), 411–18; C. Schaar, "Each Stair Mysteriously Was Meant," *English Studies* LVIII (1977), 408–10; and George Wesley Whiting, *Milton and This Pendant World* (1958; rpt. New York, 1969), chap. 3.

44. Allegorical irony, as I have identified it, is a figurative counterpart of dramatic irony. The perspectives of a character or the narrator are at implicit variance, then, with some allegorical significance of the situation. The potential of allegory to convey meaning that differs from the literal sense provides the conditions necessary for this effect.

45. Ralph Cudworth, *A Sermon Preached . . . at Westminster* (Cambridge, 1647), pp. 19–20. On the bounds of knowledge for Milton, see Dennis H. Burden, *The Logical Epic: A Study of the Argument of "Paradise Lost"* (London, 1967), chap. 6; Howard Schultz, *Milton and Forbidden Knowledge* (New York, 1955), pp. 173–83; Steadman, *Renaissance Hero*, chap. 3; and Svendsen, *Milton and Science*, index, s.v. "Knowledge."

46. John M. Steadman, "Tantalus and the Dead Sea Apples (*Paradise Lost*, X, 547–73)," *JEGP* LXIV (1965), 35–40, stresses the similarities rather than the differences between Tantalus and the devils. The implicit Tantalus allusion supports epistemological reading, for he had often exemplified the fate not only of greed but of intellectual transgression, through his betrayal of the gods' secrets or testing of their omniscience, so that Spenser's Tantalus is partially an "Example . . . of mind intemperate" (II, vii, 60). See Nohrnberg, *Analogy*, pp. 333–42.

47. See W. B. Hunter, "Milton on the Incarnation," in *Bright Essence: Studies in Milton's Theology*, ed. W. B. Hunter, C. A. Patrides, J. H. Adamson (Salt Lake City, 1971), p. 139.

48. Cf. *Aeneid*, IV, 219–78, the closest analogue; also *Iliad*, XXIV, 333–470, and *Odyssey*, V, 28–148. On the motif, see Blessington, *Classical Epic*, pp. 25–34, and Thomas M. Greene, *The Descent from Heaven: A Study in Epic Continuity* (New Haven, 1963), pp. 363–87.

49. Cf. the serpent's biblical promise that the forbidden fruit clears eyes, providing divine knowledge (Gen. iii, 5) and, e.g., IX, 705–12, 1070–75; XI, 411–20; XII, 273–74.

50. Cf. Torquato Tasso, *Giudizio sovra la sua Gerusalemme da lui medesimo riformata*, in *Le Prose Diverse di Torquato Tasso*, ed. Cesare Guasti (Firenze, 1875), I, p. 500: "I use allegory most in those parts of my poem in which I have departed furthest from history, esteeming that where the literal sense stops the allegorical and the other senses must substitute for it" (cit., trans. Bernard Weinberg, *A History of Literary Criticism in the Italian Renaissance*, 2 vols. [Chicago, 1961], II, p. 1057). Cf. also Milton's nephew Edward Phillips, "Preface," in *Theatrum Poetarum* (London, 1675), sigs. **5[b]–**6[a]: "it is not a meer Historical relation, spic't over with a little slight fiction . . . which makes a *Heroic Poem* but it must be rather a brief obscure or remote Tradition, but of some

remarkable piece of story, in which the *Poet* hath an ample feild to in large by feigning of probable circumstances, in which and in proper Allegorie, Invention . . . principally consisteth, and wherein there is a kind of truth, even in the midst of Fiction; for whatever is pertinently said by way of *Allegorie* is Morally though not Historically true." See further John M. Steadman, *The Wall of Paradise: Essays on Milton's Poetics* (Baton Rouge, 1985), pp. 143–50; and Weinberg, I, pp. 433; II, 1019, 1029–31, 1046–47, 1054–57, 1066–67.

51. Renaissance discussions of the relation of allegory to poetry tended to focus on the Horatian poetic functions of pleasure and utility. Though considered variously pleasurable, allegory could subtly fulfill the instructional purpose without interfering with reception of other textual pleasures. Allegory was especially apt for epic, then, insofar as epic was conceived as an encyclopedic genre with the highest moral and doctrinal aims. See Weinberg, *History*, I, pp. 101, 104–05, 109, 115, 168, 198, 257–58, 487; II, pp. 671–72, 685, 821, 872–73, 1060.

52. See Michel Foucault, *The Order of Things: An Archaeology of the Human Sciences* (New York, 1971), pp. 17– 76; Thomas P. Roche, Jr., *The Kindly Flame: A Study of the Third and Fourth Books of Spenser's "Faerie Queene"* (Princeton, 1964), pp. 3–31; and Steadman, *Biblical and Classical Imagery*, pp. 57–68.

SIN, EVE, AND CIRCE: *PARADISE LOST* AND THE OVIDIAN CIRCE TRADITION

Judith E. Browning

IN HER ARTICLE "Milton and the Renaissance Circe," Leonora Brodwin identifies two interpretive traditions of the Circe figure: the allegorized Circe of the Renaissance mythographers, and the Circe of the Renaissance literary tradition.[1] The former, influenced largely by the mythographer Conti, interprets the figure "as an allegorization of the archetypal Circe, who transforms intemperate men into beasts but can be resisted by the divine gift of moly (symbolizing right reason or temperance)." This Circe is associated closely with Ovid's account. The Renaissance literary tradition, however, interprets Circe "from the larger perspective of the full Homeric story." This literary tradition, begun by Ariosto and further developed by Tasso and Spenser, depicts not only the "archetypal, swinish metamorphosis, but two additional and progressively less embruting temptations, the second temptation of effeminating sex and the third of enervating idleness." Brodwin's thesis is that Milton's primary use of Circe throughout his work follows the Homeric tradition in distinguishing the three temptations and "focusing upon the higher appeals, which his successive treatments reformulate in increasingly elevated moral terms." She contrasts the "easy moralizing" of Circe by the mythographers with the more sophisticated treatment of the figure in the Homeric text (pp. 21–23).

Although it is true that modern scholars have paid exclusive attention to Conti and his followers in their analysis of the Circe of the Renaissance, there is in *Paradise Lost* a distinct influence from the mythographers' Circe that has not been adequately discussed. Milton's use of the Ovidian Circe tradition reflects an equally sophisticated treatment of the figure; his understanding of this tradition demonstrates much more than "easy moralizing."

Milton refers to the Ovidian Circe tradition repeatedly throughout *Paradise Lost*, specifically in relation to the characters Sin, Satan, and Eve. Inherent in this Ovidian tradition is the archetypal conflict between reason and appetite within the individual—largely reflected in a medieval Catholic anthropology. By referring to this tradition, Milton is able to contrast the medieval Catholic understanding with that of his own strictly held belief in Protestant Reformed anthropology. Through the character Sin, Milton revises the Ovidian Circe tradition into a new philosophical context—that of the Protestant Reformation understanding of the fall.

The focus of the scholarship on Milton and Circe has been *Comus*. Critics who analyze Circe in relation to *Paradise Lost* concentrate primarily on Eve as a Circean femme fatale.[2] Douglas Bush, however, identifies the larger significance of the Circe theme for Milton's major works. According to Bush, this theme "occupies the center of [Milton's] four major poems. No myth left a deeper or more permanent impression upon him."[3] Yet Bush claims that Milton's use of the allegorized myth ends with the masque; he finds no instance of allegorized myth in *Paradise Lost*. Brodwin's article is by far the most thorough treatment of the subject. She argues that the Circean temptation within *Paradise Lost* becomes translated into political terms—"when man 'permits' 'unworthy Powers to reign / Over free Reason,'" tyranny results (p. 55). This tyranny is symbolized by the Circean cup of servitude. Brodwin analyzes the ways in which Satan and Adam are tempted in Eve's presence to renounce their higher commitments and allow "unworthy powers to reign."

Instead of seeing Satan as victim of one sort or another of the Circean Eve, I argue that the initial Circe figure in Book IX is indeed Satan. Further, Eve becomes the Circe of the tradition only in her postlapsarian condition. Milton's revision of the Ovidian Circe tradition, however, occurs in relation to the character Sin.

In the almost exhaustive iconographic studies of Milton's Sin and Death, critics have noted the influence of Ovid's Scylla in relation to Sin. A number of critics have analyzed the theological implications of the allegory as well (generally with the understanding that the allegory functions as theological parody).[4] Most recently, Samuel Stollman has presented a different perspective on the theology of Sin and Death. He argues that Sin and Death and their encounters with Satan act out Milton's antinomian view of the Mosaic law and its impediment to the attainment of Christian liberty. Stollman concludes that "whatever other allusions and correlatives Milton has brought together, he has included Paul's warning in Romans of the consequences of perpetuating the Mosaic Law."[5] Although I agree with Stollman concerning the significance of Paul for our understanding of Milton's treatment of Sin and Death, I argue that Sin's mythological "allusions" are also essential to our understanding of Milton's Reformed theology. In his treatment of Sin in Books

II and IX, Milton revises the role of the ancient seductress figure from the Ovidian tradition into a philosophically Reformed context.

Brodwin demonstrates how the Homeric source goes beyond Ovid in the various levels of temptations, of which "swinish metamorphosis is only the most debased." In order to argue that Milton refers specifically to the Ovidian Circe in *Paradise Lost,* however, we must review more precisely the distinctions between the two accounts.

I

Homer and Ovid present significant variations in the interpretation of the character of Circe. Homer's Circe is a rather gracious hostess who, after initially enslaving Eurylochos's party and later being conquered by Odysseus, entertains him and his men for a year. Unlike Ovid's lustful witch, this Circe has a "rather lofty disinclination for ordinary men, who serve no other purpose than to stock her already extensive herds."[6] Once Odysseus proves himself by withstanding the power of Circe's "malevolent guiles" (to use Hermes's words as he gives Odysseus the gift of moly), Homer's Circe proves a gracious companion.[7] When it is time for Odysseus to leave, Circe does not try to detain him. She instead responds, "Son of Laertes and seed of Zeus, resourceful Odysseus, / you shall no longer stay in my house when none of you wish to" (X, 488–89). Circe then gives to her mortal lover her last gift—the black ram and ewe which she secretly leaves tethered to his ship on the day of his departure.

The Circe of Ovid, however, is not so gracious. In Ovid's story, there are two episodes involving Circe. The first is a brief account of Odysseus's visit to Circe's isle. The focus of this episode is on the bestial metamorphosis of Odysseus's men. As Brodwin notes, Ovid mentions that Mercury (Hermes) gave Ulysses advice in addition to moly, but doesn't specify what that advice is. "Similarly, [Ovid] offers no explanation of why Ulysses and his men stayed on with Circe for a year" (26). In the second episode, the sea god Glaucus comes to Circe to request aid for his rejected pursuit of Scylla. Ovid tells us that no one has "desires more prone" to passion than Circe; whether the cause originates "in her selfe alone," (being the daughter of the sun) or whether Venus, in her "angrie influence, / In that her Father publisht her offence," causes this.[8] Instead of offering aid to Glaucus, Circe offers him herself and demands that he "scorne her that scorns thee" (XIV, 37). Glaucus, however, rejects Circe and she in turn takes vengeance on Scylla. Circe travels to the bay frequented by Scylla and pollutes it with her monster-breeding drugs. When Scylla enters the water and beholds her "hips with barking dogs imbract" (XIV, 64), she flees from them in fear. Only as she runs does she discover that her thighs, legs, and feet have been replaced with Cerberean jaws. Glaucus, who still loves Scylla, flees from Circe; Scylla, however, remains fixed on that spot (XIV, 65–80). Odysseus's crew then provides Scylla with the first opportunity for revenge; in her hatred of Circe, Scylla deprives Odysseus of his companions.

Apart from the contrasting interpretations of Circe herself, there are a number of significant differences in the depiction of Scylla. Unlike Ovid's story, Homer's account of Skylla and Charybdis has little to do with Circe's charms. Homer's Circe in fact warns Odysseus about the monsters he will soon encounter on his journey. In Homer, Skylla and Charybdis are the two treacherous rocks which Odysseus must pass through. On one of the rocks lives Skylla, whose voice is only loud as a "new-born puppy," although she herself is an evil monster (XII, 87–88). Thus, where Ovid's Scylla is a rather innocent victim of Circe's spite, Homer's Skylla is simply a monster who already exists without any real account of her origins, apart from Circe's one reference to Krataiis, who "is the mother of Skylla and bore this mischief for mortals" (125). The associations among Circe, Scylla, and the Sirens vary as well. In Homer's account, the creatures who come closest to being seducers are the Sirens, "the enchanters of all mankind" who lure unsuspecting sailors to abandon their journey and remain on the island where the beach is "piled with boneheaps / of men now rotted away" (45–46). Homer's Sirens, like Ovid's Scylla, are thus specifically associated with seduction and with death. Homer's Skylla, however, is associated only with death. Upon encountering the rock of Skylla, "never can sailors boast aloud that their ship has passed her / without any loss of men, for with each of her heads she snatches / one man away and carries him off from the dark-prowed vessel" (98–100).

The elements that later became associated with the Renaissance mythographic tradition demonstrate the victory of Ovid's interpretation of the myth over Homer's: the Circe myth became a story of the conflict between virtue and sensuality resulting in seduction, metamorphosis, or death.[9]

Milton adapts a number of elements from this Ovidian Circe tradition to *Paradise Lost.* The first major area concerns the theme itself of seduction and metamorphosis. Although some of this occurs in Book IV, we see this theme interwoven into the action primarily in Book IX. The second major influence of the Ovidian Circe concerns more specifically the figure of Scylla.

Although always associated with Circe, Ovid's Scylla engendered her own tradition, of which Spenser's Errour and Milton's Sin are late adaptations. The Renaissance versions of Scylla associate her Circean "pollution" with her inability to withstand "bewitching pleasure."[10] As the tradition goes, Scylla, first seduced by appetite, in turn seduces others to their death. Her half-woman/half-monster body represents the archetypal conflict between reason and appetite dwelling within the individual. These Renaissance versions of Scylla and Circe embody a conception of the human will more closely associated with medieval Catholicism than with Protestantism. In Milton's adaptation of these figures, a basic philosophical conflict thus emerges between fundamentally different anthropologies.

What is the medieval anthropology inherent in the Circe tradition and how does it conflict with Protestant Reformed anthropology? Before we examine Milton's depiction of the Circe tradition within *Paradise Lost*, we must answer this question.

II

One of the first known uses of the word ἀλληγορια occurs in a fragment from the stoic philosopher Cleanthes, dating approximately from the third century B.C. The word *allegory* is used here in reference to *moly*, the gift Hermes gives to Odysseus that enables him to withstand Circe's enchantment. In discussing the significance of Cleanthes's use of the word *moly*, Apollonius states, "Cleanthes the philosopher says that Reason is indicated allegorically, by which the impulses and passions are mollified."[11] This third-century reference to Hermes's gift indicates how ancient the association is between the story of Circe and the allegorical battle between reason and appetite within the human soul.

The history of Circe is expounded by such ancient authors as Homer, Hesiod, Dionysius of Miletus, Herodian, Apollonius of Rhodes, Pausanias, Ovid, Virgil, Pliny the Elder, and Strabo. It is later developed and elaborated upon throughout the Middle Ages and the Renaissance. Each adaptation of the story reveals the same conflict between virtue and sensuality within the human condition. Those who are given the gift of moly from the gods (or exercise their reason) will be able to withstand the wiles of Circe, whereas those who succumb to their baser natures will be metamorphosed into creatures of appetite. This understanding of the will as a faculty of the mind which one has power to control is part of the Platonic understanding so prevalent in the Middle Ages.[12]

There are a number of important similarities between the Platonic understanding of the will inherent in the Circe tradition and medieval Catholic anthropology. We see this most clearly in the medieval Catholic understanding of the Fall. Briefly stated, the medieval Catholic understanding of the Fall is that humanity was endowed with two gifts at the time of creation: the first natural and the second supernatural. At the point of the Fall, the supernatural gift was removed, but the natural gift remained. Thus, in medieval Catholic anthropology, man's higher faculties are not significantly impaired after the Fall. Although the will is affected by the Fall, the natural gifts remain untouched. Because these natural gifts (or higher faculties) remain intact, humanity therefore has the ability to improve its condition.[13]

Although it would be incorrect to say that the Platonic understanding of the battle between reason and appetite and the medieval Catholic understanding of the battle between will and appetite are the same, there are elements that both share. It is clear that both are on the side of human optimism and both are opposed to the Reformed understanding of grace.

During the Protestant Reformation, the understanding of the power of the will changed profoundly. John Calvin and Martin Luther presented a different understanding of human nature. In the *Institutes of the Christian Religion*, Calvin discusses this ancient Greek concept of the power of the will:

> The philosophers (obviously with substantial agreement) imagine that the reason is located in the mind, which like a lamp illumines all councels, and like a queen governs the will. For they suppose that it is suffused with divine light to take the most effective counsel; and that it excels in power to wield the most effective command. On the other hand, they imagine that sense perception is gripped by torpor and dimness of sight; so that it always creeps along the ground, is entangled in baser things, and never rises up to true discernment. They hold that the appetite, if it undertakes to obey the reason and does not permit itself to be subjected to the senses, is borne along to the pursuit of virtues, holds the right way, and is molded into will. But if it subjects itself to the bondage of the senses, it is so corrupted and perverted by the latter as to degenerate into lust. In their opinion those faculties of which I have spoken above – understanding, sense, appetite, or will . . . have their seat in the soul. These philosophers consequently declare that the understanding is endowed with reason, the best ruling principle for the leading of a good and blessed life, provided it sustains itself within its own excellence and displays the strength bestowed upon it by nature. But they state that the lower impulse, called "sense," by which man is drawn off into error and delusion is such that it can be tamed and gradually overcome by reason's rod.[14]

The philosophers' understanding of the power of the will Calvin here refers to is clearly that depicted in the ancient Circe story. Based on this understanding of reason and appetite, certain virtues and vices are considered to be within our power. As Calvin states, "we seem to do what we do, and to shun what we shun, by free choice." According to Cicero, Calvin notes, "because every man acquires virtue for himself, no wise man ever thanked God for it." For the philosophers, reason is therefore a sufficient guide for right conduct, and the will, though "incited by the sense to do evil things," has free choice and "cannot be hindered from following reason" as its leader (p. 258).

Calvin, Luther, and the Reformers present a different philosophical understanding of the will: the acceptance of one's complete helplessness to improve upon his condition without God. Their understanding of the will is that it is utterly devoid of power to overcome the appetite or passion that exists within the flesh. This is because the power that "infected" the flesh after the fall is so great that the will alone cannot combat it (*Institutes*, p. 249). Christ alone can abolish the power of sin which "crept in" through Adam and corrupted his posterity (p. 250). Only when one understands his own helplessness to improve upon his condition will he then be able to truly understand God's grace.

The Reformed understanding of the Fall is then quite different from that of the medieval Catholics. The Reformers rejected the distinction between natural and supernatural gifts. In their view, humanity stands or falls as a whole. For the Reformers, the Fall left humanity utterly devoid of any ability to improve upon its condition without the help of God. In the Reformed anthropology, man's natural faculties have become impaired and his will exists within a state of bondage. Calvin declares that "to regard Adam's sin as gluttonous intemperance (a common notion [in the medieval Catholic understanding]) is childish. As if the sum and head of all virtues lay in abstaining solely from one fruit, when all sorts of desirable delights abounded everywhere" (*Institutes*, p. 245). The Reformers understood Adam's sin to be the result of the more dangerous sins of reason. The emphasis on the sins of reason, as opposed to the sins of the flesh, further distinguishes the Reformed from the medieval Catholic anthropology.

The Renaissance versions of Circe and Scylla are closer philosophically to the medieval Catholic than to the Reformed anthropology. Sandys's description of Scylla reflects this medieval anthropology:

> Scylla represents a Virgin; who as long as chaste in thought, and in body unspotted, appears of an excellent beauty, attracting all eyes upon her, and wounding the Gods themselves with affection. But once polluted with the sorceries of Circe; that is, having rendered her maiden honour to be deflowred by bewitching pleasure, she is transformed to an horrid monster. And not so only, but endeavors to shipwrack others. . . . That the upper part of her body is feigned to retaine a human figure and the lower to be bestiall; intimates how man, a divine creature,

inbued with wisdome and intelligence, in whose superiour parts, as in a high tower, that immortall spirit resideth, who only of all that hath life erects his lookes unto heaven, can never so degenerate into a beast, as when he giveth himself over to the lowe delights of those baser parts of the body, Dogs and Wolves, the blind and savage fury of concupiscence.[15]

Sandys's reference here to the upper and lower parts of the body reflects the Platonic scale of values present in this medieval anthropology. His description of Circe shows even more clearly this blend of Platonic and medieval Catholic understanding. Here we see the Christianizing of Circe:

[Circe is daughter of Sol and Persis in that lust proceeds from heat and moisture; and luxury, getting] the dominion, deformes our soules with all bestiall vices, alluring some to inordinate Venus; others to anger, cruelty and every excesse of passion . . . [Circe's charms] are not to bee resisted, but by the divine assistance, Moly, . . . which signifies temperance. So the fortitude and wisdome of Ulisses, preserves him in the midst of vices . . . [Some of his companions are destroyed, others are] converted into beasts by Circe: their headstrong appetites, which revolt from the soveraignty of reason (by which wee are onely like unto God, and armed against our depraved affections) nor ever returne into their Country (from whence the soule deriveth her coelestiall originall), unlesse disinchanted, and cleansed from their former impurity. For as Circe's rod, waved over their heads from the right side to the left: presents those false and sinister perswasions of pleasures, which so much deformes them: so the reversion thereof, by discipline, and a view of their owne deformity, restores them to their former beauties.[16]

The medieval versions of Circe and Scylla do not in any way reflect the Reformed understanding of the radical nature of sin corrupting the higher faculties of the mind. They are instead seen as paradigms of the dangers of concupiscence resulting in the fall of humanity.

III

The most explicit reference to the Ovidian interpretation of Circe in *Paradise Lost* is found in the "Cerberean mouths" that surround Sin when Satan encounters her at the gates of hell in Book II. This reference to Ovid's Scylla has long been noted by scholars, and Sin's iconography has been studied in relation to the woman-serpent and viper traditions.[17] What sets Milton's Sin apart from these more general traditions, however, is the event of her metamorphosis. In this detail, we are referred to the Circe of Ovid. In Ovid, the woman-seductress figure and the metamorphosis of the victim are combined in the myth of Circe.

In Book II, Sin cannot accurately be described as a Circe figure. (She is not actually seducing anyone nor does she have any poison.) In the account that she gives of herself to Satan, however, she is indeed the traditional seductress figure. Thus when Satan, baffled at the name "Father," demands to know the identity of these monsters, Sin replies:

> Hast thou forgot me then, and do I seem
> Now in thine eye so foul, once deem'd so fair
> In Heav'n, when at th' Assembly, and in sight
> Of all the Seraphim with thee combin'd
> In bold conspiracy against Heav'n's King,
> All on a sudden miserable pain
> Surpris'd thee, dim thine eyes, and dizzy swum
> In darkness, while thy head flames thick and fast
> Threw forth, till on the left side op'ning wide,
> Likest to thee in shape and count'nance bright,
> Then shining heav'nly fair, a Goddess arm'd
> Out of thy head I sprung: amazement seiz'd
> All th' Host of Heav'n; back they recoil'd afraid
> At first, and call'd me Sin, and for a Sign
> Portentous held me; but familiar grown,
> I pleas'd, and with attractive graces won
> The most averse, thee chiefly, who full oft
> Thyself in me thy perfect image viewing
> Becam'st enamor'd, and such joy thou took'st
> With me in secret, that my womb conceiv'd
> A growing burden. (II. 747–67).[18]

Like the Renaissance interpretation of Ovid's Scylla or Fletcher's Hamartia, Sin "with attractive graces" seduces Satan and the fallen angels. Yet Sin is consistent with the ancient female monster of lust only in the story she recounts to Satan concerning her origin. When she appears at the gates of hell in Book II, she is no longer such a character. She is instead a figure existing within a condition of bondage. She has been subjected to the rule of her son, and she has no control over her own body. While Death in Book II demonstrates the attributes of gluttony and lust, Sin is not as clearly distinguished. (Upon Death's birth, his first impulse is to devour his mother—only the premonition that she would prove a "bitter morsel" prevents him from consuming her.) The figure Sin most closely parallels in Book II is the mythological Scylla, the metamorphosed victim of Circe. Yet this is not the Scylla of the mythographers, "in whose superior parts, as in a high tower, that immortall spirit resideth." Sin is utterly helpless to free herself from her condition. Her behavior instead parallels the Reformed understanding of the helplessness of the sinner and the radical nature of sin. Sin prefigures the condition of the sinner after the Fall.

Given this particular understanding of Sin in Book II, one may ask why Sin would represent human sinners before she represents the power of sin in general. The reason is explained in the nature of allegory. Milton does not present the story of Sin and Death in Book II in the logic of a narrative account, but in the form of allegory. Sin can therefore prefigure the bondage of the human condition before the event of the Fall in the same way the devils in Book I prefigure the sins of fallen humanity. The power of Milton's allegory is that he illustrates the bondage of the sinner in a way that cannot be narrated after the Fall in Book IX.

The most important parallel between Sin and Reformed theology in Book II, however, is found in the event of Sin's birth. In order to understand this parallel, we turn to the classical origin of the birth of Sin found in the cephalic birth of Athena from the head of Zeus:

> But Zeus himself gave birth from his own head to bright-eyed Tritogeneia . . . who delights in tumults and wars and battles. . . . But Zeus lay with the fair-cheeked daughter of Okeanos and Tethys apart from Hera, . . . deceiving Metis although she was full wise. But he seized her with his hands and put her in his belly, for fear that she might bring forth something stronger than his thunderbolt: therefore did Zeus, who sits on high and dwells in the aether, swallow her down suddenly. But she straightaway conceived Pallas Athena: and the father of men and gods gave birth by way of his head on the banks of the river Trito.[19]

Milton's allusion to the birth of Athena in Book II has a Reformed motivation. In Milton's understanding, the origin of sin on earth occurs as a result of pride (a sin of reason) as opposed to the sin of cupidity (a sin of the flesh). J. Huizinga distinguishes between these two philosophical understandings in discussing the medieval theories of the reasons for the Fall:

> Medieval doctrine found the root of all evil either in the sin of pride or in cupidity. Both opinions were based on Scripture texts. . . . It seems, nevertheless, that from the twelfth century downward people begin to find the principle of evil rather in cupidity than in pride. The voices which condemn blind cupidity, "la cieca cupidigia" of Dante, become louder and louder. Pride might perhaps be called the sin of the feudal and hierarchic age.[20]

In the Middle Ages, pride became a symbolic sin (associated with the pride of Lucifer) and assumed a metaphysical character (Huizinga, p. 19). Cupidity, however, had no symbolic character: it was a purely worldly sin. Although pride was considered to be the root of all sin, gluttony was the sin of Adam and Eve.[21] As previously noted, Calvin addresses this medieval understanding of sin as the result of lust or gluttony:

Because what God so severely punished must have been no light sin but a detestable crime, we must consider what kind of sin there was in Adam's desertion that enkindled God's fearful vengeance against the whole of mankind. To regard Adam's sin as gluttonous intemperance (a common notion) is childish. . . . Indeed, Augustine speaks rightly when he declares that pride was the beginning of all evils. For if ambition had not raised man higher than was meet and right, he could have remained in his original state. (*Institutes*, pp. 244–45)

The Reformers clearly understood the Fall to be associated with the sins of reason as opposed to the sins of the flesh.

Sin's origin from the mind of Satan and the subsequent relationship that occurs between them are similarly associated with pride. When Satan first conceives of rebellion in heaven, the result of that conception is the figure of Sin springing forth from his head. Similarly, when the goddess Sin is seduced in heaven, it is not the result of lust, but of pride. Satan sees in his daughter his own "perfect image" (II, 764), and for that reason he becomes "enamor'd" and takes such joy with her in secret that her womb conceives a "growing burden." The origin of Sin is therefore more closely aligned with a Reformed than a medieval Catholic understanding.

When Sin makes her second appearance in the poem, however, she is no longer the metamorphosed victim of Circe, but the victimizer. What has occurred between Books II and X is the Fall. The function of Sin in the poem appears, therefore, to be determined by the theologically significant event of the Fall on earth.

In Book X, we meet Sin and Death again at the gates of hell. Sin is convinced of Satan's success on earth for she feels a new strength coming over her:

> Methinks I feel new strength within me rise,
> Wings growing, and Dominion giv'n me large
> Beyond this Deep; whatever draws me on,
> Or sympathy, or some connatural force
> Powerful at greatest distance to unite
> With secret amity things of like kind
> By secretest conveyance. (X, 243–49)

The relationship between Sin and Death here is very different from the relationship that existed at our first encounter with them in Book II. Death is no longer Sin's "inbred enemy" and Sin is no longer viewed as a "bitter morsel" by her son. In Book X, they speak to each other in terms of filial affection brought about by the unity of a common cause. Sin calls Death her "shade inseparable" and suggests that together they "found" a path from hell to earth. Death responds:

> Go whither Fate and inclination strong
> Leads thee, I shall not lag behind, nor err
> The way, thou leading, such a scent I draw
> Of carnage, prey innumerable, and taste
> The savor of Death from all things there that live:
> Nor shall I to the work thou enterprisest
> Be wanting, but afford thee equal aid. (X, 265–71)

As Summers suggests, Sin and Death are here the perfection of romantic love: "bound by secret sympathy," each lover is inseparable from the other.[22] Death will now follow closely behind his mother and offer her "equal aid." The relationship has changed because of the event of the Fall.

When Sin and Death arrive in Paradise, Sin asks her son what he thinks of their new empire. Death complains: all of this "too little seems / To stuff this Maw, this vast unhide-bound Corpse" (X, 600–01). Sin then tells her son to

> Thou therefore on these Herbs, and Fruits, and Flow'rs
> Feed first, on each Beast next, and Fish and Fowl,
> No homely morsels, and whatever thing
> The Scythe of Time mows down, devour unspar'd,
> Till I in Man residing through the Race,
> His thoughts, his looks, words, actions all infect,
> And season him thy last and sweetest prey. (X, 603–09)

Humankind must therefore be properly seasoned by Sin before they can be fare for her son. Death learns that it is only through his mother's work that he can reign. Unlike the antagonistic relationship that existed in Book II, the relationship in Book X is one of cooperation; Sin and Death must now work together in order to carry out their various functions on earth.

After the Fall, Sin realizes her full potential. She is no longer the Scylla victim of Book II, subject to the abuse and rule of her son; neither is there any suggestion of her continued torture by the "Cerberean" mouths that surround her. In Book X, we find the allegorized presence of Circe—all of the basic components of the myth are present. Sin is here the infecting agent whose function it is to make humanity thrall to appetite. She no longer offers her poison as a drug, but is herself the poison. Unlike the ancient Circe figures, Sin's potion is no longer external. Circe's contagion here becomes original sin.

After the fall of Adam and Eve, the parallels between the earthly and the diabolical couples become apparent. The unity of the earthly couple during and immediately after the Fall echoes the new unity and inseparability of Sin and Death as they prepare to journey to earth in Book X. Before Adam eats of the fruit, he declares: "So forcible within my heart I feel / The Bond of Nature draw me to my own, / My own in thee, for what thou art is mine; / Our state cannot be sever'd, we are one, / One flesh" (IX, 955–59). And Eve, just after the Fall, rejoices in the unity of their fallen state. Adam and Eve then experience lust for the first time. Their senses become inflamed with "amorous intent" as they take "largely of thir mutual guilt the Seal, / The solace of thir sin, till dewy sleep / Oppress'd them, wearied with thir amorous play" (IX, 1042–045). When they awake, the euphoria of the fruit has worn off and we are given a picture of the new relationship between Adam and Eve:

> They sat them down to weep, nor only Tears
> Rain'd at thir Eyes, but high Winds worse within
> Began to rise, high Passions, Anger, Hate,
> Mistrust, Suspicion, Discord, and shook sore
> Thir inward State of Mind, calm Region once
> And full of Peace, now toss't and turbulent:
> For Understanding rul'd not, and the will
> Heard not her lore, both in subjection now
> To sensual Appetite, who from beneath
> Usurping over sovran Reason claims
> Superior sway. (IX, 1121–131)

As Summers states, "if we have missed the colloquial tones of real men and women before, we can find them in the altered style of the fallen Adam and Eve when they accuse each other" (*The Muses's Method*, p. 60). Understanding and will are now subject to "sensual appetite," for sin has become internalized. Adam and Eve, like the body of Sin, have become enthralled to themselves.

Because of the pervading corruption wrought by Sin on humankind and on earth, Adam and Eve can no longer remain in Paradise. Thus acknowledging, the Father tells his Son:

> Those pure immortal Elements that know
> No gross, no unharmonious mixture foul,
> Eject him tainted now, and purge him off
> As a distemper, gross to air as gross,
> And mortal food, as may dispose him best
> For dissolution wrought by Sin, that first
> Distemper'd all things, and of incorrupt
> Corrupted. (XI, 50–57)

Sin's distempering of the earth implies that she has the power not only to infect the earth with disease, but also to cause derangement of the reasoning powers of the mind.

The Circean pollution of the earth is further described by God the Father who views the scene in Paradise with his Son:

> See with what heat these Dogs of Hell advance
> To waste and havoc yonder World, which I
> So fair and good created
> . . . .
> I suffer them to enter and possess
> A place so heav'nly, and conniving seem
> To gratify my scornful Enemies,
> That laugh, as if transported with some fit
> Of passion, I to them had quitted all,
> At random yielded up to their misrule;
> And know not that I call'd and drew them thither
> My Hell-hounds, to lick up the draff and filth
> Which man's polluting Sin with taint hath shed
> On what was pure, till cramm'd and gorg'd, nigh burst
> With suckt and glutted Offal. (X, 616–33)

In this passage, the figure of Sin which here pollutes and taints the earth is now within humanity. Thus throughout Books XI and XII the archangel Michael refers continually to the human condition governed by appetite: "Some by violent stroke shall die . . . by Intemperance more,"

> In Meats and Drinks, which on the Earth shall bring
> Diseases dire . . . that thou may'st know
> What misery th' inabstinence of Eve
> Shall bring on men (XI, 472–78)

> Since thy original lapse, true liberty
> Is lost, which always with right Reason dwells
> Twinn'd, and from her hath no dividual being:
> Reason in man obscur'd, nor not obey'd,
> . . . .
> upstart Passions catch the Government
> From Reason, and to servitude reduce
> Man till then free. (XII, 83–90)

By Book XII, though the figure of Sin has disappeared, the effects of her drugs yet remain. The ancient seductress figure of Circe has become internalized.[23]

Luther describes original sin as a "poison" which is "infused into our nature" at birth.[24] He maintains that humankind is "born from unclean seed and from the very nature of the seed we acquire ignorance of God, smugness, unbelief, hatred against God . . . and similar grave faults." Luther continues:

> These are so deeply implanted in our flesh, and this poison has been so widely spread through the flesh, body, mind, muscles, and blood, through the bones and the very marrow, in the will, in the intellect, and in reason, that they not only cannot be fully removed but are not even recognized as sin. (P. 166)

This understanding of sin as a poison infused into our nature at birth is exactly parallel to Milton's depiction of Sin in books X through XII. Milton has revised the medieval Circe figure into a Reformed context.

Were it not for the presence of the Circe tradition in Book IX, my argument concerning Milton's Reformed revision of the Circe figure in the poem could come to a close. As is so often the case with this poem, however, one finds a paradox at almost every turn. The appearance of the Ovidian Circe in Book IX indeed contains a number of Reformed elements in the account of the Fall. In some significant events, however, Milton does fall back on the traditional Catholic model. When this occurs, I argue that the reasons for the apparent lapse has to do with inherent difficulties within the theological tradition itself.

IV

In Book IX of *Paradise Lost,* Milton refers us to the theme of the Circe tradition in a number of ways. Although Eve's fall appears to be patterned closely on the Platonic battle between reason and appetite, it does not actually follow this ancient scheme. Eve's fall is philosophically closer to the Reformed understanding of the issue. The Circean characteristics do occur, however, in Eve's postlapsarian condition.

Before we look at the parallels between Eve and Circe in Book IX, we must look more closely at the character of Eve. The suggestion of Eve's vulnerability to the wiles of Circe begin as early as Book V.

In Book V, Eve awakes from a troubled dream. She tells Adam of a voice she assumed was his which had called her "forth to walk." The voice said:

> Why sleep'st thou Eve? Now is the pleasant time,
> The cool, the silent, save where silence yields
> To the night-warbling Bird, that now awake
> Tunes sweetest his love-labor'd song; now reigns
> Full Orb'd the Moon, and with more pleasing light
> Shadowy sets off the face of things; in vain,

> If none regard; Heav'n wakes with all his eyes,
> Whom to behold but thee, Nature's desire,
> In whose sight all things joy, with ravishment
> Attracted by thy beauty still to gaze. (V, 38–47)

Eve rises and finds herself directed to the forbidden tree, "where she finds one "shap'd and wing'd like one of those from Heav'n." Eve observes the angel praising the virtues of the tree when he suddenly plucks the fruit and eats. She is first with "damp horror chill'd," until the angel addresses her:

> Here, happy Creature, fair Angelic Eve,
> Partake thou also; happy though thou art,
> Happier thou may'st be, worthier canst not be:
> Taste this, and be henceforth among the Gods
> Thyself a Goddess. (V, 74–78)

The angel then brings her the fruit and she eats ("the pleasant savory smell / So quick'n'd appetite, that I, methought, / Could not but taste, V, 84–86). The fruit enables Eve to experience "appetite" or passion for the first time:

> Forthwith up to the clouds
> With him I flew, and underneath beheld
> The Earth outstretcht immense, a prospect wide
> And various: wond'ring at my flight and change
> To this high exaltation. (V, 86–90)

Eve's dream thus informs the reader of her particular vulnerability. The dream foreshadows the euphoria she and Adam will experience immediately after the Fall in Book IX.

There are a number of parallels to the Circe myth in the above scene. First is the idea that Eve is seduced through the ear; she is lured into following a voice she believes to be the voice of Adam. As Milton has combined the seduction of the Sirens with the Circe myth in both *Comus* and *Samson Agonistes*, he does so here as well. Once lured to the fruit, Eve is then seduced through her appetite to eat. (Her seduction also occurs when the "Full Orb'd" moon reigns, the time when, according to Comus, "Venus now wakes, and wak'ns Love" [123–24]). The angelic figure, here clearly a type of Circe figure, succeeds in seducing Eve with his poisonous fruit. The effect of this fruit resembles the effect of Circe's poison; both cause metamorphosis of the victim. In this dream, Eve's appetite overrules reason, and she therefore experiences the intoxication of passion.

The battle between reason and appetite is alluded to continually in Eve's seduction scene. It is important to note, however, that Eve's fall is not due to appetite overcoming reason, the orthodox allegorical interpretation of the Circe myth in the medieval understanding; Eve's reason is simply deceived. After Eve's fall, however, she becomes a Circe figure patterned on the medieval seductress figure. It is then Adam's fall which follows the medieval pattern of appetite overcoming reason.

In Book IX Satan bemoans his "foul descent" into a beast. He enters into the mouth of the sleeping serpent, possessing his heart and head with "act intelligential," and awaits the coming of Eve into the garden. When he encounters Eve, the language shifts to the Petrarchan language of seduction. The serpent moves toward Eve,

> not with indented wave,
> Prone on the ground, as since, but on his rear,
> Circular base of rising folds, that tow'r'd
> Fold above fold a surging Maze, his Head
> Crested aloft, and Carbuncle his Eyes;
> With burnisht Neck of verdant Gold, erect
> Amidst his circling Spires, that on the grass
> Floated redundant: pleasing was his shape,
> And lovely. (IX, 496–504)

As Satan moves in "wanton" wreaths toward Eve, his intention is to seduce her eye. Eve first hears the rustling leaves, but "minded not," "as us'd / To such disport before her through the Field, / From every beast, more duteous at her call, / Than at Circean call the Herd disguis'd" (X, 519–22). After the reference to Circe, Satan, who is "bolder now," approaches Eve:

> Oft he bow'd
> His turret Crest, and sleek enamell'd Neck,
> Fawning, and lick'd the ground whereon she trod.
> His gentle dumb expression turn'd at length
> The Eye of Eve to mark his play; he glad
> Of her attention gain'd, with Serpent Tongue
> Organic, or impulse of vocal Air,
> His fraudulent temptation thus began. (IX, 524–31)

Before Satan even begins to speak, the Circean overtones are clear.

The reference to Circe in this scene does not immediately implicate Eve as a Circe figure. Eve's relationship to the beasts in the garden is unlike Circe's relationship to her beasts. This reference instead brings to our attention the theme of the myth: the battle between the temptations of the appetite and the virtuous will. The Circe figure in this episode is Satan (Satan is here both Circe figure and beast). Like Circe, he appeals directly to "appetite," hoping thereby to seduce Eve's mind.

Using almost the exact words of praise in Eve's dream, Satan addresses Eve concerning the issue of her wasted beauty in Paradise. Instead of responding to Satan's words, Eve is shocked at the fact that the "Tongue of Brute" can speak. She knows that beasts were created without reasoning ability or speech and asks,

> How cam'st thou speakable of mute, and how
> To me so friendly grown above the rest
> Of brutal kind, that daily are in sight?
> Say, for such wonder claims attention due. (IX, 563–66)

Satan responds that he was first "as other Beasts that graze / The trodden Herb, of abject thoughts and low" (IX, 571–72), until one day he discerned "A goodly tree far distant to behold" (576). As he drew near to the tree, his appetite was aroused: "more pleased my sense / Than smell of sweetest Fennel, or the Teats / Of Ewe or Goat" (580–82), and he resolved to satisfy his "sharp desire" (584). Although he saw other beasts "with like desire / Longing and envying" (592–93) to eat, he was able to reach the fruit and eat his fill:

> I spar'd not, for such pleasure till that hour
> At Feed or Fountain never had I found.
> Sated at length, ere long I might perceive
> Strange alteration in me, to degree
> Of Reason in my inward Powers, and Speech
> Wanted not long, though to this shape retain'd.
> Thenceforth to Speculation high or deep
> I turn'd my thoughts, and with capacious mind
> Consider'd all things visible in Heav'n,
> Or Earth, or Middle, all things fair and good. (IX, 596–605)

In this scene, we find that Satan has inverted the logic of the order of events that occur in the Circe myth. In the myth, Circe offers her potion to the unsuspecting sailors who in turn become metamorphosed into beasts. The only one able to withstand Circe's "wiles" is Ulysses, and he is able to do so through the gift of moly. In the later tradition, Circe, as an external figure of concupiscence, transforms those into beasts who have allowed appetite to usurp reason. Therefore, in the place where there was once a "human count'nance, / Th' express resemblance of the gods," Circe's (or Comus's) drink fixes instead "the inglorious likeness of a beast" (*Comus*, 68–69, 528). In the above encounter, Satan, by succumbing to appetite, claims to have found reason. His argument concerning the value of the fruit is thus based on the premise that since he, a dumb brute, has received the reasoning powers of man, Adam and Eve, by eating this same fruit, will therefore become as gods.

Before Eve even eats the forbidden fruit, we find that her reason has been deceived by Satan's logic:

> He ended, and his words replete with guile
> Into her heart too easy entrance won.
> Fixt on the Fruit she gaz'd, which to behold
> Might tempt alone, and in her ears the sound
> Yet rung of his persuasive words, impregn'd
> With Reason, to her seeming, and with Truth. (IX, 733–38)

Once Eve's reason is deceived, she supposes that the serpent is telling the truth and that God must therefore not understand the true value of the fruit: by eating the fruit, the serpent has clearly not died.

Eve's fall is not due to appetite overcoming her reason: Her reason here is simply deceived. Once she eats the fruit, however, she undergoes a Circean metamorphosis into a creature of appetite. Although her body retains its human form, her mind becomes corrupt. She thus "Greedily . . . ingorg'd without restraint" and becomes "hight'n'd as with Wine, jocund and boon" (IX, 791, 793). Her internal transformation is made evident in the series of sins she now for the first time experiences: selfishness (803), passion (830–31), and idolatry (833–36). As she greets Adam, Eve's first words are a lie: "Hast thou not wonder'd, *Adam*, at my stay? / Thee I have misst, and thought it long, depriv'd / Thy presence, agony of love till now / Not felt" (IX, 856–59). In the encounter between Adam and Eve following this initial transformation, Eve herself finally becomes a Circe figure. Her words to Adam are filled with lies and the Petrarchan language of passion. Even her appearance is altered: "in her Cheek distemper flushing glow'd" (887). Eve has become a creature of concupiscence.

In Adam's fall, there is no evidence that his reason has become corrupt. The narrative voice in fact specifically tells us that Adam was "not deceiv'd"; he was instead "fondly overcome with Female charm" (IX, 998–99). Adam's sin is the result of appetite overcoming reason, as opposed to the Reformed understanding of the Fall being the result of the sins of reason. Adam's fall therefore appears to be patterned more closely on the medieval scheme.

Most critics would concur that Milton's concept of unregenerate humanity is clearly Reformed as opposed to medieval Catholic. If this is the case, why would we find elements from the medieval Catholic Circe tradition in Milton's account of the Fall in Book IX? I suggest that at least part of the reason for this has to do with the inherent difficulties in effectively narrating the Reformed understanding of the Fall. As previously discussed, Protestants understood the great act of disobedience to be the result of the sins of reason rather than the sins of concupiscence. This would require Milton to demonstrate how it is psychologically plausible for a perfect being to disobey the one command through a rational, as opposed to a lustful, act, and to make this act sufficiently evil (in the Reformed understanding of radical corruption). The most plausible reason for Milton's treatment of Circe in Book IX, therefore, is that these inherent difficulties in the subject matter were too great. For the story of temptation and fall, Milton was forced to rely on the traditional classical and medieval narrations of seduction.

The medieval seductress tradition of Circe lends itself to a psychologically realistic depiction of the Fall. It is more plausible for Milton to show Adam being "overcome with Female charm" than it is to show his corruption occurring as the result of pride or the sins of reason. Similarly, Eve's fall is more psychologically plausible being the result of deception than the result of corrupt reason. In his story of the Fall, Milton therefore chooses psychological realism over strict conformity with Reformed anthropology.

Although Brodwin has clearly demonstrated the influence of the Homeric text on the corpus of Milton's work, including *Paradise Lost*, I argue that Milton understood and used the Ovidian text in a similarly sophisticated manner. In his revision of Scylla and Circe in Books II and X, Milton demonstrates how the external temptress from the mythographic tradition becomes interiorized after the Fall. In Book II, Sin represents the self-enthralled individual—she provides the perfect theological model for the "wretched man" of Romans, chapter 7, who is similarly unable to save himself from his condition.[25] After the Fall, in Book X, Sin becomes herself the Circean cup of poison, infecting humanity to create fare for her son. No longer the external temptress offering her potion to unsuspecting sailors, she is an interiorized figure manifesting the Reformed understanding of the power of original sin.

While others maintain that the Circe of Book IX is Eve in her pre- as well as postlapsarian condition, I have argued that the Circean behavior is demonstrated only in the postlapsarian Eve. Although Eve's Circean tendencies are demonstrated as early as Book IV, she becomes the seductress only after the Fall. This is because the link between Circe and Eve is the presence of sin.

Circe is the product of fallen nature—on both the angelic and human levels. When Satan first experiences sin in heaven, he gives birth to the seductress who would soon infect humanity. After Eve becomes "infected" by Sin, she inherits the power of the ancient seductress to continue the tradition. This transfer of power cannot occur, however, until Eve partakes of Circe's cup. The allegorized figure of Circe in Book X thus provides a meaningful structure upon which the actions of Satan, Adam, and Eve in Book IX can be interpreted.

Golden Gate University

NOTES

1. Leonora Brodwin, "Milton and the Renaissance Circe," in *Milton Studies* VI, ed. James D. Simmonds (Pittsburgh, 1974), pp. 21–83.

2. See S. A. Demetrakopoulos, "Eve as a Circean and Courtly Fatal Woman," *MQ* IX (1975), 99–107; Wolfgang E. H. Rudat, "'Thy Beauty's Heav'nly Ray': Milton's Satan and the Circean Eve," *MQ* XIX (March 1985), 17–19. Rudat argues that "Milton endows Eve with the Circean power to transform Satan into a phallic serpent"—one who is sexually aroused by Eve's attractiveness (18).

3. Douglas Bush, *Mythology and the Renaissance Tradition in English Poetry* (New York, 1957), p. 265.

4. On Ovid's Scylla, see Davis Harding, *Milton and the Renaissance Ovid* (Urbana, Ill., 1946), pp. 95–98; J. F. Gilliam, "Scylla and Sin," *PQ* XXIX (July 1950), 344–47; John M. Patrick, "Milton, Phineas Fletcher, Spenser, and Ovid—Sin at Hell's Gates," *N&Q*, new series, III (September 1956), 384–86, and *Milton's Conception of Sin as Developed in "Paradise Lost,"* monograph series VII (Logan, Utah, 1960), pp. 37, 45–51; Bush, *Mythology and the Renaissance Tradition*, p. 284; John M. Steadman, "Tradition and Innovation in Milton's 'Sin': The Problem of Literary Indebtedness," *PQ* XXXIX (1960), 93–105; Robert C. Fox, "The Allegory of Sin and Death in *Paradise Lost*," *MLQ* XXIV (1963), 354–64; and Richard J. DuRocher, *Milton and Ovid* (Ithaca, 1985), pp. 204–16. Of these critics, DuRocher presents the most extensive analysis of Spenser's Errour and Milton's Sin as late adaptations of Ovid's Scylla.

On the theological implications, see Balachandra Rajan, *"Paradise Lost" and the Seventeenth-Century Reader* (1947; rpt. Ann Arbor, 1967), p. 50; Fox, "Allegory," 354–64; and Robert B. White, "Milton's Allegory of Sin and Death: A Comment on Background," *MP* LXX (1973), 337–41. For a contrasting view of the trinity-parody theory, see Maureen Quilligan, *Milton's Spenser: The Politics of Reading* (Ithaca, 1983), pp. 85–88. Quilligan argues that one sees a criticism of the idea of the Trinity implicit in an allegorical reading of the relations among Satan, Sin, and Death, because "this kind of reading is the very sort that Milton's (and Spenser's) allegory in fact works against" (88). According to Quilligan, Sin and Death ape God's creation of Adam and Eve.

Although parody of the Trinity may have been part of Milton's intention, the Trinity theory leaves too much unexplained about the behavior of Sin and Death, particularly in Book X. I argue that the fundamental tradition behind Milton's allegory is found in Ovid.

5. Samuel Stollman, "Satan, Sin, and Death: A Mosaic Trio in *Paradise Lost*," in *Milton Studies* XX, ed. James D. Simmonds (Pittsburgh, 1986), 101–20, citing pp. 101, 102.

6. Signior Ciovanni Battista Gelli, *The Circe*, trans. Thomas Brown, with an introduction by Robert Adams (Ithaca, 1963), p. xxxviii.

7. *The Odyssey of Homer*, trans. Richard Lattimore (New York, 1965), X, 289. All further references within the text are to this edition.

8. Ovid. *Metamorphoses*, trans. George Sandys (London, 1626), XIV, 25–28, p. 282. All references to Ovid are from this edition.

9. Merritt Hughes, "Spenser's Acrasia and the Circe of the Renaissance," *JHI* IV (October 1943), 378, notes that the victory of Ovid in the mythographers' tradition may be due to their ignorance of Homer.

10. George Sandys, *Ovid's "Metamorphosis": Englished, Mythologized, and Represented in Figures*, qtd. in Harding, *Milton and the Renaissance Ovid*, p. 97. Harding uses Sandys's interpretation of Scylla as an example of the Renaissance interpretation of the figure.

11. R.P.C. Hanson, *Allegory and Event: A Study of the Sources and Significance of Origen's Interpretation of Scripture* (London, 1959), p. 37.

12. In *Summa Theologica*, Thomas Aquinas discusses the will as one of the higher faculties of the mind. See *The Summa Theologica of St. Thomas Aquinas*, trans. Fathers of the English Dominican Province (London, 1912), part 1, third number, QQ.LXXV–LXIX. See also the discussion of Circe in Don Cameron Allen, *Mysteriously Meant: The Rediscovery of Pagan Symbolism and Allegorical Interpretation in the Renaissance* (London, 1970), pp. 226–28 and 292–301.

13. See Thomas Aquinas, *Summa Theologica*, Part 1, third number, XCV, first article.

14. John Calvin, *Institutes of the Christian Religion*, 2 vols., trans. Ford Lewis Battles, ed. John T. McNeill (Philadelphia, 1967), p. 257. Hereafter cited in the text as *Institutes.*

15. George Sandys, qtd. in Harding, *Milton and the Renaissance Ovid*, p. 97.

16. George Sandys, qtd. in Rosemond Tuve, *Images and Themes in Five Poems by Milton* (Cambridge, Mass., 1957), p. 132.

17. For the most complete discussion of these traditions, see Patrick, *Milton's Conception of Sin*, pp. 32–51; Steadman, "Tradition and Innovation"; and Michael Yost, "Milton's Sin and Her Pelican Daughters," *Renaissance Papers* (1972), 37–42.

18. All quotations of Milton's poetry are from *John Milton: Complete Poems and Major Prose*, ed. Merritt Y. Hughes (New York, 1957).

19. Hesiod, "Theogony," trans. Norman O. Brown (New York, 1953), II, 924–26; 929e–929r, qtd. in Philip J. Gallagher, "'Real or Allegoric': the Ontology of Sin and Death in *Paradise Lost*," *ELR* VI (1976), 328–29.

20. Johan Huizinga, *The Waning of the Middle Ages* (London, 1924), p. 18.

21. Morton W. Bloomfield, *The Seven Deadly Sins* (East Lansing, Mich., 1952), p. 223.

22. Joseph H. Summers, *The Muse's Method: An Introduction to "Paradise Lost"* (London, 1962), p. 62.

23. S. A. Demetrakopoulos, "Eve as a Circean and Courtly Fatal Woman," 103, calls the metamorphosed humanity described by Michael in Book XII the "grotesque herd that Eve's Circean powers finally produce on earth." Although indirectly related to Eve, I would argue that this "grotesque herd" is the work of Sin.

24. Martin Luther, *Luther's Works: Lectures on Genesis, Chapters* 1–5, ed. Jaroslav Pelikan, (St. Louis, 1958), vol. I, 169.

25. In Romans vii, 14–25, Paul describes the bondage of the sinner who lives under the law. In verse 23 he states, "O wretched man that I am! Who shall deliver me from the body of this death"? The controversy generated by these autobiographical passages concerns whether Paul is speaking from the perspective of regenerate or unregenerate humanity. The Reformers argue that Paul is speaking from the regenerate perspective; he provides an example of the Christian who is unable to redeem himself. For the Reformers, the process of justification therefore becomes wholly an act of grace.

DANCE AND THE NARRATION OF PROVIDENCE IN *PARADISE LOST*

Catherine I. Cox

In *Christian Doctrine* Milton explains that God's "first and most excellent SPECIAL DECREE" was the begetting of his Son.[1] Following numerous biblical proofs, Milton then turns to God's second decree, an implied decree respecting the angels. Milton supports his belief in the existence of angels by referring to Ephesians i, 9–10, a passage describing God's plan for the eventual unification of heaven and earth: "For he has made known to us in all wisdom and insight the mystery of his will, according to his purpose which he set forth in Christ as a plan for the fulness of time, to unite all things in heaven and all things on earth." Although the passage does not specifically refer to angels, they are implied by the phrase "things in heaven." The passage thus associates the revelation of God's providential plan, "the mystery of his will," with the heavenly creatures who traditionally celebrate God's goodness through song and dance. In Book V of *Paradise Lost,* Milton gives narrative form to his sequencing of special decrees in *Christian Doctrine,* for Raphael follows his story of God's announcement of his Son with a description of a dance of angels, a celebration that images and reveals the providential care of God and the harmony of his divine mind.

Images of dancing indeed interlace Milton's great epic to demonstrate visually and, at times, emblematically his assertion of "Eternal Providence." Since the most elaborate and philosophically significant description of dance comes in the mystical festival of angels following the announcement of the Son's anointment, I will begin by examining the image as an emblem of Providence and then will use the angelic dance as a point of comparison when examining less ethereal dances—those of prelapsarian creation, of hell, and of postlapsarian life. Since dancing is used to develop the concept of Providence, I will treat the dance event not as an isolated image or allusion but as an integral part of the larger narrative and philosophic context.

In order to convey to Adam both the magnificent joy and the unspoken tension pervading heaven at the announcement of the Son's priority, Raphael describes the heavenly reactions to the Father's decree:

So spake th' Omnipotent, and with his words
All seem'd well pleas'd, all seem'd, but were not all.
That day, as other solemn days, they spent
In song and dance about the sacred Hill,
Mystical dance, which yonder starry Sphere
Of Planets and of fixt in all her Wheels
Resembles nearest, mazes intricate,
Eccentric, intervolv'd, yet regular
Then most, when most irregular they seem:
And in thir motions harmony Divine
So smooths her charming tones, that God's own ear
Listens delighted. (V, 616–27)[2]

The most important aspect of the dance of the blessed is its emphasis on harmony and joy as mutual and reciprocal actions. The angels partake of God's joy in his Son and return their love through song and dance. The heavenly dance thus becomes the visual complement to music, conveying to the eye as music conveys to the ear the harmony and grace of divine wisdom and love. Indeed, in Raphael's description, sound and motion merge, for the harmony in the dancers' motions "smooths her charming tones," pleasing the ear of God. Leo Spitzer's remarks help to emphasize the significance of order as love in Milton's dance of the blessed: "According to the Pythagoreans, it was cosmic order which was identifiable with music; according to the Christian philosophers, it was love. And in the *ordo amoris* of Augustine we have evidently a blend of the Pagan and Christian themes: henceforth 'order' is love."[3]

Thus Milton's celestial dance images the Father's greatest act of love and provision — the begetting of his Son. The idea of harmony that Raphael's circles calls first to mind is the classical model which understands harmony to be not the blending of sounds in a chord but rather sounds in a continuum or scale. John Hollander explains: "The Greek *harmoniai* were scales, or melodic schemata; in general, *harmonia* is to be thought of as referring to *melody* rather than to vertical tonal aggregates."[4] The angels wheeling before the throne of God like "starry spheres" resemble the sirens of *The Republic* who stand each on a (planetary) rim and "send forth one sound, one note to form a symphonic harmony" (Hollander, p. 307). Renaissance polyphony builds on this ancient, homophonic model, by interlacing various melodic strands. While polyphony introduces depth, the musical experience remains essentially linear. Mortimer Frank explains, "To be sure, these melodies, when joined polyphonically, had to harmonize, but melodic rather than harmonic beauty was a composer's primary stylistic goal."[5] Like classical homophony and

Renaissance polyphony, the angelic dance, through its rhythm, gestures, and formations, accentuates and enriches the ideas of time and space, the measures by which Providence moves. Milton here follows in the tradition of St. Augustine, who speaks of world harmony as "a hymn scanned by God, since God allots the convenient things to the convenient time." Spitzer explains that for Augustine, "The poem of the world, like any poem can only be understood in time by a soul which endeavors to understand the action of Providence, which itself unfolds in time (*De ordine*, II, xix, 50–1); only the "ordinate soul" (the soul which is aware of the *numeri*) can understand the harmony of God" (pp. 29, 31).

Milton's use of harmony as visualized in the dance, however, suggests not only melodic but also chordal harmony. While Raphael's "mystical" dance, like Dante's dance of the blessed in the *Paradiso*, stresses eternal communion and constancy through images of circles, the dance is not without complexity and tension. Frank suggests that Milton both appreciated and employed the idea of harmony in its more modern, homophonic sense. By contrasting the new harmony to the classical idea, Frank emphasizes the tension that is essential to the innovative harmony gaining popularity in Milton's day: "When Plato wrote 'You cannot harmonize . . . that which disagrees' he expressed a view contradicted by seventeenth-century musical practices, practices that Henry Peacham recognized in asking: 'How doth music amaze us when of sound discords she maketh the sweetest harmony?'"[6]

Two paintings by Italian Renaissance masters may help us understand Milton's angelic dance as it celebratres God's design to draw harmony from discord. In Botticelli's *Mystic Nativity* (fig. 1), angels circle, hand in hand, above a nativity scene. This nativity, so close to the many pictorial representations of Christ's birth, is inspired by Revelation, chapter xii. Frederick Hartt discusses its imagery:

> so Botticelli dreams—we will all be brought to where the mystic Woman of Revelations 12 has found refuge with her child in the Wilderness, all devils will be chained under the rocks (we see this in the lowest foreground), angels will embrace us, and we may dwell in safety. . . . In the heavens above, twelve angels carrying olive branches from which dangle crowns, dance in a ring, the age old symbol of eternity.[7]

While the imprisoned devils lend tension to Botticelli's composition, the dominant images are the crèche and the dancing angels. The graceful and delicate ring of angels itself seems a crown of victory to be won at the end of time. In yet another way, Fra Angelico's *Last Judgment* (figs. 2 and 3) expresses the tension within God's providential design, for God's

Figure 1. Sandro Botticelli, *Mystic Nativity*, 1500. (Courtesy of The National Gallery, London.)

Figure 2. Fra Angelico, *Last Judgment*, ca. 1400–55. (Courtesy of Museo di San Marco, Florence.)

Figure 3. Dance in the Celestial Meadow, detail of Fra Angelico's *Last Judgment*. (Courtesy of Museo di San Marco, Florence.)

elect join with angels to dance in the celestial meadow. Their graceful round mirrors the orb of adoring angels above, encircling the throne of Christ. The dance thus reflects God's transcendent order—his defeat of chaos and his promise to unite "all things in heaven" and "all things on earth." The composition's balance, a centering of the figure of Christ above two contrasting scenes, lends a sense of order even to hell. On Christ's right hand, demons herd sinners into the infernal pit; while on his left, angels invite Christians to dance. Roland Frye describes the communal implications of this heavenly dance: "When the blessed souls just emerged from open graves, join hands with angels for a beautifully serene dance, we again have symbols of community" (fig. 3).[8]

Like Botticelli's and Fra Angelico's mystical scenes, Milton's heavenly dance stresses consonance, order, and community, while warning of a rupture that only God's love can heal. Raphael indeed begins the description not by emphasizing harmony but by stressing the tension arising from God's decree: "So spake the Omnipotent, and with his words / All seem'd well pleas'd, all seem'd, but were not all" (616–17). Satan's seeming mirth is his first act of dissemblance—the spiritual bifurcation that takes a grotesque and horrid shape in the births of his offspring Sin and Death. Through Satan's mirthful disguise, the heavenly dance incorporates the first conscious deception, indeed the first mask/masque. Though there is no individualizing of Satan throughout the festivities, we can assume that he does participate in the dance of the blessed as well as in the mystical feast that follows. We are told in fact that he does not "dislodge" himself from the faithful angels until midnight. Michael Fixler comments on the holy celebrations following the announcement of God's Son: "now the chief worshipper, next to the Son himself, feigns adoration and in being false implicitly holds within him the whole train of evil and idolatry which was to follow."[9] The emphasis on Satan's seeming pleasure at God's decree contrasts the authentic delight of God as he enjoys the music of celebration: "that God's own ear / Listens delighted" (626–27).

God, who foresees all things, is not disturbed by the presence of a dissembler in the divine dance, for, as Raphael tells Adam, things are "yet regular / . . . most when most irregular they seem" (623–24). The emphasis in Raphael's words is again on *seeming* though not on purposeful dissemblance. *Seeming* now means apparent dissonance and suggests the difference between God's knowledge and that of his creatures. The "maze" when looked on from the eternal perspective is an aesthetic additive, but from the temporal perspective, that is from the point of view of one inside the "maze," God's grand design may be difficult to discern.

A corollary to the dance's mystery exists in the medieval philosophy of music: "Divine providence has "mix'd" the tones in such a manner that man cannot guess the result: thus music although rational is mysterious (as Plato had said). . . . Mankind has no insight into the arcana of the God-ordained, pre-established musical harmony" (Spitzer, p. 35). Hoping to give Adam a perspective more closely divine, Raphael describes the joy of the dance and the "seeming pleasure" of Satan. In Ben Jonson's court masque *Pleasure Reconciled to Virtue*, the character Daedalus describes the significance of the maze that gives beauty to the masque and knowledge to its viewer:

Then, as all actions of mankind.
Are but a laborinth or maze,
So let your dances be entwined,
Yet not perplex men, unto gaze;

But measured, and so numerous too,
As men may read each act you do.
And when they see the Graces meet,
Admire the wisdom of your feet.

For dancing is an exercise
Not only shows the mover's wit,
But maketh the beholder wise,
As he hath power to rise to it.[10]

The labyrinthine pattern of Jonson's masque suggests human errors and wandering as well as a path of wisdom.[11] So, too, in Milton's early *A Masque Presented at Ludlow Castle*, the wanton dances and shrouded forest, which the lady calls a "leavy Labyrinth," symbolize the complex, bewildering path of life and the knowledge and victory to be gained by sustaining one's faith to the journey's end:

Heav'n hath timely tri'd their youth,
Their faith, their patience, and their truth,
And sent them here through hard assays
With a crown of deathless Praise,
To triumph in victorious dance
O'er sensual Folly and Intemperance. (970–75)

While the darkened forest and the antic revels in Milton's masque symbolize the difficult trials of every Christian, the triumphal dance at the play's close and the presentation of the children to their father and mother imply an encompassing, compassionate order. In just this way the maze of Raphael's description proleptically indicates the fall and the Father's provision for salvation. And so the "mazes intricate, / Eccentric, intervolv'd" become a circle at the dance's end: "Forthwith from dance to sweet repast they turn / Desirous; all in Circles as they stood" (V, 622–23, 630–31).[12] After feasting, the angels disperse in order to sleep, and the circle of angelic harmony fades into the image of the "Unsleeping eyes of God."

Masolino's fresco *The Eternal* (fig. 4), although gothic in its iconographic simplicity, images a scene close to that described by Raphael. From the Baptistery ceiling in Castiglione Olona, the figure of God looks down with large, bulging eyes, his hands outstretched to reveal the wounds of his Son. The crossed bands on the Father's garment likewise suggest the redeeming power of the cross. The fresco design — the heavy, dark circle fringed by angels surrounding the deity — itself suggests an eye. The nine angels, corresponding to the nine spheres whereon Plato's sirens sang in full harmony, float in adoring stillness fixing their eyes on their maker, a gesture of praise, vigilance, and reciprocal love. In a similar way, Raphael's description of angels who awaken alternately to circle the throne of God with "Melodious Hymns" enhances the ideas of harmony and vigilance. The announcement of the Son's priority is thus followed by reassurance through three closely linked circular images, the dance of Providence, the communion feast, and the omniscient eyes of God.

The masque of the stars in Book III closely replicates this heavenly dance. Yet while harmony and grace are accentuated as in the angels' round, the dissonance intensifies as we move farther from the divine mind. The dance of the stars emphasizes the idea of correspondence: "The golden Sun in splendor likest Heaven" (572). The harmony of the universe with the sun as its monarch reflects the harmony of heaven, and both dances replicate the love and grace of God. As Satan enters the sphere of the universe in Book III, he is immediately awed by the dance of stars and the brilliance and power of the sun:

> above them all
> The golden Sun in splendor likest Heaven
> Allur'd his eye: Thither his course he bends
> Through the calm Firmament; but up or down
> By centre, or eccentric, hard to tell,
> Or Longitude, where the great Luminary
> Aloof the vulgar Constellations thick,
> That from his Lordly eye keep distance due,
> Dispenses Light from far; they as they move
> Thir Starry dance in numbers that compute
> Days, months, and years, towards his all-cheering Lamp

Figure 4. Masolino, *L'eterno Padre e angioli, sffresco nella volta*, ca. 1435. Baptistery Castiglione Olona. (Courtesy of Alinari/Art Resource, New York.)

Turn swift thir various motions, or are turn'd
By his Magnetic beam, that gently warms
The Universe, and to each inward part
With gentle penetration, though unseen,
Shoots invisible virtue even to the deep. (III, 571–86)

While Milton may "hesitate" in this passage between the Copernican and Ptolemaic views of the universe, as Merritt Y. Hughes remarks in his note on line 575 (p. 272), the focal image of the dance is certainly the sun. Phrases like "the great Luminary" and "his Lordly eye" intensify the association between the earthly sun and the Son of God. The celestial dance and the dance of the spheres, with their emphasis on monarchical figures, remind us of the court masques of the sixteenth and seventeenth centuries, in which dancers performed for the honor and delight of royalty, whose thrones were often raised on a dais at one end of the ballroom. Just as the angels perform for the honor of God, the dance of the spheres pays homage to the sun/Son. They "towards his all-cheering Lamp / Turn swift their various motions, or are turn'd / By his Magnetic beam"[13] (582–83). Whereas the heavenly dance is given temporal dimension only for human comprehension, the dance of the stars and planets celebrates temporal measure and generation: the "Starry dance" moves "in numbers that compute / Days, months, and years" (580–81). The sun's generative beam reminds us of both the Son's effective power in creation and the spiritual insemination that is the light of conscience: The sun/Son's beam "gently warms / The Universe, and to each inward part / With gentle penetration, though unseen, / Shoots invisible virtue even to the deep" (583–86).[14]

The last four words are highly suggestive, for they point back to the opening lines of the passage where the sun's light "Allur'd [Satan's] eye" (573). It seems that more than physical light draws Satan's attention to the sun. It is perhaps the sun's spiritually "Magnetic beams" (583), the beams of conscience and also of grace. Although the Father has explained the fallen angels' inability to convert in Book III, the passage hints at the possibility that the Son's mercy might extend to Satan himself—"even to the deep" (586). But Satan, in order to join in the harmonic circle, must, like the stars, praise the creative agent and bow his diminished head, and this Satan will not or cannot do. Satan's sense of attraction to the sun/Son anticipates his inner struggle in Book IV before rededicating himself to malice and revenge. The sun's attraction thus accounts for the sadness and bitterness when Satan, refusing to submit, cries out: "O Sun, to tell thee how I hate thy beams / That bring to my remembrance from what state I fell" (IV, 37–38).

As the image of the dancing stars evokes a sense of harmony, tenderness, and creative potency, the flight of Satan is obscure, oblique, and eccentric: "but up or down / By centre, or eccentric, hard to tell, / Or Longitude" (574–76). The fallen angel flying precariously among the stars becomes a part of the total choreographic design. Satan is not merely dancing with feigned pleasure as in the heavenly round; he is an antimasque figure in his grim and wild state.

This tormented, self-deceived angel, buffeted by the winds and lost among the stars, reminds us of his fallen legions imprisoned below, who console themselves while awaiting their champion with "Vain wisdom" and "partial" song. The attempts of the fallen angels to imitate the harmony of the blessed are indeed similar to those of Comus's riotous crew, who suppose themselves capable of mirroring the dance of stars:

> We that are of purer fire
> Imitate the Starry Choir,
> Who in their nightly watchful Spheres,
> Lead in swift round the Months and Years. (111–14)

The incantatory revel of Comus and his followers, however, more closely resembles the dances of fairy elves and witches than the dance of stars: "Come knit hands, and beat the ground / In a light fantastic round" (143–44). Just so, the songs and rhetoric of the fallen angels charm the listeners only to entangle them more fully in "wandring mazes" as they "reason'd high / Of Providence, Foreknowledge, Will, and Fate, / Fixt Fate, Free will, Foreknowledge absolute, / And found no end, in wand'ring mazes lost" (II, 558–61). Because they, like the bestial crew of Comus, have subjected reason to passion, pride, and sensual delight, the fallen angels are now as fluid and ambivalent in their physical forms as they are lost in the mazes of their thoughts. One moment they seem "In bigness to surpass Earth's Giant Sons" and the next are "less than smallest Dwarfs" (778–79). Though Satan attempts to hide his malignity by using the guise of a cherub (just as Comus puts on the garb of a shepherd), Uriel eventually recognizes him for an enemy when Satan gestures grotesquely atop Mt. Niphates: "and on th' *Assyrian* mount / Saw him disfigur'd, more than could befall / Spirit of happy sort: his gestures fierce / He mark'd and mad demeanor" (IV, 126–29). Uriel's vision, unlike God's all-seeing eyes, has recognized Satan late. Satan's deception thus lends a foreboding quality to his masked presence as he joins the paradisal dance.

As we approach Eden, the generative values associated with the dance grow stronger still, for all of nature seems to participate in a procreative and innocent dance:

The Birds thir choir apply; airs, vernal airs,
Breathing the smell of field and grove, attune
The trembling leaves, while Universal *Pan*
Knit with the *Graces* and the *Hours* in dance,
Led on th' Eternal Spring. (IV, 264–68)

The association of the world's creation with dancing goes back, according to E.M.W. Tillyard, to the early Greek philosophers who envisioned creation as "an act of music." The metaphor was then adopted by medieval writers, such as Isidore of Seville who tells us: "Nothing exists without music; for the universe itself is said to have been framed by a kind of harmony of sounds, and the heaven itself revolves under the tones of that harmony."[15]

As early as *On the Morning of Christ's Nativity*, Milton associates musical harmony with the story of creation:

Such music (as 'tis said)
Before was never made,
But when of old the sons of morning sung,
While the Creator Great
His constellations set,
And the well-balan'ct world on hinges hung,
And cast the dark foundations deep,
And bid the welt'ring waves their oozy channel keep. (116–23)

Here music suggests a power that creates by placing ("on hinges hung") and containing ("their oozy channel keep"). The balanced phrasing and rhymed couplets reinforce a sense of structuring by restraint. The creation story of *Paradise Lost*, however, swells in baroque fullness, expressing the flow and playfulness of becoming as well as the sacredness of being. The songs of birds mingle with the hymns of angels to create a harmony that blends the "Lydian airs" of *L'Allegro* with the "Prophetic strain" of *Il Penseroso*. Complementing this joyous music, each natural thing springs to life filled with spontaneous energy and motion as though called to dance. The creation of the plants emphasizes through active verbs a sense of the world's dynamic order and copious grace:

Forth *flourish'd* thick the clust'ring Vine, *forth crept*
The smelling Gourd, *up stood* the corny Reed
Embattl'd in her field: and th' humble Shrub,
And Bush with frizzl'd hair implicit: last
Rose as in a Dance the stately Trees, and *spread*
Thir branches hung with copious Fruit.
(VII, 320–25, emphasis added)

Like the plants, the prelapsarian animals move in harmony and joy. Just as the angels praise God through their masque and the stars pay homage to the sun/Son, the animals frolic about Adam and Eve as if to express their obedience and love:

> About them frisking play'd
> All Beasts of the Earth, since wild, and of all chase
> In Wood or Wilderness, Forest or Den;
> Sporting the Lion ramp'd, and in his paw
> Dandl'd the Kid; Bears, Tigers, Ounces, Pards
> Gamboll'd before them, th' unwieldy Elephant
> To make them mirth us'd all his might, and wreath'd
> His Lithe Proboscis. (IV, 340–47)

The dance of nature, though initiated by the abstract Word, must continue through the sexual responses of its creatures. Thus as the providential dance enters the realm of Paradise, it loses its abstract quality. The dance is no longer the symbolic reflection of the divine mind as in the masque of angels. It becomes vivid, sensual, and at times threatening. Without a desire for the chase, the animals exercise through sport and play. The elephant then wreathes his "Lithe Proboscis," forming at once the circle of nature's harmony and a symbol of the phallus. The circular image of harmony and generative power, however, is soon exchanged for the false circle as the narrator brings into focus the twisting coils of the snake: "close the Serpent sly / Insinuating, wove with Gordian twine / His braided train, and of his fatal guile / Gave proof unheeded" (IV, 347–50). As we come closer to the temptation, the disturbing element within the cosmic dance takes a more tangible and sinister form. The mazelike pattern of the heavenly dance and the eccentric flight of Satan entering the masque of the stars find a natural and frightening corollary in the "Gordian twine" of the serpent.

The contrast between innocent sexual play and sinister sexual guile is more poignantly felt in the bower scenes as Adam and Eve join in the dance of procreation. As Adam says in Book VIII, their nuptials were celebrated by the stars and by the hills, birds, gales, and airs of the earth with music and a gentle, dancelike sympathy:

> To the Nuptial Bow'r
> I led her blushing like the Morn: all Heav'n,
> And happy Constellations on that hour
> Shed thir selectest influence; the Earth
> Gave sign of gratulation, and each Hill;
> Joyous the Birds; fresh Gales and gentle Airs

Whisper'd it to the Woods, and from thir wings
Flung Rose, flung Odors from the spicy Shrub,
Disporting, till the amorous Bird of Night
Sung Spousal, and bid haste the Ev'ning Star
On his Hill top, to light the bridal Lamp. (VIII, 510–20)

Adam's words "And happy Constellations on that hour / Shed thir selectest influence" remind us of the dance of the stars at the world's creation: "and the *Pleiades* before him danc'd / Shedding sweet influence" (VII, 374–75). The consummation of the love of Adam and Eve completes the creation of the world itself, and so their nuptial, like the creation of the heavenly bodies, is celebrated through dance. Thus Adam and Eve become the center of nature's dance just as God is the center of the heavenly dance and the sun/Son is the center of the dance of the spheres.

This blessed and protected night sharply contrasts the sinister though beautiful description of Adam and Eve's evening in the bower following Satan's appearance in Paradise. We recall that a hymn of praise celebrating God's care and protection precedes the entry of the sinless couple into the bower:

how often from the steep
Of echoing Hill or Thicket have we heard
Celestial voices to the midnight air,
Sole, or responsive each to other's note
Singing thir great Creator; oft in bands
While they keep watch, or nightly rounding walk,
With Heav'nly touch of instrumental sounds
In full harmonic number join'd, thir songs
Divide the night, and lift our thoughts to Heaven. (IV, 680–88)

The image of the angels' vigilant rounds corresponds to the never-sleeping eyes of God following the Dance of the Blessed in Book V. Realizing the presence of Satan in the Garden, the mention of angel bands keeping watch reminds us not only of God's Providence but also of Eden's vulnerability. The narrator then describes Adam and Eve as they enter the lush and gorgeous bower hand in hand: "Thus talking hand in hand alone they pass'd / On to thir blissful Bower" (IV, 689–90). The image of the sinless couple holding hands suggests the concord and the intimacy of married love. Roland Frye tells us that the image of holding hands is rarely seen in Renaissance art except in depictions of a dance: "The natural joining of hands may be found in representations of the dance, where it was indisputably common, but it almost never appears under other circumstances."[16] In *The Boke Named the Gouernour*, Sir Thomas Elyot explains the symbolism of men and women joining hands in the act of dancing:

In euery daunse, of a moste auncient custome, there daunseth to gether a man and a woman, holding eche other by the hande or the arme, whiche betokeneth concorde. Nowe it behouethe the daunsers and also the beholders of them to knowe all qualities incident to a man, and also all qualities to a woman lyke wyse appertaynynge.

A man in his naturall perfection is fiers, hardy, stronge in opinion, couaitous of glorie, desirous of knowlege, appetiting by generation to brynge forthe his semblable. The good nature of a woman is to be milde, timerouse, tractable, benigne, of sure remembrance, and shamfast. Diuers other qualities of eche of them mought be founde out, but these be most apparaunt, and for this sufficient.

Wherefore, whan we beholde a man and a woman daunsinge to gether, let us suppose there to be a concorde of all the saide qualities, beinge ioyned to gether, as I haue set them in ordre. And the meuing of the man wolde be more vehement, of the woman more delicate, and with lasse aduancing of the body, signifienge the courage and strenthe that oughte to be in a man, and the pleasant sobrenesse that shulde be in a woman. And in this wise *fiersenesse* ioyned with *mildenesse* maketh *Seuertie; Audacitie* with *timerositie* maketh *Magnanimitie.*[17]

An engraving of the dance by Giacomo Franco (fig. 5) displays these ennobling qualities, for the woman appears compliant, poised, and serene while the man looks bold and assertive. The idea of harmony extends to the social arena in *Grand Ball* by F. A. (fig. 6), as couples promenade hand in hand to form a circle. The trust and concord between male and female provide the necessary support for community.

Elyot's lines and the engravings of Franco and F. A., as they praise the complementary virtues of male and female exhibited in dance, may remind us of Adam's plea to God for a human mate that will bring him completion and company, "Of fellowship I speak / Such as I seek, fit to participate / All rational delight, wherein the brute / Cannot be human consort; they rejoice / Each with thir kind, Lion with Lioness; / So fitly them in pairs thou hast combin'd" (VIII, 389–94). While the story of Adam's sense of completion in his human mate and his growing submission to Eve unfolds gradually in *Paradise Lost*, the narrative emerges in a single moment in Joannes Saenredam's *Adam and Eve* (fig. 7), one of the rare visual depictions of Adam and Eve joining hands. While not technically a dance, Adam's stylized pose with right leg extended, left shoulder lowered, and head inclined toward Eve, suggests the courtesy and affection displayed by dancers. Though hands are joined, the male and female roles are clearly reversed, for Adam's stance expresses com-

Figure 5. Giacomo Franco, engraving for *Il Ballarino di Fabritio Caroso da Sermoneta*, Venice, 1581. (Courtesy of Tobin Collection, McNay Art Museum, San Antonio, Texas.)

Figure 6. F. A., *Grand Ball at a Residence in Vienna in 1566*. (By permission of The British Library, London.)

Figure 7. Joannes Saenredam, *Adam and Eve*, ca. 1600, in *The Kitto Bible*, 1850? (Reprinted by permission of The Huntington Library, San Marino, California.)

pliance and submission while Eve, leading Adam with outstretched arm, uplifted head, and body turned beautifully and fully to her audience's view, displays surety and power. The interlaced fingers lend tragic poignancy to the scene, for the intimacy and love between male and female is precariously poised. We know that Adam's steps toward the tree will soon separate hands and hearts.

We develop a similar tragic awareness as Milton's Adam and Eve enjoy their last night of perfect love. As they enter the bower hand in hand, they are sinless and together complete. They combine both the masculine and the feminine virtues in perfect concord. Their entrance into the bower, however, is like the first step into a mazelike and disturbing dance, a dance that moves from the sweet revels of love to a dream in which identities blur and Satan, a second partner, hides behind the voice of Adam: "Close at mine ear one call'd me forth to walk / With gentle voice, I thought it thine" (V, 36–37). Although beautiful in its copiousness, the interwoven and shaded bower portends psychic danger:

each beauteous flow'r,
Iris all hues, Roses, and Jessamin
Rear'd high thir flourisht heads between, and wrought
Mosaic; underfoot the Violet,
Crocus, and Hyacinth with rich inlay
Broider'd the ground, more color'd than with stone
Of costliest Emblem. (IV, 697–703)

The word *mosaic*, meaning a complex and intricate design, comes from the Greek μοῦσα, meaning *muse*, and so implies both music and dance. The phrase "wrought Mosaic," however, seems emphatic and jarring, for *wrought* does not suggest music but the hammering and beating of metals, and is particularly harsh when referring to flowers. The phrase "costliest Emblem" is also suggestive, for it not only refers to the richness of colors and visual design but also proleptically suggests the cost or penalty of the Fall and the sacrifice to be paid for redemption. The bower then is a mazed and gorgeous covering as well as a moral emblem of the fragile quality of innocent love.

The narrator interlaces his description of the bower not only with flowers but also with disturbing allusions. He recalls the time when Eve was first brought to her bridal bed more lovely than Pandora:

Pandora, whom the Gods
Endow'd with all thir gifts, and O too like
In sad event, when to the unwiser Son
Of *Japhet* brought by *Hermes*, she ensnar'd

Mankind with her fair looks, to be aveng'd
On him who had stole *Jove's* authentic fire. (IV, 714–19)

The box, a symbol of female sexuality, is for Japhet both mysterious and fatal. Although the narrator opposes Eve's innocence to Pandora's treachery, the allusion suggests the fraud and seduction that lie ahead. As Adam and Eve move "handed" into the recesses of the bower, their purity of love is contrasted to the beguiling and hypocritical lovers of the fallen world:

into thir inmost bower
Handed they went; and eas'd the putting off
These troublesome disguises which wee wear,
Straight side by side were laid, nor turn'd I ween
Adam from his fair Spouse, nor *Eve* the Rites
Mysterious of connubial Love refus'd. (IV, 738–43)

After exalting married love as a "mysterious Law . . . Founded in Reason, Loyal, Just, and Pure," the poet turns from the hard tone of pronouncement to the image of playful and delicate lovemaking: "Here Love his golden shafts imploys, here lights / His constant Lamp, and waves his purple wings, / Reigns here and revels" (IV, 763–65).[18] The narrator assures us that Adam and Eve's revel at this moment is not like those which we might imagine in our postlapsarian state:

not in the bought smile
Of Harlots, loveless, joyless, unindear'd
Casual fruition, nor in Court Amors
Mixt Dance, or wanton Mask, or Midnight Ball
Or Serenate, which the starv'd Lover sings
To his proud fair, best quitted with disdain. (IV, 765–70)

As the narrator fervently disclaims the lascivious dances, he nonetheless appropriates them to the scene. The images seem to wait on the other side of consciousness, just beyond the shelter of the purple-winged amoretto. The weight of the catalogs makes the revel of holy, wedded love appear ephemeral and fragile at best. Through the accumulation of images—the guardian angels, the "inwoven shade," the allusion to Pan and Pandora, and the lengthy descriptions of profane and lustful dancing—we sense the presence of the arch antimasquer near at hand: "him there they found / Squat like a Toad, close at the ear of *Eve*" (IV, 799–800).

Elyot describes in the myth of Proteus some features of masking that are appropriate to Satan in the larger providential dance:

> Some interpretours of poets do imagine that Proteus, who is supposed to haue turned him selfe in to sondry figures, as some tyme to shew him selfe like a serpent, some tyme like a lyon, other whiles like water, a nother time like the flame of fire, signifieth to be none other, but a deliuer and crafty daunser, which in his daunse coulde imagine the inflexions of the serpente, the softe and delectable flowynge of the water, the swifnes and mounting of the fire, the fierce rage of the lyon, the violence and furie of libarde. (*The Gouernour*, chap. XX, p. 215)

Similar to Proteus's elusive and subtle dancing, Satan rhythmically shifts from the form of cherub to that of cormorant, mist, toad, and finally serpent.[19] Satan's slippery metamorphoses provide the mazelike pattern which only Christ can shape into the circle of harmony at the world's end.[20]

An emblem by George Wither entitled "Through many Spaces, Time doth run" (fig. 8) may in a simple manner image Milton's complex treatment of the providential dance in *Paradise Lost.* Wither uses images of the dance and the uroborus, the serpent devouring its tail, to symbolize the concept of Providence. Similar to Plato's dance of the spheres in *The Republic* and his description of the creation of planetary bodies in *Timaeus*, the planets and seasons wheel around in "everlasting rings." The four seasons mentioned in Wither's poem tell us that we are in a fallen world, and the emblem gives visual confirmation of the fact by including contrasting landscapes within the frame. The barren branches represent winter and the birds and luxuriant vegetation symbolize spring. Comfort, however, comes in our knowledge of the continuance of the seasonal cycle. Spring comes with the "Resurrections" of natural things. The word *resurrections*, suggesting the mysteries of Christ's sacrifice and the hope of eternal life, climaxes the verse paragraph on the dance of the spheres. The seasonal "roundells," the poet tells us, "shew the Mystery / Of that immense and blest *Eternitie*" (19–20). Just as the providential dance in Milton's epic includes wandering and labyrinthine movement, so in Wither's poem the round (which is also a "scrowle") progresses by "Vnfolding" and "Infolding." The poet concludes by stressing the round's ultimate mystery: "Tis that which is, but, cannot uttered be" (30). The uroborus in the emblem indicates that jarring contraries are reconciled through Providence. Evil works ultimately to God's good, and the cycle of seasonal change will be transformed through the resurrection of Christ into the holy round of eternity.

Before entering the serpent, Satan again describes the dance of the spheres but this time with a strong Ptolemaic emphasis:

> O Earth, how like to Heav'n, if not preferr'd
> More justly, Seat worthier of Gods, as built

Through many ſpaces, Time *doth run*,
And, endeth, *where it firſt* begun. 157

ILLVSTR. XXIII. *Book.3*

OLd *Sages* by the Figure of the Snake
(Encircled thus) did oft expreſſion make
Of *Annuall-Revolutions*; and of things,
Which wheele about in *everlaſting-rings*;
There *ending*, where they firſt of all *begun*,
And, there *beginning*, where the *Round* was *done*.
Thus, doe the *Planets*; Thus, the *Seaſons* doe;
And, thus, doe many other *Creatures*, too.
By minutes, and by houres, the *Spring* ſteales in,
And, rolleth on, till *Summer* doth begin:
The *Summer* brings on *Autumne*, by degrees;
So ripening, that the eye of no man ſees
Her Entrances. That *Seaſon*, likewiſe, hath
To *Winter-ward*, as leaſurely a path:
And, then, cold *Winter* wheeleth on amaine,
Vntill it brings the *Spring* about againe,
With all thoſe *Reſurrections*, which appeare,
To wait upon her comming, every yeare.
Theſe *Roundells*, helpe to ſhew the *Myſtery*
Of that immenſe and bleſt *Eternitie*,
From whence the CREATVRE ſprung, and, into *whom*
It ſhall, againe, with full perfection come,
When thoſe *Additions*, it hath fully had,
Which all the ſev'rall *Orbes* of *Time* can add.
It is a full, and fairely written *Scrowle*,
Which up into it ſelfe, it ſelfe doth rowle;
And, by *Vnfolding*, and, *Infolding*, ſhowes
A *Round*, which neither *End*, nor *entrance* knowes.
And (by this *Emblem*) you may partly ſee,
Tis that which *IS*, but, cannot uttred be.

Each

Figure 8. George Wither, "Through many Spaces, Time Doth run" in *A Collection of Emblemes Ancient and Moderne*, 1635. (Courtesy of The Newberry Library, Chicago.)

With second thoughts, reforming what was old!
For what God after better worse would build?
Terrestrial Heav'n, danc't round by other Heav'ns
That shine, yet bear thir bright officious Lamps,
Light above Light, for thee alone, as seems,
In thee concentring all thir precious beams
Of sacred influence: As God in Heav'n
Is Centre, yet extends to all, so thou
Centring receiv'st from all those Orbs; in thee,
Not in themselves, all thir known virtue appears
Productive in Herb, Plant, and noble birth
Of Creatures animate with gradual life
Of Growth, Sense, Reason, all summ'd up in Man. (IX, 99–113)

Perhaps due to his fervent grief or to a perverted sense of value, Satan raises earthly grace and beauty above heavenly virtue. While the earlier description of the dance of the spheres emphasized the seminal power of the sun/Son, Satan's tribute centers on the earth's feminine qualities of receptivity and fertility. Impregnated by the precious celestial beams, the earth gives birth to plants and animals and accounts for the rational and spiritual growth of "Man." The geocentric dance stresses the glory and procreative abundance of the earth, the globe that Satan, masked as a phallic serpent, believes himself poised to uncreate.

With this description of the earth's life-giving power, we feel an intense sadness that this harmonious and perfect dance must soon end. As Satan enters the serpent, his coiling motion, unlike the dance of the spheres, images false harmony, indeed a dance of death. Like the minstrel grave diggers and jesting skeletons of the dance of death, Satan invites opposites to take hands and follow. After tasting the forbidden fruit, Adam will not merely take Eve's hand but will seize her hand in order to lead her to a new kind of revel, one filled with "contagious Fire," "exhilirating vapor," and "mutual guilt." The lascivious play of Adam and Eve after tasting the fatal fruit and the seductive dances of their children as seen in the prophetic scenes of Books XI and XII have as their model not the revels of heaven but the distorted and hypnotic dances of hell.

Following the Fall, Satan flies back to hell to bring news of his magnificent triumph, but as he reaches the pinnacle of that "bad eminence" he finds his celebrants and soon himself twisting and hissing—a mass of horrid asps. No more is hell's song partial as before the Fall, nor can it charm the senses to a brief suspension of hell (II, 552, 556). All is hissing and buzzing. The maze that provided interest and beauty to the heavenly dance finds its counterpart in this parody of harmonic movement—mazes not merely "intricate" and "intervolved" but grotesque in their restless, compulsory involutions. And the counterpart to the "communion sweet" following the heavenly dance is the gluttonous engorging of apples that transubstantiate into ashes.[21]

The fallen angels' hissing and swarming brings to horrid completion an earlier image of parodic triumph. When Satan calls his fallen legions to rise from the burning lake, they come "Thick swarm'd, both on the ground and in the air / Brusht with the hiss of rustling wings. As Bees / In spring time" (I, 767–69). In his poem *Orchestra*, Sir John Davies tells us that military marches should be viewed as a bold and manly dance. His soldiers march with "perfect measure" in "well-set ranks" in "Quadrant forme or semicircular" into "well-order'd war."[22] Contrasting this valiant directness, Satan's soldiers move as indistinguishable insects or "smallest dwarfs" crammed into a "narrow room." The quality of insubstantiality and vagueness in the word *seem'd*—"they but now who *seem'd* / In bigness to surpass Earth's Giant Sons" (777–79, emphasis added)—is carried into the metaphor of the dancing elves:

> like that Pigmean Race
> Beyond the *Indian* Mount, or Faery Elves,
> Whose midnight Revels, by a Forest side
> Or Fountain some belated Peasant sees,
> Or dreams he sees, while over-head the Moon
> Sits Arbitress, and nearer to the Earth
> Wheels her pale course; they on thir mirth and dance
> Intent, with jocund Music charm his ear;
> At once with joy and fear his heart rebounds. (I, 780–88)

The dreamy quality of the elfin dance anticipates the subtle strategy that the fallen angels will eventually support. Indeed, the unwary peasant who "sees, / Or dreams he sees" the faery dance closely parallels Eve's visual and auditory experience when sleeping in the bower. The pygmy dance works on the subconscious of the peasant, filling him with conflicting feelings of joy and fear. Eve describes her sense of the dream as one lifting her to "high exaltation" and as quickly letting her sink into depression and fear.

The satanic dance takes on a far more horrifying character in the description of Sin and the hellhounds that kennel in her womb. The hounds are said to be more ugly than

> the Night-Hag, when call'd
> In secret, riding through the Air she comes
> Lur'd with the smell of infant blood, to dance
> With *Lapland* Witches, while the laboring Moon
> Eclipses at thir charms. (II, 662–66)

Like the hellhounds, which move rapaciously in and out of Sin's womb, the witch's flight suggests a kind of narcotic masturbation. The hag's ride "through the Air" connotes the way witches would force hallucinogens into their systems either vaginally or anally to achieve mystical flight to the black sabbaths. Like a hound, the Night-Hag depends on the olfactory sense to guide her to the scene of infant sacrifice. She is secretly called, "Lured with the smell of infant blood." By blaspheming the sacrifice of Christ through the parodic slaying of an innocent babe, the witches empower their spells. The shifting moon, who was arbitress in the elfin dance, now takes a more vigorous role, "laboring" and eclipsing as the witches perform their ghastly dance. With its brutal narcissism, violating all that does not image the self, the witches' revel becomes the complete inversion of the heavenly dance, which celebrates the reciprocal love of God and angels. The dance of the blessed images Providence and implicitly the concept of free will. Rhythm and graceful movement are a joyful expression of the freedom of life. The dance of the pygmy elves and the Night Hag's obscene, incantatory rites function to imprison the human will, to shut down the passages of sight, as in hypnosis, and stir the passions to sin.

As the dances blaspheme the sanctity of Christ's sacrifice, they suggest the waste and futility of demonic energy. We recall the vain worshippers of Moloch in the Nativity ode, whose frenetic dances are wasted in worship of a banished god: "In vain with Cymbals' ring / They call the grisly king / In dismal dance about the furnace blue" (208–10). The cymbals resonate emptiness, for Moloch, who demands the sacrifice of children, has fled at the news of Christ's birth. So, too, the dance of Hecate, as it celebrates the slaying of innocents, parodically suggests the crucifixion and evil's ultimate futility in the providential design.

When Adam ascends the mountain with the angel Michael to see and hear the prophecy of human history, he views dances not far removed from those associated with hell. Adam had been told by Raphael the joys of the heavenly dance; now, again for educational purposes, he views a dance of a different kind. To remember Milton's early plans to portray the prophetic visions as a masque is to accentuate the musical and rhythmical suggestiveness of scenes such as the seduction of the sons of God by the daughters of men and the spiritual corruption of Sodom. Some vestiges of the original masque may be found in the description of the seductive advances of the daughters of men:

> they on the Plain
> Long had not walkt, when from the Tents behold
> A Bevy of fair Women, richly gay

In Gems and wanton dress; to the Harp they sung
Soft amorous Ditties, and in dance came on:
The Men though grave, ey'd them, and let thir eyes
Rove without rein, till in the amorous Net
Fast caught, they lik'd, and each his liking chose;
And now of love they treat till th' Ev'ning Star
Love's Harbinger appear'd; then all in heat
They light the Nuptial Torch, and bid invoke
Hymen, then first to marriage Rites invok't;
With Feast and Music all the Tents resound.
Such happy interview and fair event
Of love and youth not lost, Songs, Garlands, Flow'rs,
And charming Symphonies attach'd the heart. (XI, 580–95)

The mention of the nuptial torch takes us back in our memories to Adam's last innocent revel of love. The privacy and caring in the male and female relationship is now exchanged for indiscriminate unions based on appetite. The "Bevy of fair Women" is an image akin to the swarming bees and faery elves of hell, an image suggesting diminution and prostitution.[23] Joannes Sadeler's engraving *Jubal* (fig. 9) illustrates the indiscriminate and frenzied quality of this fallen dance. Bending to the desires of promiscuous dancers, workers in the foreground forge musical instruments. Two amoretti assist these laborers while three others dance gleefully in the background, supporting the revels of bare-breasted women and exhilarated men.[24] We respond with sadness to this scene, for the pastoral, intimate, and graceful world of Saenredam's *Adam and Eve* has yielded to city life, where bodies grow gnarled and bent with labor and age and where the young submit to sexual license and delusive gaiety. In *Paradise Lost* Adam's response to the visionary dance is particularly interesting, for like the sons of Lamech he is charmed by the dance and caught in the "amorous Net" of love. The fallen Adam cannot distinguish between the "amorous Ditties" sung to the harps of wanton women and the angelic symphonies heard nightly from his bower in Paradise. So Adam, like Dante rounding the gyres of hell, must be taught by his spiritual mentor the correct responses to the things he sees.

By the end of the poem, however, Adam and Eve have both obtained some understanding of Providence and of the parts they will play in God's eventual uniting of "all things in heaven and all things on earth." They grieve for the destruction that will proceed from their sins and rejoice in God's promise of restoration through the "Promis'd Seed." Eve tells us that she knows all that Adam has seen. Her understanding, however, has come through a dream rather than through discursive narrative. Eve's dream, implying a passive and intuitive way to truth and grace,

Figure 9. Joannes Sadeler I (1550–1600) after Marten de Vos, *Jubal* in *The Kitto Bible*. (Reprinted by permission of The Huntington Library.)

complements Adam's more active, intellectual experience on the mountain. Thus the events of Books XI and XII, by distinguishing the virtues or ways of knowing particular to each sex, rejoin the male and female figures for the providential dance. The final lines of the poem suggest the couple's delicate and cautious steps into the next movement of human history. Adam and Eve's hands are again joined in concord, though their "wand'ring steps" and "solitary" journey indicate the uncertainty and loneliness of their advance:

> The World was all before them, where to choose
> Thir place of rest, and Providence thir guide:
> They hand in hand with wand'ring steps and slow,
> Through *Eden* took thir solitary way. (XII, 646–49)

The phrase "Providence thir guide" now bears a new significance, for the archangel, after leading Adam and Eve hastily through the gates of Paradise and down the cliff to the "subjected Plain," disappears. No longer do angels stand near at hand to teach the couple holy steps. The images of a "flaming Brand" and of "dreadful Faces throng'd and fiery Arms" emphasize the new relation between angels and humanity. Angels will no longer watch over the couple who are the sum of Paradise but will vigilantly guard Paradise from their reentry. Adam and Eve are irrevocably cut off from the music of angels and the dance of innocent nature. Though they must now negotiate God's complex maze without direct guidance, they do not move in total blindness, but according to their own intellect and faith. Indeed, Providence now moves largely into their hands: "The World was all before them, where to choose." To help explain the extension of this concept at the close of *Paradise Lost*, we may recall Sir Thomas Elyot's description of the movement of the dance signifying Providence. While acknowledged as an attribute of God, Providence is considered primarily a human virtue: "Prouidence is whereby a man not only foreseeth commoditie and incommoditie, prosperitie and adversitie, but also consulteth, and therewith endeuoureth as well to repelle anoyaunce as to attaine and gette profite and advuauntage" (*The Gouernour*, chap. XXIII, p. 246).

In *Christian Doctrine* Milton similarly claims that God has made us governors of matters moral and religious: "Obviously if religious matters were not under our control, or to some extent within our power and choice, God could not enter into a covenant with us, and we could not keep it, let alone swear to keep it" (YP VI, p. 398). Milton supports this assertion by referring to 2 Chronicles xv, 12, 14, a passage blending the ideas of covenant and musical celebration. Adding to his references verse

Figure 10. Henry Fuseli, *The Expulsion* in F. J. Du Roveray's edition of *Paradise Lost*, 1802. (Reprinted by permission of The Huntington Library, San Marino, California.)

15, which brings a sense of closure to the passage, we discover the word *rest*, a word figuring prominently in the closing lines of Milton's epic:

> And they entered into a covenant to seek the Lord God of their fathers with all their heart and with all their soul. . . . And they sware unto the Lord with a loud voice, and with shouting, and with trumpets, and with cornets. And all Judah rejoiced at the oath: for they had sworn with all their heart, and sought him with their whole desire; and he was found of them: and the Lord gave them rest round about.

The covenant drawn by God at the close of *Paradise Lost* is held in Eve's final words: "By me the Promis'd Seed shall all restore." Adam and Eve's slow, deliberate steps to the subjected plain signify their agreement to God's covenant. Unlike the tribe of Israel, the triumphal tone is subdued by a sense of incredible loss and the perplexity of facing choices never imagined before. The passage indeed suggests the lyrical and elegiac tones of strings and woodwinds rather than the crisp, sharp sounds of brass. Adam and Eve now must provide for themselves and create their own world. Though largely estranged from God, they ironically become more godlike, for they are choreographers of as well as performers in the cosmic dance. In his illustration of the expulsion (fig. 10), Henry Fuseli beautifully images the quality of dancing in Milton's last lines. Fuseli has removed Adam and Eve from the social arena of the masque to the intimate and romantic world of ballet. The archangel has turned his back to the couple, who move forward, painfully, but with tenderness and grace. The masque may reflect the cosmic scheme, but the ballet reveals the cosmos of male and female as they alone create, in the face of death and with the hope of eternity, a new earth. Thus, with the deliberate and sorrowful steps of Adam and Eve, dance becomes the ultimate form of incarnation, for human flesh now embodies the spiritual message of guilt and grace.

Corpus Christi State University

NOTES

I would like to thank Ira Granville Clark, Susan Elaine Marshall, and Peter E. Medine for their invaluable suggestions during the revisions of this essay and the National Endowment of the Humanities for offering me the opportunity to study with John T. Shawcross at the Arizona Milton Institute.

1. *Complete Prose Works of John Milton*, 8 vols., ed. Don Wolfe et al. (New Haven, 1953–82), vol. VI, pp. 166–67, hereafter cited as YP.

2. *John Milton: Complete Poems and Major Prose*, ed. Merritt Y. Hughes (New York, 1957). All references to Milton's poetry will be to this edition.

3. Leo Spitzer, *Classical and Christian Ideas of World Harmony: Prolegomena to an Interpretation of the Word "Stimmung,"* ed. Anna Granville Hatcher (Baltimore, 1963), pp. 19–20. Discussing the masque's relation to order and love, John C. Meager quotes a significant passage from Lucian's *Peri Orchesos*, "Dance came into being contemporaneously with the primal origin of the universe, making her appearance together with Love—love that is age-old." In *Method and Meaning in Jonson's Masques* (Indiana, 1966), p. 85.

4. John Hollander, *The Untuning of the Sky: Ideas of Music in English Poetry, 1500–1700* (Princeton, 1961), p. 27.

5. Mortimer H. Frank, "Milton's Knowledge of Music," in *Milton and the Art of Sacred Song*, ed. J. Max Patrick and Roger H. Sundell (Wisconsin, 1979), p. 85.

6. Frank, "Milton's Knowledge of Music," pp. 92–93.

7. Frederick Hartt, *History of Italian Renaissance Art: Painting, Sculpture, Architecture* (New Jersey, 1979), p. 349.

8. Roland Mushat Frye, *Milton's Imagery and the Visual Arts: Iconographic Tradition in the Epic Poems* (Princeton, 1978), p. 100.

9. Michael Fixler, "Milton's Passionate Epic," in *Milton Studies*, I., ed. James D. Simmonds (Pittsburgh, 1969), p. 175.

10. Ben Jonson, *Pleasure Reconciled to Virtue*, in *Ben Jonson's Plays and Masques*, ed. Robert M. Adams (New York, 1979), p. 370.

11. Renaissance dance masters, philosophers, and poets often justify dancing as an art and an exercise that instructs in virtue both those who dance and those who watch. In *Method and Meaning in Jonson's Masques*, John C. Meagher writes: "The dance teaches both dancer and spectator, the former by giving order and discipline to expressive movement, the latter by drawing the attention and admiration to the same; both are perfected in the thing expressed through the order and excellence of the expression" (p. 99). "The ballet," Meagher continues, "is by its *nature* emblematic of virtuous and right order in general. . . . The same is true in reverse of deliberately awkward dances, such as Jonson uses for antimasques . . . [which] give a general portrayal of vice or deformity" (pp. 100–01).

12. According to Stephen Orgel, *The Jonsonian Masque* (Massachusetts, 1965), p. 35, "Grotesquerie and disorder are characteristics of 'misrule,' and relevant enough to the season of masques and revels. But even in the early disguisings, the antic masque was controlled by a larger structure, superseded—physically, if not always logically—by the court dances." Milton's heavenly dance closely follows the neoclassical style of Inigo Jones. Orgel writes of the change in the style and nature of the antimasque occurring after 1625. During the reign of King James, Ben Jonson's conception of the antimasque dominated the collaborative efforts of Jonson and Jones. For Jonson, the antimasque was comical, satiric, and bold. Under the reign of Charles, Jones's view held favor and the antimasque became greatly subdued. It was at times represented not by characters but by a maze within the court dance or by descriptions of antic dances. Orgel supports his point by quoting a passage from *Loves Triumph through Callipolis:* "All which, in varied, intricate turns, and involv'd mazes, exprest, make the Antimasque: and conclude the exit, in a circle" (pp. 79–80).

13. The association of the Son of God with dance may be found in the apocryphal

Acts of John, where Christ sings a hymn at the Last Supper and invites his apostles to dance:

> 95. 12. "I will pipe,
> Dance, all of you."—"Amen."
> . . . .
> 16. "To the Universe
> belongs the dancer."—"Amen."
> 17. "He who does not dance
> does not know what happens."—"Amen."
> . . . .
> 96. 28. "Now if you follow
> my dance,
> 29. see yourself
> in Me who am speaking,
> . . . .
> 31. You who dance, consider
> what I do, for yours is
> 32. This passion of Man
> which I am to suffer."

In E. Hennecke's *New Testament Apocrypha*, vol. 2, ed. W. Schneemelcher (London, 1965), pp. 229–30. This passage associates the dance with the passion of Christ and suggests a magical avenue to knowledge: "He who does not dance / does not know what happens." In *Classical and Christian Ideas of World Harmony*, Leo Spitzer comments on this text, pp. 27–28.

14. Readers familiar with Ficino will respond to the magical suggestiveness of Milton's treatment of the dance of stars. In *The Transcendental Masque: An Essay on Milton's "Comus"* (New York, 1971), p. 65, Angus Fletcher explains:

> For the celestial bodies possess number, organization, order in the highest degree, and above all, brilliance, which presents to the eye of the beholder an inherently magical sight. The stars dazzle . . . while the planets wander in their special ways, to be watched and understood as magical mirrors reflecting the wanderings of men on earth. The science of the stars include a range of occult lore, astrological in the main, which can be regarded as the source of divine *influence* over heroic action. Thus Ficino, according to [E. D.] Walker [in *Spiritual and Demonic Magic*], revived in *De Vita Coelitus Comparanda* a theory of astrological influence, ultimately stoic in origin, which postulates a cosmic spirit (*spiritus mundi*) flowing through the whole of the sensible universe, and thus providing a channel of influence between the heavenly bodies and the sublunar world.

15. Quoted in Tillyard, *The Elizabethan World Picture* (London, 1943), p. 94.

16. Frye, *Milton's Imagery and the Visual Arts*, p. 283.

17. Sir Thomas Elyot, *The Boke Named the Gouernour*, ed. Henry Herbert Stephen Croft, vol. I. (1531; rpt. London, 1883), pp. 235–38.

18. Here Milton suggests a similar though more delicate and intimate revel than the innocent wedding festivities of *L'Allegro:*

> There let *Hymen* oft appear
> In Saffron robe, with Taper clear,

And pomp, and feast, and revelry,
With mask, and antique Pageantry. (125–28)

19. Orgel, *The Jonsonian Masque*, p. 10, explains that Proteus is "the spirit of the masque, the embodiment of the idea of disguising," and represents to the Elizabethans "the great enemy Mutability."

20. I credit this idea to my colleague at the 1988 Arizona Milton Institute, Larry Langton of Metropolitan State College, Denver, Colorado.

21. After the Fall, the stars, planets, and all terrestrial life, which had formerly moved in harmonic order, join the antimask. Michael Lieb selects those passages that best reveal this dramatic alteration from graceful and creative movement to chaotic and "uncreative" action: "Cosmically, the process of uncreation manifests itself in various ways. The sun moves in such a manner as to 'affect the Earth with cold and heat / Scarce tolerable,' thereby creating winter and summer (X, 651–56). The moon and other planets form a type of uncreative union, a 'joyning' in 'Synod unbenigne; (X, 656–61). . . . Within the confines of the earth a return to Chaos likewise ensues." Lieb illustrates with the passage:

Beast now with Beast gan war, and Fowl with Fowl,
And Fish with Fish; to graze the Herb all leaving,
Devour'd each other; nor stood much in awe
Of Man, but fled him, or with count'nance grim
Glar'd on him passing. (X, 710–14)

In *The Dialectics of Creation: Patterns of Birth and Regeneration in "Paradise Lost"* (Massachusetts, 1969), pp. 205–06.

22. Sir John Davies, *Orchestra*, in *The Poems of Sir John Davies*, ed. Robert Krueger (Oxford). Edited from the texts of 1596 and 1622, stanza 87, p. 113.

23. For John T. Shawcross the "Bevy of Fair Women" suggests prostitution and the temptation "concupiscentia oculorum," which is part of the second temptation of Jesus in *Paradise Regained*. Lecture at the 1988 NEH Arizona Milton Institute, The University of Arizona, Tucson, 1988.

24. Roland Frye discusses this engraving in *Milton's Imagery and the Visual Arts*, pp. 304–06.

STANDING ALONE ON THE PINNACLE: MILTON IN 1752

Ashraf H. A. Rushdy

Upon the slippery tops of human state,
  The gilded pinnacles of fate,
Let others proudly stand, and for a while,
  The giddy dangers to beguile,
With joy and with disdain look down on all,
  Till their heads turn, and down they fall.
—Abraham Cowley

No man stands more by himself than does Milton.
—George Dawson

THE ACTION OF *Paradise Regained* does not constitute an identity test. Two hundred and fifty years of literary explication have somehow made this idea the ascendant dogma of critical interpretation. I hope to show how damaging this dogma is to understanding Milton's narrative and theology. The idea of an "identity contest" has achieved that rare place in critical debate where it is both premise and conclusion, both the question asked and the answer given. I believe that it is the wrong question and the wrong answer.[1] To demonstrate this, I must return to the origin of the criticism of this poem and assess how modern exegesis has buttressed mistaken premises therein first proposed.

The modern critical assumptions about *Paradise Regained* as a whole, and of the pinnacle scene in particular, were established in the first variorum edition of the poem, originally published in 1752. We must return therefore to the annotators of that edition to discover the critical tradition concerning the issues that the pinnacle scene allegedly raises and resolves. Calton expresses the full gamut of these assumptions and might profitably be quoted at length. He writes:

In the Gospel account of the temptation no discovery is made of the incarnation; and this grand mystery is as little known to the Tempter at the end as at the beginning. But now, according to Milton's scheme, the poem was to be clos'd with a full discovery of it: there are *three* circumstances therefore, in which the poet, to serve his plan, hath varied from the accounts of the Gospels. 1. The critics have not been able to ascertain what the . . . *pinnacle* . . . was, on which Christ was set by the Demon: but whatever it was, the Evangelists make no difficulty of his standing there. This the poet (following the common use of the word *pinnacle* in our own language) supposeth to be something like those of the battlements of our churches, a pointed spire, on which Christ could not stand without a miracle. 2. In the poem, the Tempter bids Christ give proof of his pretensions by standing on the pinnacle, or by casting himself down. In the Gospels, the last only is or could be suggested. 3. In the Gospel account the prohibition *Thou shalt not tempt the Lord thy God* is alleged only as a reason why Christ (whose divinity is concealed there) must not throw himself down from the top of the temple, because this would have been *tempting God*. But in the poem it is applied to the Demon, and his attempt upon Christ; who is thereby declar'd to be the *Lord his God*.[2]

From these three circumstances Calton concludes that Milton has Jesus reveal to Satan the mystery of the Incarnation. But Calton's conclusion is also his presupposition: that Jesus reveals and Satan acknowledges the secret of the Incarnation. As concerns *Paradise Regained*, this conclusive presupposition has become perhaps the most widely held of critical orthodoxies in our century.

Calton founds a legacy to which so estimable a critic as Earl Miner adds weight when he argues that "the working-out of that mystery [of the Incarnation] constitutes the action of *Paradise Regained*."[3] What I hope to argue here is that this view and all three of Calton's circumstantial theses are untrue to the poem. While ultimately, of course, the evidence to disprove these ideas will have to come from the poem, we might simply note here that the Incarnation was the one mystery of Christianity which Milton chose not to discover even to himself. The subject of Christ's two natures, Milton comments, "is too profound a mystery, in my judgment at least, to warrant any positive assertion respecting it." And "since God has not revealed the mode in which this union is effected, it behoves us to cease from devising subtle explanations, and to be contented with remaining wisely ignorant."[4] True, *Paradise Regained* is Milton's one extended meditation on the Incarnation, but nowhere in the poem does Milton attempt to dispel the *mystery* of that event — and certainly nowhere does either Milton or Jesus clarify the issues of that mystery for Satan. To what extent Milton entered into that mystery I leave to my conclusion. Now we may turn to the critical tradition.

Although there is no unanimity among the critics of the poem, we may nonetheless discern and speak of a distinct and regnant orthodox reading of the pinnacle scene. It is an interpretation that both builds upon and supports the beliefs fostered by the preceding action in the narrative. That orthodox reading may be described briefly thus: Satan has heretofore been kept from knowing the Son's identity by Jesus' nonaffirmative answers. Because the poem is an "identity contest," Satan must not discover until the concluding scene that Jesus is the Son of God. So there must be a revelation of Jesus' status at the pinnacle: as Miner terms it, a "religious epiphany without an apotheosis" (*Restoration Mode*, p. 281). In order to assert this reading, it is necessary to argue that (1) standing on the pinnacle is humanly impossible; (2) a miracle sustains Jesus in his stand; (3) this miracle expresses the divinity of the Son; and (4) this miracle gives Satan the knowledge of the Son's divinity. Finally, what is presupposed in this reading is that there is a chasm between the previous temptations and this final one, for whereas Jesus could not reveal his divinity before, he is able to reveal it now. I hope, in this study, to show that each of these four arguments misrepresents the poem's plot, and that the presupposition of a chasm between the second and third temptations is a critical casuistry involving a severe falsification of Milton's design. As it is only upon these four arguments and baseless presuppositions that the interpretation of the poem as an identity contest may stand, the leveling of this base will, I hope, demonstrate how unjustified this interpretation is. We may begin by examining the first argument.

I

Satan takes up Jesus and sets out for Jerusalem, the tower, and the final temptation:

> There on the highest Pinacle he set
> The Son of God; and added thus in scorn:
> There stand, if thou wilt stand; to stand upright
> Will ask thee skill; I to thy Fathers house
> Have brought thee, and highest plac't; highest is best,
> Now shew thy Progeny; if not to stand,
> Cast thy self down; safely if Son of God:
> For it is written, He will give command
> Concerning thee to his Angels, in thir hands
> They shall up lift thee, lest at any time
> Thou chance to dash thy foot against a stone.
> To whom thus Jesus: also it is written,
> Tempt not the Lord thy God, he said and stood. (IV, 546–58).[5]

The word *set* may mean to be placed in either a stationary or a sitting position.[6] The orthodox interpretation of this scene assumes that standing on the pinnacle is humanly impossible. Either, then, Jesus is set in a crouching position of some sort, from which situation he stands when he articulates his answer to Satan's temptation, or he is set standing, but is maintained in this stand by God's invisible hand. In either case, the critics argue, in standing Jesus is either the instigator or recipient of a miracle, and he therefore (in either case) demonstrates his divinity.[7] Let us take up these issues individually: first, whether standing is possible or not; second, whether Jesus stands as an act or maintains the standing position in which he had been set; third, whether Jesus demonstrates any degree of divinity in his stand by a miracle.

Those who argue that standing is humanly impossible do so despite a dearth of evidence from either tradition or the poem. We might begin by noting that in the tradition of English commentary, almost all exegetes suggest that standing on the pinnacle is quite possible. Lancelot Andrewes goes so far as to argue that only such as have a "light and giddy brain" would be unable to stand on the pinnacle.[8] Calton noted that Milton somehow altered the significance of the pinnacle without altering the word itself: "the poet (following the common use of the word *pinnacle* in our own language) supposeth to be something like those of the battlements of our churches, a pointed spire, on which Christ could not stand without a miracle." Calton argues in effect that somehow Milton is able to invest the word used in Scripture with added (and contradictory) significance merely by the force of his personality. As to the first point, the English commentators use the word *pinnacle* without this supposition, thus making Calton's suggestion spurious.

The second point, though, is more susceptible to consideration. Milton does use the word *spire* in his elaboration. Barbara Lewalski holds that in this lay the difference between seventeenth-century exegetes and Milton. Whereas most of the "exegetes understood that Christ was placed upon a narrow ledge of the Temple, where he would be able to stand," Milton has Satan place Jesus "on the topmost spire where by human power alone he cannot stand" (*Brief Epic*, pp. 306–07; cf. p. 317). We may dispute this reading on two points. Initially, at least one commentator took into consideration the issue of the pinnacle as a spire. Isaac Colfe elaborates on Josephus's comment on the pinnacle thus: "That is, in the top it was rough with most sharp golden spires, least it should be defiled with the birds sitting thereon: but thus cannot the Pinnacle be here taken, but rather by this Pinnacle wee must (although digressing from the proprietie of the word) understand, the battlements wherewith the flat roofe of the Temple was compassed about, that none might fall therefrom."[9] Secondly, and more to the point, Milton does not have Satan place Jesus on the spire. The temple appears far off "like a Mount / Of Alabaster, top't with Golden Spires." The spires are part of the simile describing only the mount of alabaster. What Satan does, on the other hand, is set

Jesus "on the highest Pinacle" (IV, 544–46). There is no reason to determine that the pinnacle of the tenor is the spire of the vehicle. It is arguably the difference between semblance and reality, a difference only Satan would wish to eradicate.

The only evidence available for determining the possibility of standing on the temple comes from two passages in the poem. In the first, wherein Jesus is set on it, we have seen that there is a difference between the spire and the pinnacle, and that Jesus is set only on the latter. The accumulated wisdom of the English exegetical tradition on the temptation sequence agrees that while the pinnacle is certainly a dangerous place to stand, it is not one where standing is impossible. The second passage is that describing the angels assisting Jesus from off the pinnacle. They fly to him and receive him from his "uneasie station" (581). John Carey argues that "'uneasy station' implies that the standing was not miraculous but a balancing feat."[10] Two recent critics have disputed this reading, claiming that Carey's theory "is implausible." The "uneasie station," Burton Jasper Weber suggests, "describes the spire himself, not Jesus' feelings: the station is 'uneasy' not because Jesus is wobbling uncomfortably but because a man cannot stand there."[11] We must demur on three counts. First, we have seen that Jesus is not set on a spire, but on the pinnacle. Second, the angels receive Jesus from "*his* uneasie station" (my italics), and the pronoun would seem to describe Jesus' posture, not the pinnacle. Third, the word "uneasie" hardly seems capable of bearing the significance of impossibility. Standing, then, is not humanly impossible. It only asks skill and is not easy.

The second question is whether Jesus stands from another posture or whether he is standing from the time Satan sets him on the pinnacle. Two narrative facts—that Satan delivers a nine-line speech while Jesus is on the pinnacle and in that speech he intimates that standing will ask skill of Jesus—suggest that standing is quite possible (if difficult, as Satan says). I would like to suggest that Jesus is standing throughout the temptation. This interpretation, I shall argue, stands where traditional ones tend to follow Satan, and fall. Let me return to the pinnacle and Satan's final temptation, and then examine the traditional reading. Satan's speech is artful and requires some explication. He addresses Jesus "in scorn":

> There stand, if thou wilt stand; to stand upright
> Will ask thee skill; I to thy Fathers house
> Have brought thee, and highest plac't, highest is best,
> Now shew thy Progeny; if not to stand,
> Cast thy self down; safely if Son of God.

When, it may be asked, does the temptation begin? Satan has admirably shrouded the whole of the speech in ambiguity. He orders Jesus to stand where he has set him ("There stand"), and then alters this imperative into a conditional ("if thou wilt stand"). He changes the conditions of standing by adding an adverbial "upright" in qualification and suggests the difficulty of the feat ("Will ask thee skill"). Having insinuated that Jesus is in the presence of the Father, Satan urges him to premature activity. This, we recall, has been the leitmotif of all the temptations. Then follows the volta: "Now shew thy Progeny." Satan places the basic scriptural temptation, "Cast thyself down," between two conditionals, one concerning standing, the other concerning Sonship. The final conditional states the safety that obtains *if* Jesus is the Son of God. But safety that obtains for what, we must wonder: for standing, for casting himself down, or both? Thus does Satan employ the rhetoric of ambiguity to hide the essence of the temptation amidst the peripheral conditionals. If either standing or casting himself down is to succumb to the satanic offer, what hope does Jesus have to obey only God? It would seem that Satan has manipulated the temptation in such a way that Jesus must choose one of the two satanic offers. Satan has made it impossible for his complete defeat to be effected. But, I argue, the situation only *seems* impossible, in the same way that Adam had thought his situation "seem'd remediless" (PL IX, 919). The traditional critical reading of this scene, though, has taken that semblance for reality.

The orthodox reading does not solve the ambiguity of Satan's speech, but succumbs to it. If Jesus is not standing, then the temptation as Satan offers it – either to stand *or* to cast himself down – leaves Jesus no choice; he must take one of the two options Satan offers. When the narrator tells us, then, that Jesus "said and stood," critics assume Jesus has followed the lesser evil.

Again, it is Calton who first accepted Satan's ambiguity as Milton's. He makes standing part of the temptation, and suggests that by standing Jesus reveals himself to Satan. Put in a less casuistical way, what he says is that by succumbing to Satan's temptation Jesus gives Satan the knowledge he wishes to have. Put yet another way, Jesus fails and shows his "Progeny" by way of a miracle. But to resort to the miraculous at this juncture would simply be admitting defeat. Milton would have agreed with Thomas Taylor when the latter writes: "Now in a time of serious humiliation to advance himselfe by a miracle, had been as seasonable as snow in harvest" *Christs Combate,* p. 116). Why, if Jesus has been successful in the previous temptations by human means, should he need or receive divine assistance in this one? This is certainly the most complex and most severely trying of the temptations, both mentally and physically. If Jesus receives divine aid at this point, only at the most difficult and crucial moment in the encounter, can he be said to emerge victor? Those who argue that Jesus receives the aid of a miracle as a sort of epiphany of his own divinity merely beg the question. Why does he discover his divinity (if he does) at the most difficult moment? Why also should he discover his divinity now, when even at the Crucifixion he feels himself forsaken? These themes will be elaborated on later.

Let us return to Satan's temptation, then, and offer a reading in which we account for Satan's ambiguity. An interpretation in which Jesus is set standing on the pinnacle from the beginning raises no such problems and offers a satisfactory resolution to the poem's various themes. Satan's initial statement ("There stand") is merely a taunt and not part of the offer. If Satan were to say "There obey God," it would likewise not be a temptation. That Satan states its difficulty ("will ask thee skill") obtains for our imaginary articulation as well: standing and obedience to God here, as elsewhere in Milton's poetry, are difficult (but not impossible). The pinnacle scene, then, acts as an icon for the whole process of the poem's action: the difficulty of standing in obedience to God in the face of the antagonist's persistent subtlety and wiles.[12] But Satan has here done something even more clever, even more subtle. He shrouds the final temptation in ambiguity and attempts to conflate the issues of standing and leaping off as if they were both parts of the temptation. But standing is no part of the temptation. The temptation begins when Satan utters that very important temporal deictic: "Now."[13] The temptation is for Jesus to show his progeny only by casting himself down. After stating the temptation, Satan places the issue of standing under the dubiety of a conditional—"if not to stand." This parallels the conditional before the temptation began—"if thou wilt stand"—and allows Satan to make ambiguous whether standing is part of the temptation or not. Jesus sees through the ambiguity and remains standing: "he said and stood." As he had done in all his interpretations of Satan's offers, Jesus sees through the peripheral and deceptive clouds in order to understand the essential defining issue of the temptation. He dispels the ambiguity and responds to the quiddity of the offer. Standing, then, is no expression of divinity; there is no miracle allowing Jesus to stand. What, then, is Jesus' status at the pinnacle? To know that, we must turn to his utterance thereon.

II

The Son's final answer to Satan, Lewalski remarks, is "notably ambiguous." She finds the alleged ambiguity artful, permitting Jesus' phrase to operate on two levels. As an answer to Satan's temptation, Jesus refers to the Mosaic source and rejects the offer to tempt his Father. As an answer to the "identity challenge," Jesus refers to himself, "indicating that he is now given to understand, at this climactic moment, the full meaning of his divine sonship—his nature as the Image of the Father—and that he is also permitted to exercise his divine power in standing where standing is impossible."[14] That Jesus' answer somehow operates at two levels is an answer to a critical debate that again began in 1752.

Calton, as we saw, argued that the Son's words in the poem differed from the Gospel account. This difference, he argued, allowed him to discover a contradictory significance in those words. Newton disagreed: "I cannot entirely approve this learned Gentleman's exposition, for I am for understanding the words, *Also it is written Tempt not the Lord thy God*, in the same sense, in which they were spoken in the Gospels, because I would not make the poem to differ from the Gospel account, farther than necessity compels, or more than the poet himself has made it." Newton argued that although Jesus did not declare himself to be God, he nonetheless expressed and demonstrated the degree of divinity demonstrating his "Progeny" that "the Tempter requir'd" (p. 182). In our century Calton has found his progeny in Elizabeth Pope, and Newton his in Arnold Stein. Pope, supporting "that remarkable critic Calton," expresses her position without hesitation, that the scene only "makes sense" if Jesus refers to himself: "'Tempt not the Lord thy God, he said, and stood,' really meant, 'Make not trial of *me*, the Lord your God'." What Milton does, she suggests, is follow the tradition of Hilary, Pseudo-Chrysostom, and Walafridus Strabus.[15] Stated quite simply, however, almost every commentary and biblical annotation in the English tradition disagrees with these three exegetes. Let me begin with the exception.

The only English commentator who departs from the tradition that Christ does not refer to himself as God, and the only one, I think, who cites Hilary (or any of the three), is John Gumbleden. But, even so, his exposition seems to confuse the issues. He first paraphrases Christ's reply: "He answered, It is *written again, Thou shalt not tempt the Lord thy God:* and in vain thou *temptest me* to tempt him." Later in his commentary, Gumbleden interprets this answer: "Meaning that as he himself might not *tempt* his Father, so neither might the Divel *tempt* him, who was the Lord his God; not *as he was a Divel*, no, *but as he was a creature.*" (*Christ Tempted*, pp. 38, 53). In the first instance, Gumbleden uses parallelism to suggest that Christ's reply refers only to God the Father, in the second to imply the sort of dual levels Lewalski suggests inform *Paradise Regained?* So even in this one exception, there is nothing to suggest that Christ refers to himself as God on the pinnacle.

The ascendant tradition in English commentary is ably exemplified by William Perkins. He paraphrases Christ's reply: "It is true indeed that God hath made many worthy promises of aide and protection to his children in his word, yet they shall not bee performed to those that presume to *tempt God*, as thou wouldest have me to doe." Or, as Thomas Bentham paraphrases it, "Thou wouldest have me to tempt God my father . . . with miracles not necessary . . . I am a man, and I wil follow mans waies." Joseph Hall echoes, "I doe not heare our Saviour averre himselfe to be a God, against the blasphemous insinuations of Sathan."[16] I suggest that Milton follows the prevalent English tradition on this issue. But it will not do simply for me to propose that Milton fits in with one tradition but not with another.[17] Let us examine the critics who argue that Jesus declares himself to be God at the pinnacle.

First of all, we may wonder at Calton's method of explication. How should Milton somehow signify a contradictory meaning to that of the Gospel account without any additional signifying gestures? And why does the phrase "the Lord thy God" in the answer to the third temptation have a meaning differing from precisely the same phrase in the answer to the second (IV, 177, 558)? The only way to avoid the implications to which these questions give rise is to pose the idea of a chasm between the second and third temptations, and the dangers to which this leads we shall presently see. Pope writes: "Christ is no longer acting under the peculiar conditions of the temptation, which made it necessary for him to speak and behave wholly as man; because the episode therefore has no exemplary function, his words can certainly be 'restricted to this particular occasion'" (*Tradition*, pp. 103–04). Joseph Hall, to the contrary, explains that this temptation does have an exemplary function: "If hee had subdued Sathan by the Almighty power of the Deitie, wee might have had what to wonder at, not what to imitate: now he useth that weapon which may be familiar unto us, that hee may teach our weaknesse how to bee victorious" (*Contemplations*, p. 34). Nor is Pope's explanation, that Milton used the order of Luke's account instead of the more traditional one of Matthew's, adequate. The difference in order does not bespeak any difference in the degree of revelation of divinity. And this is universally testified to by the commentators on the scene.

The Temptation scene, according to exegetical tradition, prefigured the Passion, and the tower scene the Crucifixion.[18] To examine Milton's interpretation of Christ's status at the Crucifixion will prove enlightening to our present interest. In *Christian Doctrine*, Milton uses Christ's prayers at the Crucifixion as evidence that the Son was not the Father and enjoyed none of the power of the Father in his human form: "If these prayers be uttered only in his human capacity, which is the common explanation, why does he petition these things from the Father alone instead of from himself, if he were God? Or rather, supposing him to be at once man and the supreme God, why does he ask at all for what was in his power?" (CM XIV, 230–31). Milton is perfectly clear on the point. Jesus is neither God, nor God-man. He is what he always is in Milton's mature theology and in *Paradise Regained:* the Son of God in human form. That is, he is both man and Son of God, neither less nor more, neither mere man nor God.

Whether or not Milton prefigured the Crucifixion in this pinnacle scene is unimportant—although it seems to me, and to many critics, that he has. What is important is that Milton believed that the Son did not possess the power of the Father, that he believed the Son must suffer in his human form in order to redeem humanity, and that he believed the Son to be successful. It is difficult to say why critics for two hundred and fifty years have denied Milton the right to express these beliefs in his narrative.

III

Although Calton and Newton disagreed about the significance of the phrase "the Lord thy God," they agreed that Jesus' "*standing* properly makes the discovery" of "his divinity." Newton was astute in using the term *divinity* in answering Calton. In our century, the debate has been conducted with a notoriously confused and wide-ranging vocabulary. One school of critics argues that when Jesus stands he is divine, meaning he is God; a second that he is divine but not God the Father; a third that he achieves a degree of divinity; a fourth that he is both God and man; and a fifth that he is "mere man."[19] Let us now examine the first four of these.

Pope, for instance, argues that because in *Christian Doctrine* Milton "seems quite willing to grant Christ the *title* of God (for what the title may be worth after he finishes defining it), we have no real grounds for supposing that he would absolutely refuse to let Jesus tell the devil that he is the Lord his God" (*Tradition,* p. 106). We must demur, however, on the grounds that Jesus has throughout the temptations referred Satan to a higher being—God, he makes clear, is higher than himself—and on the grounds that Jesus has used exactly the same phrase to refer to God in answer to the second temptation as to the third. The rhetoric of the *Christian Doctrine* is not simple; on the issue of the status of the Son, Milton vacillates between nominalism and something like realism. But he denies that the Son is essentially the Father, that the Son is equal to the Father, or that in any way but a nominal one the Son and God are one. In any case, in this poem, Jesus nowhere else refers to himself as God, and never so much as hints that he may be God, in essence or even in name.

Those who argue that the Son is divine but not God at the pinnacle are correct only insofar as they accept that Jesus is also divine but not God at each and every point in the narrative. If they argue that he is only now, on the pinnacle, divine, then they rely on the difference between the second and third temptations, and that reliance, we shall see, is based on a satanic perspective. For if, as we argue, there is no miracle manifest in the final temptation, then there is no reason to argue that there is an alteration in the degree of Jesus' divinity. The same argument holds for the third case: that Jesus displays some degree of divinity on the pinnacle.

The most popular argument is that Jesus is both God and man. But how does one then explain Jesus' unrelenting acquiescence to God? He has submitted his intellectual discipline to him (I, 293), his choice of means and time for establishing the kingdom (III, 433–40), his glory, his will—in short, his life. What is the value of that acquiescence if he is submitting to himself? It is on this point, we saw, that Milton relied in explaining Jesus' status at the Crucifixion: that it would have been of little avail if it had not been done by human volition. If based on mere nominalism, though, then the argument may be upheld that the Son is both God and man.

The fifth school argues that the Son is "mere man." The denigratory adjective *mere* is Satan's, of course. It was, as I shall argue in the conclusion, an adjective Milton expressly repudiated. Although the Son is not "mere man," he *acts* on the pinnacle as a man. He is neither the agent nor the recipient of a miracle, for a miracle is exactly what Satan tempts him to perform. To act as a man does not, though, argue that Jesus is not divine. I suggest that he is now exactly what God had first said he was: man and Son of God. And he has been that since God declared in the first book that Jesus was "This perfect Man, by merit call'd my Son" (I, 166). He remains that when the angelic chorus ends the poem by declaring him the Son of God, whether in celestial repose or human pose:

> True Image of the Father whether thron'd
> In the bosom of bliss, and light of light
> Conceiving, or remote from Heaven, enshrined
> In fleshly Tabernacle, and human form. (IV, 593–96)

In either habit, state, or motion, he is "still expressing / The Son of God, with Godlike force indu'd." His "merit" is to act under the limitations of humanity, and by fulfilling the covenant of obedience within those limitations to exalt humanity to the status of sonship. On the pinnacle he does so, both as man and as Son of God. So the final similes describing Satan's fall attest.

The first simile describes the victory of Hercules over Antaeus, and the second the riddling contest between the Sphinx and Oedipus:

> And as that *Theban* Monster that propos'd
> Her riddle, and him, who solv'd it not, devour'd;
> That once found out and solv'd, for grief and spight
> Cast her self headlong from th' *Ismenian* steep,
> So strook with dread and anguish fell the Fiend. (IV, 569–73)

On the one hand, the first simile describes the conquest of Antaeus by "Joves Alcides," or in other words by a Son of God. The second simile, on the other hand, refers to Jesus as man in two ways. The first is that the direct answer to the Sphinx's riddle, "once found out and solv'd," is "man." The second is that as the Sphinx was foiled by the man, Oedipus, so is Satan foiled by the man, Jesus.[20] Jesus is man and Son of God. He has been presented in that unified duality from the beginning of the narrative to its conclusion. This perhaps is Milton's gesture of acquiescence to the mystery of the Incarnation: a nominal acceptance of the irreducible wondrousness of the turning point in cosmic history. Milton gives us a Jesus who is, from the baptism, evidently divine, and who expresses that divinity in meritorious obedience to God. I leave to later a more precise account of Jesus' divinity in this poem, its origins and meaning. Now we may attempt to answer one final argument concerning Jesus on the pinnacle.

He stands. I argue that he stands of human volition and by human power. Some critics who do not assert that Jesus is God on the pinnacle nonetheless assert that God is present in that scene. Jesus, they argue, is upheld by God's invisible hand. God, I argue, does not make an entry at this moment in the scene, either covertly or overtly. Some critics feel God makes a covert entrance into the action at this time in the guise of a kind of deus ex machina. Dick Taylor argues that after Jesus makes a "moral decision," God "enters with his grace . . . and performs himself the miracle that holds Christ standing aloft on the impossible foothold of the pinnacle." Weber argues that Taylor's reading may be justified on "structural grounds." God's covert entrance has been prepared for, he argues, "by the symmetrical incidents in the introduction and conclusion of the poem. As Satan's opening council (1.33–118) is balanced by his final return (4.577–80), and the angels' first hymn (1.168–82) by their second (4.593–635), so God's appearance at the opening (1.126–

67) is balanced by his closing appearance—his descent to perform the miracle."[21] Weber discovers a greater symmetry than truly exists in the poem. For example, why does he not refer to Satan's second council (II, 147–234)? Because it offends the easy balance for which he argues. Milton "chose not to describe or even to mention God's descent," Weber suggests, because it allows our "focus to remain on Jesus, whose moral victory is more important than the divine judgment which validates it." Weber's terms are troubling, for they are not clear. It is worth our while to clarify them.

In Milton's theology there are two levels of graceful operation. At the first level, God is immanent throughout the universe, a formal and final cause of its being (CM XV, 21). At the second level, he infuses his chosen with greater spirit by the "motions" of grace. So in *Paradise Lost*, Adam and Eve receive prevenient grace to remove the stony from their hearts and lead them to repentance. Samson receives "rousing motions" that lead him from the torpor of his self-pity to the activity of God's champion. In *Paradise Regained*, the Spirit descends in the form of a dove at the baptism. Here it might be worth digressing slightly to discuss Milton's theology on the issue of the origin and degree of Christ's divinity.

The descent of the Spirit in the form of the dove at the baptism, Milton writes, "seems to have been nothing more than a representation of the ineffable affection of the Father for the Son, communicated by the Holy Spirit under the appropriate image of a dove, and accompanied by a voice from heaven declaratory of that affection" (CM XIV, 367). God's affection visits Jesus in the form of a dove, but remains his throughout his life in the essence of the Spirit. It is an affection that abides both as an operative power and a vocation in which to apply that power. Milton writes: "I am inclined to believe that the Spirit descended upon Christ at his baptism, not so much in his own name, as in virtue of a mission from the Father, and as a symbol and minister of the divine power." This divinity of the Son allows him the capacity to participate in the godhead. But in the ordeal of his temptation he manifests nothing but human powers—his divinity always latently available, never applied. The important thing I must note here is that in Milton's theology Jesus receives his divine power at the baptism, not at the pinnacle. There is no epiphany at the pinnacle. In *Paradise Regained* the "motions" symbolic of God's grace are expressed in the Spirit in the form of the dove.

This is what takes Jesus into the desert—"the Spirit leading"—and what Jesus recognizes as the "strong motion" leading him there (I, 189, 290). Whereas Samson and the fallen pair require motions that rouse them to repentance or proper activity, Jesus receives motions that are merely indicative of the spiritual manifestation of his life. William Kerrigan makes a serious error when he suggests that "rousing motions come to Christ on the pinnacle."[22] None such do come, for Jesus does not need to be roused. He has been the beneficiary of divine power from the baptism, he has expressed his Sonship through only human power up until now, and he does so now. By arguing that such a continuity informs the career of Jesus in this narrative, I am arguing once more against the critical tradition begun in 1752.

IV

Both Newton and Calton note that Milton wishes Jesus to discover to Satan his "Progeny." In order to argue that Jesus has heretofore not been allowed to express this divine power, but is now enabled and bid to do so, it is necessary to argue that there is a discontinuity between the second and third temptations. In modern critical debate, this argument has often taken the form of denying that the pinnacle scene is a temptation.

The third temptation of *Paradise Regained*, argues Tillyard, "is strongly contrasted with the second," and in comparison "is not really a temptation at all but the rout of Satan."[23] This alleged sense of contrast is in no small part based on Satan's own statement of intent: "Therefore to know what more thou art then man, / Worth naming Son of God by voice from Heav'n, / Another method I must now begin" (IV, 535–37). Elizabeth Marie Pope notes that this final encounter of the two main figures "is not even a temptation in the ordinary sense at all." She writes: "Milton says specifically that Satan has not come back with a 'new *device:* they *all* were spent,' and makes it clear that he is trying '*another* method' to determine whether Christ is God or man. The whole episode, in fact, has become simply a last desperate test of identity, Milton's resolution of the doubt motif. But the scene on the pinnacle is so brief and so highly condensed that it is a little difficult to see at first glance in just what this test was to consist."[24] Initially, it must be pointed out that although it is indeed Milton who says that Satan has no new device (IV, 440), it is Satan (and most emphatically not Milton) who "makes it clear that he is trying "'another method,'" and from Satan we might expect only limited clarity and a great deal of untruth. Secondly, I fail to see the logic of Pope's argument in yoking together Milton's and Satan's statements as if they are concordant, rather than contradictory. If Milton says that Satan has no new devices, and Satan says he is about to try another method, either Milton or Satan is wrong. Either Satan will try another method, demonstrating in that case that he has a new device, or Satan will not try another method because, as Milton said, he has no new devices. Have we here the alleged tension A.J.A. Waldock claimed to discover in *Paradise Lost* between Satan's acts and the narrator's descriptions of them?[25] Satan, I hope to show, is lying, and that removes the suspicion of any real or supposed tension between the narrative and its narration. But it will not do for me to claim Satan's mendacity on the grounds of the author's assertion. It will be necessary for me to demonstrate that Satan does not attempt another but uses his old and only method.

Satan has stated before this that he desires knowledge of Jesus' status, that he would apprehend the spiritual significance of Sonship. With "fear abasht" he says to Jesus:

> Be not so sore offended, Son of God;
> Though Sons of God both Angels are and Men,
> If I to try whether in higher sort
> Then these thou bear'st that title. (IV, 196–99)

It is nothing less than infuriating to watch Satan's intellect in action. He first states what he knows and then shrugs off the obvious ramifications of his statements in a doubtful gesture. I was only trying to know who "thou art, whose coming is foretold," Satan continues, because you are to "me most fatal" (204–05).

If the agenda of the Son of God consists, as Satan says, in a prophesied advent in which he destroys Satan, then Satan has already noted that this Jesus, who was proclaimed from heaven before his very eyes at the baptism, is the one foretold. In the first consistory, he had sadly told his compeers that they must "bide the stroak of that long threatn'd wound" (I, 59). He elaborates: "For this ill news I bring, the Womans seed / Destin'd to this, is late of woman born (I, 64–65). Satan has no doubts that Jesus is the one foretold, nor any doubt that the person he encounters in the desert is the same person he had watched at the baptism. What he does is create doubt as to Jesus' status by willfully casting himself and his compeers into a state of Pyrrhonism. He has manufactured doubts in the consistory, and he manufactures them now. He offers the banquet to Jesus: "What doubts the Son of God to sit and eat? . . . What doubt'st thou Son of God? sit down and eat." And the Son answers those doubts: "I can at will, doubt not, as soon as thou, / Command a Table in this Wilderness" (II, 368–84).

Just before Satan's apology quoted above (IV, 196–99), Jesus had twice claimed to be "the Son of God" in answering the offer of the kingdoms:

And dar'st thou to the Son of God propound
To worship thee accurst
. . . .
Wert thou so void of fear or shame,
As offer them to me the Son of God,
To me my own. (IV, 178–91)

That this Son of God is the one who will destroy his kingdom Jesus made obvious to Satan: "Know'st thou not that my rising is thy fall, / And my promotion will be thy destruction? (III, 201–02). Satan, then, has all the evidence he needs. What Satan has heard from God and from the Son himself, that Jesus is the Son of God, ought to remove his suspicions. But he is still skeptical: "For Son of God to me is yet in doubt."

Calton believes that, because Satan poses his questions in terms of degree of significance, Satan's doubt and the evidence of Jesus' Sonship may be reconciled. Calton notes: "On the terms of the annunciation Christ might be the Son of God in a sense very particular, and yet a mere man as to his nature: but the doubt relates to what he was *more than man, worth calling Son of God*, that is worthy to be called *Son of God* in that high and proper sense, in which his sonship would infer his divinity" (Newton, pp. 177–79). First, what more could Satan desire by way of knowledge? Jesus has said that the promotion of his kingdom would lead to the destruction of Satan's, the prerogative solely of the Son of God ("in that high and proper sense"). Second, Satan, although he has the opportunity to discern the "sense" of the term *Son of God*, chooses to confuse himself, as he had perplexed those who visited his oracles, "with double sense deluding" (I, 435): "For Son of God to me is yet in doubt." The term, he complains, "bears no single sence" (IV, 514). In answering the offer of Athenian philosophy, Jesus had added a criticism of Pyrrhonic philosophy even though Satan had not offered it. The words Jesus uses there are hugely significant here: "A third sort doubted all things, though plain sence" (IV, 293). But Calton's argument rests on his presupposition that Satan wished to discover Jesus' divinity, and concludes that Jesus reveals this on the pinnacle. We have already seen the fallacy of that presupposition. Let us return to the idea that the final temptation is none.

Satan claims that he will begin a new method to discover the significance of that ascendant term, *Son of God*. But Satan has already evinced a reluctance to accept Jesus' Sonship in the face of "plain sence." Satan does not have another method. He attempts on the pinnacle what he has attempted in each offer thus far: to corrupt Jesus by provoking him to faithlessness. Every temptation has been to forego God's time in favor of human expediency and to forego God's means in favor of human means: in a word, each has been a temptation of faith.

This third temptation, then, to answer Pope and Tillyard, is certainly a temptation and, moreover, one not qualitatively different from the previous temptations. While Satan wishes Jesus to think that there is a contrast between the second and third temptations, it is important for us to recognize that there is no difference. As Richard Ward writes, Satan "endeavours one and the same thing by contrarie meanes, his craft more clearly shining forth hereby."[26] It is the same craft he displays in attempting to suggest that both standing on and casting oneself off the pinnacle comprise the final temptation. Satan, that is, works by both contraries and similarities.

The modern critical reading suggests that Satan requires and receives a miracle to dissipate his doubts. But Satan, as we have seen, has no honest doubts; he doubts merely as a ploy. Although I agree with Pope that the pinnacle temptation is "Milton's resolution of the doubt motif," I do not agree with her interpretation of that resolution. But her interpretation is the ascendant modern one, and, as I argued, might be traced back to the origin of formal criticism of the poem, Newton's variorum edition of 1752. It is difficult to see why critics have eagerly believed Satan when he, and he alone, makes a radical distinction between the previous temptations and the pinnacle temptation. It is difficult to say why critics have chosen to destroy the integrity of Milton's fabular design by imposing a kind of disfigured plot on its serene face. In order to show that the plot of *Paradise Regained* does not follow this sort of simplistic melodramatic program, but is rather designed on another, more concordant with the preceding action, I will turn to the issue at the crux of the poem: Satan's knowledge.

V

The pinnacle scene, Pope argues, was the final resolution to the doubt motif. The fit conclusion was that Satan must be made aware of Jesus' true identity, and not "go away unsatisfied and dubious" (*Tradition*, pp. 94, 40). I have argued elsewhere that Satan's Pyrrhonism is irremediable.[27] Because it is in effect the blasphemous sin against the Holy Spirit, Satan's sin of doubting is visited by immortal nescience. Let us return to the narrative to discover whether Satan knows or does not know Jesus at the pinnacle. As Jesus pronounces his scriptural text, standing, Satan "smitten with amazement fell" (IV, 559). Lewalski takes this "amazement" to indicate that, in total defeat, Satan "knows his victor as before he knew his conqueror in heaven and will know him again in this role at the end of time."[28]

Knowledge, I assume, is to some degree a possessing of sense. If, however, we examine Satan's final glimpse of the Son of God in his defeat in heaven, we see that Satan and the rebel crew fell "Insensate, hope conceiving from despair" (*PL* VI, 787). Both the word used to describe their intellectual status — *insensate*, which Dr. Johnson defines as "Stupid; wanting thought" — and the indirect exposition of their folly — believing in the nonsense that from despair could be wrought hope — demonstrate that Satan and his crew fall in a state hardly to be described as one of knowledge. Returning to *Paradise Regained*, we note that Satan had been presented with evidence of Jesus' Sonship before the pinnacle scene, at the baptism. He had willed himself to a literal interpretation of the dove and had denied the authority of God's voice. He doubts the validity of the spirit latent in the Son, of the expression of the Holy Spirit, and the authority of God: it is, as I have argued, the blasphemy against the Spirit.

The argument that Jesus reveals his status to Satan at this point in the narrative, but not before, is based on the argument that the final temptation is different from those preceding it (an argument whose false suppositions we have already examined). First of all, the Son has not been silent about his status before this. As I noted above, he answers the second temptation by declaring twice that he is "the Son of God" (IV, 178, 190). Satan has seen the form of the Spirit, heard the voice of God, and discerned the glimpses of spirit in the Son (I, 83, 85, 91–93). But he has cast all these under doubt. His is a consumptive skepticism, one that leads him from doubt to amazement.

We might allow Thomas Bilson to offer us a better appreciation of his crucial word. Amazement, Bilson argues, is not astonishment, for Christ may be astonished, as he is in Mark xiv, but he may never be amazed. For "all vehement amazing for the time depriveth a man of *motion, sense,* and *speech.*" It also, he argues, deprives a man of understanding. Dr. Johnson defines it, in its first signification, as such a "confused apprehension as does not leave reason its full force."[29] Having used doubt to will himself into a state of nescience as to the spiritual significance of the Son's advent, Satan now suffers the consequences of his blasphemy. As he had willed himself into a literal interpretation of the dove, so now he is unable to have any but a literal understanding of Jesus on the pinnacle. That is, he sees the literal standing but does not understand the spiritual station. At the first consistory, Satan had noted that Jesus exhibited two existential states: "Who this is we must learn, for man he seems / In all his lineaments, though in his face / The glimpses of his

Fathers glory shine" (I, 91–93). In conformity to his Pyrrhonist philosophy, Satan allows the semblance but denies the essence. Why, then, should critics argue that somehow Satan is pardoned this breach of essential sense and allowed an insight into the spiritual significance of the Son, his station and his mission? It is certainly not true to Milton's attitude, either in his prose or his poetry.

Satan denies the Son's right to rule heaven, and is punished with an obdurate insensate state. God asserts that though his grace is open to all, "They who neglect and scorn, shall never taste; / But hard be hard'n'd, blind be blinded more, / That they may stumble on, and deeper fall" (*PL* III, 199–201). In his prose, Milton notes that Jesus "amuses" his tempters, excluding them from the knowledge they desire because of the malice of their attempts. To amuse means to "confound, distract, bewilder, puzzle." Elsewhere, Milton suggests that Christ answers the Pharisees with enigmatic riddles ("to amaze them yet furder") because they "were not fit to be told" the spiritual facts.[30] Satan, quite obviously, is not fit to be told, for his attempt to misdeem the Son was malicious, as was his attempt to corrupt Job (I, 424–26). It is not inspired by an honest wish to know, but to afflict; and for that malice he is visited with unrelenting blindness as to the significance of spiritual things.

Now, this is not to say that Satan is wholly ignorant of the significance of the Son. Milton, I have demonstrated, did not attempt to penetrate the mystery of the Incarnation in his theological tract. He rested secure in the knowledge that he who worked the atonement of man was both the Son of God and man, or, after (and only after) conceding a diffuse usage of the word, *God* and man.[31] In *Paradise Regained*, Milton does not proceed much further in the mystery. He again rests in asserting that there is a dual nature in Jesus. He presents a hero who expresses himself in this action as a man and is by merit the Son of God.

Milton does offer, in the poem, one other insight into the nature of the Son's incarnation. Although clothed in fleshly tabernacle, as the angels put it, he still exudes spirituality. By having Satan express this truth, moreover, Milton demonstrates Satan's blasphemy against the Holy Spirit. Satan says of Jesus: "man he seems / In all his lineaments, though in his face / The glimpses of his Fathers glory shine." Though he expresses it so beautifully here, because of his sequent denial of the force and validity of that spirit, because of his malice, and because of his Pyrrhonism, Satan cannot understand the idea of spirit residing in the form of flesh.

Satan states that he has found Jesus' actions thus far befitting the utmost to which "mere man" may aspire (IV, 538). He tempts him, then, to discover "what more" than mere man he is. If, as we argue, Jesus does not display any virtue that he has not heretofore evinced, then perhaps he is "mere man"? Such, however, would be the satanic interpretation. Milton argues that the nature of Christ is human, but not "merely human" (*merum hominem*), that it is divine, but not in the same degree as the Father is divine. He calls him "God," but not until he has defined that key term to indicate that the Father has no part of the Incarnation: "The reasons, therefore, which are given to prove that he who was made flesh must necessarily be the supreme God, may safely be dismissed" (CM XV, 260–63, 272–73). Mary Ann Radzinowicz argues that in the poem, "the Son *is* mere man." Milton, she states, asserts a "functional relationship" over a "consubstantial relationship" between God and "any beings entitled to be called His sons."[32] Perhaps, then, with this in mind, Radzinowicz's insight might more accurately be rephrased to say that the Son *acts* as mere man. Milton tended to avoid the copula when discussing the Son; as the angels say, he *expresses* Sonship.

In this way, we do not deny Milton's insistence on the mystery of the Incarnation. The resident spirit, carrying with it the divine power and the mission in which that power is to be manifest, informs the Son. And, for Milton, this was the utmost of human comprehension of the Incarnation: that the flesh might be invested with divine power in order to counter the diabolical element inherent in the carnal.[33] The merit of Jesus in obeying God bespeaks his spiritual power, his divinity. Satan does not see the merit, cannot understand the obedience, and hence cannot apprehend the divinity. He sees only the act of a "mere man." We, though, see the divinity in the act.

Although he does not understand the divine man at the pinnacle, Satan will comprehend to a degree the role the Son is to play in cosmic history, but to a very small degree. And, more importantly, he will not learn it from the Son during this temptation sequence. Let us once more return to that extremely informative first encounter between the adversaries. In answer to Satan's boast of his oracular aid to humans, Jesus declares that Satan cannot know God's expressed will:

> when his purpose is
> Among them to declare his Providence
> *To thee not known*, whence hast thou then thy truth,
> But from him or his Angels President. (I, 444–47, my italics)

Let us compare this to the final scene. Having lifted Jesus from his uneasy station, fed him, and sung his victory, the angelic chorus addresses Satan:

> But thou, Infernal Serpent, shalt not long
> Rule in the Clouds; like an Autumnal Star
> Or Lightning thou shalt fall from Heav'n trod down
> Under his feet: for proof, e're this thou feel'st
> Thy wound, yet not thy last and deadliest wound
> By this repulse receiv'd
>
> . . . .
>
> hereafter learn with awe
> To dread the Son of God: he all unarm'd
> Shall chase thee with the terror of his voice
> From thy Demonaic holds, possession foul
> Thee and thy Legions, yelling they shall flye,
> And beg to hide them in a herd of Swine. (IV, 614–26)

Satan has a chasm in his intellectual capacity disabling him from entertaining divine verities in their immediate manifestation. When God determines, Satan is suffered to express that truth in the same way he does all actions tending to promote providential designs—"contrary unweeting" (I, 126). Only after he has himself expressed it, without understanding it (it is to him "not known"), does the truth appear to make itself manifest to him. I say "appear" because there is no evidence that Satan does have the truth. He only claims to have it: "Then to thy self ascrib'st the truth foretold" (I, 453).

It is important that Satan does not comprehend any truth of God's Providence through its activity. He becomes aware of it only after, and only through either God or the angels. In the final scene of the narrative, Satan likewise does not learn the truth of Jesus' station through the Son's acting out of God's Providence, or through the Son's manifestation of that grace, but only at the very end, and only through the angels. This time, of course, it is the truth of God's "living Oracle" that is expressed and only partially understood.

The angelic chorus alludes to the one scene in the Gospels in which Jesus will again meet the devils, where he exorcises them from the unclean man in Capernaum (Luke iv, 31–37; Mark i, 21–28). As Jesus approaches the man the devils call out, "I know thee who thou art; the Holy One of God." Jesus then commands them out. It is, in both Mark's and Luke's gospel, the first of Jesus' miracles. The angels suggest that Jesus shall "command" the devils out of the possessed man into "a herd of Swine" as a prelude to the final conquest of Satan and his crew. Jesus has not manifested himself by miracle in the temptation sequence, and so Satan does not comprehend the spirit residing within. By alluding to a scene outside the action of the narrative, and a scene in which Jesus will perform his first miracle, the angels demonstrate how Satan's intellectual capacities still lag behind. The resolution of the doubt motif, then, is not effected within the action of *Paradise Regained.* Although we are made aware that he shall possess some degree of knowledge of the spiritual power of his queller, at a later time, in the narrative proper he concludes his career in a state of senseless amazement—a state, that is, in which the mind, as Dr. Johnson said, is in a condition of such "confused apprehension as does not leave reason its full force." Being amazed, then, Satan lacks reason, and without reason comprehension is impossible. If, then, Satan is unable to comprehend the Son, in the truly spiritual significance of that term, can we say that he is able to identify him? It would appear that there is, quite simply, no contest.

University of Calgary

NOTES

I would like to thank the Social Sciences and Humanities Research Council of Canada for providing me with a fellowship enabling me to pursue the research for this essay.

1. See Irene Samuel, "The Regaining of Paradise," in *The Prison and the Pinnacle: Papers to Commemorate the Tercentenary of "Paradise Regained" and "Samson Agonistes,"* ed. Balachandra Rajan (Toronto, 1973), pp. 111–34, esp. 126, for a fine argument debunking the fallacy of the "identity contest."

2. *"Paradise Regain'd." A Poem in IV Books*, ed. Thomas Newton (London, 1752), p. 181; note is by Calton. Criticism of *Paradise Regained* formally began with Richard Meadowcourt's treatise, *A Critique on Milton's "Paradise Regain'd"* (London, 1732), issued in a revised second edition, retitled *A Critical Dissertation with Notes on Milton's "Paradise Regain'd"* (London, 1748); antedating Meadowcourt, John Dennis has some cogent comments about the poem in his "The Grounds of Criticism in Poetry" (1704), anatomized in *Milton: The Critical Heritage*, ed. John T. Shawcross (London, 1970), pp. 134–35. Nonetheless, I maintain that Newton's 1752 variorum edition is the formal origin of modern criticism because it has acted on and become institutionalized into the discipline as neither Dennis's nor Meadowcourt's treatise can be said to have done.

3. Earl Miner, *The Restoration Mode from Milton to Dryden* (Princeton, 1974), p. 273.

4. *Christian Doctrine* XV, 279, 273, in *The Works of John Milton*, 18 vols., ed. Frank Allen Patterson et al. (New York, 1931–40). All future quotations from Milton's prose will be taken from this edition, hereafter cited as CM.

5. All quotations from *Paradise Regained* will be taken from the first edition (London, 1671); all quotations from *Paradise Lost* will be taken from *John Milton: Complete Poems and Major Prose*, ed. Merritt Y. Hughes (Indianapolis, 1957).

6. Dr. Johnson gives sixty-six significations for the verb form, of which the first is to put in any "situation," and the second to put in any "state" (cf. the twenty-fourth,

"to station"). The OED gives over 154 significations for the verb form, of which the first is "to cause to sit" and the eleventh "to place."

7. Modern critics who argue that standing is "humanly impossible" include Georgia Christopher, *Milton and the Science of the Saints* (Princeton, 1982), p. 220; Karl Franson, "'By His Own Independent Power': Christ on the Pinnacle in *Paradise Regained,*" *MQ* XIV (May 1980), 55–56; E. L. Marilla, *Milton and Modern Man* (University, Ala. 1968), p. 60; Elizabeth Marie Pope, *"Paradise Regained": The Tradition and the Poem* (Baltimore, 1947); Arnold Stein, *Heroic Knowledge: An Interpretation of "Paradise Regained" and "Samson Agonistes"* (Minneapolis, 1957); Barbara Lewalski, *Milton's Brief Epic: The Genre, Meaning, and Art of "Paradise Regained"* (Providence, 1966); Burton Jasper Weber, *Wedges and Wings: The Patterning of "Paradise Regained"* (Carbondale, Ill., 1975).

8. Andrewes, *Seven Sermons Upon the Temptation of Christ in the Wilderness,* V, 518, in *The Works of Lancelot Andrewes,* 10 vols. (Oxford, 1865). Cf. Bentham, *A notable and comfortable exposition, upon the Fourth of Matthew, concerning the Tentations of Christ* (London, c. 1578), pp. E_6^r–E_7^v; Isaac Colfe, *A Comfortable Treatise concerning the temptations of Christ* (London, 1592), p. 94; William Cowper, *The Combate of Christ with Satan* (1609) in *The Workes of Mr. William Cowper* (London, 1623), pp. 617–18; Daniel Dyke, *Michael and the Dragon, or Christ Tempted and Sathan foyled* (London, 1616), pp. 279–80; Thomas Fuller, *A Comment on The eleven first Verses of the fourth Chapter of S. Matthew's Gospel. Concerning Christs Temptations* (London, 1652), pp. 68–69; John Gumbleden, *Christ Tempted: The Divel Conquered. Or, A short and plain Exposition on a part of the fourth Chapter St. Matthew's Gospel* (London, 1657), p. 33; Joseph Hall, *Contemplations Upon the Historie of the New Testament* in *The Works of Joseph Hall* (London, 1628), p. 34; William Perkins, *The Combate Betweene Christ and the Devil displayed* in *The Workes of . . . Mr. W. Perkins,* 3 vols. (Cambridge, 1616–18), III, 389–90; Thomas Taylor, *Christs Combate and Conquest* (Cambridge, 1618), pp. 228, 229; John Udall, *The Combate betwixt CHRIST and the Devill* (London, 1588), p. F_8^r; Richard Ward, *Theologicall, Dogmaticall, and Evangelicall Questions, Observations, Essays, Upon the Gospel of Jesus Christ, According to St. Matthew* (London, 1640), p. 102. The one exception is Thomas Bilson, *The Survey of Christs Sufferings for Mans redemption* (London, 1604), p. 309, but he is heterodox to the English tradition in a variety of ways; see Pope, *Tradition,* p. 86; *The Poems of John Milton,* ed. John Carey and Alastair Fowler (London, 1970), pp. 1161–62.

9. Isaac Colfe, *A Comfortable Treatise,* p. 94. Colfe suggests that the pinnacle, then, is not such as Josephus describes. See Josephus, *The Jewish War,* ed. Gaalya Cornfeld (Tel Aviv, 1982), p. 360, V, v, 6. For discussions of the physical logistics of the temple in relation to Josephus's description, see W. A. McClung, "The Pinnacle of the Temple," *MQ* XV (January, 1981), 13–16; *Poems,* ed. Carey and Fowler, p. 1161; Walter MacKellar, *A Variorum Commentary on The Poems of John Milton,* vol. 4 (London, 1975), pp. 238–39; *Paradise Regained,* ed. Charles Dunster (London, 1795), pp. 255–56; Pope, *Tradition,* pp. 102–03.

10. *Poems,* ed. Carey and Fowler, p. 1162; cf. John Carey, *Milton* (New York, 1970) p. 128; Mason Tung, "The Patterns of Temptation in *Paradise Regained,*" *Seventeenth-Century News* XXIV (1966), p. 59n6: Jesus stood by "simple human skill."

11. Weber, *Wedges and Wings,* p. 61; cf. Hugh MacCallum, *Milton and the Sons of God: The Divine Image in Milton's Epic Poetry* (Toronto, 1986), pp. 256, 258.

12. MacCallum, *Sons of God,* pp. 257–58, notes likewise that standing is an "expression and symbol of perfect obedience." To insist that standing on the pinnacle is miracu-

lous seems to argue, then, that obedience requires a miracle; and this is to argue what Milton persistently denies.

13. In Dryden's *Absalom and Achitophel*, Achitophel tempts Absalom with the same themes as Satan does Jesus (to glory, human activity, carpe diem), and makes the actual temptation begin, "*Now, now* she meets you with a glorious prize" (244–60, my italics).

14. Lewalski, *Brief Epic*, p. 316, A.S.P. Woodhouse, "Theme and Pattern in *Paradise Regained*," *UTQ* XXV (1955–56), p. 181, argues that this statement is "Christ's supreme act of obedience and trust, and it is also the long awaited demonstration of divinity." Arnold Stein, *Heroic Knowledge*, pp. 128, 224–25, is strongly opposed to this view. See Stanley Fish, "Inaction and Silence: The Reader in *Paradise Regained*" in *Calm of Mind: Tercentenary Essays on "Paradise Regained" and "Samson Agonistes" in Honor of John S. Diekhoff*, ed. Joseph Anthony Wittreich, Jr. (Cleveland, 1971), pp. 42–43, for an attempt in resolving these disparate views by suggesting that Jesus ceases at this point to have "an independent existence," that he becomes "God to the extent that *he*, as a consciousness distinguishable from God, is no more." Fish's argument is based on the fact that the Son here uses the Scriptures to renounce his own personality: "The man who wraps himself in Scriptures, as Christ does here, becomes an adjunct of them and ceases to have an independent existence." But Jesus has cited Scripture twice before this; why is it he loses his identity only at this point in the narrative?

15. Pope, *Tradition*, p. 103. I think Calton evinces his desire to edit Milton into orthodoxy when he suggests emending God's reference at Book I, line 122, from "This man of men, attested Son of God" to "This man, *of Heav'n* attested Son of God"; *Paradise Regained*, ed. Newton (1752), p. 13; cf. pp. 15–16.

16. Perkins, *The Combate*, in *Workes*, III, 393–94; Bentham, *A notable and comfortable exposition*, pp. $E6^r$–$E7^v$; Hall, *Contemplations*, in *Works* (1628), p. 34. Cf. Dyke, *Michael and the Dragon*, p. 301; Fuller, *A Comment*, pp. 68–69; Thomas Taylor, *Christs Combate*, pp. 268–69; Jeremy Taylor, *The Life of Our Blessed Lord and Saviour Jesus Christ* in *The Whole Works of the Right Rev. Jeremy Taylor D.D.*, 15 vols., ed. Reginald Heber (London, 1822), vol. II, p. 187.

17. While Milton's gestures in this part of the poem do conform to the prevalent English tradition on this issue, I am not in any way suggesting that Milton *adhered* to the English tradition, or, indeed, to any "tradition" at all. As with all the elements of Milton's thought, what he inherited he reformed. Moreover, Milton held that tradition, which he called a "broken reed" and a "muddie pool," "hath had very seldome or never the gift of perswasion" (CM III, 99).

Milton's attitude to a tradition of hermeneutics is likewise iconoclastic, as well as being somewhat confusing. In 1644, he eschewed the "Papistical way of a literal apprehension against the direct *analogy* of sense, reason, law, and Gospel" (CM IV, 9); yet, the next year he condemns those who "would ingrosse to themselves the whole trade of interpreting, [and] will not suffer the clear text of God to doe the office of explaining it self" (IV, 83). In 1649, he posed as a willful hermeneut: "For in words which admitt of various sense, the libertie is ours to choose that interpretation which may best minde us of what our restless enemies endeavor, and what wee are timely to prevent" (V, 68). In his *Christian Doctrine*, Milton writes in the tenth chapter of the first book that we are "to interpret the text in its plain and obvious meaning, without attempting to elicit from it more than it really contains" (XV, 153), and in the thirtieth chapter of the first book, "Scripture is the sole judge of controversies; or rather, every man is to decide for himself through its aid, under the guidance of the Spirit of God" (XVI, 269, cf. 271–75). It is worth noting that the first reference in the *DDC* is in Skinner's hand, the second in Picard's; see Maurice

Kelley, *This Great Argument* (Princeton, 1941), pp. 22–25. Milton's strategy of interpretation seems to fluctuate between positions that have in recent debates been called the affective and the intentional fallacies. (I would like to thank Professor Joseph Wittreich for generously providing me with valuable advice on this and other points.)

18. See Lewalski, *Milton's Brief Epic*, pp. 313–14; *Paradise Regained*, ed. Dunster (1795), p. 256. Cf. Ward, *Theologicall*, p. 84; Bernard, *Saint Bernard His Meditations: Or Sighes, Sobbes and Teares upon our Saviour Passion*, 4th ed., trans. W. P. (London, 1631), p. 378; Colfe, *A Comfortable treatise*, p. 29; Joseph Hall, *The Passion Sermon* (London, 1609), pp. 44–45; Andrewes, *Seven Sermons*, in *Works*, V, 516–17; Cowper, *The Combate*, in *Works*, p. 606; Gumbleden, *Christ Tempted*, pp. 15, 50, 77; Thomas Taylor, *Christs Combate*, "Epistle Dedicatorie"; Jeremy Taylor, *The Life*, in *The Works*, vol. II, pp. 201, 244, 253.

19. Representing the five schools, seriatim, are (1) Ralph Waterbury Condee, "Milton's Dialogue with the Epic: *Paradise Regained* and the Tradition," *Yale Review* LIX (1970), 374; Jesus achieves triumph at the pinnacle "by anti-epic restraint. He conquers evil simply by being God"; cf. George deForest Lord, *Poetic Traditions in the English Renaissance* (New Haven, 1982), p. 235: "in refusing to tempt God, Jesus manifests that he *is* God." (2) Edward W. Tayler, *Milton's Poetry: Its Development in Time* (Pittsburgh, 1979), p. 173; cf. Joan Malory Webber, *Milton and His Epic Tradition* (Seattle, 1979), pp. 195, 198: she writes, initially, that in "the sense in which he and his Father are one, Jesus is God in fact," then qualifies, that "He is one with God, but not equal to God." (3) Franson, "'By His Own Independent Power,'" p. 55. (4) Gordon Teskey, "Balanced in Time: *Paradise Regained* and the Centre of the Miltonic Vision," *UTQ* L (1981), 276–77. (5) Mary Ann Radzinowicz, *Toward "Samson Agonistes": The Growth of Milton's Mind* (Princeton, 1978) p. 332.

20. For two contrary interpretations of the similes, see Lewalski, *Milton's Brief Epic*, p. 319, and Kathleen M. Swaim, "Hercules, Antaeus, and Prometheus: A Study of the Climactic Epic Similes in *Paradise Regained*," *SEL* XVIII (1978), 137–53.

21. Dick Taylor, Jr., "Grace as a Means of Poetry: Milton's Pattern for Salvation," *Tulane Studies in English* IV (1959) p. 88. Weber, *Wedges and Wings*, p. 66.

22. Kerrigan, *The Sacred Complex: On the Psychogenesis of "Paradise Lost"* (Cambridge, Mass., 1983), p. 119.

23. E. M. W. Tillyard, *Milton*, (1930; rev. ed. New York, 1966), p. 277.

24. Pope, *Tradition*, p. 94, her italics. Cf. MacCallum, *Sons of God*, pp. 253–54, who argues that the "formal period of temptation" ends with the Son's words at Book IV, lines 494–95. He suggests that Satan still retains his power over the body of Jesus in the pinnacle scene, but that this power "is now exercised in direct defiance of the Son's command."

25. A.J.A. Waldock, *"Paradise Lost" and Its Critics* (Cambridge, 1947), pp. 65–96, esp. p. 78.

26. Ward, *Theologicall*, p. 102. Stanley Fish, "Things and Actions Indifferent: The Temptation of Plot in *Paradise Regained*," *Milton Studies* XVII, ed. Richard S. Ide and Joseph Wittreich (Pittsburgh, 1983), p. 177, argues that it is also the reader's task "to penetrate to that sameness amidst so many signs of difference."

27. In "'In Dubious Battle': Skepticism and Fideism in *Paradise Regained*," *Huntington Library Quarterly* LIII, 2 (1990), 95–119. Cowper, *The Combate*, in *The Workes*, p. 620, argues that Satan is incapable of penitence because he has sinned the Sin against the Holy Ghost. He argues from that position to the pinnacle: "for presumption hee could not stand, for obstinacie he cannot rise."

28. Lewalski, *Brief Epic*, p. 318; cf. Rajan. "To Which Is Added *Samson Agonistes*," in *The Prison and the Pinnacle: Papers to Commemorate the Tercentenary of "Paradise Regained" and "Samson Agonistes" 1671–1971* (London, 1973), p. 101.

29. Bilson, *Survey*, pp. 369, 409–21, 467–68, 479–82. I affirm nothing about Bilson's distinction, which he himself belies later, attributing to astonishment all the mental dysfunctions he had attributed (supposedly) solely to amazement. I only note that amazement is indicative of senselessness, Satan's fate. I cite other examples of the use of "amazement" in "Of *Paradise Regained:* The Interpretation of Career," in *Milton Studies*, XXIV, ed. James D. Simmonds (Pittsburgh, 1988), pp. 269, 275 n13. It might be noted that the word assumes an important place as both Adam and Eve fall (*PL* IX, 552, 614, 640); Samson says he shall strike the Philistines with "amaze" (*SA* 1645), and that benighted group, we recall, is "Insensate left, or to sense reprobate, / And with blindness internal struck" (1685–86).

30. *Tetrachordon* (1645), in CM IV, 186; *Doctrine and Discipline of Divorce* (1643), in CM III, 456.

31. For Milton's christology, see CM XIV, 176–357 and XV, 251–83.

32. Radzinowicz, *Towards "Samson Agonistes,"* pp. 331–32; cf. Jack Herring, "Christ on the Pinnacle in *Paradise Regained*," *MQ* XV (October 1981), p. 98.

33. We must keep in mind that Milton was a mortalist. See *Christian Doctrine* in CM XV, 214–51. Cf. Harold Fisch's introduction to his edition of Richard Overton's *Mans Mortalitie* (Liverpool, 1968); cf. Fisch's *Jerusalem and Albion: The Hebraic Factor in Seventeenth-Century Literature* (London, 1964), pp. 152, 168; Christopher Hill, *Milton and the English Revolution* (London, 1977), pp. 317–23.

DISORIENTATION AND DISRUPTION IN *PARADISE REGAINED*

Jeffrey B. Morris

IN "THINGS AND ACTIONS INDIFFERENT," Stanley Fish comments off-handedly that the doctrine of things indifferent "holds the key to the structure (if that is the word) of *Paradise Regained*." What is surprising here is not the newly discovered "key," for there have been many such keys, but the parenthetical qualification questioning whether the poem has structure at all. This question has important implications for critics who have argued over the fundamental arrangement of the poem and the organizational principle supporting it. It casts doubt upon Barbara Lewalski's argument that the poem's structure depends on the biblical brief epic form, or Arnold Stein's thesis that the "permeating conceptual form" depends on the theme of "weakness that is proved strength." It makes us wonder whether we should demolish Tillyard's "imaginary church," and it certainly allows us to further doubt Arthur Barker's tentative observation that "the three temptations . . . seem to provide the poem with its structure."[1]

All these critics, Fish included, are responding to difficulties in the poem best summarized by J. B. Broadbent in "The Private Mythology of *Paradise Regained*": "The narrative is arbitrary. Mary, the apostles, and Belial appear early and no more. . . . Books III and IV split a conversation."[2] Many readers have experienced these difficulties and have tried to overcome them by reading structure into the poem; consequently, they have produced diverging opinions on the poem's structure, some of which are recorded above. Instead of rationalizing a structure by suppressing and highlighting evidence, or doubting whether the poem has a structure at all, I would like to approach the issue in a new way; I suggest we embrace the phenomena described by Broadbent and examine our responses to them. The arbitrary narrative, the rapidly appearing and disappearing characters, and the unexpected book breaks naturally leave us confused about the arrangement of scenes and the purpose of certain characters. Because these factors lead to a general confusion about the direction of the narrative, we can characterize our primary sensation toward the poem as one of disorientation.

The term *disorientation* needs further explanation, but we must first examine how we orient ourselves toward a text. As we read *Paradise Regained* or other works, our imaginations are engaged in creating the time, setting, and characters we confront on the page. As Wolfgang Iser puts it in "The Reading Process: A Phenomenological Approach," "the literary text activates our own faculties, enabling us to recreate the world it presents."[3] Our imaginations recreate the setting and sequence of actions in order to realize more fully the meaning of the work. It is, in other words, a way of orienting ourselves to a particular text and its ideas. But we do not limit our means of orienting ourselves merely to recreating the setting and sequence of actions. We also orient ourselves to a work through, for example, characterization. Characters' actions and reactions will often affirm earlier suspicions of how events will turn out or foreshadow what is to come, thus providing us with a sense of direction. In other words, characters contribute to the reader's ongoing process of "establishing . . . interrelations between past, present and future" (Iser, p. 278). Lastly, we often look for ways to orient ourselves to a work by searching for keys to the work's organization in the unfolding sequence of events.

These various factors, however, can not only encourage our orientation toward a work but hinder it as well. Such is the case in *Paradise Regained.* Milton limits our sense of space, time, and direction, especially in the first halves of Books I and II, through scantly described scenes and rapid scene shifts. And as a consequence of these limitations, we have difficulty imagining where we are and where we are going. Also, in placing a heavy emphasis on monologue, Milton discourages our tendencies to orient ourselves to a text by noting how characters react to each other. And yet another way in which he disorients us is by using book breaks to discourage our efforts to impose an organizational scheme on the poem. These difficulties, among others, have caused many critics to condemn the poem and a few critics to encourage us to read it with patience, even to endure it in a Christlike manner. However, I will argue that these disorienting factors do not diminish the poem's quality, but enhance it. Through the disorientation caused by Milton's handling of various scenes, characters, and the general progression of the narrative, we find ourselves oriented toward the poem's main character—Christ. In other words, the poem's formal disorientation leads to a more theological orientation, and the problems of structure are not faults or limitations but necessary steps for apprehending the higher purposes of the poem.

In the early sections of Books I and II, frequent scene changes and bare descriptions undermine any sense of stability that can be offered through setting. A quick count shows that in the first 293 lines of Book I, our location shifts four times. We begin with Christ's baptism at the River Jordan. Then we move quickly to Satan's midair kingdom where he announces the coming of Christ to his cohorts. Next we are in heaven, where we listen to God speak, and then we return to the desert to hear Christ. Recounting the early scenes demonstrates that a great deal happens in a very short space, but it is not the amount of action alone that disorients us. As any reader of *Paradise Lost* knows, Milton frequently transports us between heaven, hell, and earth. But in that poem we stay in any given place for the length of one book (books usually twice as long as those in *Paradise Regained*), and sometimes longer. The more time we have to imagine ourselves in a scene, the better we are able to associate ourselves with it. But in the early sections of Books I and II of *Paradise Regained*, the short scenes give us little time to perceive ourselves in any one place. Based on our knowledge of *Paradise Lost*, we expect to have enough time to familiarize ourselves with the scene at hand. This expectation is frustrated, however, and this frustration promotes our sense of disorientation.

Additionally, the abruptness of the transitions between scenes accentuates the speed and seemingly random manner in which we move, as a detailed examination of the opening lines will show. The poem opens with an invocation and the narrator's summarized account of the baptism. The narrator gives us few specific details, and actually tends to move away from the more particular terms to more general ones, preferring to call John the Baptist "the great Proclaimer" and Christ "the Son of *Joseph*."[4] He even condenses Luke's account of God's words, and thus we only learn that God "From Heav'n pronounc'd him his beloved Son" (I, 32). The brief and undetailed description of the baptism does not provide us with a concrete picture of what occurs, thus preventing us from developing a vividly imagined setting that would make us comfortable with the scene or help orient us toward the drama taking place before us. Immediately following God's proclamation, the poem shifts its focus from the baptism scene to Satan, who witnesses the baptism. As soon as our viewpoint has shifted to him, Satan

with envy fraught and rage
Flies to his place, nor rests, but in mid air
To Council summons all his mighty Peers,
Within thick Clouds and dark tenfold involv'd,
A gloomy Consistory; and them amidst
With looks aghast and sad he thus bespake. (I, 38–43)

These lines rapidly transport us from the Jordan to the midair throne, forcing us to adjust quickly to a new setting. But our adjustment is hindered by another sparsely detailed description, this time of Satan's kingdom, which is nothing more than clouds "tenfold involv'd." Satan then informs his peers that their enemy has arrived on earth, recounts the baptism, and proposes, to the host's unanimous approval, that he must return to earth to tempt Christ by fraud. At this point the narrator gives us a clearer sense of direction by marking the end of the scene: "So to the Coast of *Jordan* he directs / His easy steps, girded with snaky wiles" (I, 119–20). The use of "so" indicates that the scene is closing, and we continue to watch Satan as he returns to earth. However, as we watch him descend, a new scene comes abruptly into focus. We suddenly find ourselves in heaven:

> So to subvert whom he suspected rais'd
> To end his Reign on Earth so long enjoy'd:
> But contrary unweeting he fulfill'd
> The purpos'd Counsel pre-ordain'd and fixt
> Of the most High, who, in full frequence bright
> Of Angels, thus to *Gabriel* smiling spake. (I, 124–29)

The movement from Satan to God is both subtle and abrupt, and our awareness that we are about to change speakers is hindered by a generalizing phrase—"the most High" instead of "God." But, more importantly, the burden of the shift falls on the relative pronoun "who." Until then, our focus is on Satan, but afterwards it is on God. This is a great amount of weight for a small grammatical connector to carry. Moreover, we have no description to help us visualize the change in scene. Thus stripped of any sense of place, we only hear one voice running into another—first Satan's, the narrator's, briefly, and then God's. God tells Gabriel how Christ will conquer "Sin and Death the two grand foes, / By Humiliation and strong Sufferance" (I, 159–60). After hearing God's proclamation, the angels break out in hymn, and then we make our way back to Christ. Here the narrator aids us with a clear but still abrupt transition between heaven and earth: "So they in Heav'n their Odes and Vigils tun'd. / Meanwhile the Son of God" (I, 182–83). Once again, "so" tells us that the scene is coming to a close. But the change in scene is once again very quick, with only the word "meanwhile" directing us to a new place.

Each of these transitions and the scenes they separate share certain characteristics. The transitions are fast and sometimes startling. The settings are virtually nonsettings in their lack of descriptiveness. Also, the quick transitions give us little sense of direction. The cumulative effect of these descriptions is to impair our abilities to envision the poem taking place in an imaginary space. However, the second half of Book I is more settled. The scene shifts end for a time as we come to the wilderness to witness the first day of the temptation. Christ rebukes Satan three times, Satan vanishes, night falls, and Book I ends. The opening of Book II, however, presents us with another series of short scenes.

Book II opens with a surprise for us. We are no longer with Christ, but back at the Jordan to hear Simon and Andrew. The opening is especially disconcerting because the main drama between Satan and Christ was beginning to move in a direction familiar to all of us through the Gospel accounts of the temptations. But the drama, like Satan, has "disappear'd / Into thin Air diffus'd." (I, 498–99). Furthermore, Book I ends with nightfall, and so we might logically expect Book II to begin with the morning of the next day. The poem, however, frustrates this basic and logical expectation by shifting the scene and beginning with "meanwhile," which could refer to any part of Christ's first day of temptation, or even the forty days preceding it. Once again, we revert to a series of quickly drawn scenes with minimal setting and rapid transitions between them.

Back at the Jordan, for instance, we learn nothing about our new setting. We hear nothing about the landscape, whether we are by the river's banks or in a town beside it. All we know is that we are at the Jordan, and the name itself must serve as our setting. First we hear Simon and Andrew resolve their worries over Christ's absence, after which we suddenly shift to Mary:

> Thus they out of their plaints new hope resume
> To find whom at the first they found unsought.
> But to his Mother *Mary*, when she saw
> Others return'd from Baptism, not her Son,
> Nor left at *Jordan*, tidings of him none. (II, 58–62)

The first two lines effectively close Simon and Andrew's scene, but we are unprepared for the abrupt shift to Mary. Also, the narrator gives us no clues as to how Mary stands in relation to Simon and Andrew. It is clear that she is at the Jordan, but we don't know if she is with Simon and Andrew or in a different region altogether. And because we do not know if Mary is with them or not, we do not know whether her speech is a reaction to theirs or independent of it. The lack of spatial detail and the quick change between the scenes disrupt our attempts to build a sense of continuity among the different parts of the poem.

Following Mary's scene are two rapid transitions that likewise disrupt our sense of continuity and direction:

Thus *Mary* pondering oft, and oft to mind
Recalling what remarkably had pass'd
Since first her Salutation heard, with thoughts
Meekly compos'd awaited the fulfilling:
The while her Son tracing the Desert wild,
Sole, but with holiest Meditations fed,
Into himself descended, and at once
All his great work to come before him set;
How to begin, how to accomplish best
His end of being on Earth, and mission high:
For Satan with sly preface to return
Had left him vacant, and with speed was gone
Up to the middle Region of thick Air. (II, 105–17)

The words "Thus Mary" bring her scene to a solid conclusion, but once again we are left unprepared for the brief look at Christ that follows. In a matter of twelve lines we move from Mary to Christ to Satan, and just as critics complain that Simon and Andrew's and Mary's scenes seem extraneous, so does the short interlude with Christ. Its only purpose seems to be to remind us that Christ is still alone in the desert while we go on to look at other scenes. The scene can also lead us to expect a meditation from Christ if we consider what the poem has done before: move us to a new scene and provide us with a new speaker. But this expectation is frustrated by another disorienting scene shift. We are not aware that we are moving on to Satan even after his name is first mentioned. Line 115 does not explicitly mark a scene change and allows us to read the line thus: Satan's disappearance has given Christ the chance to reflect on his mission. But what has really happened is that we have been transported to Satan's midair council. After the council, Satan returns to the wilderness, and, after Christ meditates on his mission, the second day of temptation begins. As with Book I, the rapid, disorienting shifts stop when Christ and Satan are both in the wilderness and the focus returns to the main drama.

By downplaying the spatial elements, by disregarding our need for concrete detail and transitions that clearly indicate shifts from one scene to another, Milton has not completely deprived us of our ability to imagine actively the fictional world that he has created, but he has certainly hindered our ability to do so. This criticism is not a new one. In his first essay on Milton, T. S. Eliot criticized him for a similar fault. Eliot said Milton's poetry did not give us the illusion of being in a specific place at a specific time seeing specific things.[5] But even Eliot admitted that Milton's tendency to downplay spatial and visual elements provided *Para-*

dise Lost with its better moments—the description of hell, for instance (p. 263). This tendency aided him in *Paradise Regained,* though not for the same reasons. In *Paradise Regained,* the spatial disorientation resulting from nondescriptiveness leads to a clearer focus on the speeches of each character, which leads us to focus on the role of Christ. From Satan's speech, we see Christ the enemy who must be defeated. From God's view, we see Christ the Son, preordained to defeat Satan and save mankind. And from the testimony of Simon, Andrew, and Mary, we have a human perspective on Christ which shows three aspects of his character: through Simon and Andrew we see Christ as both comforter and spiritual leader; through Mary, we see humanity's faith in Christ as the son of God. While this complex image of Christ might have been presented without the disorienting shifts, that very disorientation actually heightens and highlights our focus upon Christ. This observation comes close to Louis Martz's suggestion that our interest in the poem arises when we watch "the movements of the narrating mind as it defines the nature of the Son of God."[6] Though focusing on the movement itself rather than on any disorientation the movement might cause, Martz realizes that our understanding of Milton's Christ depends on the activity of the mind itself as it freely roams among the events of Christ's life and those of his followers. Consequently, this movement reduces attention to setting and shifts between scenes, and, by downplaying setting and scene, Milton moves us away from those elements of narrative that we habitually rely on to help us find meaning. Without these elements, we must find our meaning more through the speeches, which direct us to the role and mission of Christ.

At first glance, the spatial disjointedness of the scenes did not seem to hold much promise for pattern or coherence. The more we move through the text, going from place to place, the more we feel we are not going anywhere. But, as we have seen, the various interruptions force us to rely heavily on the characters' speeches, all of which center upon their experiences with Christ. In addition to the poem's spatial disjointedness, confusing time references in the opening scenes of Books I and II reinforce our feelings of disorientation and heighten our focus on Christ's character. As we move through the first four scenes, we find that three involve the baptism. We have already seen how the opening narrative describes the event. But, later in the poem, Satan adds to the narrator's testimony:

> I saw
> The Prophet do him reverence; on him rising
> Out of the water, Heav'n above the Clouds

Unfold her Crystal Doors, thence on his head
A perfect Dove descend, whate'er it meant,
And out of Heav'n the Sovran voice I heard,
This is my Son belov'd, in him am pleas'd. (I, 79–85)

Satan's account, of which only half appears here, is more detailed than the opening narration. The crystal doors and a close paraphrase of God's words as reported in Luke help complete our view of this moment in Christ's life. But the more fully developed and longer description at this point also reverts our attention back to the events we already witnessed in the opening lines. Christ's account of the very same event is also more detailed than the narrator's version and once again reverts to that past moment:

And last the sum of all, my Father's voice,
Audibly heard from Heav'n, pronounc'd me his,
Mee his beloved son, in whom alone
He was well pleas'd. (I, 283–86)

The opening scene of the baptism is informed by three viewpoints, the testimony of each serving as a fragment trying to complete a picture of the whole which centers on Christ. All these testimonies occur in different places in the poem, yet they all bring us back to the same moment. And not only do they return us to the same moment, they help us to learn more about the Christ that Milton portrays. For instance, God's proclamation about his son becomes clearer with each retelling of the event. First, from Satan's viewpoint, we hear how God said that Christ is his son in whom he is pleased. In comparison, Christ's version of the event adds one significant detail — in Christ alone is God pleased. Christ's own retelling further distinguishes Christ's relation to God and comes closer to the gospel tradition. In this way we learn about Christ from different angles; sometimes we get new information, sometimes we see overlapping. At any rate, the movements forward in time with intermittent reflections backwards unsettle our sense of the whole time frame in which these events take place. Nevertheless, while the shifts disturb us on a temporal level, on a thematic one they form a more complex view of Christ's life and mission.

Recreating a text as we read it demands more than just reconstructing the spatial and temporal settings through which the characters move. It also means recreating the characters and the relationships between them. The early scenes of Books I and II in *Paradise Regained* consist of monologues that introduce us to the poem's characters. But perhaps, because they do speak in monologues, these characters do not interact in any way that furthers the main story. The overall effect of these monologues, each succeeding the other for no clear reason, each providing its own particular viewpoint, is a feeling of disjointedness and lack of direction. To further enhance our discomfort with their roles, nearly all speakers address specifically defined audiences who respond vaguely or not at all to their interlocutors. We anticipate their responses and expect them to shape the direction of the poem, yet these expectations are thwarted time after time. For instance, Satan addesses a specifically defined audience when he returns to his kingdom after Christ's baptism. But when Satan first addresses his band of rebels and tells them that the enemy has arrived and must be ruined as Adam was, their reply is condensed by the narrator:

> his words impression left
> Of much amazement to th' infernal Crew,
> Distracted and surpris'd with deep dismay
> At these sad tidings; but no time was then
> For long indulgence to their fears or grief:
> Unanimous they all commit the care
> And management of this main enterprise
> To him their great Dictator. (I, 106–13)

Even though Milton obviously wants to keep the rebels' role to a minimum and not offer us a grand council similar to that in Book II of *Paradise Lost*, he overcompensates and leaves us at an extreme distance from the action. Instead of having the rebels express their distraction and surprise, Milton merely tells us they were so. Similarly, we do not know how they expressed their unanimous consent to allow Satan alone to carry out the enterprise. The crew's minimal role calls into question their need to be addressed at all. Satan could have spoken his piece as a soliloquy and resolved by himself to return to earth. Therefore, Satan's auditors have no essential role whatsoever, yet their appearance would lead us to expect that their role should have something to do with the direction and shape of the poem. That expectation, however, is frustrated.

The relationship between God and his angelic host is not much better. The narrator tells us that God is speaking to Gabriel, thus raising our expectations of hearing a dialogue. In place of Gabriel's response to God's speech, however, we hear the angels break out in a hymn little tied to the substance of God's speech. This sequence has two consequences. First, we wonder what happened to Gabriel. Why was he singled out as God's auditor yet never allowed to have his own response? Again, the sequence of speeches denies our expectations to hear an exchange between characters. Second, the nature of the angelic hymn, which is more a commentary on God's goodness and power than a specific response to God's providence, enhances the overall disjointedness of the monologues.

Until Satan and Christ meet in the wilderness, the only part of Book I that comes close to an exchange between characters is Christ's monologue, in which he recounts an exchange with Mary. Through Christ's monologue, we hear how Mary announced to him that he was God's son. But as with all the monologues so far, Mary's speech indirectly engages Christ's words: "These growing thoughts my Mother soon perceiving / By words at times cast forth, inly rejoic'd, / And said to me apart: High are thy thoughts" (I, 227–29). Mary's reply is not in response to any particular thing that Christ said. Rather, it is a response based on her overall perceptions of her son. Further complicating matters is that she is not really speaking to Christ at this moment; Christ is recounting what she once said to him. But as Christ was once Mary's auditor, we again expect to know what Christ's reaction was when she revealed to him that he was God's son. We could imagine him surprised, incredulous, or trusting, but his specific reaction never comes to light in the poem. Instead, Christ becomes the scholar. Having heard his mother, Christ says, "straight I again revolv'd / The Law and Prophets" (I, 259–60). His response is to turn to Scripture, not to reply directly to Mary, and therefore our ability to reconstruct the exchange between Mary and Christ is hindered by Christ's omission of his direct response to his mother. Once again, the overriding impression continues to be one of disjointedness, where the characters speak and respond in ways that resist the reader's establishing any logical sequence of events.

As with Book I, the characters of Book II do not further the main action of the narrative, chiefly for the same reason—they speak words that elicit no reactions. Simon and Andrew's portion of the poem is a monologue in chorus, not a dialogue, and, apparently, their monologue is directed toward no particular audience, for none is mentioned. Therefore, their words do not seem to affect anyone in a way that makes much difference to the poem's direction. Conceivably, Simon and Andrew's monologue could exist as a poem by itself, and conversely, *Paradise Regained* would be much the same without it. It creates its own tension separate from the main action of the poem. The source of this tension is Christ's absence, and Simon and Andrew express the impact of their loss: "Alas, from what high hope to what relapse / Unlook'd for are we fall'n!" (II, 30–31). But as they continue to meditate on Christ and pray to the Father, they find solace:

> But let us wait; thus far he hath perform'd,
> Sent his Anointed, and to us reveal'd him
>
> . . . .
>
> Let us be glad of this, and all our fears
> Lay on his Providence. (II, 49–54)

And so the monologue creates its own resolution as well, but neither the resolution nor the tension relates in any clear way to the heart of the poem, the temptations of Christ. While we often rely on characters' actions and reactions to orient ourselves to the work's direction, Simon and Andrew's monologue only serves to keep us from any sense of the poem's direction. So too does Mary's speech, which follows Simon and Andrew's. Her monologue also creates a tension and resolution independent of the rest of the poem. We see her initial calm give way to "Motherly cares and fears" (II, 64), and in her distress she remembers Christ being lost once before, only to be found in the temple. This memory leads her to intuit that his absence is due to a divine mission, and that he has disappeared only to go about "His Father's business." Although her meditation indirectly alludes to Christ's mission in the wilderness (he is indeed about his father's business), her speech as well as her very existence in the poem appears extraneous. Again, our expectations that her speech will somehow lead us toward the main action of the poem are thwarted.

While characters often help us perceive patterns and meaning in a work, it would seem that not all characters do so in *Paradise Regained.* The relationships between characters are not what they first seemed, and the characters themselves seem extraneous and speak on irrelevent matters. In both these cases, our expectations are frustrated because the poem's characters do not respond to each other in ways that further the main action of the poem. Instead, they contribute to the disjointed sense of some of its sections. However, in their disjointedness there is still unity within them that focuses our attention on Christ. Even though Satan's council does not appear as a council for us because of the severely limited role of Satan's cohorts, it still serves as an opportunity to see Satan's perspective on his enemies and to learn his plans for fighting them. Instead of the grand debate we see in Book II of *Paradise Lost*, we hear only enough to understand that Christ's coming has elicited a certain response from Satan and the rest of hell. In giving us a fuller view of the council, one that would have better oriented us to Satan's reactions and plans, Milton would have drawn farther away from his focus on Christ. Similarly, God's speech relates to his plans for Christ's triumph over Satan, and the angels' hymn rejoices over God's providence. But at the same time it sings of God's intent in a manner that once again brings our attention back to Christ: "Victory and Triumph to the Son of God / Now ent'ring his great duel, not of arms, / But to vanquish by wisdom hellish wiles" (I, 173–75). Despite the disjointedness caused by not hearing Gabriel as expected and by the hymn that only briefly comments on God's message, the angels once again help us focus on part of Christ's life and purpose—help us understand that it is through wisdom and not physical force that the battle was won over Satan. Christ's nature is foregrounded again when he tells of his exchange with Mary. True, had Milton chosen to have Christ tell of his reaction to Mary's pronouncement, the section would not have been so disjointed and we would have had the opportunity to feel more comfortable with the flow of narration. However, in omitting this matter and having Christ tell how he sought corroboration for his mother's revelation, Milton forces our attention more clearly on Christ's nature and his mission.[7] In those regards, Christ's reaction to Mary's speech would have less to tell us than Christ's investigation of Scripture. Therefore, the disorientation we may feel at this disjuncture leads to a fuller vision of Milton's Christ.

More perplexing are the opening scenes of Book II. As we have seen, they hinder our abilities to reconstruct the temporal and spatial settings of the poem, yet they also have the problem of seeming irrelevant. The characters in these scenes speak of matters which do not directly illuminate the central conflict of the poem, and once they finish they never speak again. Many critics have held these scenes to be irrelevant to the poem, but I agree with those who find them relevant. Tillyard, for instance, explains that Simon, Andrew, and Mary emphasize faith in God's promises, the same faith that Christ also must have to resist Satan (*Milton*, p. 325). In "Why is *Paradise Regained* so Cold?" Alan Fisher claims that the basic connection between these scenes and the rest of the poem lies in the theme of endurance. "Milton," says Fisher, "sets up a parallel between the enduring 'we' must do and the enduring of the poem's only other mortals."[8] As Tillyard and Fisher show, reflection will produce solutions to the problem of these "irrelevant" scenes, and key to both of these solutions is that Christ is the exemplar for humanity. As Simon and Andrew pray for the return for the Messiah, their sudden insight to wait, be patient, endure, and have faith is created by their meditation upon Christ. Similarly, Mary finds solace as she thinks of how Christ goes about doing his father's work. Of all the scenes in the poem, only these two offer us humanity's perspective on Christ. And although the scenes appear disruptive and irrelevant to the poem's main conflict for a variety of reasons, the sense of disruption may actually help us to focus on that perspective. As we realize we are in a new place, listening to new speakers, we search for anything familiar that will help us establish relations between what we are witnessing now and what has gone before. In reorienting ourselves, we find that the only familiar element is once again Christ. The perspective has certainly changed; it is not God's, Satan's, or even Christ's view that we see. Instead, it is a perspective more akin to our own as humans without the understanding that God, Satan, or Christ would have. In offering us this perspective, Milton adds another dimension to his vision of the poem's main character and his influence on our lives.

To this point we have examined only the early scenes of Books I and II, for it is in these places that we are most disoriented by rapid shifts and unconnected monologues. However, our disorientation extends to subsequent sections of the poem, even those that are relatively stable. In order to examine disorientation in these sections, we must look at yet another way in which *Paradise Regained* discourages us from our normal ways of orienting ourselves to a text. In novels and longer poems, we often search for patterns that unify large portions of the work. To this end we often look to a work's chapters, or, in the case of *Paradise Regained*, its books. Though chapters and books are sometimes divided arbitrarily, we normally expect the divisions in the work to mean something, to reveal an internal organization that will help us comprehend a large section of the work. There are often other means through which we try to recreate the larger movements of a work—the phases of a character's life, for instance, or the time in which the narrative takes place in a given setting. In *Paradise Regained*, the three days of temptation also create large segments through which we can orient ourselves to the poem. However, Milton has arranged the books and the days so that these two elements work against each other, and consequently we are surprised to find books ending in strange places in relation to the days.

The first book escapes this problem. Book I takes us from Christ's baptism to the end of the first day of temptation, and, quite logically, it ends with the sun setting on the first day. Book II, however, presents difficulties. Because of the structure of Book I, we may expect that Book II will open with the morning of the second day. But, as we discussed earlier, that expectation is frustrated and we witness the apostles' and Mary's speeches, which are not firmly located in time. The second day finally does get under way, and, based on the pattern we witnessed in Book I, we may expect Book II likewise to end with the second day of temptation. This does not happen, however, and nothing in the action of the poem, the setting, or the speech itself, prepares us for the end of the book. The division comes as an interruption, and the narrator's first line of Book III indicates no awareness of it: "So spake the Son of God." Similarly, the division between Books III and IV also cuts across the second day of temptation, though Book III does have a better sense of closure as the narrator steps in to interrupt the conversation: "So spake *Israel's* true King, and to the Fiend / Made answer meet, that made void all his wiles. / So fares it when with truth falsehood contends" (III, 441–43). His commentary, no matter how didactic, at least offers a feeling of closure. Nevertheless, nothing in the setting or in the characters' actions prepares us for the division, and the sense of surprise is more dominant than the formal attempt at a conclusion for the book.

Because of these unexpected breaks between books and the disproportionate stress given to the second day of temptation, the poem resists our attempts to find consistent patterns within the books. This is not to say, however, that solutions have not been suggested for these difficulties. They have, and in great numbers. But whatever solution is put forth, it testifies to the underlying disorientation we feel when we encounter the book breaks, and it is that sensation that we encounter before we try to formulate a solution to the problem. As A.S.P. Woodhouse confesses, he had to read the poem several times before he realized its structural principle.[9] However, as Woodhouse's confession makes clear, our more immediate reaction to the unexpected book divisions is puzzlement, and this perhaps encourages a distrust of the poem because it appears to sabotage its own structure. In resisting our attempts to comprehend larger elements of its structure, the poem places more stress on its smaller elements, the series of speeches surrounding and including the central conflict between Christ and Satan. And, as we have seen, all the speeches heighten our focus on Christ's mission. Just as the poem achieves a heightened focus on Christ by discouraging us from imagining settings and time frames, the disorientation caused by the unexpected book breaks discourages us from envisioning the poem's overall structure, thereby placing more emphasis on the speakers, who give us a complex, even if fragmented, view of Christ's mission and role in the world.

Not only do these confusing book divisions and constantly shifting scenes and voices ultimately lead to a heightened focus on Christ, they also lead us to empathize with him and his strategy for defeating Satan. Paradoxically, our empathy depends on the narrator's moving us quickly from scene to scene and creating unexpected divisions in his work. By doing so, Milton does more than downplay the formal features of his poem in a way that highlights its content; he limits our roles as readers. Normally, we enjoy an active, meaning-making role of the kind Alan Fisher ascribes to us in "Why is *Paradise Regained* So Cold?" (p. 199). Iser's view of our reading activity agrees with Fisher's: "By grouping together the written parts of the text, we enable them to interact, we observe the direction in which they are leading us, and we project onto them the consistency which we, the readers, require" (*The Implied Reader*, p. 284). Although Milton cannot completely stop our active role in recreating the imaginary world that the text presents, nor our tendency to project consistent patterns onto it, he deters those faculties to a noticeable degree. Throughout *Paradise Regained*, but especially in the opening scenes of Books I and II, Milton hinders our abilities to see a coherent pattern in the poem by disrupting our senses of time, space, plot, and organization. Thus, our abilities to act on the poem are limited as the poem moves us about as it sees fit, much in the same way that Satan moves Christ physically from place to place. This similarity between us and Christ is not immediately obvious, yet this similarity allows us to sense an affinity with the poem's main character. For both ourselves and Christ, our usual ways of moving through an environment, whether real or textual, are limited by circumstances.

Although Christ's subjection to Satan's movements and our subjection to the narrator's produce a sort of kinship between Christ and us, we must also be aware of our differences in order to appreciate Christ's ability to resist Satan. Throughout the poem, the narrator has forced us to view a sequence of scenes briefly, listen to characters who have no immediate relation to the main action, and confront seemingly arbitrary organizational divisions. The disorientation we have felt as a consequence of the narrator's action expresses itself in all the critical activity surrounding the poem's problems with structure. In the poem, however, we witness Christ. He too has been moved much like we have, yet he registers no signs of agitation or disorientation. In various sections of the poem, Satan moves Christ from place to place without giving him any indication of where they are going. From the initial desert scene, Satan takes Christ to the top of a high mountain, whereby Christ can see the kingdoms that Satan plans to offer him (III, 251–52). Once there, Satan directs Christ's attention (and ours) to different regions of the world—Assyria, Parthia, Rome. Yet after Satan offers him Parthia, Christ "answer'd thus unmov'd" (III, 386). After his temptation of the kingdoms fails, Satan again moves Christ back into the desert (IV, 394–97). But the narrator takes pains to mention how unaffected Christ was by Satan's action: "Our Savior meek and with untroubl'd mind / After his airy jaunt, though hurried sore, / Hungry and cold betook him to his rest" (IV, 401–03). Despite the "airy jaunt," his cold and hunger, Christ remains untroubled and ready for rest.

Nevertheless, some critics have condemned Christ's character in the poem for being unaffected and unmoved. For instance, Lawrence Hyman in "The Reader's Attitude in *Paradise Regained*" writes that we are distanced from Christ because he is unaffected by the pleasures and glories offered by Satan. However, Milton's portrayal of Christ can lead to a different conclusion. In "Inaction and Silence: The Reader in *Paradise Regained*," Fish writes that the reader is continually disappointed in Christ's lack of action.[10] However, unlike Hyman, Fish sees the poem as leading not away from Christ, but toward him. We move toward him, according to Fish, because our disappointment leads to our deliverance from poetry and all language to a "union with God" (pp. 26–27). But, as we have seen, it is through experiencing—not rejecting—poetry that we move toward Christ in *Paradise Regained*. Milton, I believe, would want us to understand God's ways through his poetry, for such was his stated intention in his opening invocation to *Paradise Lost:*

> What in me is dark
> Illumine, what is low raise and support;
> That to the highth of this great Argument
> I may assert Eternal Providence,
> And justify the ways of God to men. (I, 22–26).

He wishes to assert Providence through poetry, not in spite of it. Nevertheless I do agree with Fish that *Paradise Regained* reduces the distance between the reader and Christ, though for a different reason. It is precisely that immovable aspect of Christ that makes him accessible, for the poem has conditioned us to achieve a similar attitude all along. Earlier in this essay we saw how Christ was the only unifying point amidst diffuse and disorienting action. The form of the poem has been creating a subtle message that points us toward Christ as the model of stability. Furthermore, the poem's efforts to disorient us have given us the opportunity to compare ourselves with Christ in order to appreciate his perfection, not despair at our differences. Lastly, in the final scenes of the poem, Milton impresses us with Christ's ability to defeat Satan and in the process persuades us to see Christ as the key to overcoming disorientation.

In Book IV, the imagery associated with Christ reinforces his stability. Milton portrays him as the calm, immovable center of chaotic, disorienting movement, which is usually associated with Satan. Book IV begins with a simile in which Satan accosts Christ

> as a swarm of flies in vintage time,
> About the wine-press where sweet must is pour'd,
> Beat off, returns as oft with humming sound;
> Or surging waves against a solid rock,
> Though all to shivers dash't, th' assault renew. (IV, 15–19)

Although the lines almost read as a tribute to Satan's perseverance, the tribute belongs to Christ, who exudes sweetness in the center of a dangerous swarm and endures as a rock against the waves (a traditional symbol of the eternal stability of Christ and his church). Another image related to the storm scene portrays Christ as unmoved while Satan whirls his storm about, but Christ is more explicitly praised:

> O patient Son of God, yet only stood'st
> Unshaken; nor yet stay'd the terror there.
> Infernal Ghosts, and Hellish Furies, round
> Environ'd thee, some howl'd, some yell'd, some shriek'd,
> Some bent at thee thir fiery darts, while thou
> Satt'st unappall'd in calm and sinless peace. (IV, 420–25)

Clearly Milton wants us to see Christ's lack of action as virtuous, even heroic. More importantly, however, we can associate disorientation with Satan, for he is portrayed in the poem as the source of chaos and disorder. This association also holds significance for our reading, because if we succumb to disorientation, even the rather mild disorientation provided by the poem, we implicitly acknowledge our fallibility under Satan. With that realization of fallibility, moreover, we recognize the need for redemption. That need, of course, is fulfilled by Christ in the pinnacle scene. Leading up to the moment of the third temptation, Satan reveals his inner disorientation. He first doubts that Christ is the son of God, then asserts that he is, or was, a son of God, and that all men, including Christ, are sons of God. He then flatters Christ by affirming what we have seen all along, that Christ is "Proof against all temptation as a rock / Of Adamant, and as a Center, firm" (IV, 533–34). Nevertheless, Satan tempts him one more time. Finally, Satan places Christ on the "highest Pinnacle" of the temple, thereby unwittingly acknowledging Christ's place. Gradually we come to see that Satan is disoriented and that we need to escape him. Christ provides us with that escape when, after the temptation, he "stood" and Satan "smitten with amazement fell" (IV, 561–62). Therefore, at the poem's end, we should no longer see ourselves as different from Christ but standing with him against Satan. By experiencing the disorientation created by the poem's structure (or lack of it), we participate more directly in the poem, for the poem makes us see Christ as the answer to the disorientation that the poem itself helps us to feel. In this light, we should not see the much-discussed structural difficulties as faults that need to be explained away. Instead, we should see them as means for helping us realize Christ's defeat of Satan.

The structural difficulties we confront in *Paradise Regained* have given rise to a vast number of attempted solutions, all of which arise from our innate need to realize a unified, well-proportioned pattern in the text. Perhaps the true difficulty lies with our approach to the poem, for the difficulty seems to be that we assume a structure even when we cannot easily recover it. Instead, we should approach *Paradise Regained* on its own terms and allow ourselves to experience the disorientation caused by having some of our basic expectations about reading frustrated. We do not understand the poem any less for responding directly to the feeling of disorientation. What I hope to have shown is that those very feelings allow us to understand better how one man could regain Paradise.

The Pennsylvania State University

NOTES

1. Stanley Fish, "Things and Actions Indifferent: The Temptation of Plot in *Paradise Regained*," in *Milton Studies*, XVII, ed. Richard S. Ide and Joseph Wittreich (Pittsburgh, 1983), p. 168; Barbara K. Lewalski, *Milton's Brief Epic: The Genre, Meaning and Art of "Paradise Regained"* (Providence, R.I., 1966), pp. 102–16; Arnold Stein, *Heroic Knowledge* (Hamden, Conn., 1965), p. 8; E.M.W. Tillyard, *Milton* (London, 1946), p. 323; Arthur Barker, "Calm Regained through Passion Spent: The Conclusions of the Miltonic Effort," in *The Prison and the Pinnacle*, ed. Balachandra Rajan (Toronto, 1973), p. 22. For an extensive description of how critics have approached structural problems in *Paradise Regained*, see Burton J. Weber, "The Schematic Structure of *Paradise Regained:* A Hypothesis," *PQ* L (1971), pp. 553–66. Weber examines two major schools of thought concerning the structure of the poem: one dramatic, the other schematic. The dramatic approach orders the poem according to the relationships and development of its characters. The schematic approach orders the poem according to the arrangement of themes.

2. J. B. Broadbent, "The Private Mythology of *Paradise Regained*," in *Calm of Mind: Tercentenary Essays on "Paradise Regained" and "Samson Agonistes" in Honor of John S. Diekhoff*, ed. Joseph Anthony Wittreich, Jr. (Cleveland, 1971), p. 77.

3. Wolfgang Iser, *The Implied Reader: Patterns of Communication in Prose Fiction from Bunyan to Beckett* (Baltimore, 1974), p. 279.

4. *John Milton: Complete Poems and Major Prose*, ed. Merritt Y. Hughes (Indianapolis, 1957), I, 18–23. All further references to Milton's poetry are to this edition.

5. T. S. Eliot, "Milton I," in *Selected Prose of T. S. Eliot*, ed. Frank Kermode (New York, 1975), pp. 259–60.

6. Louis Martz, *Milton: Poet of Exile*, 2nd ed. (New Haven, 1986), p. 254.

7. Martz, ibid., p. 262, makes a similar point about how Milton subordinates the quality of characters *as* characters to his own narrative purposes. Observing that Milton's voice will occasionally disrupt the illusion of character, Martz says that "the 'characters' of this poem exist, not for their own points of view, but as occasions, as channels, by which the narrative voice can make its way."

8. Alan Fisher, "Why Is *Paradise Regained* So Cold?," in *Milton Studies*, XIV, ed. James D. Simmonds (Pittsburgh, 1980), p. 207.

9. A.S.P. Woodhouse, "Theme and Pattern in *Paradise Regained*," *UTQ* XXV (1956), p. 170.

10. Lawrence Hyman, "Inaction and Silence: The Reader in *Paradise Regained*," *PMLA* LXXXV (1970), p. 498; Fish, *Calm of Mind*, p. 28.

"SUNG AND PROVERB'D FOR A FOOL": *SAMSON AGONISTES* AND SOLOMON'S HARLOT

Laura Lunger Knoppers

IN MILTON'S *Samson Agonistes*, female sexuality has ostensibly brought the champion of Israel to blindness and imprisonment and undermined any hope for Israel's deliverance. Such at least is the claim of Samson and the Chorus, who together objectify and demonize Dalila as a "deceitful Woman," "specious Monster," "Traitress," "Hyaena," "pois'nous bosom snake," "sorceress," and "manifest Serpent." Samson and the Chorus see Dalila as a subversive threat to family, state, and religion — a threat which must be countered by male wisdom and authority.

A number of critics have taken Samson's view of Dalila as Milton's own and have denounced her as the "worst of all possible wives."[1] F. Michael Krouse assumes that a sufficient assessment of Dalila is to say that the antifeminism is traditional, not personal. More recently, John Guillory is concerned to ascertain the historically specific nature of seventeenth-century antifeminism in *Samson Agonistes*. Joseph Wittreich has rightly queried this positing of an unreflective link between text and context.[2] Wittreich's recent work challenges our sense of Samson's heroism by showing how *Samson Agonistes* interacts with various seventeenth-century redactions of Samson in political and religious writings; but he does not show what writings on women and marriage Milton engages and what changes he makes.[3] Although readers have long sought an interpretive key to Milton's Dalila, few sources have been found to illumine this puzzling and problematic female character.[4] The text remains opaque.

I want to argue that the harlot and fool of Proverbs vii provide a crucial and previously unrecognized source for Milton's redaction of Samson and Dalila. Contextualizing Milton's use of Proverbs vii reveals that he draws on and interrogates seventeenth-century discourse on the harlot. Through limited and self-interested characters who use proverbial wisdom to justify and excuse their own faults, Milton seeks to demonstrate the need for discipline, not of the sexually transgressive woman, but of the male self.

I

Solomon's harlot and fool would have been familiar to Milton's readers not only from the Proverbs text, but from domestic handbooks, marriage sermons, and biblical commentaries in seventeenth-century England. This domestic discourse constructs the normative woman, the good wife of Proverbs xxxi, by her defining opposite, the harlot or strange woman of Proverbs vii. Writings on marriage not only publish the signs of female sexual transgression, but in doing so also demonstrate the need for male wisdom to "decypher" and avoid the danger. Hence, John Wing in *The Crowne Conjugall* looks to Solomon "to set forth and discover the compleate state of *a good Wife*, and *an evil*. . . . The *wisdom* of heaven, and the *wisest* on earth are fittest, to decypher both these before us." More precisely, the wisdom of Solomon will provide "*either* the uncoveringe of the *sinfulnesse* and *shame* of the *evill* and *adulterous woman*, that her *filthy nakednesse* appearing, she may be *abhorred* of all men: *Or*, the *commendation* of her that is *good* and *gracious*, that she might be *manifested* in her excellency and men might be enamoured with her."[5]

Transgressive female sexuality is inscribed in the clothing, speech, and behavior of the harlot.[6] In his commentary on Proverbs, Robert Cleaver notes the signs of Solomon's harlot. The first sign is:

> her apparell, wherein she was tricked, and trimmed, unbeseeming the modestie of a sober Matrone, or the honestie of a chast woman. The second is, her inward deceit and guilefulness in that she was of *a subtil heart*. The third is, her unwomanly disposition, and properties: she is a babler, and full of tattle, she is stubborne, perverse and rebellious to God and her husband, she is a gadder abroad, and every where given to allure and corrupt all those whom she can intice into her companie.[7]

Michael Jermin succinctly sums up the nature and significance of these signs in his Proverbs commentary: "wantonesse of apparel, a brawling stubbornnesse of speech, an idle gadding abroad, are no signes of a good mind."[8] Ironically, this secret always gives itself away. The outward appearance of the harlot conceals and yet reveals her true inner state:

> She is base in shamelessness, glorious in her apparell, painted in her cheeks. For because she cannot have the true comelinesse of nature, by false drawings she borrows the shew, not the truth, of an affected beauty. Secondly, after the outward clothing of her body, the inward clothing of her heart is noted, and she is sayd to be *subtile of heart*. (Jermin, p. 139)

Paradoxically, this discourse simultaneously displays the harlot and forbids the reader (who presumably is male) to look at her. Marriage sermons such as *The Crowne Conjugall* warn their readers against the "carnall eye," adducing the examples of Adam, Samson, and the fool from Proverbs vii:

There is no *bondage* greater, then that where-into the *unlawfull liberty* of the *eye*, hath brought many; no *slavery baser*, or more *miserable*, scarce any comparable to it. *Solomons* youncker was catcht so, and how contemptible his state was, is betrayed in two base (but *welbefitting*) *similes*, to wit, of (*a foole going to the stockes, and an Oxe to the slaughter*), this, arguing how *pernitious* his condition was, the other how *reproachfull*. (Wing, p. 201)

The husband must control his gaze: "Seeing therefore so it is, that the miscarriage of this *little* member may be so *great*, and that the Lord hath yet shewed a use of it, that is *so good*, let us be suitors to him that made our eies, to manage them, that they may be kept within the limits of his Law (*not beholding vanity*)" (Wing, p. 206). But despite these warnings, the marriage tracts and sermons display the harlot in vivid, even lurid detail. Disrobing the harlot, so that she is revealed in her "filthy nakednesse," this discourse both incites and condemns the "carnal eye."

Similarly, domestic discourse both publishes and forbids giving ear to the speech of the harlot. Cleaver explains that "the principall meanes whereby she did perswade him was *her speech*, which was both large and delightful; for she used many arguments; she answered all objections, her habite, her catching and kissing of him no doubt did worke upon him, but the poyson which did most intoxicate him was from her tongue" (p. 119). Jermin's commentary on Proverbs likewise dwells on the tongue of the harlot: "First, *she is lowd*, for the tongue of an harlot is as common as herself, it is ready for all ears, it is as lowd as herself is lewd" (p. 139). The reader is urged to hearken not to the harlot but to Solomon's words of wisdom, "as if he should have said, Give eare to mee my sons, and listen not to the harlot, whom God forbiddeth you to heare, and to whom if you hearken, you may evidently foresee your owne ruine in this simple young mans destruction" (Cleaver, p. 120). The voice of the harlot is particularly dangerous as she allures the fool into adultery "by her dissembling and inchanting speeches":

Now the better to cover her plot, and that he should not suspect her treacherie, and mischievous purpose, she pretendeth first, pietie and devotion towards God, to whom she had offered sacrifice . . . and secondly, great love, and good affection towards him, whom she much desired to bee better acquainted with, and to make partaker of her beneficence and kindness. (Cleaver, p. 117)

The words of wisdom to which the reader must hearken include, paradoxically, the enticing words of the harlot.

The threat of the harlot as a "defining other" serves to mandate and legitimate male wisdom and authority even while this wisdom is (necessarily) never sufficient. The threat remains; it cannot be erased. *A Good Wife, Gods Gift* notes that "many have good skill in chusing of wares, in valuing of lands, in beating a bargaine, in making a purchase, that are yet blinde buzzards in the choice of a wife. Yea the wisest that are may bee soone here over-reached."[9] Cleaver sets out the paradigmatic, recurrent nature of the seduction and threat: "Yea many strong men have been slaine by her, whereof one amongst the rest was Samson" (p. 121). The domestic tracts define their power and function as negative and prohibitive: "both to keepe men out, that are in danger to be overtaken, and to get men out, that are already intangled in the miserable snares of the wicked woman" (Wing, p. 19). But such power is also positive, producing in its problematic form the transgressive female sexuality which then requires (male) regulation and control.

Domestic discourse not only warns against and sets out to control unruly females, but also constructs and disciplines male subjectivity, instilling wisdom which will counter the ongoing threat of the harlot. John Wing, in his preface "To the Reader," exhorts his readers to acquire wisdom, praying "that thou mayest be enriched by thy reading of holy treatises; and be made more wise to know, and willing to doe what is good, and what the Lord requireth of thee." These clergymen, writing on women and marriage, establish their own wisdom and authority, paradoxically, by deferring to biblical wisdom: "the wisdom that we speake of is not naturall, but fetched from the fountaine of all wisdom, God himselfe; who by his word giveth unto us pure light to walke by, not in the church alone, nor in publike societie of men onely, but even within the secret of our owne walles."[10] They thus extend church discipline to domestic discipline, to behavior within the reader's "owne walles." By constructing as perennial the threat of the unruly woman, domestic discourse enforces external and internal discipline of sexuality and shapes male subjectivity by defining it against the transgressive female other.

II

Recurrent references in *Samson Agonistes* to examples, proverbs, wisdom, folly, and wise men foreground the proverbial status of Samson and Dalila and engage the current domestic discourse of the harlot. Milton's extensive and significant use and reworking of Proverbs vii in *Samson Agonistes*, previously unremarked by critics, is crucial to an understanding of Samson and Dalila. Unlike the Proverbs account, or contemporary versions of Solomon's harlot, *Samson Agonistes* gives a voice to the fool—Samson himself. As the work opens, Samson interprets his past experience as a paradigmatic fall from wisdom to folly through the flattery and seduction of a deceitful woman. Samson recognizes and laments his lack of wisdom: "O impotence of mind, in body strong! / But what is strength without a double share / Of wisdom?"[11] Samson's foolishness leaves him subject to the scorn and gaze of all: "Within doors, or without, still as a fool, / In power of others, never in my own" (77–78). His foolishness, however, was not literal adultery, but the violation of a sacred pledge, "and for a word, a tear, / Fool, have divulg'd the secret gift of God / To a deceitful Woman" (200–02). Nonetheless, he sees himself as having proverbial status: "tell me, Friends, / Am I not sung and proverb'd for a Fool / In every street" (202–04). Like the betrayed fool, Samson is in despair, wishing only for "speedy death, / The close of all my miseries, and the balm" (650–51).

Samson's depiction of himself as fool places much of the blame on Dalila, the "deceitful Woman" who seduced him. Describing Dalila's betrayal of him to the princes and magistrates of her country, Samson implicitly shifts the blame to female sexuality, as Dalila is "vitiated" (deflowered or violated, *OED*) with gold (389). In recounting his own fall, Samson uses animal imagery similar to that in Proverbs vii, and he blames the "lascivious lap" of a "deceitful Concubine":

> At length to lay my head and hallow'd pledge
> Of all my strength in the lascivious lap
> Of a deceitful Concubine who shore me
> Like a tame Wether, all my precious fleece,
> Then turn'd me out ridiculous, despoil'd,
> Shav'n, and disarm'd among my enemies. (535–40)

Charging Dalila with lust, harlotry, and deceit, Samson draws on the full arsenal of weapons from the discourse of the harlot—despite the fact that Dalila is his wife, not his concubine; that his not her lust was proverbial; that he was never deceived; and that his downfall was not sex but the telling of a secret.[12] He nonetheless adduces himself as proverb or example, to listen to wisdom and beware of the harlot.

Having given a voice to the fool himself, *Samson Agonistes* further revises domestic discourse by having the harlot return to confess her misdeed and ask for a second chance. Yet when Dalila comes sailing into *Samson Agonistes,* the Chorus almost immediately types her as the strange woman or harlot. They recall the Proverbs account and foreground the signs of the harlot in her apparel, her coming into the street, her perfume, and her foreign nature:

> But who is this, what thing of Sea or Land?
> Female of sex it seems,
> That so bedeckt, ornate, and gay,

Comes this way sailing
Like a stately Ship
Of *Tarsus*, bound for th' Isles
Of *Javan* or *Gadire*
With all her bravery on, and tackle trim,
Sails fill'd, and streamers waving,
Courted by all the winds that hold them play,
An Amber scent of odorous perfume
Her harbinger, a damsel train behind;
Some rich *Philistian* Matron she may seem,
And now at nearer view, no other certain
Than *Dalila* thy wife. (710–24)

The Chorus shifts the reader's gaze to the female body, or rather to clothing which both conceals and reveals the harlot. In the scopic economy of the Chorus, Dalila's female sexuality is enhanced and made visible. By drawing on the discourse of the harlot, they are able to survey, objectify, and (implicitly) judge.

Dalila, then, shows the first sign of the harlot in her "attire" (Prov. vii, 11). Depicted as a "bedeckt, ornate, and gay" ship, Dalila is the defining opposite of the virtuous wife of Proverbs xxxi, often pointed to in domestic discourse, who "is like the merchants' ships, she bringeth her food from afar" (14). In his popular marriage sermon *The Merchant Royall*, Robert Wilkinson delineates not only the qualities of a ship that a good wife should have but those she should not. Wilkinson particularly warns against "too much rigging," in lines which strikingly recall the description of Dalila as ship:

> Oh what a wonder it is to see a ship under saile, with her tacklings, and her masts, and her tops . . . and so bedeckt with her streames, flags, and ensignes, and I know not what; yea but a world of wonders it is, to see a woman created in Gods image, so miscreate oft times and deformed, with her French, her Spanish, and her foolish fashions . . . with her Plumes, her Fannes, and a silken Vizard, with a ruffe like a saile, yea a ruffe like a rainebow, with a feather in her Cap like a flag in her top, to tell, (I thinke) which way the wind will blow.[13]

Significantly, Wilkinson sees this lavish apparel as indicating sexual transgression and he links the wife-ship which "cannot be housed" with the harlot of Proverbs vii: "for it is a note of the unchast woman, that her *feet cannot abide in her house, but now she is without, now in the street, and lies in wait at every corner*, Prov. 7.11.12" (sig. C3). Milton's Dalila thus shows another sign of the harlot in that "her feet abide not in her house" (Prov. vii, 11 KJV).

Finally, when she persists in pleading her case with Samson, Dalila shows the third sign of the harlot: "She is loud and stubborn" (Prov. vii, 11). As she comes "to behold / Once more thy face, and know of thy estate" (741–42), Dalila echoes the voice of the harlot, who flatters the fool, "Therefore came I forth to meet thee, diligently to seek thy face, and I have found thee" (Prov. vii, 15). She speaks smooth flattering words of love, claiming that "the jealousy of Love" (791) caused her actions and pleading that "Love hath oft, well meaning, wrought much woe, / Yet always pity or pardon hath obtain'd" (813–14). Her extended plea of patriotism and piety also recalls Solomon's harlot, who has "peace offerings" with her, having just "paid [her] vows" (Prov. vii, 14). Dalila alleges patriotism as a motive for her yielding to the importunities of the Philistine magistrates, princes, and priest:

> at length that grounded maxim
> So rife and celebrated in the mouths
> Of wisest men, that to the public good
> Private respects must yield, with grave authority
> Took full possession of me and prevail'd;
> Virtue, as I thought, truth, duty so enjoining. (865–70)

There are sexual overtones even here, as proverbial (male) wisdom "took full possession of" and "prevail'd" with the yielding Dalila. Dalila's encounter with Samson has as its crux a thinly veiled sexual offer. Dalila offers solace, as she tries to take Samson home: "Life yet hath many solaces, enjoy'd / Where other senses want not their delights / At home in leisure and domestic ease" (915–17). The echo of Solomon's harlot, who offers to the fool the deceptive solace of love, indicates the danger: "Come, let us take our fill of love until the morning: let us solace ourselves with loves" (Prov. vii, 18). The secret of Dalila's continued harlotry seems to give itself away in her clothing, behavior, and, above all, her speech.

Because Samson hears in Dalila the voice of the harlot, he invariably and harshly rejects everything she has to offer, refusing to believe her confession until her true nature is revealed. Samson uses his new knowledge of the harlot to expose and reject the guilt inscribed in the female body: "These false pretexts and varnish'd colors failing, / Bare in thy guilt how foul must thou appear?" (901–02). The "filthy nakednesse" of the harlot is again simultaneously displayed and condemned. Despite his earlier assertion of foolishness, Samson now sees himself as having gained the knowledge or wisdom to recognize and resist Dalila's sexual snares:

> Nor think me so unwary or accurst
> To bring my feet again into the snare
> Where once I have been caught; I know thy trains

Though dearly to my cost, thy gins, and toils;
Thy fair enchanted cup, and warbling charms
No more on me have power, their force is null'd,
So much of Adder's wisdom I have learn't
To fence my ear against thy sorceries. (930–37)

Samson particularly refuses to listen to the voice of the harlot and hearkens instead to the words of wisdom to "Remove thy way far from her, and come not nigh the door of her house" (Prov. v, 8). He now diverges from the fool in Proverbs; having gained the "Adder's wisdom," he will not enter her house: "This Gaol I count the house of Liberty / To thine whose doors my feet shall never enter" (949–50). Maintaining that Dalila is lying, Samson threatens her verbally and physically until she at last confesses what he takes as the truth of her character.

The woman who strays outside the house, talks, and wears fancy clothes is finally "revealed" to be plotting the overthrow of all authority—domestic, political, and religious. Like Solomon's strange woman, Dalila's lips "drop as an honeycomb," but "her end is bitter as wormwood, sharp as a two-edged sword" (Prov. v, 3–4). Rejected by Samson, Dalila finally lashes out and embraces her public role:

Nor shall I count it heinous to enjoy
The public marks of honor and reward
Conferr'd upon me, for the piety
Which to my country I was judg'd to have shown.
At this who ever envies or repines
I leave him to his lot, and like my own. (991–96)

Samson and the Chorus see Dalila as "a manifest Serpent by her sting / Discover'd in the end, till now conceal'd" (997–98). The dangers of the harlot have been, it seems, providentially averted.

Dalila's perfidy is confirmed by the Chorus, which (analogous to the writers of domestic tracts or to the Proverbs narrator) comments on the action and speaks proverbial wisdom, but paradoxically denies that it will do any good. Throughout *Samson Agonistes*, the Chorus views Samson as the proverbial strong man inevitably deceived and felled by a wicked woman: "Tax not divine disposal; wisest Men / Have err'd and by bad Women been deceiv'd / And shall again, pretend they ne'er so wise" (210–12). According to the Chorus, wisdom cannot discern the vicious woman:

Whate'er it be, to wisest men and best
Seeming at first all heavenly under virgin veil,
Soft, modest, meek, demure,

> Once join'd, the contrary she proves, a thorn
> Intestine. (1034–38)

Nor is wisdom sufficient to find the virtuous woman: "Favor'd of Heaven who finds / One virtuous, rarely found, / That in domestic good combines; / Happy that house!" (1046–49). The Chorus, like Samson, seems to spend a lot of time inveighing against female waywardness, which only seems to proliferate. Wisdom or knowledge seems destined to fail. But using this failure as support, the Chorus argues for coercive male power: "Therefore God's universal Law / Gave to the man despotic power / Over his female in due awe" (1053–55). The Chorus applauds Samson's verbal and threatened physical violence, his show of "despotic power" against the threat of his contrary wife.

Yet is Dalila the real threat to Samson? Or has she ever been? By placing proverbial discourse on the harlot in the mouths of limited, self-interested characters, Milton exposes such "wisdom" as a displacement of blame and responsibility. Samson has been undone, not by Dalila, but by his own folly. By his own admission, Samson "with a grain of manhood well resolv'd / Might easily have shook off all her snares: / But foul effeminacy held me yok't / Her Bondslave" (408–11). What the Chorus does not recognize, and what Samson only in part intuits, is that control over women is necessary for the self-control of men.

Samson's exposure and rejection of Dalila is thus problematized. Intervening in contemporary domestic discourse, *Samson Agonistes* reveals that the signs of harlotry—voice, appearance, and behavior—are unreliable, constructed, and not unique to women. Samson hears in Dalila the voice of the harlot, but he does not hear very well. Early in the drama, Samson hears "The tread of many feet steering this way" (111) and concludes, wrongly, that his enemies are approaching. When the Chorus first speaks, Samson can only "hear the sound of words, thir sense the air / Dissolves unjointed ere it reach my ear" (176–77). Nor does the Chorus hear infallibly: near the end of the drama, they cannot decide whether the "hideous noise" (1509) that they hear is good or bad and wrongly deduce that Samson's eyesight is "by miracle restor'd" (1528).

Further, *Samson Agonistes* reveals that eyesight can be deceiving. Samson, of course, cannot see Dalila at all. But the Chorus who can gives two contradictory descriptions: Dalila as a haughty and decked-out ship or "with head declin'd / Like a fair flower surcharg'd with dew" (727–28). The body most on display—Samson's blinded, imprisoned body—is also variously interpreted. The Chorus sees Samson's prostrate, unkempt body as sign of "one past hope, abandon'd, / And by himself given over"

(120–21). But they also recognize the unreliable, shifting gaze: "Or do my eyes misrepresent?" (124). Samson's visitors see inscribed on his body the signs of mutable fortune, the power of Dagon, the victory of the Philistines, and God's desertion. Samson reads in his body defeat and failure; he expects to die "Betray'd, Captiv'd, and both my Eyes put out, / Made of my Enemies the scorn and gaze" (33–34). Samson appears to be the defeated and now useless fool. But he isn't.

Nor are the signs of behavior trustworthy or stable in *Samson Agonistes*. In going to the Philistine temple, Samson seems to be violating Israelite law, obeying the Philistines, and bringing praise to Dagon. But his victory over the Philistines proves otherwise. The Israelite Chorus, which judges by appearance, is surprised that one "blind of sight, / Despis'd and thought extinguish't quite" (1687–88) can be so miraculously reborn. These often-mistaken representations of Samson's body reveal the unreliability of signs. Samson and the Chorus condemn Dalila on the basis of signs which have been exposed as arbitrary, shifting, and radically unstable. The signs of the harlot, despite the claims of Samson and the Chorus, remain opaque—as attested to by the long critical tradition of violent disagreement over Dalila's motives and true nature.

Further, although he rejects Dalila's excuses that she acted from womanly nature, Samson describes her as an animal, a trap, a witch, and thus objectifies her as a nonhuman thing which by nature acts in certain ways. Milton reveals that proverbial wisdom does not so much uncover as construct the harlot. Samson repeatedly thwarts Dalila's confession and constrains her to speak the "truth": rejecting her in the home, he pushes Dalila toward the public role that is then used to confirm her harlotry.[14]

Finally, Dalila shares the signs of harlotry with the male characters, particularly with Samson. All of Samson's visitors have sought him out to offer (mistaken) solace, and have not been accused, as Dalila is, of treachery and hypocrisy. Ironically, Samson himself shares the gender-coded signs of the harlot. He too had been pridefully decked out like a ship, "Gloriously rigg'd" (200). His self-confessed downfall was "Shameful garrulity" (491), transgressive speech. And finally, Samson has been spiritually unchaste, having "yielded, and unlock'd her all my heart" (407) and given up his "fort of silence to a Woman" (236). The harlotry most threatening to Samson is his own; like the strange woman of Proverbs, he "forgetteth the covenant of [his] God" (Prov. ii, 17). In constructing and rejecting Dalila as a harlot, Samson displaces and rejects his own spiritual harlotry.

Samson's rejection of Dalila has the effect of mastery and detachment of desire; since he can now "fence [his] ear" (937) against the voice of the harlot, Samson has, in effect, renounced his harlotry. He thus can expect his voice to be heard by God whose "ear is ever open" (1172). Samson describes his spiritual bond in language with sexual overtones. Assured of "Favor renew'd," he is wary of "prostituting holy things to Idols" (1357–58), is concerned with God's "jealousy" (1375), and feels "rousing motions" (1382). The threat of the harlot, most importantly, enables Samson to master and redirect his own desire.

At the end of the tragedy, Manoa still wants to see Samson as a proverbial example of the destruction wrought by a wicked woman: he predicts that virgins will visit Samson's tomb, "only bewailing / His lot unfortunate in nuptial choice, / From whence captivity and loss of eyes" (1742–44). But the work as a whole points not to Dalila's sexuality but to Samson's own folly as the primary danger. As with domestic discourse, *Samson Agonistes* constructs a defining other which both threatens and legitimates control. But Milton replaces the harlot with the fool as the object of the gaze and then depicts how this foolishness can be overcome by repentance, renewed self-discipline, and submission to God. Milton draws on and significantly reworks the depictions of Solomon's harlot to demonstrate the need for male discipline, not of the transgressive female, but of the self.

Tragedy, as Milton defines it in his preface to *Samson Agonistes*, has the moral function of raising "pity and fear, or terror, to purge the mind of those and such like passions, that is to temper and reduce them to just measure" (Hughes, p. 549). Yet in publishing Samson's secret folly and the resulting shame and destruction, *Samson Agonistes* ensures that the emotions of fear and pity are never fully purged—the threat remains, contained and deployed in discourse. The tragedy does not simply warn against, but produces in its problematic form, the male folly which mandates self-discipline and submission to divine wisdom. By deploying the perennial threat of male folly, *Samson Agonistes* instills internal discipline, shaping male subjectivity by defining it against the transgressive *male* other. Milton deconstructs the discourse of the harlot, to turn from male wisdom to the "unsearchable dispose / Of highest wisdom" (1747–48). Only divine wisdom, for Milton, provides the solution to the threat of foolishness and harlotry—of both male and female, Samson and Dalila.

The Pennsylvania State University

NOTES

Research support for this essay was provided by the Institute for the Arts and Humanistic Studies, The Pennsylvania State University.

1. See, for example, Thomas Kranidas, "Dalila's Role in *Samson Agonistes,*" *SEL* VI (1966), 125–37; Mary S. Weinkauf, "Dalila: The Worst of All Possible Wives," *SEL* XIII (1973), 135–47; and, most recently, Ricki Heller, "Opposites of Wifehood: Eve and Dalila," in *Milton Studies* XXV, ed. James D. Simmonds (Pittsburgh, 1988), pp. 187–202. A minority of critics take the opposite stance. Early defenses of Dalila were made by William Empson, *Milton's God*, rev. ed. (London, 1965), pp. 211–28 and Irene Samuel, "*Samson Agonistes* as Tragedy," in *Calm of Mind: Tercentenary Essays on "Paradise Regained" and "Samson Agonistes,"* ed. Joseph A. Wittreich (Cleveland, 1971), pp. 235–57. More recently, see John Ulreich, "'Incident to All Our Sex': The Tragedy of Dalila" in *Milton and the Idea of Woman*, ed. Julia Walker (Urbana, Ill., 1988), pp. 185–210.

2. F. Michael Krouse, *Milton's Samson and the Christian Tradition* (Princeton, 1949), pp. 102–03; John Guillory, "Dalila's House: *Samson Agonistes* and the Sexual Division of Labor," in *Rewriting the Renaissance: The Discourses of Sexual Difference in Early Modern Europe*, ed. Margaret W. Ferguson, Maureen Quilligan, and Nancy J. Vickers (Chicago, 1986), pp. 106–22; Joseph Wittreich, *Feminist Milton* (Ithaca, 1987), pp. 143–46.

3. Joseph Wittreich, *Interpreting "Samson Agonistes"* (Princeton, 1986).

4. Dalila has been compared to such negative paradigms as Cleopatra and the Whore of Babylon. See Barbara K. Lewalski, "*Samson Agonistes* and the 'Tragedy' of Apocalypse," *PMLA* LXXXV (1970), 1058–59; Milton Miller, "A Contrary Blast: Milton's Dalila" in *Drama, Sex and Politics, Themes in Drama* VII, ed. James Redmond (Cambridge, 1985), pp. 93–108; and Guillory, "Dalila's House," pp. 112–15. Stella Revard argues for a more positive paradigm in "Dalila as Euripidean Heroine," *Papers on Language and Literature* (Summer 1987) XXIII, no. 3, 291–302.

5. John Wing, *The Crowne Conjugall or The Spouse Royall* (London, 1620), pp. 21, 16.

6. On the deployment of female sexuality as a disciplinary technology, see Michel Foucault, *The History of Sexuality, Vol. I: An Introduction*, trans. Robert Hurley (New York: Vintage, 1980). See also Peter Stallybrass, "Patriarchal Territories: The Body Enclosed," in *Rewriting the Renaissance*, pp. 123–29.

7. Robert Cleaver, *A Brief Explanation of the whole Booke of the Proverbs of Salomon* (London, 1615), p. 115.

8. Michael Jermin, *Paraphrasticall Meditations, By Way of Commentarie, Upon the Whole Booke of the Proverbs of Solomon* (London, 1638), p. 140.

9. Thomas Gataker, *A Good Wife, Gods Gift: and A Wife Indeed. Two Mariage Sermons* (London, 1623), p. 10.

10. John Dod and Robert Cleaver, *A Godly Forme of Household Government* (London, 1621), Sig A2.

11. *Samson Agonistes*, lines 52–54, in *John Milton: Complete Poems and Major Prose*, ed. Merritt Y. Hughes (Indianapolis, 1957), hereafter cited parenthetically in the text.

12. That Dalila's earlier betrayal of her husband was verbal and emotional rather than physical adultery would, however, only make it worse for Milton. Throughout his prose tracts on divorce, Milton is concerned with emotional rather than physical faithfulness and compatibility, and he even redefines fornication as enmity, faithlessness, or dis-

obedience of *mind* (of wife to husband or man to God). See *Complete Prose Works of John Milton*, gen. ed. Don M. Wolfe et al., Vol. II, ed. Ernest Sirluck (New Haven, 1959).

13. Robert Wilkinson, *The Merchant Royall. A Sermon Preached at White-Hall before the Kings Majestie* (London, 1613), Sig C4).

14. On this point, see Ulreich, "Incident To All Our Sex," pp. 190–96.

SUICIDE AND REVENGE: *SAMSON AGONISTES* AND THE LAW OF THE FATHER

Gregory F. Goekjian

> O Lord God, remember me, I pray thee, and strengthen me, I pray thee, only this once, O God, that I may be at once avenged of the Philistines for my two eyes. . . .
>
> Let me die with the Philistines. (Judg. xvi, 28–30)

THE TWO PRAYERS at the end of the Samson story in Judges are never heard in *Samson Agonistes*. One can imagine many reasons for this omission, including the dramatic convention of offstage death and the Puritan preference for silent prayer. But it also seems clear that these prayers are totally inappropriate to the interpretation of Samson's death embraced by the Chorus. The focus of these prayers on the self, on personal vengeance and the desire to die, are at variance with the divine witness the Chorus finds in Samson's death. Yet like the canonical Christian interpreters of the Samson story, Milton's Hebrews find in Samson's great act witness to God's rightful preeminence, Samson's filiality, and Israel's legal foundation.[1] What was blind is illuminated, what doubted, proved, and, in similitude to the phoenix, what was "Deprest, and overthrown, as seem'd . . . Revives, reflourishes."[2] As the Chorus asserts at the end, the evidence of this reversal is no less than God's, who

> to his faithful Champion hath in place
> Bore witness gloriously; whence *Gaza* mourns
> And all that band them to resist
> His uncontrollable intent;
> His servants he with new acquist
> Of true experience from this great event
> With peace and consolation hath dismist,
> And calm of mind, all passion spent. (1751–58)

Rarely has tragic closure been asserted so absolutely.

But it is just this assertive force that has led to critical doubt about a play that throughout calls into question patriarchal order and the law of God on which that order is based. The overdetermined ending serves to divulge the ambiguities and displacements in the text that it might be intended, through its force, to dissolve. Does Manoa's conclusion that "*Samson* hath quit himself / Like *Samson*" (1709–10) suggest that there is no higher comparison, or is it evasive tautology, a rhetorical mask of doubt? Is Samson's claim that he is "Sole Author" and "sole cause" (376) of his fall a reviving recognition of his responsibility to God, or is it an expression of existential despair? Is the Chorus' jubilant celebration of God's witness to what is, after all, his own power the ultimate proof of God's authority or a sublimation of its absence? To ask such questions is to admit a good deal of suspicion, but suspicion is a primary motivation of tragedy and of this tragedy in particular. What is disturbing about *Samson*—antithetical to the "calm of mind" the Chorus proclaims—is that it seems to demand and then to ratify an absolute choice between conclusions it has placed in opposition. The choric interpretation of Samson's act is right or it is wrong, and choice between the two ordains the meaning of the play and of Samson's "great act."[3]

The choice becomes increasingly difficult with time, not only because reading has become suspicious of binary opposition, of authority, and of faith, but also because such opposition implies a particular view of the relationship between history and authority. To read *Samson* with the Chorus is to create an author in reaction against the tumult of his time, one who looks back, with blind confidence or nostalgia, to the authoritative, closural values of a Christian humanist past. To read against the Chorus implies a despair about the future, whereby Samson or any authoritative hero can only hope to fall again.[4] The closure provided by the first choice has been the more attractive to traditional criticism, for if we look backward we may find that Milton's work "subsumed the whole history of humanism in one grand restatement at the moment of its demise." If forward, we find the "great bogey" with which Romanticism and feminism have struggled.[5]

In this essay I want to suggest that the oppositions may not be so opposed, nor the choices so direct. Both are based on the relationship we understand to exist between Samson and God, yet that relationship implies one between Samson and men as well, and whereas the play constantly raises the question of Samson's divine relationship, in God's absence it can only manifest such a relationship in mortal terms. In *Samson* those terms are primarily legal and domestic, testing the hierarchy of God and man through its manifestations in human law and familial ties. Both of these related structures imitate the divine hierarchy, and, in their inadequacy, they may suggest the difference of God's law from man's, man's inability to accede to the law, or, conversely, the strength of divine providence in spite of human weakness. Whatever choices we or the Hebrews make, they are always blind choices, based on an interpretation of absence rather than presence.[6] Furthermore, the choices to some degree displace the truth, for they are always mimetic, based on desire for the truth rather than on knowledge. Throughout the play, Samson as well as the rest of the characters make their choices in imitation of the choices of others.

The text's own model of interpretation—of choice—suggests that some suspicion is warranted. Unlike the Samson of Milton's source in Judges, who voices clearly two desires—to have his revenge and to die—Milton's Hebrews can only countenance one. Told by the messenger that Samson died "by his own hands," Manoa asks, "Self-violence? what cause / Brought him so soon at variance with himself?" (1583–85). The messenger's interpretation, based on his eyewitness of the event, is that the cause was "Inevitable . . . / At once both to destroy and be destroy'd" (1587–88), to which Manoa responds, "O lastly overstrong against thyself! / A dreadful way thou took'st to thy revenge" (1590–91). Manoa suspects suicide: Samson, "at variance with himself," has wished for death throughout the play. The messenger's invocation of inevitability is no real help, for Samson chooses to pull down the temple, and if he chooses to destroy, he chooses to be destroyed as well.[7] But Manoa suppresses suicide: the logical conclusion to the exchange would be that Samson has found a dreadful way to *die*, yet Manoa finds *revenge* on the Philistines instead. In the messenger's subsequent description of Samson's end, no supporting evidence of a pure revenge motive is brought forth, and the fact that its validity is based on an "eyewitness" (1594) thoroughly discredited by the play's controlling trope is emphasized by the messenger's report of Samson's last words, a grisly pun on visual evidence: "Now of my own accord such other trial / I mean to show you of my strength, yet greater; / As with amaze shall strike all who behold" (1643–45). Yet the Chorus picks up the revenge motif and moves farther away from the "variant" of suicide: "O dearly bought revenge, yet glorious" (1660). And this leads Manoa to indulge in a further and concluding assertion when he declares Samson "on his Enemies / Fully reveng'd . . . / With God not parted from him, as was fear'd, / But favoring and assisting to the end" (1711–20).

Although in Judges Samson's desire for death seems clearly subordinate to his ringing prayer for vengeance, in *Samson Agonistes* the desire is raised to its most desperate level—suicide—only to be absolutely displaced. It seems clear that for Manoa and the Chorus suicide is a possibility to be both recognized and willfully rejected, for to admit suicide as a motivation for Samson's act would be to admit the possibility of despair, a reversal of Samson's witness to God and the Law.

It seems equally clear that the object of Samson's revenge must be, for Manoa and the Chorus, the Philistines, for the only other possible objects are the Hebrews themselves and, of course, God. Yet in the course of the play there is no evidence to warrant the choric conclusions; in fact, just the reverse is indicated. Before Samson's death, revenge on the Philistines is never a consideration. In fact, the term is used three times and always in reference to Philistine revenge on Samson for his former acts of mayhem. The antagonists Samson recognizes throughout the play are not the Philistines, whose enmity he understands, but the Hebrews and God, whose actions he does not (for example, lines 237–76, 1211–16). What is evident is a desire for death which Samson expresses repeatedly, to the point that Manoa feels obligated to warn him, "let another hand, not thine, exact / Thy penal forfeit from thyself" (507–08). The Hebrews' rush to judgment, with its displacement of unacceptable motives, may well suggest a sublimation of their fear that Samson's death denies the authority, order, and witness they would have it reestablish.[8]

To consider the story of Samson in the mid-seventeenth century is virtually to consider the nature of suicide. Suicide was, as S. E. Sprott contends, "a practical and urgent problem in the Puritan way of religious life," reflected in the almost epidemic increase in its incidence during the interregnum.[9] At least three full books had appeared on the topic between 1637 and 1653, and it was a common topic in treatises throughout the period. In most of them, the Samson story (or question) took a proud place as scriptural example, most often of a divinely inspired exception to the strict Augustinian suicide prohibition. Samson's suicide might be considered a result of a direct command from God, or it might be used to indicate the permission of suicide if committed in the interest of God's glory. The latter is the greatest source of Puritan concern, wherein, since Scripture is not clear on the proscription of suicide, promotion of God's glory could be prompted by inner light, which might be subject to manifold vagaries. As Sprott puts it, "suicide in the Puritan era was not a mere occasion of theological fascination; it was an occupational hazard of the religious calling" (p. 51).

Yet one need not have been a Puritan to take an even more radical position. In *Biathanatos* John Donne argues that suicide, as an act of charity, may be permissible and perhaps even mandatory as an imitation of Christ's death. In fact, this argument is the basis of Donne's claim that Samson is a type of Christ. In effect, Donne's argument is that suicide, an act of self-will, may be an imitation of Christ's self-willed death.[10]

The indistinction (or perhaps indifference) between self-will and mimetic (self) will, complicated by the temporal inversion of typological understanding, comes very close to the argument in *Samson*. Samson's "self-violence," though judged by the Chorus to be "inevitable" in the course of his revenge, is clearly such an ambiguous act of self-will, even as the Chorus struggles interpretively to deny self-motivation in Samson's act. And this ambiguity seems fully intentional on Milton's part. At moments when we might expect illumination about Samson's motivation (Samson's "rousing motions," or in his prayer just before death), the issue is raised only to be obscured, displaced, or sublimated, deflected by revenge. And revenge itself is altered by the Hebrews, who reject the motive of personal vengeance "for my two eyes" in favor of witness to God's power and the consequent reification of Hebrew law, for personal revenge would also be an abrogation of God's power.

The displacement of suicide by revenge and the insistence on the Philistines as revenge's object may share an interpretive motive, conscious or not—the choric sublimation of a suspicion that Samson's "great act" may just as evidently be seen to violate the greatest and most deadly prohibition of all, a renunciation of the Father. To argue for the possibility of such a motive is to argue for undecidability, and I would like to suggest that the undecidable is precisely the locus of tragic heroism in *Samson Agonistes* and perhaps in its author as well. To act without knowing, even to write without knowing, may be to risk the ultimate violation of truth in truth's pursuit.

If readings of the text are undecidable, this in turn argues a certain textual ambivalence. Perhaps the best way to phrase the question this raises is to ask whether Samson finds God's resolution to the situation, his own "self-satisfying solution," or perhaps both. The situation bears a close resemblance to Freud's reading of the mythos of Christianity, an Oedipal deconstruction of patrilineal order:

> In the Christian myth man's original sin is undoubtedly an offence against God the Father, and if Christ redeems mankind from the weight of original sin by sacrificing his own life, he forces us to the conclusion that the sin was murder. . . . The reconciliation with the father is the more thorough because simultaneously with this sacrifice there follows the complete renunciation of women, for whose sake mankind rebelled against the father. But now also the psychological fatality of ambivalence demands its rights. In the same deed which offers the greatest possible expiation to the father, the son also attains the goal of his wishes against the father. He becomes a god himself beside or rather in place of the father.[11]

In citing Freud in the context of *Samson* I do not mean to suggest that Samson is necessarily a type of Christ or even that Freud's theory is adequate to the play. Yet "renunciation of women," "psychological fatality of ambivalence," and especially displacement of the father do accurately summarize the play's most profound though least pronounced actions. And if Samson is a type, he may be typical not of Christ, but of Miltonic man, enmeshed in the events of history and proscribed by law.

The choric interpretation of *Samson*'s meaning at the end is not a singular event. A pattern of displacement, and even doubled displacement, with the object of sublimating or suppressing a fear that order, divine or temporal, has been lost, may in fact be the play's major action.[12] The "temptations" of Manoa, Dalila, and Harapha all seek to place or replace a Samson whose neutered condition has displaced them as father, wife, or Philistine champion, whether or not the tempters are aware of it. Samson himself, of course, is virtually the representation of displacement, defined and self-defined by his separation from, and to, God.

The choric assertion of closure and order to which God "hath in place / Bore witness gloriously" (1751–52) is predicated on the unexpected return of the hidden God who has been manifest throughout the play only in terms of negation and prohibition: whenever Samson begins to rationalize the disintegration brought about by his fall, rationalization that leads inevitably to a wish for death, "Tax not divine disposal" (210) prohibits the interpretive logic that could put Samson — however despairingly — to rest. He is tormented by thoughts that "present / Times past" (21–22), "Myself my sepulchre, a moving Grave" (102). God's prohibitive, hidden "presence" decenters Samson throughout. "Separate to God" (31), Samson is also separated from the order of men, undefined by present or past, life or death. His search for what the Chorus calls a "self-satisfying solution" (306) is the search for an end to displacement.

At the end of the play, even as the Hebrews assert the finality of Samson's answer to the question of "whose god is God" (1176), the patriarchal order on which it is based is undercut by an exception. Manoa's closing vision of such a stable order is "A Monument . . . / With all his Trophies hung and Acts enroll'd," excepting only "His lot unfortunate in nuptial choice, / From whence captivity and loss of eyes" (1734–44). The exception of nuptial choice from the list of Samson's commemorable acts might simply suggest Manoa's disappointment in a worldly tarnish on his son's divine trophies, were it not for the fact that the laws of marriage and the power of women play such a large part in Samson's struggle.

Historically, the interdependence of domestic with civil and religious hierarchy is not only one of Milton's constant themes, but one, like suicide, pronounced to a crucial degree by his age. The reformation and the violent dissolution of monarchy had put severe pressure on the hierarchies of English society, particularly at the domestic level. Maureen Quilligan contends that "Radical Protestants were thrown back on the one social unit that might still stand—the nuclear family. . . . Increasing authority of the husband over the wife is a conservative social move designed to act as a safety valve on the revolutionary energies unleashed by the Reformation: if there were to be no more bishops and no more kings, yet there were still to be, finally and irrevocably, patriarchs."[13] I find this analysis of history particularly appropriate to *Samson*, for in drawing a reactionary conclusion (the overassertion of domestic patriarchy) from the *failure* of the system on which it is based, it mirrors the assertiveness of the choric conclusion about Samson's death, based, as I think it is, on a suspicion of Samson's failure. Furthermore, the disturbance of domestic patriarchy is precisely the ground on which *Samson* preares us for the choric conclusion. The contradictory (and perhaps ambivalent) displacement of suicide by its opposite, a glorious revenge which is made possible only by a further displacement of the object of revenge, is predicated on the violation of patriarchal order argued in the text.

The central presence of Dalila in the play speaks most loudly and overtly to the problem of patriarchal disruption, of course: her displacement of Samson as matrimonial hierarch is a source of the play's action, of Samson's impotence, and of his own self-accusation of "foul effeminacy." Whether or not Samson redeems his position by the slaughter of the Philistines (as Manoa must convince himself that Samson does), she is only the most obvious example of the situation. More subtle and more troubling is the case of Manoa himself, for just as Samson is separate to God, Manoa is separate to Samson, a father whose paternity is unsettled from within by his son's divine filiality and further decentered by the apparent absence of God manifested in Samson's fall. At the outset of the play, however, confined by the same divine prohibitions that decenter Samson, he cannot quite name the source of his distress:

> Nay, what good thing
> Pray'd for, but often proves our woe, our bane?
> I pray'd for Children, and thought barrenness
> In wedlock a reproach; I gain'd a Son,
> And such a Son as all men hail'd me happy;
> Who would be now a Father in my stead? (350–55)

Manoa has always been Samson's "second" father, a function of his son's special relationship to God. At Samson's fall he attempts to reassert his paternity in an effort to "replace" the father made absent by Samson's failure. But unable to name God in his suit for paternity, Manoa names the Philistines, invoking an economic strategy to ransom Samson from his Philistine captors.

The strategy, of course, is itself doomed to failure, preempted by news of Samson's death.

> O all my hopes defeated
> To free him hence! but death who sets all free
> Hath paid his ransom now and full discharge.
> What windy joy this day I had conceiv'd
> Hopeful of his Delivery, which now proves
> Abortive. (1571–76)

The language in which Manoa expresses his grief exemplifies the displacement that marks the play's action throughout. The "real" transaction, as both Samson and Manoa have understood, is between Samson and God, and although Manoa can caution his son to "let another hand . . . exact / Thy penal forfeit" on the ground that "perhaps / God will relent and quit thee all his debt" (507–09), his own need to reestablish paternity has demanded an opposite turn:

> I however
> Must not omit a Father's timely care
> To prosecute the means of thy deliverance
> By ransom or how else. (601–04)

Although Manoa's conscious intention to buy Samson's freedom from the Philistines seems clear enough, when Samson responds he seems to find subtler implications in his father's words. Ignoring the overt economic strategy, Samson, pricked perhaps by the "penal forfeit" and "deliverance" of Manoa's expression, contrasts what is overt to the much more painfully covert—"the body's wounds and sores" to those which "secret passage find / To th'inmost mind" (607–11). There,

> Thoughts my Tormentors arm'd with deadly stings
> Mangle my apprehensive tenderest parts
>
> . . . .
>
> Thence faintings, swoonings of despair,
> And sense of Heav'n's desertion.
> I was his nursling once and choice delight,
> His destin'd from the womb. (623–34)

In the maternal and infantile figures of the interchange between Samson and Manoa, the terms of Freud's interpretation of Christianity begin to converge. The confusion of paternity with maternity, the implicit desire for the silence of "nursling" infancy, and particularly the sense that Samson's despair has been caused by "Heav'n's desertion," all contribute to our sense of Samson's ambivalence—perhaps fatal ambivalence—about his situation.

Admittedly, much of the weight of the argument I am developing is borne by language, the figures by which Samson and Manoa express their "inmost mind." Yet it is precisely language that may be the key to the play's psychological action. The nominal reference in Samson's speech is God, but the sense of desertion includes Manoa as well. Throughout the play, Samson associates Philistine power and his own neutered condition with both woman and gold: the Philistines, Samson contends, "durst [not] attack me, no not sleeping, / Till they had hir'd a woman with their gold" (1113–14).[14] Manoa's plan to ransom Samson substitutes Dagon's economy for God's, and it reveals the same associations: to repay Samson's "rigid score" to God, Manoa would pay gold to the Philistines. But the language in which he couches his economic strategy reveals the further and perhaps less conscious motive to replace woman in Samson's life by appropriating the role of the absent mother, and Samson's response in the nostalgic terms of infancy suggests he may recognize in his father's words the despair of an occulted paternity in its abortive attempt to recuperate a lost authority.

Such an attempt is a maneuver not lost on feminist theorists. Hélène Cixous, for example, argues that "a will: desire, authority, you examine that, and you are led right back—to the father. You can even fail to notice that there's no place at all for woman in the operation! In the extreme the world of 'being' can function to the exclusion of the mother. No need for the mother—provided there is something of the maternal: and it is the father who acts as—is—the mother."[15]

Consciously or not, to Manoa or Samson in "th' inmost mind" and manifest in their language, woman is not simply an agent of Philistine power, but a threat to right order in herself, and the attempt to appropriate her power serves to reify the force of its threat. Manoa may not hear the impact of his words, but Samson surely finds no hope in them. Once doubly fathered and doubly established in the world, Samson finds himself outside both the divine and the natural order—blind, impotent, fatherless, rejected by a God who "now hath cast me off as never known" (641). Bereft of hope in himself, his only source of stability is blind adherence to the law, with which he will attempt to counter Dalila and Harapha. The problem is, of course, that the law is based on the very patriarchal order Samson would have it replace.

These encounters, both "placed" in *Samson* much as suicide is displaced, constitute an indictment of the law and of the power from which it springs even as they verbally maintain it. That Samson understands the legal and political basis of Dalila's physical "temptation" is obvious in his responses, which first to last focus on the matrimonial nature of her "treason," "Against the law of nature, law of nations" (890). In the legalization of the relationship between Samson and Dalila, Milton creates a full parallel to the hierarchic disruption he has begun with the absence of the Father and the paternal abdication of Manoa, a threatened reversal of the patriarchal order at its most basic, domestic level. Samson's citations of the law — Hebrew, Philistine, and natural — overtly reject Dalila's quest for authority over her husband. Yet, in the process of rejection, Samson recognizes not only the nature of her power, but the possibility of its appropriation after Manoa's example. Herman Rapaport has observed that Dalila is the representative of feminine discourse, a secondary "castrated" discourse Samson must learn to accept in order to achieve his great act: "in Milton's play, the castration at the hands of Dalila is not only a prerequisite for repetitions of radical separation that Samson must endure . . . but also constitutes a way of access to the great display of power Samson achieves at the end of the drama when he breaks the columns and thereby symbolically castrates the temple of the heathen Philistines."[16] We should recall here, however, that displaced though it may be, the death of God's champion may be as "castrating" to God as the fall of Dagon's temple is to Dagon. If Dalila teaches Samson faith in the law, it is a law of displacement and appropriation as much as a constituted prohibition of God's.

The law I have in mind, of course — alluded to in my title — is the Freudian "law" by which self-sacrifice in the name of the Father achieves, simultaneously, displacement of the father and appropriation of his power through the "psychological fatality of ambivalence." As Jacques Lacan argues, Freud was led "to link the appearance of the signifier of the Father, as author of the Law, to death, even to the murder of the Father, thus showing that although this murder is the fruitful moment of the debt through which the subject binds himself for life to the Law, the symbolic Father, in so far as he signifies this Law, is certainly the dead Father."[17] In the symbolic Oedipal operation, which Lacan calls the "name-of-the-Father," the unbearable sense of competition of the subject son in his desire to occupy the position of the father leads to a symbolic identification with the father, the source of the law. For Lacan, to embrace the law is to embrace the father symbolically — in language — and also to displace the father (the Other), and his implicit threat, to the order of symbol. In the sacrifice of the differentiated self, the son takes on the power of the father.

The ambiguous undercurrent of this operation in the play—an ambivalent struggle for patriarchal authority—is suggested by Milton's treatment of the Judges story. The intensity of Samson's sexuality is evident throughout, primarily through reference to his desexing "Like a tame Wether" (538). Yet the Oedipal stresses most common to psychological interpretation of sexuality are "deliberately" denied. The absence of a mother and the legalizing of Samson's exogamous sexual relationships make "normal" Oedipal interpretation a matter of implication only. What they achieve, however, is a reemphasis on the paternal "revenge" motif of the Oedipal triangle by leaving empty the place of the mother in the operation and inserting woman into the patriarchal struggle from the outside. Samson's exogamy is matrimony in *Samson,* not only a marriage outside his tribe, but into the law of Dagon and the Philistines. Marriage to Dalila thus becomes a threat to the Hebrew patrilineal order both sexually (as a replacement of the mother) and as an inserted disruption of Hebrew law by a Philistine.

Manoa's recuperative strategy of economic ransom for Samson is yet another example of repressive displacement in the play. Manoa has abrogated paternity in order to appropriate the power of the absent (m)other, and Dalila expropriates patriarchal power through unmanning of her husband—reversing the order of authority: in their actions Samson may learn the efficacy of a much more dangerous symbolic appropriation of the power of God.

In the course of these "temptations" Samson may recognize his returning strength, but it is a strength that must alienate him from God as much as it draws him back to his former glory. For the source of his strength springs from its antithesis, his symbolic "castration" not only by Dalila but by his father as well. His power is, as John Guillory argues, "the paradox of the castrated male, who becomes limitlessly powerful because *beyond the law.*"[18] This metamorphosis of impotency into potency mirrors the attempts of both Manoa and Dalila, and it may find its fullest expression in the concept of suicide so forcefully repressed by the Chorus. For suicide, seen in these terms, is the ultimate form of self-castration, an ambivalent assertion of powerlessness as absolute power.

Samson's awareness of such a paradox, and his ambivalence toward it, is manifest in his confrontation with Harapha, a combination of impotent bickering about the demands of the various codes of law that bind the two champions and the bravado of insupportable threat in the name of the law. Its climax, Samson's offer of "mortal fight, / By combat to decide whose god is God" (1175–76) — a mortal decision on divinity — suggests that the nadir of his despair and the apex of his pride may be undifferentiable to him.[19]

Samson's exaggerated reliance on legalism as he approaches his death suggests such undifferentiation, even though his words describe a revived faith in divine hierarchy and the inviolable power of God.[20] The confrontation with Harapha is a demonstration of both the power of hierarchy and the law and their inadequacy. Harapha is motivated by a frustration very similar to Samson's: he is a champion whose place in the hierarchy of champions he is unable to prove because of Samson's blindness and its "meaning" in the law. Like Manoa and Dalila, he has been displaced by Samson's fall, but unlike them he has no recuperative strategy beyond eyewitnessing Samson's condition — to see "If thy appearance answer loud report" (1090). Harapha's problem, as he sees it, is that he was "never present on the place / Of those encounters, where we might have tried / Each other's force" (1085–87), and Samson's neutered state places the giant between two contradictory codes of law. Philistine law declares Samson a league-breaker, murderer, and robber, "Due by the Law to capital punishment" (1225), but the code of honor by which Harapha claims his championship forbids battle: "To combat with a blind man I disdain, / And thou hast need much washing to be toucht" (1106–07). To kill Samson would be to establish Harapha's primacy and to fulfill the Philistine law, but to do so would also destroy the basis of his claim to championship. Unmanned by Samson's unmanning, Harapha is laughed from the stage for his impotence. Harapha may be a coward, but he is a coward in the law.[21]

Samson's own sense of contradictory restrictions is evident in his proposal for a scene of battle: "Therefore without feign'd shifts let be assign'd / Some narrow place enclos'd, where sight may give thee, / Or rather flight, no great advantage on me" (1116–18). Assigned limits, the requisite ring for a "fair" fight, both support and deny the fight's "divine" decision. Furthermore, Harapha's sense of literal displacement ("never present on the place") elicits from Samson the definition of placement as closure that has been implicit all along, and that will be echoed in the choric conclusion that God "to his faithful Champion hath in place / Bore witness gloriously." The "narrow place enclos'd" is precisely the end of displacement desired by all of the characters, the stable definition of order, be it expressed as tomb, home, marriage bed, or field of battle. Perhaps for Samson it is all of these: it is the place where suicide and revenge converge as well.

Following his engagement with Harapha, Samson is approached by the Philistine Officer who demands that he perform before Dagon, in direct contradiction to Hebrew law. Samson first declines and then suddenly agrees on the grounds of "rousing motions" he will never define. But immediately preceding his agreement he articulates the contradictory displacement that has been his lot throughout the play:

> the *Philistian* Lords command.
> Commands are no constraints. If I obey them,
> I do it freely; venturing to displease
> God for the fear of Man, and Man prefer,
> Set God behind: which in his jealousy
> Shall never, unrepented, find forgiveness.
> Yet that he may dispense with me or thee
> Present in Temples at Idolatrous Rites
> For some important cause, thou needst not doubt. (1371–79)

If Samson obeys the Philistines, he will venture to displace (set behind) a jealous, unforgiving God, yet if he accepts God's dispensation, he will, effectively, obey them. By implication, although Philistine command is no constraint, God's dispensation *is.* To conform to divine dispensation, Samson must venture the unforgivable, for to bring down the Philistine hierarchy, "where all the Lords and each degree / Of sort, might sit in order to behold" (1607–08), Samson must also bring down Samson, by his own hand.

As the critical conflict over the "meaning" of Samson's "rousing motions" never fails to demonstrate, the "self-violence" of Manoa's suspicion is always a possibility in Samson's fulfillment of God's dispensation. The question is whether Samson is motivated by God or himself. Motivated by God, Samson's self-violence is as inevitable as the Chorus decrees, an event consequent to revenge on the Philistines. It is a suicide justified in the way Augustine justifies it. But if motivated by self, it is a displacement of God: in fulfilling his reiterated desire to die, Samson would act in place of God, not because of him. In such a case, the inevitable, subsequent event would be the death of the Philistines, and, more importantly, the implicit revenge would not be directed primarily against the Philistines but against God. Samson accepts his neutered self (his selflessness) and acts as God's instrument, or he celebrates the freedom from the law it implies. He overthrows the hierarchy of God's enemies (including their associated values — the power of woman and gold), or he becomes his own god. To decide between these binary oppositions is to depend absolute difference from the indifference of momentary choice.

It is not a long step from the ambiguity of Milton's hero to a sense of the ambivalence of the author, the psychological ambivalence inherent in the law of the Father as articulated by Freud and Lacan. This should not be surprising, of course, since all of Milton's great work threatens to displace its divine subject through mimesis, the Derridean re-presentation that calls presence into doubt even as it reifies presence. Read through the eyes of a post-Christian cultural historian like Freud, Samson's pre-enactment of the Christian myth proclaims that his "second fall" and his "regeneration" are not opposites, but one and the same act. To choose such an act of ambiguity and ambivalence as the source of tragic heroism argues a vision of the world wherein all order is at risk, and where the right ordering of the world may even risk calling into doubt the divine hierarchy on which it is predicated.

But a theory of Milton's ambivalence is not necessary to an understanding of his *Samson.* In all of his major work—on divorce, on regicide, on the nature even of good and evil, right and wrong—he insists repeatedly that the apparent right choice may be wrong, or simply not right enough. Milton could have decided for us, of course, but as critical conflicts over the play attest, he did not. Instead, Milton's tragedy foregrounds the contradictions inherent in Samson's potentially doubled motivations. What is clear, I think, is that what the Chorus sees, despite its claim of God's witness, is a merely human, symbolic act. For revenge on the Philistines is valuable only symbolically, an overcoming of the wrong many by the right one. It is an act of hierarchical restoration which leads to a closure and stasis that creates only a monument to the past. What the Chorus will not see is that to find only such closure is itself a mark of the Fall, a mimesis limited to the potentialities of fallen men, a safe, singular, and merely visible heroic act. Yet what Samson does is something much greater. In his suicide he risks the appropriation of God's power in an effort to reify that power in a world that has lost sight of it, for whereas revenge is an imitation of Philistine action (death for "my two eyes"), suicide is an imitation of God, an act wherein despair is indistinguishable from absolute faith, an act that rejects the visible hierarchies of men in the faith that truth will out. It is an act of radical iconoclasm wherein Samson is himself the icon to be destroyed.

If the Chorus misreads Samson's death it does so in the spirit of Christian humanism, wherein mimesis may be closural and revenge is a sufficient end to struggle. And the choric reading might well have been Milton's, for he was not, of course, a post-Christian mythographer like Freud. Yet his choice of an act of such ambivalence as the source of tragic heroism and his ambiguous representation of it argue a vision of a world in which all order is at risk. If he reads with the Chorus, he ignores what he has observed in the world, that "certainly then that people must needs be mad or strangely infatuated that build the chief hope of their common happiness or safety on a single person; who, if he happen to be good, can do no more than another man; if to be bad, hath in his hands to do more evil without check than millions of other men."[22]

Samson embraces the contradictions of his world, and in doing so he finds a radical resolution to the problem of maintaining a "proper" religious, political, and social hierarchy in a world wherein all such hierarchies are called in doubt. This can be summed up, I think, in the Miltonic recognition that to assert God one must risk God's death, a risk that is heroic precisely because it cannot be fully justified in human terms. The choric analogy between Samson and the phoenix at the end of the play may be both more and less appropriate than the Chorus realizes: in his solution to the struggle with God and his own powerlessness, he is very much "Like that self-begott'n bird" (1699), for his act is one that suggests enormous personal potency. But the revival and reflourishing the Chorus claims, through which the Hebrews interpret that potency, remain hopeful assertions, and Samson is more than a monument to the past or a hope for the future. In suicide, he may figure forth the death both of Christ and of traditional Christian order. His existence, whether as judge, husband, champion, or icon, has led only to misreading of the texts of politics, society, and faith among God's chosen, and it is perhaps appropriate that they misread his death as well.

Samson Agonistes implies that interpretation of the past leads to no certain understanding of the future—in Philistia or, perhaps, in England. Rather, the text suggests that, blind though Milton was, his work was "inwardly illuminated" by the full range of contradictions and displacements that constituted the heroic tragedy of his age, and that, with Samson, one can only take its promise on faith.

Portland State University

NOTES

1. See, for example, Augustine, *De civitate Dei* I, 17–27, for the originating orthodox position on suicide, including the exception of Samson from the suicide prohibition.

2. *Samson Agonistes* 1699–1704, in *John Milton: Complete Poems and Major Prose*, ed. Merritt Y. Hughes (New York, 1957). All Milton citations to follow are from this text.

3. Perhaps the most interesting major studies representing these familiar positions

are those of Mary Ann Radzinowicz, *Toward "Samson Agonistes": The Growth of Milton's Mind* (Princeton, 1978), wherein even so suspect a tautology as Manoa's "*Samson* hath quit himself / Like *Samson*" is found to positively unite the catharses of Samson and Manoa (pp. 105–07), and Joseph Wittreich, *Interpreting "Samson Agonistes"* (Princeton, 1986), wherein *Samson* is read in contrast to *Paradise Regained.* "From one point of view," writes Wittreich, "*Samson* contains the sad reality, the elemental despair that issues forth from the failed idealisms of *Paradise Regained;* from another, it is as if *Samson* contains the illusion and *Paradise Regained* the true reality" (p. 348).

Another familiar critical solution to the dilemma of choice is to define a doubleness throughout the play. See, for example, Joseph Summers, "The Movements of the Drama," in *The Lyric and Dramatic Milton*, ed. Summers (New York, 1965); Stanley Fish, "Question and Answer in *Samson Agonistes,*" *Critical Quarterly* XI (1969), 237–64; and R. A. Shoaf, *Milton, Poet of Duality* (New Haven, 1985); Kathleen M. Swaim, "The Doubling of the Chorus in *Samson Agonistes*, in *Milton Studies*, XX, ed. James D. Simmonds (Pittsburgh, 1985), pp. 225–45. Although I, too, find doubling in the play, I want to suggest that it is more than textual, and is motivated by the demands of the age and Milton's own deep suspicion of closural answers. In this regard, see Stanley Fish, "Spectacle and Evidence in *Samson Agonistes,*" *Critical Inquiry* XV (1989), 556–86, wherein Samson, in his climactic act, is found to hazard action "without any clear sense of what it means or of its exact relationship to God's ultimate design" (579). I agree with a great deal of Fish's interpretation, and particularly with the idea that Samson does not act on direct evidence of God's will, but I do not share Fish's sense of Samson's freedom in the act.

4. The critical urge to unify a play that, since Dr. Johnson at least, has been perceived to be disunified seems overwhelming. Attempts to unify *Samson* temporally most often take the form of typological interpretation, but as I have argued in "Deference and Silence: Milton's Nativity Ode," in *Milton Studies*, XXI, ed. James D. Simmonds (Pittsburgh, 1985), pp. 119–35, typology is functionally a method of reading rather than of writing, and too often typological readings of Milton suggest that he was writing precisely to be read typologically. This is true of Wittreich, *Interpreting "Samson Agonistes"*, and, to a lesser degree, William Kerrigan, *The Prophetic Milton* (Charlottesville, Va., 1974), wherein the eternal time and earthly temporality fix the limits of the play. Such a temporal distinction is also implicit in Barbara Lewalski's "*Samson Agonistes* and the 'Tragedy' of the Apocalypse," *PMLA* LXXXV, 1050–62. Although critical of the doubling of political allegory, Lewalski finds unity in a typological doubling wherein "Israel of old" is the type of the Christian Elect. In *From Shadowy Types to Truth* (New Haven, 1968), William G. Madsen finds Samson situated between "the old dispensation of the Letter and the new dispensation of the Spirit" (p. 196). Although wary of a direct identification between Samson and Christ, it is still the Christian story that makes sense of the play for Madsen. Anthony Low, *The Blaze of Noon* (New York, 1974), is less susceptible to a strictly typological interpretation, but to make his case for *Samson* as Christian tragedy, he makes a curious distinction between Samson's action and his "passive" suffering (p. 227).

5. The first view is O. B. Hardison's in *English Literary Criticism: The Renaissance* (New York, 1963), p. 11; the second is Virginia Woolf's in *A Room of One's Own* (New York, 1929), p. 118, a source of many feminist readings of Milton. It is also implicit in the conception of literary history that lies behind Harold Bloom's "anxiety of influence." For a sensible Marxist discussion of the centrality of the social and cultural revolution of Milton's time to his work, see Christopher Kendrick, *Milton: A Study in Ideology and Form* (New York, 1986).

6. John C. Ulreich, Jr., "'Beyond the Fifth Act': *Samson Agonistes* as Prophecy,"

in *Milton Studies*, XVII, ed. James D. Simmonds (Pittsburgh, 1983), contends that the play's "stubborn refusal to yield a 'self-satisfying solution' (306), reflects Milton's persistent iconoclasm. He declines to allow any mere image to stand as true" (p. 281). Although I agree with this understanding of the play, I do not think it is necessary to take Ulreich's further step of declaring the play to be "prophecy" in order to unify it on iconoclastic grounds.

7. The concept of inevitability is called into question by its implicit connection to necessity which, we might recall, is "the Tyrant's plea" in *Paradise Lost* (IV, 394).

8. Choric sublimation of Samson's wish to die is evident throughout the play, but nowhere is it more pronounced than after the confrontation with Harapha, where Samson's contention that "my deadliest foe will prove / My speediest friend, by death to rid me hence, / The worst that he can give, to me the best," is followed by the incongruous choric introduction to a further binary choice between "plain Heroic magnitude of mind" and "patience": "Oh how comely it is and how reviving" (1262–68).

9. S. E. Sprott, *The English Debate on Suicide: From Donne to Hume* (La Salle, Ill., 1961), p. 35.

10. *Biathanatos: A Modern Spelling Edition*, ed. Michael Rudick and M. Pabst Battin (New York, 1982), p. 182: "When, therefore, he felt his strength in part refreshed, and had by prayer entreated the perfecting thereof, seeing they took continual occasion from his dejection to scorn and reproach his God, burning with an equal fervor to revenge their double fault and to remove the wretched occasion thereof, he had, as a very subtle author says, the same reason to kill himself which he had to kill them, and the same authority, and the same privilege and safeguard from sin. And he died, as the same man says, with the same zeal as Christ, unconstrained; for in this manner of dying, as much as in anything else, he was a type of Christ."

11. *The Basic Writings of Sigmund Freud*, trans. and ed. A. A. Brill (New York, 1938), p. 861.

12. If such absence of order, and the choric repression of absence (absenting of absence) is readable in the play, Johnson's complaint of a missing middle may indeed have an answer. See *Rambler*, 140 in *The Yale Edition of the Works of Samuel Johnson*, Vol. V, ed. W. J. Bate and Albrecht B. Strauss (New Haven, 1969), p. 376.

13. Maureen Quilligan, *Milton's Spenser: The Politics of Reading* (Ithaca, N.Y., 1983), pp. 224–25.

14. See also lines 399, 829–31, 958–59 for further examples of the association between woman and gold. The implication of the association is, I think, that when woman overtly becomes a commodity (like gold), she becomes a threat to the patriarchal order, disrupting its economy in which her role as a covert commodity is central. Manoa's inadvertant exposure of the relationship serves to further alienate Samson from Hebraic order.

15. Hélène Cixous, "Sorties," in *New French Feminisms: An Anthology*, ed. Elaine Marks and Isabelle de Courtivron (New York, 1981), pp. 91–92.

In an enactment of a pattern Luce Irigaray, "Veiled Lips," trans. Sara Speidel, *Mississippi Review* XI, no. 3 (Winter/Spring, 1983), 98–99, finds in the *Eumenides* (and by implication in all tragedy), the father appropriates the mother's role because femininity is "an indispensable intermediary for the father in making his law prevail." "Femininity," according to Irigaray in her reading of Nietzsche and Aeschylus, "appeases anger, calls for the forgetting of bloodshed, lulls vengeance with her eloquence, promises tokens of esteem, honors, a cult, rites, sacrifices, a religious silence." Significantly, such results are very close to those envisioned by Manoa at the end of the play (1733–44).

I have referred to these as maternal images, and it is strange to think of Dalila as a maternal figure, I think, only until we remember how estranged the mother always is in Milton. As early as the "Fair Infant," Milton could dismiss the mother as existing—"named"—only insofar as she ceases lamenting the "false imagin'd loss" of her child and accepts her role as the vehicle of God's offspring. Only in *Paradise Regained* does the mother play a significant part, and there, although Mary begins with the same complaints as Manoa about being honored by God only to suffer loss and tribulation, she ends her lament not with Manoan action, but with silence: "My heart hath been a storehouse long of things / And sayings laid up, portending strange events" (*PR* II, 103–04).

16. Herman Rapaport, *Milton and the Postmodern* (Lincoln, 1983), pp. 163–64.

17. Jacques Lacan, *Ecrits: A Selection*, trans. Alan Sheridan (New York, 1978), p. 199.

18. John Guillory, "The Father's House: *Samson Agonistes* in its Historical Moment," in *Re-membering Milton: Essays on the Texts and Traditions*, ed. Mary Nyquist and Margaret W. Ferguson (New York, 1987), p. 166.

19. Again *Paradise Lost* furnishes a parallel text that suggests Milton's attitude toward the possibility of such an empirical and evident result. Michael warns Adam, "Dream not of thir fight, / As of a Duel, or the local wounds / Of head or heel" (XII, 386–88).

20. Here again the thrust of intention on the part of the speaker is undercut by the terms he uses, as in Manoa's "maternal" discussions of Samson's ransom.

21. Although Harapha is often found to be an image of the earlier braggart Samson, it is rarely noted that Harapha's abstention from battle on the grounds of Samson's uncleanness is parallel to Samson's own Nazarite abstemiousness, which has been just as confusing to Samson. See, e.g., lines 541–62.

22. John Milton, *The Ready and Easy Way to Establish a Free Commonwealth*, in Hughes, p. 886.

"SEEKING JUST OCCASION": LAW, REASON, AND JUSTICE AT SAMSON'S PERIPETY

Daniel T. Lochman

DESPITE ITS AMBIGUITIES and complexities, Milton's position on law has been treated often in general studies and in those more narrowly focused on *Samson Agonistes*. Yet most studies leave unexplained the relationship between law—in its civil, ecclesiastical, Mosaic, and Christian forms—and the reason which informs liberty. Moreover, the relation of the rational faculty to justice, the informing principle of law, remains largely undeveloped. Yet it is precisely such interconnections that are implied in the case of Milton's Samson, a Danite and Nazarite, a "judge," an executor of God's justice, and a daunted and questionable hero tormented by debilitating "thoughts." The conflicts implicit in constraints imposed by law, reason, and justice come to a point of crisis at Samson's peripety, when the "glory late of *Israel*, now the grief" resurrects himself to revived action in the world, "seeking just occasion" to support God's justice whatever the consequence for his personal salvation.[1]

Milton is apt to view divine and secular law with suspicion so long as it seems to threaten individual faith and action. Due to this inherent potential for conflict between law and liberty, Milton normally contrasts the Christian era, rooted in free exercise of will, with all forms of legalism that impose inflexible conditions, a "barbarous tyranny" on its adherents.[2] In poetry and prose Milton repeatedly affirms that mankind must participate actively in discerning and choosing between good and evil: true judgment, we learn in *De Doctrina Christiana*, derives most certainly from the "evidence of Scripture" which persuades "reason into assent and faith" (CM XIV, p. 11). In *Paradise Lost*, the Father makes it plain that he will endow fallen humanity with a free will informed by "Umpire Conscience" and a softened heart (III, 189, 195) though he knows that the lapsed parents and their children will choose to ignore the good these guides imply. In *The Doctrine and Discipline of Divorce*, Milton more particularly lists "four great directors" which are God's guides for humanity in a fallen world—reason, charity, nature, and good example. To these internal capacities of judgment he adds the external guidance of God's laws.[3] Together, the four "directors" and the accompanying law constitute means by which mankind, if it so chooses, may discern good and evil and determine just action.

For Milton, reason and law, whether of divine or human origin, should never be limited to blind and rigid principles or legalisms; rather, both should be open to possibility without stricture.[4] In *The Doctrine and Discipline of Divorce,* Milton states unambiguously that "all sense and equity reclaimes that any Law or Cov'nant how solemn or strait soever, either between God and man, or man and man, though of Gods joyning, should bind against a prime and principall scope of its own institution, and of both or either party cov'nanting" (YP II, p. 245). That is, no law or covenant may force or condone violations of its intended purpose; as a consequence, the spirit of law must always predominate over the letter. Later in the same work, Milton illustrates how this principle might be put to use by arguing that the law binding partners in marriage may and indeed *must* be rescinded if marital happiness turns to perpetual misery, discord, and unhappiness—if the original intent of the law, marital happiness, has been abrogated by incompatibility (YP II, p. 247). In such a case, the judgment of the marriage partners, with the support of legal authority, must be trusted to determine the relative good or evil of marriage and divorce regardless of legal precedent and formal codes.

In other cases, however, the possibility of accurate judgment becomes complicated. Milton sometimes suggests that the ability to choose, to judge, is difficult in a lapsed world despite the internal and external guides; in daily life, judgment often seems more problematic than in situations involving clearly delineated good and evil. Although absolute values such as marital harmony may override legal formulas of marriage and poles of good and evil may be clearly demarcated as in *Paradise Lost* and *Paradise Regained,* there remains a huge field of mundane choice that appears inaccessible to absolutes, devoid of the clear aura of sanctity and profanity in the general confusion of a fallen, mixed world. In *Samson,* we enter a landscape remote from paradisical Eden, remote even from the hopeful sadness of the first parents' "wand'ring steps" taken with "Providence thir guide" at the expulsion (PL XII, 647–48). The Book of Judges provided Milton with an archetypal and striking pattern of behavior rooted in failed human judgment; its narrative catalogues corruption and idolatry that alternate depressingly and cyclically with seemingly savage assertions of God's promise to his chosen people.[5] In such a world, as we learn in *Areopagitica,* humankind exercises limited judgment only, and the measures that distinguish good from evil become opaque (YP II, pp. 514–15); the "great directors" fall useless. For Milton, corruption of judgment is a legacy of the Fall, a consequence of the weakness of the lapsed "directors" and law in a world seemingly dominated by relative truths. In *Areopagitica* he explains the result:

> Good and evill we know in the field of this World grow up together almost inseparably; and the knowledge of good is so involv'd and interwoven with the knowledge of evill, and in so many cunning resemblances hardly to be discern'd, that those confused seeds were impos'd on *Psyche* as an incessant labour to cull out, and sort asunder, were not more intermixt. It was from out the rinde of one apple tasted, that the knowledge of good and evill as two twins cleaving together leapt forth into the World. (YP II, p. 514)

After the Fall, the twinned good and evil echo Dalila's "double-mouth'd" truth; Kathleen Swaim rightly observes that Milton's good often seems perilously close to evil from limited, human points of view.[6]

Still, the "great directors"—reason, charity, nature, and good example—may assist in the discernment of good and evil among those illumined by the spirit and doctrine of the New Testament.[7] Joan Bennett ("Liberty Under the Law," p. 145) notes that Milton extends the use of rational judgment to the Israelites and Gentiles in the time of the Mosaic law, even though the chosen people preferred self-imposed servitude to liberty requiring exercise of reason and revelation. Yet, as the dramatic poem reveals and as Milton reminds us in his prose, reason is often faulty: Samson's early "buzzing" and "swarming" thoughts constitute a distracting and corrosive mental state that impedes his spiritual development. It remains to be seen whether the more energized (if still unregenerate, as the revisionists would have it) Samson exercises reason, and, if so, to inquire of its nature. Indeed, William Kerrigan, echoing some earlier studies, argues that reason plays no significant part in Samson's determination to attend the profane rites at Dagon's temple; rather, he sees the character's actions as the work of God's power through grace.[8]

Many argue that the dramatic poem affirms an ultimate regeneration of its hero or, as the revisionists claim, that it depicts tragic, unredeemed violence and revenge. In my view, Samson emerges from the catastrophe as a hero tainted and nearly—not completely—corrupted by a world confused by disturbingly proximate good and evil.[9] At the conclusion Samson seems neither clearly elect nor reprobate, as attest those much-discussed, confusing images of dragons, eagles, the phoenix, and the confusingly profane wishes of Manoa for "eternal fame" (1717) and of the Chorus for "glorious" revenge upon their enemies, now "heaps of slaughter'd" (1660, 1530).[10] Instead, the dramatic poem concludes with

Samson at the point of judgment, leaving the audience to affirm providence and "calm of mind" in the face of unnervingly violent deeds and opaque truths; it teases out the readers' admission that no matter how fearsome the design, "All is best, though we oft doubt, / What th' unsearchable dispose / Of highest wisdom brings about" (1745–47). In a Hebraic world with dimly lined polarities—in a world where moral sign posts are even less clear than in the fallen society described in *Areopagitica*—evil may seem proximate to, even interchangeable with, what is good. Milton creates a setting and situation whose apparent shapeless ambiguity is echoed by the physical blindness of its hero and the moral blindness of an error-prone Chorus, by an arid and imprisoning atmosphere, by characters capable of beguiling Samson through sensuousness, apparent sincerity, and seeming right thinking, by a hero anxious for death and capable of deliverance achieved only through destruction. Because *Samson* is concerned with human existence long after Eden and before the advent of Christ, memories of the "paradise within thee, happier far" (*PL* XII, 587) have dimmed to the point of extinction.

Insofar as Milton's poem questions the possibility and nature of judgment in a lapsed world, it explores the human ability to make choices freely—the possibility and nature of judgment in its psychological and legalistic senses. For Milton the legitimating force of law may conflict with the principle of liberty. Law implies a potential infringement on the spontaneous moral act and faith which, Milton argues in *On Christian Doctrine*, ought to follow from trial of reason and conscience (CM XV, pp. 112–63). The tension between law and liberty is echoed in the ambiguity of the word *judgment*,—a word bearing distinct, potentially conflicting legalistic and psychological senses: it refers both to personal determination of truth and falsehood through mental faculties and to the imposition of formal, codified determinations in a legal process. Both senses seem to have influenced the Protestant view of the biblical judges; the Argument to the Book of Judges in the Geneva Bible defines the rulers described therein as "executors of Gods iudgements . . . raised up, as it semed best to God, for the gouernance of his people."[11] The judges and their earthly judgments are linked to an absolute truth resident, from the point of view of Genevan Protestantism, in God, the sole arbiter of justice. Similarly, in the twelfth book of *Paradise Lost*, lines 315–20, Michael speaks of judges who will save the fallen Israelites. The latter become "penitent" for their faithlessness through their suffering at the hands of their enemies, and judges become the means of the reassertion of providence whether willing or not.[12] The activity of the biblical judges manifests the will of God through the alignment of human reason with Providence, even if divinely appointed actions conflict, as they often do, with customary strictures of positive or religious law.[13] What is at issue in Milton's poem is a question of motivation: does Samson perform his catastrophic act as a consequence of independent and free judgment based on reason, the intervention of some external power such as grace, or combined judgment and grace?

Analysis of Samson's peripety (that is, his determination to accompany the officer to the temple) indicates that reason plays a major, if not absolute, role in his exercise of judgment; however, the unique force of his reason is negative, iconoclastic, deconstructive in that it breaks down prior conclusions rooted in unwarranted assumption, legal absolutes, and destructive ratiocination. Paradoxically, Milton's judge conforms to God's law by opening himself to limitless potentiality and by abandoning strictures resulting from rigid logic and legal precedent. At the moment of reversal, Samson judges with an eye to the potential of Providence, unconstrained by prior cases of human or divine law.

In anticipation of this transformation, Milton's dramatic design offers a context wherein hypotheses, expectations, and initial judgments are repeatedly frustrated by conditions in the real world. At least until the episode with Harapha, the work is dominated by a sense of unfulfilled expectations. The aura of failure encompasses not only the pitifully fallen Samson but also the faithless Israelites, and, finally and ironically, the Philistine overlords. The circular, despairing logic of the fallen hero in his prologue and introductory speeches is preliminary to and consistent with the more widespread disappointments of his countrymen and enemies: eddies of despair, hope, and frustration are common in the stasima of the Chorus and in the discourse of Manoa and Dalila even as Samson's emphatic laments form the work's center. Before his revivification, Samson wallows in a state of mixed self-pity, despair, humiliation, pride, and doubt of Providence. He compares his promise to deliver "*Israel* from *Philistian* yoke" to the lapse embodied in his literal "yoke." A debased slave "Eyeless in *Gaza*," he convinces himself that he wears his enslaving collar because he has published God's secrets to the profane (38–42; see also 266–72, 1212–19). The prologue and episodes with the Chorus and Manoa reveal Samson as a self-torturer, one whose "Thoughts" are "Tormentors" that flit from one "chief" complaint to another. In "Swoonings" of melancholic despair, he blames himself, his country, and implicitly God and Providence for his blindness (67), his personal shame (196), and the "Dishonor, obloquy" that have infected Israel and the reputation of God (448–59). Yet this personal failure and guilt is merely the center of a series of related failures felt not just by

Samson but also by all the "chosen" who inhabit the desert of the mind closed to grace. The Chorus recognizes belatedly its share of responsibility for the political servitude which Samson could not cast off (237–40, 277–90). Manoa asserts the need to vindicate God's name "Against all competition" (476) although he is obsessed with "timely care" (602) for the nurture of a son whom he suspects is a corrupt failure and an affliction upon his family name; he discredits Samson's claims that "Divine impulsion" motivated a desire for the woman of Timna. Dalila, though "With all her bravery on" (717), fails to achieve either domestic control over a submissive husband or a positive reputation as a political heroine, and the overblown Harapha is unable to cut a convincing figure as a threat against Samson in a physical agon, much less as contender on points of law. In short, the world of Samson is one characterized by failed expectations on personal, social, and religious levels, and the cumulative weight of this collective error casts doubt on a Providence which seemingly permits God's adherents to fail, the perverse to triumph. Corruption seems equally endemic to Danite and Philistine, and both individual and society, Danites as well as Philistines, are blind to the will of God.

Repeatedly, in *Samson*, wishes, assumptions, and expectations are overturned, bringing into question the nature of God's power and justice in a fallen world. "Just are the ways of God / And justifiable to Men," the Chorus confidently affirms, but, as Fish has noted, the Danite men soon fall into a tangle of confused and implausible "justifications."[14] With "vain reasonings," they argue that a *just* God must give the Nazarite hero dispensation to "seek in marriage that fallacious Bride" and to set "his people [including the Chorus] free" by achieving revenge on the Philistines (294–324); they presuppose that God's judge must always be just, and they require that God's will conform to their assumption. No other explanation, according to the Chorus, could account for Samson's seeming violation of "National obstriction" (312), a norm, their argument suggests, which even God may not violate. Implicit is the Chorus's doubt of God's purpose in permitting the deliverer to marry one who is unclean and unchaste—God and/or his promised hero must, it seems, be at fault, even if the fault may be papered over with a "dispensation."[15]

The potential for an inversion of divine justice, with God's justice become unjust, exists in the text and margins of *Paradise Lost* and *Paradise Regained* as well as *Samson*. It is a product of two world orders, one good and one evil, that Milton locates first in Satan's sin and then in the sin of the first parents. Given the two orders, absolute norms become relative and involve a choice for one system or another, for God or evil, based on one's rational estimate of the *probability* of the true good derived from law, conscience and its aforementioned "directors"—reason, charity, nature, good works—or prophetic inspiration. With the assistance of law and reason, an individual's choice is not arbitrary, but it may easily be confused by competing, contrary orders of things. Dalila, for example, seems justly to claim that pressures imposed by church and state influenced her decision to enthrall her husband (849–70), and, as John Ulreich has argued recently, her feelings of "conjugal affection" (739) may hint at Christian charity, "an incarnation of heavenly Love."[16] Harapha's list of legal complaints about Samson, though received with blind hostility, justly raises grave, unanswered questions concerning the legality of God's so-called "*faithful* Champion" (1751; my emphasis).

Indeed, such seemingly reasonable challenges to Samson and the God he represents are implicit in a lapsed world where the tyranny of evil seems relatively just. As Michael explains to Adam in *Paradise Lost* when the latter is dismayed by the vision of Babel, those who are fallen are not devoid of "reason" understood as logical and ratiocinative faculties, but in them the place of reason as authority has been inverted and perverted by the passions.[17] The cacophony of language at the tower of Babel is God's proper judgment upon "Authority usurpt" when men seek control over other men (XII, 66). Michael observes that humanity will lose "true Liberty" following the "original lapse"; the political state will mirror psychology, now prone to a corrupt inversion of "right Reason," "twinn'd" with Liberty, and the passions:

> Reason in man obscur'd, or not obey'd,
> Immediately inordinate desires
> And upstart Passions catch the Government
> From Reason, and to servitude reduce
> Man till then free. Therefore since hee permits
> Within himself unworthy Powers to reign
> Over free Reason, God in Judgment just
> Subjects him from without to violent Lords;
> Who oft as undeservedly enthral
> His outward freedom: Tyranny must be,
> Though to the Tyrant thereby no excuse.
> Yet sometimes Nations will decline so low
> From virtue, which is reason, that no wrong,
> But Justice, and some fatal curse annext
> Deprives them of thir outward liberty,
> Thir inward lost. (XII, 86–101)

Although Michael goes on to observe that from this "vicious Race" will emerge "one peculiar Nation" "select" above the rest, he maintains that political tyranny, including Harapha's and the Philistines', is a just consequence of humanity's "upstart" passions. These require the ministration of "strict Laws" and the "puissant deeds" of judges like Samson and kings like David (*PL* XII, 304, 319–22) to clarify the existence of sin and its rectification to virtue, that is, "reason." The repeated subjection of the Israelites to the oppressive rule of their enemies constitutes a "Judgment just" and the proper effect of the cause – the Israelites' willing choice of the rule of the passions rather than of "right Reason." In their depravity, neither an enslaved psyche nor corrupt society lacks reason or the choice it permits.[18] The Chorus, Manoa, even Dalila and Harapha, like Satan in *Paradise Lost* and *Paradise Regained*, are sometimes capable of telling, even just argumentation. Concern therefore centers not on the existence of reason but the exercise of "right" reason.

What constitutes this "right" reason which is the same as "virtue," elsewhere equated with "moral law" and related to law proper, God's law, "natural logic," and the law of nature?[19] Adam and Michael outline its characteristics in the summary of Adam's knowledge and the requirements of the "paradise within." Right reason involves a willing acceptance of things as they are; conversely, seeking beyond the limits of what is proper is "folly" (*PL* XII, 560). Moreover, genuine knowledge requires a rational admission that obeying and loving God with fear are the "best" modes of acting, that God's Providence may involve inversions of conventional estimates of strength and weakness, that "suffering for Truth's sake" is "fortitude." Reason ought to culminate in opening oneself to Providence and in performing God's will in "Deeds" "answerable" to one's knowledge. As Michael teaches Adam, reason rooted in opening oneself to God surpasses the restrictive operations of reason derived from formal systems of classification and teleology:

> This having learnt, thou hast attain'd the sum
> Of wisdom; hope no higher, though all the Stars
> Thou knew'st by name, and all th' ethereal Powers,
> All secrets of the deep, all Nature's works,
> Or works of God in Heav'n, Air, Earth, or Sea,
> And all the riches of this World enjoy'dst,
> And all the rule, one Empire. (XII, 575–81)

As we learn also from the Son's denial of Satan's temptations in *Paradise Regained*, power, possession of wealth, and unlimited knowledge ring hollow unless preceded by rational choice to follow the will of the true God; an exercise of proper ratiocinative faculties follows upon the prior determination to follow good rather than evil. The choice to dispose oneself to God becomes, then, the substance of "right" reason, true "virtue." Such reason follows upon the rejection of competing claims to obedience, whether offered by Satan, by the world, by Dagon, by Manoa's paternal, domestic care, by the seductive charms of Dalila, or by the legalistic claims of Harapha. "Right" reason, that reason which is most closely linked to one's moral act and spiritual destiny, determines choice for or against God. It clears away all conflicting, distracting passions and subordinate rational faculties by focusing on the central question of one's willed disposition toward God. In this sense, reason is iconoclastic, removing impediments generated by the rational faculty itself, at the same time that it is receptive to the fullness of God's will, bridging from discursive reason first to a receptivity and then to a passive intuition of right and wrong, good and evil.

Samson's transition from circling despair to determined action has been traced often: the reviving strong man moves from the languor of his initial lethargy to provocations and threats directed at Dalila and Harapha. The judgment evoked from the poem's audience to this revivification has been varied; and this diversity itself suggests that the problem of accurate judgment in *Samson* extends outward from the biblical judge to readers attempting to make sense of good or evil within the confining limits of the dramatic poem. Milton's work encourages its readers to force its action violently into absolute categories of tragedy or comedy, the protagonist into heroic or villainous character, the agon into matter of good *or* evil, though a final determination of good or evil in the work seems as difficult for the audience as for Samson, the Chorus, and Manoa. Finally, the difficulty if not impossibility of absolute judgment forces both audience and Samson to an acceptance of God's will: whether the choice to go to Dagon's temple is for good or ill in light of the protagonist's personal salvation, the act he perpetrates, no matter how violent or disturbing, must lie within the broader purview and will of God if God, the source of justice, is just and if his acts are justifiable.

In the episode with the officer, Samson clears away modes of thought which had previously confined him to reflect fixedly on his past promise and present misery, and he begins to see that, though fallen, he is not necessarily excluded from his promised destiny.[20] The determination to attend the heathen festival and thereby to violate his law's prohibition brings Samson in line with Providence, a possibility raised in the episode with Harapha, when he tells the accusing giant, "[I] despair not of [God's] final pardon / Whose ear is ever open; and his eye / Gracious to re-admit the suppliant" (1171–73). It is after this recognition of God's ongoing promise of pardon and grace that Samson is emboldened to challenge Harapha's "verdict" (1228) and to intimidate the "Tongue-doughty Giant" (1181). For a moment, he comprehends that a gracious God can accept one who repents and confesses his wrong, whatever his state, but he is unable to sustain that vision when, in lines 1262–64, he slips back to "swoonings of despair" (632), recalling his earlier state of melancholic fixation on "speedy death" (650). Zigging and zagging between reviving hope and spinning despair, he knows that his humiliation and death wish need not, indeed cannot, prevent the prophesied liberation of his people.

When the officer first commands Samson to attend Dagon's "solemn Feast" (1311), the resurgent strong man still appeals to the Mosaic law in its prohibition of Philistine rites; "for that cause," he judges, "I cannot come" (1321). With this response Samson reveals his persistent inclination to measure moral acts against the constraints of law. Just as he had accepted the "strictest vow of purity" as a Nazarite (319), so Samson here upholds the Hebraic legal tradition, applying its maxims as universals to individual cases. From this assumption of the inviolability of the Mosaic law – a reasonable assumption for an Israelite – Samson deduces that he must not violate the law by attending rites devoted to a profane god and blasphemous religion; therefore, three times he clearly states that he has no intention of accompanying the officer.

Samson had used a similar legalism to justify his second marriage: the marriage to the woman of Timna that "motion'd was of God" (222) becomes the universal which he applies subsequently to his more questionably inspired "motions" for the "manifest Serpent," Dalila – "I thought it lawful from my former act" (231). Whatever his claims for "intimate impulse" (223), Samson could easily rationalize his marriages – depending on his audience, the marriage to the woman of Timna might be part of a plan to destroy Philistines or an impulse driven by lust and God's will.[21] Whether or not Samson succeeds in justifying this second marriage – whether he is justified in his desire to lead his spouse to true belief or whether the marriage was sinful – it is clear that his argument rests on shaky logic. In his response to the officer and in his rationalizations for marriage, Samson's appeal to legal precedence as a means of establishing conduct rings hollow. Like Dalila's law of love, which "always" admits "pity or pardon" (814) and like the Chorus's mysogynistic claim for "God's universal Law" of male "despotic power" (1053–54), Samson's affirmations of universals in a lapsed world seem willful and dangerous.[22]

The officer, a representative of government upheld by the Philistine legal code and replete with its visual signs of "Scepter or quaint staff" (1303), forces Samson to make a choice from which his former reclusiveness in the prison had protected him. Samson is here at an interesting crossroads. He must judge whether to go to the temple or not. There seems to be no middle ground, and the tension becomes explicit when the Chorus observes that "matters are now strain'd / Up to the height, whether to hold or break" (1348–49). In this dilemma, as I have indicated, Samson's first instinct is to retreat to standards imposed by fixed law, and from that inflexible point of view to conclude that he "cannot" attend Philistine rites.[23]

When he considers the likely alternative to his participation — the punishment he is likely to undergo at the hands of his tormentors — his refusal remains firm. He believes that he must either go to perform the tricks of the side-show — like the Philistine "Sword-players," "Gymnic Artists, Wrestlers, Riders, Runners, / Jugglers and Dancers, Antics, Mummers, Mimics," though "tir'd, / And over'labor'd" from his toil at the mill — or refuse and thereby bring new "distress," an "occasion of new quarrels" upon himself (1323–32). In either case, Samson faces renewed affliction, but he refuses to go, preferring familiar conflict to the possibility of new public shame, the dehumanizing folly which has already transformed the canny riddler to one "proverb'd for a Fool / In every street" (203–04).

He indicates that he "will not come" for a third time when he considers his "conscience and internal peace," the "great directors" of moral act. The threat of humiliation of mind and the exhibition of his "sorrow and heart-grief" (1339), the knowledge that he must profanely "play before thir god, / The worst of all indignities" (1340–41) are all points sufficient to lead Samson to refuse "absurd commands" (1337). The desire for stability if not calm of mind compels him to avoid the emotional and mental disturbance that his attendance would surely evoke — he prefers suffering in known servitude to the imagined horrors of the Philistine crowds.

Law, reason, and conscience together lead Samson to the same reasonable conclusion, yet despite all these tangible reasons for *not* attending, within sixty lines Samson abruptly reverses himself and determines after all to attend the "Idolatrous Rites" (1378). How can one account for such an abrupt transformation?

To effect this change, Samson removes impediments to the "rousing motions" mentioned at line 1382. In response to the Chorus's imperative "Consider" (1348), Samson introduces a series of questions which reinforce and repeat his intention to refuse to go: the exchange seems to justify his refusal to himself as well as to the Chorus. His first step toward reversal takes the form of a rhetorical question — a verbal structure that implies the *possibility* of doubt even when the conclusion seems probable; unlike the deductive syllogism, which is capable of asserting universal conclusions, the rhetorical question implies contingency. Samson considers "Shall I" — and at first apparently intends to assert that he will *not* — "abuse this Consecrated gift / Of strength, again returning with my hair / After my great transgression, so requite / Favor renew'd, and add a greater sin / By prostituting holy things to Idols; / A *Nazarite* in place abominable" (1354–59). The judge frames a question — not an absolute assertion — which leaves room to doubt the necessity of describing a violation of the Nazarite code and the law as an "abuse" and "transgression." The rhetorical force of the question undercuts its implied answer, permitting the hero to hint at the *possibility* of avoiding new transgression despite violation of the Nazarite code.

Samson's seeming rejection of acts which violate law is followed by a second repudiation of acts likely to result in personal humiliation and impurity: "how vile, contemptible, ridiculous, / What act more execrably unclean, profane" (1361–62) than participation in the festival? Unlike his previous assertion to the officer, however, Samson frames his argument in a rhetorical question which again prevents flat denial at the same time that it apparently strengthens Samson's intention not to participate in Dagon's rites.

Finally, Samson considers the conditions that frame his decision. He poses questions whose intent is to prove that he has no "constraint" to go to the temple unless dragged (1370–71); therefore, he concludes, "the sentence holds" which proscribes participation at idolatrous ceremonies. It is at this point — as he considers the Philistines' need to use force to drag him to the site and the possibility that he could be forced after all if God so willed — that his thinking seems to take a new direction. If he is free to *choose* not to go, he possesses a power of choice which he had not previously admitted; and, though he may choose not to go, he may choose to go, even with God's sanction. When Samson affirms that "commands are no constraints" (1372), his rational mode shifts from the rhetorical question to the conditional — a logical structure which may limit statements to a rigid causal sequence if used syllogistically or open thinking to new, speculative possibilities.[24] In context, the conditional's terms anticipate a recognition of liberty that undercuts the prescriptive force of law and reason. The form of the conditional — focused on future possibility rather than the inflexible terms of the past — allows choice: "*If* I obey [the Philistine commands], / I do it freely" (1372–73; my emphasis). This consideration of the *possibility* of going to the temple offers alternatives formerly concealed behind rhetorical questions, and at this point the confining letter of the law and the rationality of the "great directors" weaken in their force.

Yet Samson considers one more narrowly logical, confining alternative. Incompletely aware of the freedom of the just, he believes he must choose in this crisis to follow God or man, good or evil,

> venturing to displease
> God for the fear of Man, and Man prefer,
> Set God behind: which in his jealousy
> Shall never, unrepented, find forgiveness. (1373–76)

Samson's alternative assumes that he may go to the temple and therefore demonstrate a fear of the Philistines and the pain they might inflict *or* that he may follow God and not go.[25] Such a formulation presupposes that God's will is identical with the law, yet it is precisely this identification that liberty and free will undercut. Samson had already rejected this identification of God with inflexible justice in his dispute with Harapha. The syntactic juxtaposition of "never" and "unrepented" place side by side an inflexible absolute and a negative whose obverse reverberates with the possibility of forgiveness through repentance and the potential for advancing God's cause without "fear of Man."

At the very moment that the alternatives between the ways of God and man seem most distinct, Samson's thinking permits a leap which negates his preceding arguments. He perceives—even if dimly—the consequences of God's freedom in Providence and the fruitlessness of judging divine will according to civil or religious law: "Yet that he may dispense with me or thee / Present in Temples at Idolatrous Rites / For some important cause, thou needst not doubt" (1377–79). At this moment, Samson erases all human rationalizations—the alternatives, conditionals, hypotheses, and deductions that have limited his thinking.[26] In this almost serendipitous recognition of God's absolute potential, Samson begins to sense the intellectual premise which he has admitted without complete, conscious comprehension—God may do what he will when he chooses with whomever he chooses, sinner or saint alike. This throwing open of possibility—the product of a process of negative, iconoclastic reasoning—creates an opportunity for Samson to consent to act. The "important cause" that enters obliquely into this recognition places "me or thee" fully within the purview and guidance of Providence.

It is no coincidence and not completely a matter of external intervention that "something extraordinary" affects Samson's "thoughts" immediately thereafter; Samson's mode of thinking has shifted from applications of precedent and law to judgment rooted in the conviction that all actions guided by Providence must be good. To arrive at this conclusion, Samson makes not inconsiderable use of reason, with the "rousing motions" linked closely to his patterns of thought. To see the motive for the "motions" as only a product of external force, as a divine or satanic intervention, is to assume that Samson can do nothing on his own behalf; the divine will becomes rigid, threatening to obliterate free will.[27] Although Milton conceals the nature of Samson's motions beneath vague language ("good courage," "presage," and predictions of a "remarkable" day), Samson's reversal indicates his new relationship to law, the Philistines, himself, and God. There is no complaint, no lamentation, only freely offered service.

When Samson offers his ironic response to the officer ("Masters' commands come with a power resistless / To such as owe them absolute subjection; / And for a life who will not change his purpose?" 1404–06), the meaning of his motions and their terrible import for the Philistines remains secret, a truth which Samson successfully hides from his enemies.[28] Nevertheless, he repeatedly affirms that his future act, whatever that might be (we cannot be certain that even Samson is aware of its nature at this point), will not violate the law or his vow: he pledges to the Chorus that he will do nothing "that may dishonor / Our Law, or stain my vow of *Nazarite*" (1385–86); he affirms before the officer that he will comply with nothing "Scandalous or forbidden in our Law" (1409); and he vows to the Chorus: "Happ'n what may, of me expect to hear / Nothing dishonorable, impure, unworthy / Our God, our Law, my Nation, or myself" (1423–25). Although these repeated assertions of the legality of his proposed action raise questions about the soundness of his decision – the appropriateness and source of his violent motions, the significance of his destruction of human life, including his own – the principle which Samson believes that he operates on – the freedom of God's will from narrow legalism – remains unassailable. Indeed, the law which *ought* to govern the individual, the nation, and religion should be commensurate with the law of God and the principles of "right" reason and nature, the "fundamental" law.[29]

The casting off of impediments to reason in the fulfillment of Providence opens Samson to serve once more as God's instrument. However we read Samson's claims for justice, the act of destruction and deliverance that he effects must accord with God's providential design – no evil, if there is evil here, can frustrate God's plan for universal justice. Although the "dispose / Of highest wisdom" may be "unsearchable" (1746), humanity may, like Samson, choose to serve God by choosing to restrain reason, to act with rather than against divine law; choice refutes the claims of fatal "necessity," the "tyrant's plea" (*PL* IV, 393).

Samson's judgment stands in contrast to more customary sorts of human judgment and judging. For Milton, the conventional office of judgeship holds little divine authority; magistracy is better obtained through judgment of an individual informed by a comprehension of God's word revealed through thought, inspiration, and the divine word.[30] Ironically, Milton's Samson exercises judgment after he has thrown off legal restrictions like those binding the decisions of the magistrate. Samson's action as judge, terrible in its enactment of divine justice against the enemies of the chosen people, is a product of rational judgment.

Iconoclastic reasoning opens Samson to the reception of justice rooted in the mystery of God's wisdom. Though one should not confuse the rough-hewn and savage figure of Samson with the pacifically wise Son in *Paradise Regained,* Samson in his own way contributes to the fulfillment of "th' unsearchable dispose" (1746). He does so not by affecting divine wisdom, which in him is admittedly "nothing more than mean" (207), but by remaining faithful to God and mindful of his promised deliverance. Brutal as his final act may be and as questionable as his personal salvation remains, Samson's use of reason to restrain reason permits him to enact God's justice.

Southwest Texas State University

NOTES

1. *Samson Agonistes*, 179, 237, in *John Milton: Complete Poems and Major Prose*, ed. Merritt Y. Hughes (Indianapolis, 1957). All subsequent references to Milton's poetry follow this edition.

2. Cf. *PL* III, 93–134; *The Works of John Milton*, ed. Frank Allen Patterson et al. (New York, 1931–1938), vol. XIV, pp. 13, 62–89, 100–03; vol. XV, pp. 112–63; hereafter cited as CM. See also John T. Shawcross, "Milton and the Covenant: The Christian View of the Old Testament," in *Milton and the Scriptural Tradition: The Bible into Poetry*, ed. James H. Sims and Leland Ryken (Columbia, Mo., 1984), pp. 165–73.

3. *Complete Prose Works of John Milton*, 8 vols., ed. Don M. Wolfe et al. (New Haven, 1953–1982), vol. II, p. 229, hereafter cited as YP. On *experience* as a generic term comprehending *good example*, see Barbara Kiefer Lewalski, "Milton's *Samson* and the 'New Acquist of True [Political] Experience,'" in *Milton Studies*, XXIV, ed. James D. Simmonds (Pittsburgh, 1989), pp. 234–37.

4. Joan S. Bennett, "Liberty Under the Law: The Chorus and the Meaning of *Samson Agonistes*," in *Milton Studies*, XI, ed. Balachandra Rajan (Pittsburgh, 1978), p. 145;

Hugh MacCallum, "*Samson Agonistes:* The Deliverer as Judge," in *Milton Studies*, XXIII, ed. James D. Simmonds (Pittsburgh, 1987), pp. 260–62.

5. John Ulreich, "Samson's Riddle: Judges 13–16 as Parable," *Cithara* XVIII (May 1979), 11–12.

6. Kathleen Swaim, "The Doubling of the Chorus in *Samson Agonistes*," in *Milton Studies*, XX, ed. James D. Simmonds (Pittsburgh, 1984), pp. 225–27. See also Virginia R. Mollenkott, "Relativism in *Samson Agonistes*," *SP* LXVIII (1970), 89–102.

7. See *De Doctrina Christiana*, CM XIV: "it is my particular advice that every one should suspend his opinion on whatever points he may not feel himself fully satisfied, till the evidence of Scripture prevail, and persuade his reason into assent and faith" (p. 11);

> "It has . . . been my object to make it appear . . . of how much consequence to the Christian religion is the liberty not only of winnowing and sifting every doctrine, but also of thinking and even writing respecting it, according to our individual faith and persuasion; an inference which will be stronger in proportion to the weight and importance of those opinions, or rather in proportion to the authority of Scripture, on the abundant testimony of which they rest. Without this liberty there is neither religion nor gospel—force (*vis*) alone prevails—by which it is disgraceful for the Christian religion to be supported. Without this liberty we are still enslaved, not indeed, as formerly, under the divine law, but, what is worst of all, under the law of man, or to speak more truly, under a barbarous tyranny." (Pp. 11–13)

See Bennett, "Liberty Under the Law," pp. 143–44.

8. See Joseph Wittreich's controversial argument against Samson's regeneration, *Interpreting "Samson Agonistes"* (Princeton, 1986), esp. pp. 3–52, 296–385, and the critical review by Philip J. Gallagher, "On Reading Joseph Wittreich: A Review Essay," *MQ* XXI (October 1987), 108–13; William Kerrigan, "The Irrational Coherence of *Samson Agonistes*," in *Milton Studies*, XXII, ed. James D. Simmonds (Pittsburgh, 1986), pp. 217–24; cf. G. A. Wilkes, "The Interpretation of *Samson Agonistes*," *HLQ* XXVI (1963), 378.

9. For a brief narrative review of recent regenerationist, revisionist, and other scholarship on *Samson*, see MacCallum, "The Deliverer as Judge," pp. 286–87 *n1*.

10. From the perversion of the Chorus's enthusiasm for slaughter, Joseph Wittreich argues backward to conclude that Samson's "last act is left ambiguous . . . with the probable implication that Milton's poem is not *about* Samson's regeneration but, instead, about his second fall" (p. 80); Stanley Fish, "Spectacle and Evidence in *Samson Agonistes*," *Critical Inquiry* XV (1989), 561–64, 572, argues instead that ambiguity means only ambiguity, not necessarily guilt.

11. *The Geneva Bible*, facs. ed. (Madison, Wis., 1969), p. 108.

12. See Mary Ann Radzinowicz, *Toward "Samson Agonistes": The Growth of Milton's Mind* (Princeton, 1978), p. 289; Christopher Grose, *Milton and the Sense of Tradition* (New Haven, 1988), 142–48.

13. MacCallum, "The Deliverer as Judge," pp. 260–63; Bennett, "Liberty Under the Law," pp. 142–43; Barbara K. Lewalski, "*Samson Agonistes* and the 'Tragedy' of the Apocalypse," *PMLA* LXXXV (1970), 1056–58, 1060–61.

14. Stanley Fish, "Questions and Answers in *Samson Agonistes*," *Critical Quarterly* XI (1969), 246. Fish's "Spectacle and Evidence" is a self-proclaimed "sequel" to this earlier article.

15. Fish, "Spectacle and Evidence," pp. 560–61, outlines a similar view of the hollowness of the Chorus's argument. Milton's own view of dispensations depends on human perspective; that is, dispensation only exists for minor issues and from human perspective

since God never violates his own laws. For cases involving God's law, there is no true dispensation, as Milton argues in affirming the legal basis for divorce (*DDD* II, 4, YP, p. 297) and "penall statutes" such as that requiring the marriage of a widow by her husband's brother (Lev. xviii, 18; *DDD* II, 5, YP, p. 299). Yet God's law embraces in itself the charity which appears to humanity as dispensation in individual cases: "a dispensation most properly is some particular accident rarely happ'ning and therefore not specify'd in the Law, but left to the decision of charity, ev'n under the bondage of Jewish rites, much more under the liberty of the Gospel" (YP, p. 299). Milton never flatly denies the possibility of dispensation, but he generally sees it as suspect, like indulgences and other human perversions of God's justice.

16. John Ulreich, "'Incident to All Our Sex': The Tragedy of Dalila," in *Milton and the Idea of Woman*, ed. Julia M. Walker (Urbana, 1988), p. 202; Lewalski, "*Samson* and the 'New Acquist,'" 239–42.

17. Cf. the *Art of Logic* (CM XI, p. 75), where logic's concern with the art of reasoning is distinguished from the nature of reason.

18. See YP II, 514, 527, for the equation of reason with choice in *Areopagitica.*

19. See Milton's *Brief Notes* (CM VI, p. 158), *Pro Populo Anglicanae Defensio* (CM VII, p. 445), *Doctrine and Discipline of Divorce* (YP II, p. 292), *Artis Logicae* (CM XI, p. 11), and *De Doctrina Christiana* (CM XII, p. 117).

20. Samson's alteration may parallel Milton's; Fish, "Spectacle and Evidence," observes that the early works of Milton establish a norm of fixed, "internal certainty" that, after *Areopagitica*, becomes identified instead with "spiritual sloth" (576).

21. Helen Damico, "Duality in Dramatic Vision: A Structural Analysis of *Samson Agonistes*," in *Milton Studies* XII, ed. James D. Simmonds (Pittsburgh, 1978), pp. 106–07.

22. Cf. MacCallum, "The Deliverer as Judge," pp. 275–76.

23. See Fish, "Spectacle and Evidence," p. 575, for a contrast between Samson's "cannot" and "will not."

24. See *SA*, 231–36, 265–68; *Art of Logic*, CM XI, 348–55. On the movement of Samson "beyond the limits of choice dictated by the intersection of the situation and the Law," see Fish, "Questions," p. 254 and Daniel T. Lochman, "'If there be aught of presage': Milton's Samson as Riddler and Prophet," in *Milton Studies*, XXII, ed. James D. Simmonds (Pittsburgh, 1986), pp. 195–97.

25. Fish, "Spectacle and Evidence," p. 577, sees Samson's backsliding as a "recoiling" from his preceding observation that he acts "freely" (1373).

26. Fish, "Questions," p. 254; "Spectacle and Evidence," p. 578.

27. Some critics, like Kerrigan, "Irrational Coherence," attribute all or nearly all the cause of Samson's reinvigoration to God's external agency through grace. Alternatively, revisionists like to see the "motions" as potentially or actually demonic and cruel (Wittreich, *Interpreting 'Samson,'* pp. 141–43), inspired by evil external agents or the product of corrupt judgment; see also Albert C. Labriola, "Divine Urgency as a Motive for Conduct in *Samson Agonistes*," *PQ* L (1971), 99–107. Even readers who focus on logic and rhetoric in *Samson* often see the motions as essentially, perhaps deliberately *irrational* (Fish, "Questions," pp. 255–57; in "Spectacle and Evidence" the irrationality becomes "obscurity," p. 571). MacCallum, "The Deliverer as Judge," asserts that Samson's decision "has been prepared for, been made apposite and meaningful, by the long process of self-examination which preceded it" (p. 281), but does not specifically examine the sequence of logical steps that leads Samson to abandon his prior assumptions and modes of thought, instead linking the motions directly to grace (p. 279). Grose, *Milton and the Sense of Tradition*, refers to Samson's "insight" as the source of enaction and notes the development

of Samson's ability to listen (188–209) but does not detail the sequence by which Samson actively dissociates himself from the constraints of the world.

28. See John Ulreich, "'This Great Deliverer': *Samson Agonistes* as Parable," *MQ* XIII (1979), 82–83, on Samson's irony as "deliberate" and a product of choice.

29. *Brief Notes*, CM VI, p. 158; *DDD*, CM III, p. 440.

30. Radzinowicz, *Toward 'Samson,'* pp. 107–08.

THE WORLDLY END OF *SAMSON*

Burton J. Weber

MANY CRITICS seem ill at ease with the political nature of *Samson Agonistes.* Several have attempted to spiritualize the play with typology, and one critic maintains that *Samson* ends with a triumph of reason rather than of force. Rejecting the view of the orthodox regeneration critics—Arnold Stein, Joseph Summers, and Anthony Low,—that in the "rousing motions" (1382) God assists Samson in his worldly mission, the providential critics try to spiritualize the climax of the play, arguing that God's motions perfect his morally imperfect agent. Critics of several viewpoints have attempted to disarm the close, contending that it is wholly or partially ironic: in celebrating a military victory, Samson's advocates do not understand his triumph.[1] But the structure of the crisis (1308–1444) and conclusion (1445–1758) of the tragedy insists that both Samson's regeneration in the middle of the play (115–1307) and the grace that God extends to the hero at its crisis are means to that earthly end that is celebrated at its close, the defense of a civil and religious freedom ordained by God.

It is convenient to use the word *grace* for God's intervention at the climax of *Samson,* but the rousing motions that the God of the tragedy sends to the tragic hero should not be equated with the grace that the God of *Paradise Lost* sends to the hero of the epic, the "motions" (XI, 91) which bring to completion Adam's spiritual regeneration. At the time Samson receives God's motions, he is already a regenerate man. Having taken the opportunities for self-correction offered in his exchanges with the Chorus and Manoa, Dalila and Harapha, the Samson who defies the Philistine officer is already the moral antithesis of the despairing man whom the Chorus viewed at dawn. In the soliloquy that opens the play, Samson alternates between a despairing doubt of God and a self-doubt so profound as to preclude all hope of change. Either God is faithless, he laments (23–42), or he himself has sinned beyond forgiveness (43–52); either God has given him a gift inadequate to his mission (53–59), or his unsuccessful strength has been punished with irreparable ruin (60–109). At the play's crisis, rejecting the summons of the lords (1320–21), Samson, by honoring the law, honors the God whose fidelity he had doubted: "O wherefore was my birth . . . foretold / Twice by an angel?" (23–29),

"Why was my breeding ordered and prescribed / As of a person separate to God?" (30–33). Answering the apprehensive Chorus (1355–62), Samson expresses confidence in God's favor: "Shall I abuse this consecrated gift / Of strength, again returning with my hair / After my great transgression, so requite / Favor renewed?" Honoring the divinely ordered separation of whose fruitlessness he had complained, Samson asks indignantly whether the temple of Dagon, a "place abominable," is a fit place for a Nazarite. Samson's initial sense that he had sinned unforgivably is reversed in his defense of his moral dignity. When the officer warns, "Regard thyself" (1333), Samson replies, "Myself? my conscience and internal peace," and declares that slavery has not debased his mind (1334–42), the mind whose "impotence" he had previously cursed (52). Having rebuffed the officer, Samson insists to the Chorus that he must use his gift for the purpose for which it was given, the resistance of tyranny: "Who constrains me to the temple of Dagon / Not dragging?" (1369–70). He is repudiating the doubts of his mission which he had expressed in the disparagement of that gift: "God, when he gave me strength, to show withal / How slight the gift was, hung it in my hair" (58–59). Samson's sense that his physical self had been vitiated is reversed in his refusal of physical indignity: "Have they not sword-players and ev'ry sort / Of gymnic artists . . . / But they must pick me out . . . / To make them sport with blind activity?" (1323–32).

Nor do the rousing motions effect a moral change in Samson: the man who accepts the second summons to the temple is morally identical to the man who refused the first. Announcing to the Chorus the change of plans to which he has been prompted, Samson insists that he will not abuse his consecrated gift nor sully his Nazarite purity: "I with this messenger will go along, / Nothing to do, be sure, that may dishonor / Our Law, or stain my vow of Nazarite" (1384–86). Responding to the second command of the lords, the riddling Samson straightforwardly repeats his declaration as a condition for his compliance: "Yet this be sure, in nothing to comply / Scandalous or forbidden in our Law" (1408–09). Samson's third riddle—"And for a life, who will not change his purpose?" (1406)—is, as Joseph Summers argues, a reaffirmation of the hero's moral dignity, though Summers's familiar reading is not the only reading possible. He argues that Samson goes to affirm what he but not the officer calls a "life," namely his conscience and internal peace. In his second riddle, "Masters' commands come with a power resistless / To such as owe them absolute subjection" (1404–05), Samson reaffirms his mission. Summers's religious reading of the riddle has been widely accepted—Samson is obeying the commands of the one master to whom he owes absolute subjection[2] — but this reading contains a pun that Milton would not have attributed to a Nazarite. *Masters'*, as the word *them* insists, is plural, and the pun therefore trifles with a central Hebrew prayer: "Hear, O Israel, the Lord our God is one Lord" (Deut. vi, 4). It is possible that in his third riddle Samson does not pun on the word *life,* but instead ironically reaffirms his "purpose": he will not change that purpose, namely to obey his conscience, in order to save his physical life. In his second riddle, where he cannot be punning, Samson must be employing a similar irony. Utilizing an ambiguity of reference, he must be declaring that, not such a man as owes the lords subjection, he only appears to obey them. This reading is supported by the analogy between this riddling declaration of obedience and Samson's riddling proclamation at the temple: "'Hitherto, lords, what your commands imposed / I have performed, as reason was, obeying'" (1640–41). He has not obeyed because obedience is reasonable but because he has had a reason appropriate for an impenitent political prisoner.

In his second riddle, then, Samson refers not to the irresistible power of God, but to the resistible power of tyrants. His first riddle, an assertion of physical dignity, completes the series of reaffirmations: "Yet knowing their advantages too many, / Because they shall not trail me through their streets / Like a wild beast, I am content to go" (1401–03). Seeming to acknowledge his helplessness as a blind man, Samson conceals with ambiguity and understatement an assertion of strength: he goes not to avoid a fight, but to avoid a fight in the open, where a blind man would be at a disadvantage; he goes in order that he may not be led like an animal in captivity, but in order that, on the contrary, he may fall upon his enemies like a lion.

If "Grace is a term that primarily concerns matters of salvation," as Dennis Danielson asserts,[3] then grace is literally depicted in *Paradise Lost,* but it is not literally depicted in *Samson Agonistes:* the rousing motions do not urge Samson to "prayer, repentance, and obedience due" (*PL* III, 191), they give him military advice. Samson received such advice in his youth: in the "intimate impulse" (223) God prompted him to violate a statute of the law of the covenant which forbade marriage to Gentiles, granted him the exemption necessary, and explained the consequences — that by marrying the woman of Timna, Samson would begin the deliverance of Israel (219–26). In his pride — as Arnold Stein has rightly observed — Samson, marrying Dalila, rationalized that he had been given not a particular dispensation, but a general exemption from the legal statute.[4] Rejecting the lords' first command, Samson stubbornly insists upon obeying a statute of the national law which forbade the presence of Hebrews at pagan rites. He remembers his proud transgression, and by resisting both the warnings of the officer and the casuistry by which the Chorus attempts to preserve the life of its friend, he demonstrates the firmness of his repentance. He becomes once more what he was in his youth, God's obedient champion, and God responds by offering in the rousing motions what he had offered in the intimate impulse. Milton calls attention to the likeness between the two events. When, in a startling non sequitur – as has been observed by Stanley Fish[5] – Samson introduces the subject of dispensation ("Yet that he may dispense with me or thee, / Present in temples . . . thou need'st not doubt" [1377–79]), the audience is reminded of the Chorus's discussion of the subject: "[God] hath full right to exempt / Whomso it pleases him by choice / From national obstriction" (310–12). The discussion is based on Samson's disclosure of the intimate impulse. In the rousing motions, God once again tells Samson to violate a statute of the national law, grants him a dispensation, and tells him the "important cause" (1379): Samson is to go to the temple of Dagon on a military mission to perform a "great act" (1389).

In the rousing motions, then, God does not guide a sinner to salvation, he guides a penitent warrior to the completion of his earthly task, "The work to which [he] was divinely call'd" (226). At the crisis of the play, Milton adapts to the worldly sphere concepts strictly applicable only to the otherworldly one, and in the offstage catastrophe which brings Samson's story to its end (1596–1659) he follows the same procedure. In *Paradise Lost* Milton depicts a literal Arminian (or even Pelagian) interplay of necessary grace and free will.[6] Adam chooses freely: "What better can we do, than . . . confess / Humbly our faults, and pardon beg" (X, 1086–89), but God's grace makes that choice possible – he must "soften stony hearts / To pray, repent, and bring obedience due" (III, 189–90). In *Samson Agonistes* Milton substitutes a necessary prompting to a military victory and an equally necessary understanding of that prompting. In Samson's rightful refusal to obey the first command of the Philistine lords, Milton indicates that Samson could not have achieved his triumph without divine guidance. In the motif of incomprehension stressed by one of the providential critics, G. A. Wilkes, he shows that no human being could have thought of God's stratagem.[7] The motif appears prominently in the first scene of the close, the scene in which the Chorus discusses with Manoa the ransoming of Samson (1445–1595); but its most poignant appearance occurs at the end of Samson's confrontation with Harapha. There the Danites, reminded of the hero of Ramath-lechi by Samson's intimidation of Philistia's champion (1268–86), are struck with second thoughts (1287–96). They remember Samson's "sight bereaved," and, comforting their friend, assure him that the metaphoric wreath of saintly patience is as noble as the literal wreath of military victory. Samson has a similar change of mood. His confidence that the "baffled" Harapha (1237) will not dare complain to the lords (1253–55) is followed by a reversion to an earlier acceptance of death in prison (573–76): "But come what will, my deadliest foe will prove / My speediest friend, by death to rid me hence" (1256–64). A moment later, Samson revives in the hope of one last encounter with the Philistines, but that hope brings him no inkling of God's means: "Yet so it may fall out, because their end / Is hate, not help to me, it may with mine / Draw their own ruin who attempt the deed" (1265–67). Milton makes clear that God's prompting is necessary for Samson's success, but, tying the play's crisis to its catastrophe, he also makes clear that Samson's comprehension of the prompting is equally necessary.

When Samson departs for the temple, he knows that he has been sent to perform a warrior's task, and he knows that he may die in the attempt: "This day will be remarkable in my life / By some great act, or of my days the last" (1388–89). But just as Samson did not know how his marriage to the woman of Timna would provoke a war, so he does not know what "great act" God has in mind, and he reasonably but wrongly supposes that he has been asked to assume a warrior's risk, the risk that he may be defeated and killed in battle. The difference between the riddles that Samson speaks before the officer and the riddles that he addresses to the Philistine lords indicates the time when Samson acquires the missing knowledge. The earlier riddles are forced upon Samson. Knowing that he may not survive his present campaign, the champion must convey to the Hebrew people that his death is not that of an impious and vengeful suicide, lest his death do more harm to Israel than his fall had done. He must explain his intentions to the friends who are to be his messengers to the people, and in such a way as to avoid the sin of his youth, the disclosure of God's secrets to an enemy. At the temple, however, about to be pressed to death, Samson displays a gallows humor as self-expressive and exuberant as the wit of a bridegroom: like his first riddle, his last riddles have no ulterior purpose. Samson's exuberance must spring from his discovery of what his "great act" will be and of what his death will mean. The play's structural patterning suggests the means of that discovery.

In the ironic proclamation of obedience that the man clad as Philistia's public servant (1615–16) addresses to the lords (1640–1642)—"'as reason was, obeying'"—Samson repeats the political defiance of his second riddle (1404–05). In his voluntary display of strength, "Now of my own accord such other trial / I mean to show you of my strength, yet greater, / As with amaze shall strike all who behold'" (1643–45), Samson repeats the covert threat of his first riddle (1401–03), "Because they shall not trail me . . . / Like a wild beast." What Samson says repeats half of his parting pledges to the Chorus: "Happen what may, of me expect to hear / Nothing dishonorable, impure, unworthy / Our God, our Law, my nation, or myself; / The last of me or no I cannot warrant" (1423–26). In "my nation," Samson concludes the series of patriotic declarations which began with his threatening reply (1347) to the officer's valediction, "I am sorry what this stoutness will produce" (1346). In his ironic proclamation of obedience Samson declares himself the champion of his "nation." In "myself; / The last of me or no I cannot warrant," Samson sums up his refusals to demean himself. He repeats the meaning of "for a life, who will not change his purpose?" (1406): he will follow his conscience though it cost him his life; and he repeats the meaning of "knowing their advantages too many" (1401–03): he will exert his strength though he die in the attempt. Introducing the final "trial" of "strength," Samson confirms the latter pledge. If Samson's words announce his fulfillment of half of his pledges, the other half must be the burden of the final thought or prayer that the messenger describes (1637–38). The moral "self" must be the subject of Samson's prayer, and the "great matter" which he ponders must therefore be his pledge to honor "God" and the "Law." In that pledge, seeming to repeat his straightforward refusals to disobey the Mosaic law (1384–86, 1408–09), Samson adds under cover of litotes ("Nothing . . . unworthy") a further implication—that he intends to fight for God as well as for country.

The messenger, unable to determine whether Samson "Prayed, / Or some great matter in his mind revolved" (1637–38), does not pause to speculate on the contents of the thought or prayer, but the audience at its leisure can consider the structural hints. Thinking of his "great act" and of the law that he had sworn to obey and uphold, Samson realizes that the legal statute from which he has been granted an exemption is the statute which he has been sent to obey: "Thou shalt not bow down to [the] gods [of the inhabitants of Canaan], nor serve them, nor do after their works: but thou shalt utterly overthrow them, and quite break down their images" (Exod. xxiii, 24). Thinking of death and of the moral "self"—the reading of the third riddle (1406) that best fits the thought is the ironic one: that Samson will not change his moral purpose to save his life—Samson realizes that his death is to be a consequence not of his failure but of his success; he prays that this noble death, which attests to his repentance, may atone for his fall. By persisting in his resolve to honor "God," the "Law," and the moral "self," Samson comes to discover what "great act" God has sent him to perform, and what kind of death God has granted him. The cooperation between God and man, which in *Paradise Lost* issues in the salvation of Adam and Eve, has a worldly outcome in *Samson Agonistes*. By understanding God's prompting, Samson at the pillars is able to complete his life, affirming his spiritual and physical dignity, and acting to defend his faith and nation.

The main objection to taking this triumph at face value has its roots in Stein's reading of Manoa's description of the Philistine lords: "the hated Philistia is divided into three parts, of which one part is humanly decent" (*Heroic Knowledge*, p. 193). Milton—the objection runs—could not have viewed the deaths of three thousand Philistines as they are viewed by Samson's advocates: some of the Philistines did not deserve to die.[8] It is possible, though, to view Manoa's description in a different light, to see the suppliant's judgment of the Philistines as a practical judgment rather than a moral one. One faction of the lords, the venal, are described as indifferent to both God and state (1464–66). A second, the "much averse," who "most reverenced Dagon and his priests," are the upholders of Philistia's god (1461–63)—a false god, as Samson demonstrates to Dalila (895–900). Milton expects the audience to surmise that the "generous" and "civil" faction are the upholders of the state, and Manoa's description corroborates the surmise: these lords propose a political settlement, a "convenient ransom" for a man who is no longer a military threat, a foe who has been "reduced" to "misery beneath their fears" (1466–71). Manoa judges the lords "civil" because, unlike the "averse," they will agree to free his son, and he judges them "generous" because they ask only a public ransom, not that mass of private bribes demanded by the "moderate seeming" (1464). Milton expects the audience to feel sympathy for the lovingly industrious father, but he does not expect it to judge as Manoa judges. He expects it to remember that, as Samson has demonstrated to Dalila (888–94) and to Harapha (1193–1219), the state upheld by these Philistine patriots is a tyranny. Irene Samuel argues that the harshest of the Philistines did not kill their enemy, but she misses the motives for keeping Samson alive, which are suggested by two of Samson's remarks about his captors: that the lords make "no small profit" from the labors (1258–61) of their "drudge" (1393), and that they have a "daily practice" of "insult[ing]" (113–14) their "slave" (1392). These suggestions are corroborated by Manoa's report. The "moderate seeming" demand "Private reward," and the "generous" and "civil" expect "some convenient ransom" (1464–65, 1471). The "much averse" are "set on revenge and spite" (1462).

Milton must have known that he would open the mouths of idolists and atheists if he did not preclude the possibility that God had prompted Samson to an ungodly deed. Preparing a careful indictment of all of Samson's slain, Milton demonstrates that God made available to the erring Philistines the same opportunities for moral change that he extended to his erring champion. Moved by the guilt and grief that Samson voiced after the departure of his father (606–32, 641–51), the Chorus prayed that God might grant to Samson a change of heart (652–66), "consolation from above," and a turn of fortune (705–09), a "peaceful end." God listened, but he granted to Samson only appropriate substitutions for the Chorus's requests. He sent for Samson's resistance the dangerous consolations of a "serpent" with a concealed sting (997–98), and he sent for Samson's rejection the chance for an ignominious "retire[ment]" before a threatening "storm" (1061). Refusing to force Samson's repentance, God instead sent him opportunities for self-correction. Anthony Low has observed God's extension to Dalila of a similar opportunity for change: "Samson's rejection is a necessary trial for Dalila. To accept her back would only be to re-establish their old relationship and to confirm her in her ways. . . . [Samson's] words carry a sting, along with their admonition to think over what she has done — and that, if anything can help, is what is needed to pierce through the armor of her self-enclosing spiritual blindness" (*Blaze of Noon*, p. 157). Samson's dismissal of Harapha, "Go, baffled coward" (1237), parallel to his rejection of Dalila (954–59), "Bewail thy falsehood," provides the giant a like opportunity to examine his life.

Her armor unpierced, Dalila does not return home stricken, nor does the "crestfallen" Harapha (1244) return to Gath in shame. Refusing their opportunities for change, both Philistines violate the law of nature, the law — as Samuel observes — by which God judges pagans.[9] Samson explicitly invoked that law in condemning Dalila's betrayal (888–90), and at her departure Dalila confirms his charges. Defending her conduct, not only does she prove herself a false patriot by her eagerness for "public marks of honor and reward" (992), but she proves herself what Samson has called her, a "smooth hyprocr[ite]" (872). She does not go to the Dagonalia to praise her gods, but to be praised by men (971–84). The law of nature is implicitly the basis upon which Samson defends himself from Harapha's charge of criminality (1193–1219), and at his departure Harapha proves himself a criminal by that law. In threatening a state punishment for Samson (1242), he shows himself the proponent of arbitrary power, the antithesis of an advocate of freedom. When Samson has atoned for his doubts of God and answered his despairing judgments of himself, God intervenes to aid him; when the Philistines refuse to obey the law of nature, God disowns them, leaving them to the deaths that they have brought upon themselves. Dalila has not achieved the ends for which she had sought a reconciliation with Samson, but there remain for her the wages of the "piety / Which to [her] country [she] was judged to have shown" (993–94). Intending to collect these, she collects instead the wages which God thinks due. Harapha, who does not dare to "appear" Samson's "antagonist" (1628), loses his last chance to save both himself and his country at the temple and earns his ignominious death.

The lords of Philistia receive their call to change in Samson's refusal to obey their first command, his appeal for the religious freedom and civil justice sanctioned by the law of nature. Shutting their ears, they importune their destruction to "Come without delay" (1395). The public servant of these lords has been thought a touching innocent, a gentle man respectful to Samson and as solicitous as Samson's father and loyal friends.[10] But in *Paradise Lost* Milton condemns not only proud Satan, but Satan's unquestioning followers. In his second riddle, "Masters' commands come with a power resistless" (1404f), Samson affirms ironically what he surmises to be the officer's beliefs. The upholder of "strenuous liberty" (268–71) finds in the civil servant what Aristotle would call a born slave. The Chorus similarly finds the officer a sycophant (1350–51). His nervous valediction, "I am sorry what this stoutness will produce" (1346), is not necessarily respectful—"stoutness" can mean "arrogance" as well as "courage"—and Milton, who provides the officer no reason to be solicitous toward a surly stranger, does suggest a motive for his evident reluctance to depart. The officer is reminiscent of such figures as the rightly nervous bearer of bad tidings in the *Antigone*.

Praising Samson's resolution to go to the temple, "By this compliance thou wilt win the lords / To favor, and perhaps to set thee free" (1410–12), the officer does not reveal a hope like that of Manoa and the Chorus. The Philistine speaks not from love but from relief that the threat of disobedience has passed, not from respect for Samson but from awe of the nobility. That awe is revealed in the officer's overestimation of his masters: not even the "civil" lords respond to the humiliation of the suppliant Manoa (1459) with such clemency as the officer describes. In warning the departing Philistine, "Perhaps thou shalt have cause to sorrow indeed" (1347), Samson gives him the same opportunity for change that he has given to parting Dalila and parting Harapha. The consequences of the officer's response are told in the messenger's description of Samson's triumph. In Judges the guide who leads Samson to the pillars is a boy, but Milton places in the messenger's narration no indication that Samson's guide is someone whom the audience has not seen. He implies that Samson's guide at the temple is the guide who led Samson to the temple, the public officer. That the officer is "unsuspicious" (1635) proves that he has not been jarred from his complacency. Like his masters, he thinks Samson reduced beneath his fears, and in leading Samson to the pillars he brings death upon himself and upon the men he serves.

Having convicted the patriots, cynics, and idolators of Philistia of hardened sin, Milton calls attention to God's sanction and supervision of their destruction. In the first scene of the play's close Milton suggests through the motif of incomprehension that the unfolding events have a divine cause. Hearing the sound of "Blood, death, and dreadful deeds" (1513), the Chorus is once more reminded of the hero of Ramath-lechi; unable, like Manoa (1503), to imagine how a blind man can triumph unless God causes "light again within [his] eyes to spring" (584), it dreams of replacing Samson's metaphoric crown of saintly patience with a literal palm of victory (1527–33). Manoa's "windy" hopes (1574) end in a double disappointment. First the father is prevented from rescuing his son by Samson's death (1573), then his heart is broken by what seems the realization of his worst fears, that both his own hopes and his son's have proven "Deceivable and vain" (349–50). Thinking that Samson has died a suicidal reprobate (1590–91), that his death has proven not the "crown" of his life but its "shame" (1579), Manoa turns his face from the painful vision: "More than enough we know" (1592).

The events at the temple, unforeseen and misunderstood even by the pious, are, Milton suggests, beyond human contriving. The contriver endorses his faithful servant by choosing between those whose "ends" are "help" to Samson and those whose "end / is hate." Touchingly oblivious to the weary sloth, the proud self-importance, and the avarice of age, Manoa reports how he "attempted one by one the lords, / Either at home, or through the high street passing, / With supplication prone" (1457–59) to accept a ransom for his son that would require his "whole inheritance" (1476). As the Philistines shout to "behold / Their once great dread, captive and blind before them" (1473–74), the Chorus shares the father's "joy" at the thought of Samson's "delivery" (1504–07). In the end, as Samson's enemies "Draw" upon themselves "their own ruin," there enters with unexpected haste—for "evil news rides post, while good news baits" (1538)—a messenger who in the end brings to those who sought to deliver Samson the news of their own deliverance. The blundering Chorus is enlightened, and Manoa receives comforts which Milton is careful to balance against the father's disappointments. Learning from the messenger's collected account that Samson's death has proven not the "shame" of his life but its "crown," Manoa retracts his fear that Samson had died ignominiously, and takes comfort in the thought of his "heroic" death: "no time for lamentation" (1708). He retracts his fear that his son had died a despairing death, and takes comfort in a "death so noble": "Nothing is here for tears" (1721–24). Bringing Samson "Home to his father's house" (1733), Manoa preserves, in the place of his son's life, his son's memory and the memory of his cause (1725–44).

The contrast of secondary characters from the play's middle provides the basis for the structure of its close. As Summers observes ("Movements of the Drama," p. 159), Samson's visitors enter two by two, the Chorus and Manoa "as comforters," Dalila "to seduce," and Harapha to "insult." Samson overcomes his initial doubts of God by atoning for the harm that his fall had done to Israel's patriots and pious. He reassures the doubting Chorus about the divine sanction of his mission, and he reassures his grieving father about the justice of God's ways. Samson overcomes his despairing self-condemnations by defeating his Philistine enemies. He learns by resisting Dalila that his "impotence of mind" (52) is not irreparable, and he learns by defying Harapha that blindness and captivity have not deprived him of his strength.[11] In the first scene of the close the visitors who come to conquer Samson receive "Ruin" and "destruction" at his hands (1514). In the last scene (1660–1758) the visitors who come to comfort Samson take comfort in the deliverance he has brought them. In this scene Milton demonstrates that Samson's victory corroborates his answers to the doubts that his fall had raised in Israel's saving remnant.

Israel's "just men long oppressed" (1269) have been primarily concerned with the failure of Samson's mission and with the ruin of the strength upon which that mission depended. First viewing the despondent Samson, they recalled his victory at Ramath-lechi and his exploit at Gaza (115–50) and lamented the "bondage" and "lost sight" (151–63) which Samson in his soliloquy had named as the "miseries" brought him by his strength (60–109). Interpreting his fall in terms of the instability of worldly fortune (164–75), they applied to Samson a view of tragedy in which the audience is meant to hear Hebraic corrections, as it were, of Aristotelian concepts. The point of these corrections is the difference between Hebrew values and the values of the pagan world, the world to which the Philistines belong. The Chorus places the nobility of the tragic hero in personal merit rather than in the aristocratic station valued by societies with kings (170–72), and, as its later questioning of Samson's marriages reveals (215–18), it thinks of *hamartia* (173) as the breaking of the statutes delivered by Moses, no common law. In the end, answered in its doubts, it replaces its tragic account of Samson's life with a heroic account, assigning heroic images to Samson's strength (1687–96), which "Might have subdued the earth" (174), and to Samson's virtue (1697–1707), once more the "mate" of that strength (173).

Though the last of these images, that of the phoenix (1699–1707), is sometimes thought typological,[12] Milton directs attention elsewhere. He prevents the audience from finding typological significance in the eagle of the preceding image (1695–96) – it is a descending, realistic eagle, not a rising, symbolic one – and even more certainly he prevents its finding typology in the first image of the series, that of the snake or "dragon" (1692–95). His play is built not on the relation of Jews to Christians, but on the contrast of Jews with pagans. Comparing Samson's assault upon the Philistines to the attack of a snake upon "villatic fowl," the Chorus enhances the snake with a heroic metonymy, "evening dragon," but shows by the realistic description that it does not believe in dragons. Comparing the assault to the attack of an eagle, it stresses the terror of that attack, likening it to an unexpected stroke, "cloudless thunder," but it rejects the tale of the eagle's magical rejuvenation, a fable of credulous pagans. Asserting that Samson's virtue is, like the phoenix, a nonpareil, the Chorus describes the Arabian bird in such a way as to suggest that it, like him "whom the Gentiles feign to bear up heav'n" (150), does not exist. Denying what is contrary to nature, the rebirth of an immolated bird, the Chorus makes clear that the phoenix, like the dragon, is merely a poetic fiction. The Danites are as Hebraic in their heroic as they are in their tragic pronouncements: even in their celebrations, Milton suggests, they would never mistake a hero for a demigod.

Discerning a moral pattern in what had seemed man's "fickle state" (164), the Chorus balances its account of Samson's rise with a fall to which Aristotle denies the name of tragedy, the punishment of the wicked. Hailing in the antistrophe of its ode of celebration (1687–1707) the return of the youthful champion, the Chorus takes note of God's participation in Samson's victory, referring in the phrase "With inward eyes illuminated" (1689) not to rational insight,[13] but to an instance of supernatural intervention which it has witnessed, the bestowal of the motions that guided Samson to his place of victory. In the strophe (1669–86) the Chorus contrasts with God's lifting up, his bringing low. Remembering the governmental theory which it has heard Samson voice to Harapha (1208–19), the Chorus sees in the fall of the Philistines God's vengeance on the "mighty of the earth" (1272), his vengeance for Samson's "bondage" and "lost sight": God has visited upon the hero's captors the same blindness and ruin which they had visited upon Samson at Dalila's house.

The Chorus believes that it has seen Samson's defeat reversed and his old mission renewed, and Milton upholds its thanksgiving.[14] The Danites have a precedent for their celebrations, the song of gratitude sung by the former slaves of Egypt for their deliverance at the Red Sea. That precedent justifies their ode: had they not rejoiced in Samson's victory they would have shown themselves to be murmurers of the desert, lovers of what Samson calls "Bondage with ease" (271). Milton carefully confines their expressions of gratitude within the bounds of justice. The Chorus rejoices only in the deaths of those responsible for the conditions of its house of bondage. As Samuel acknowledges in passing, "the arched roof . . . smites only responsible Philistine heads"—"Lords, ladies, captains, counsellors . . . priests," the "choice nobility and flower" of Philistia (1653–54).

But though the Chorus is chiefly concerned with Samson's mission and strength, the plight of God's champion has raised in it doubts of God's fidelity, and it has been moved by Samson's guilt. Responding to his call for death's "benumbing opium" (617–32), the Chorus prays for the "secret refreshings" which will enable Samson to bear his tormenting thoughts (652–66), and, recalling what Samson's father had said about God's treatment of those whom he had "chosen . . . / To worthiest deeds" (368–69), it protests in Manoa's absence, and in Manoa's stead, God's abandonment of those whom he had "solemnly elected" (678): "thou oft / Amidst their highth of noon / Changest thy countenance and thy hand, with no regard / Of highest favors passed / From thee on them, or them to thee of service" (682–86). In the end its doubts are answered, and it expresses its gratitude in a heartfelt (if characteristically inaccurate) hyperbole, "All is best" (1745). It sees (1745–54) that by mysterious ways God's "unsearchable dispose" has brought his prophecy to pass, and in the achievement of God's "uncontrollable intent" the Danites find the answer to their complaint: "Oft [God] seems to hide his face, / But unexpectedly returns / And to his faithful champion hath in place / Bore witness gloriously" (1749–52). Their prayer for the assuagement of Samson's guilt is rewarded with the assuagement of their own "passion" (1755–58), the grief that they had shared with the "afflicted" (660). That grief is allayed, however, not by the means for which they had prayed, divine impulsion, but by the means by which God had granted their prayer for Samson, the "new acquist / Of true experience" (1755–56).

God's desertion and Samson's sin have been the primary concern of Manoa, however, rather than of the Chorus. Appalled by Samson's ruin, Manoa complained of God's betrayal, ending in the words remembered by the Chorus: "Alas, methinks whom God hath chosen once . . . / if he through frailty err, / He should not so o'erwhelm, and as a thrall / Subject him to so foul indignities, / Be it but for honor's sake of former deeds" (368–72). Manoa also complained that his own hopes had proven delusive, that the son whom God had given him as a blessing (356–60) had brought "shame" to himself and to his "father's house" (444–47). But as Manoa's reproaches to his son are the scoldings of a loving father, so his complaints of God are not the blasphemies of a man of these latter days. By his horror and indignation at the thought of the Dagonalia—"So Dagon shall be magnified, and God . . . / Disglorified, blasphemed, and had in scorn / By th' idolatrous rout" (440–43)—Manoa proves that his reproaches are the loving familiarity of a man whose god may be met at the next oak or bush—though, unlike his son, Manoa has met only God's angel. In his expression of dismay, the father acknowledged but extenuated Samson's sin: "if he through frailty err." The extenuation, voiced to God, so to speak, concealed a persistent worry, and Manoa could not help voicing it to Samson. Even when comforting his despairing son—"[God] can . . . / Cause light again within thy eyes to spring" (583–84)—he could not forbear adding, "Wherewith to serve him better than thou hast" (585).

In the end, the messenger's narration brings consolation to Manoa, and the first part of Manoa's final speech (1708–24) is a testimony to the allaying of his religious fears. At the end of the first section (1708–20) Manoa, counting his blessings, tells their sum: "And what is best and happiest yet, all this / With God not parted from [Samson], as was feared, / But favoring and assisting to the end" (1718–20). He sees that God has kept his promises to his son, and he sees that God's gift to himself has proven a "grace," that the son for whom he had prayed (356–57) has not brought "reproach" to himself and "father's house" (444–47), but "To himself and father's house eternal fame" (1717). When he declares that his son has left the Philistines "years of mourning, / And lamentation to the sons of Caphtor" (1712–13), and declares that Samson has brought "Honor" and "freedom" to Israel (1714–15), he is thinking of the evils he had dreaded, the blasphemies of the Dagonalia, chargeable to Samson. God's name has been vindicated, he declares: Samson has been the means by which the "magnif[ying]" of Dagon has doomed Philistia and the "Disglorif[ying]" of God (440–43) saved Israel. Rejoicing that Samson has "quit himself / Like Samson . . . on his enemies / Fully revenged" (1709–12), Manoa retracts the charge against God remembered by the Chorus, that Samson had been overwhelmed with indignities. In "Fully revenged," Manoa remembers his exclamation upon hearing the messenger's first fragmentary reports, "A dreadful way thou took'st to thy revenge" (1591).

The Danites had also remembered those words, and had countered, "O dearly bought revenge, yet glorious!" (1660); but Manoa's point is not the same as theirs. By its expansion of "glorious"—"Living or dying thou hast fulfilled / The work for which thou wast foretold / To Israel" (1661–63)—the Chorus makes clear that it is distinguishing between personal revenge and that legitimate use of force in public affairs which it had heard Samson defend to Harapha: "My nation was subjected to your lords? / It was the force of conquest; force with force / Is well ejected when the conquered can" (1205–07). Manoa, however, is concerned with what the rise of his son and the fall of Israel's oppressors prove about God's favor to Samson. Supposing that his son, desiring to kill himself, had spitefully also decided to end the lives of his enemies (Milton calls to mind the prayer of the Samson of Judges), Manoa had thought of his son's death as a final indignity, a final sign of God's abandonment. Now, recognizing his mistake, Manoa refers in "Fully revenged" to God's vengeance for Samson's "foul indignities," and declaring that Samson has "heroicly . . . finished / A life heroic" (1710–11) he repudiates his complaint of God's ungrateful degradation of the "chosen" (368–72). In the second section of his religious affirmation (1721–24), Manoa recalls another of his responses to the messenger's fragmentary reports, "O lastly over-strong against thyself!" (1590). The Chorus had also remembered those words and after hearing the messenger's full account had defended Samson's exertion of his strength: the hero lay "self-killed" but "Not willingly," it had declared, "victorious among [his] slain" (1664–65). Manoa, however, is concerned with Samson's moral "weakness," with an evidence of sinful despair which would have deserved "contempt, / Dispraise, or blame." Taking comfort in Samson's "noble" death, Manoa recognizes his son's atonement.

But Manoa's plan of ransom testifies to his concern for the failure of Samson's mission and for the ruin of Samson's strength. Manoa has wished to lighten Samson's "miseries," his blindness and his "Life in captivity / Among inhuman foes" (60–109)—"It shall be my delight to tend his eyes" (1490)—and he has wished to lighten the shame of Samson's defeat—"And view him sitting in the house, ennobled / With all those high exploits by him achieved" (1491–92). That he has shared the Chorus's dismay at the fall of the champion is attested by his hopes and dreams: he had hoped that God would make further use of Samson "in some great service" (1495–99), he had dreamed that God would "restore [Samson's] eyesight to his strength" (1502–03). In the end Manoa's hopes are realized, though not in the way that he had dreamed, and though he cannot lessen his son's sufferings (nor forget them), he can keep alive Samson's memory and his cause. The tomb that Manoa plans to build is the opposite of the tomb that Dalila had imagined for herself (980–90). The father who was willing to spend his "whole inheritance" to ransom his son now spends to preserve his son's memory. The monument of Dalila's imagining, a mark of her fame, exposes her reason for offering to ransom her husband: she had dreamed of receiving what she has been forced to renounce (971–82), a fame among the Hebrews equal to her fame among the Philistines, a universal praise. Dalila's monument is a monument to values whose hollowness Samson, appealing to the law of nature, had exposed (888–890); Manoa's monument is a monument to Samson's values. The antithesis between the tombs serves to focus the antithetical fates of Samson's Hebrew comforter and his Philistine enemy: God destroys a monument to Philistine "piety" (993), conceived in self-love, and commissions in its stead a work of love, a monument to Israelite patriotism.

As Milton justifies the patriotism of the Chorus, so he honors the patriotism of Manoa.[15] He devises a means for praising the burial of Samson. In the Jeremian complaint with which the Chorus responds to Samson's lamentation, the Chorus first repeats Manoa's initial expressions of dismay, then amplifies its own first expression, "O mirror of our fickle state." It adds to its example of Samson's fall (164–169) two ignominious fates at the hands of men (692–96), the condemnation of heroes by "unjust tribunals" and the death of God's champions in battle or their capture by unworthy foes. It closes with an indignity bestowed by God, a premature old age of poverty and illness visited upon virtuous men (697–700). The passage is notable for its topical references, its references to the fate of Puritan leaders, and to the "painful" gout of a man "not disordinate," to his "poverty," and to the premature blindness of his "crude old age" (697–702). Though the doubts are not allowed to stand (1660–65), the moving realistic details stay in the mind. When the Chorus tells Manoa that his son has been "made older" by "eyesight lost" than the father who means to "nurse" him (1488–89), the audience recalls the description of a "crude old age": it notices that what Manoa has to offer Samson living, though better than Samson's other sorry choices, is a fate of which a guiltless man might complain. But, it sees what Manoa has to offer Samson dead is beyond reproach. When Manoa plans to display Samson's trophies, "legend[s]," and memorial verses (1736–37), the audience recalls the Chorus's contempt for the "condemnations" of heroes by the "ingrateful multitude" (696); it sees in Manoa a preserver of greatness in a mean and forgetful world. When Manoa says, "Let us go find the body where it lies . . . and from the stream / With lavers pure . . . wash off / The clotted gore" (1725–28), the audience recalls the Chorus's horror that the bodies of heroes have been left as "carcasses / To dogs and fowls a prey" (693–94); it sees that Manoa is a civilized man in a world of barbarians.

Milton devises even stronger praise for the builder of Samson's monument. Critics who belittle the celebrations of Samson's triumph (or the triumph itself) sometimes cite the historical argument of Parker, that the biblical judges did not accomplish the liberation of Israel.[16] Milton, though, who altered Samson's life, emphatically denying the account of his death in Judges, alters his time as well, incorporating into the story from Judges the giant from 2 Samuel: "I dread him not, nor all his giant brood, / Though Fame divulge him father of five sons, / All of gigantic size, Goliah chief" (1247–49). Milton tells the audience that Samson's victory is only one generation from David's final defeat of the Philistines; thus, when Manoa in the second part of his final speech describes his tomb for Samson—"Thither will all the valiant youth resort, / And from his memory inflame their breasts / To matchless valor and adventures high" (1738–40)—the audience receives his words as a prophecy. It surmises that David, a boy too young to bear arms, drew courage from the example of the "Despised" captive and read in the destruction of the Philistines the sign of Israel's triumph. Milton honors the preserver of Samson's memory by giving him a necessary role in the victory of Samson's cause.

By his "great act," Samson confirms what in his atonement he had told his friends and father about the sanction of his mission and about the trustworthiness of God, and the celebrations of the Chorus and Manoa testify to the importance of the end for which Samson has struggled and for which God has aided him. At only one point in the close is there an instance of the kind of irony that might undermine the testimony, an irony which points to the limitations of Samson's advocates, and which differs from the ironies of incomprehension, pathetic in tone. This irony occurs at the point at which the opening hyperbole of the Chorus's final speech—"All is best" (1745)—intersects with what Low (*Blaze of Noon*, p. 131) remarks to be the odd concluding turn of Manoa's final speech: "The virgins also shall . . . / Visit his tomb with flowers, only bewailing / His lot unfortunate in nuptial choice, / From whence captivity and loss of eyes" (1741–44). The speakers here disagree on an issue raised by the problem of the fortunate fall in *Paradise Lost*, the question of whether God's good purposes require the sins of his creatures. Two of the providential critics, Wilkes and Rajan, answer "yes": ignoring Stein's reading of Samson's decision to marry Dalila, they argue that Samson's marriage, prompted by God, is a partial evil justified by the universal good revealed at the close.[17] This devotional view, expressed by the Chorus, is denied by Manoa, who believes that Samson would have lived a happier life had he not sinned: "lot unfortunate," like "if he through frailty err" (369), is a euphemism (*nil nisi bonum*). Had Samson not married Dalila, Manoa believes, he would have triumphed without captivity and loss of eyes, and, living to bury his father, would have judged Israel in a heroic, noble, and happy old age.

Theologically, Manoa is correct. The ending of *Samson* contains far less good than a necessary and divinely sanctioned sin should produce, and when the Chorus, imagining that Samson's eyesight has been restored, recalls the battle of Ramath-lechi, it reminds the audience of what further good might have been expected. God, by deflecting a roof beam, might have saved Samson during his last great battle as, with a miraculous fountain (581–83), he saved him after his first. The audience sees that in not fulfilling the Chorus's dream God is again correcting a theological error. Rewarding the regenerate Samson, God grants him the best of the fates now available to him. Before God bestowed the rousing motions, Samson had had three choices of death. He could have died at the house of Dalila, a relapsed sinner; he could have died at the prison house, a sinner accepting his wages; he could have died at his father's house, a sinner penitent but ruined. What God offers is an alternative to these three sorry choices, a noble death at the house of Dagon. The limitations of the offer are related to Samson's fall, as Manoa supposes, and as Low observes: "In one action Samson makes final payment for his sin and is given a chance to achieve his purpose in life: thus he is both rewarded and punished. God finds a way . . . to combine justice with mercy to the detriment of neither" (*Blaze of Noon*, p. 88).

The irony in Manoa's words arises from the means by which he arrives at his theological insight. When the father speaks of his son's "frailty," he refers to what he believes to be Samson's principal fault, his deluded belief that God had prompted his marriages. Manoa's view of the matter arises from Samson's misrepresentation. Explaining to the Chorus about the intimate impulse, Samson says that his parents "knew not / That what [he] motioned was of God" (221–22); at the time of its occurrence, then, Samson did not mention God's prompting to his father. When Manoa says, "thou didst plead / Divine impulsion" (421–22), he must be referring to what Samson told him at the time of his second marriage: having deceived himself that he had been given more than a single exemption from the national law, Samson must thereupon have deceived his father, equating the unsanctioned second marriage with the sanctioned first. Manoa never learns the facts that would have ended his puzzlement, the facts that Samson explains to the Chorus (219–233) — that his triumph at Ramath-lechi issued from a marriage arranged by God but that the opposite of that triumph, the defeat at the house of Dalila, issued from a marriage which was not divinely prompted. Manoa, therefore, never loses his puzzlement, and when he imagines the flowery tributes to his son, he thinks of all the Hebrew maidens from whom he might have chosen a wife for Samson, and shakes his head again at Samson's inexplicable frailty.

Manoa, then, derives a theologically correct conclusion from erroneous facts, while the Chorus, which knows the facts, draws an erroneous conclusion. The irony points to the limitations of the celebrants of Samson's victory, but so gentle an irony cannot be Milton's means of discrediting their celebrations. Rather, at the end of the play, Milton touches upon a theme dear to Stein, the relation of the hero to his community (*Heroic Knowledge*, pp. 194–202). The limitations revealed in the Chorus and Manoa are limitations which the men themselves would acknowledge, knowing that they are not, like Samson, men "chosen" or "solemnly elected." But Samson does not despise them, as his opening tribute to the Chorus indicates (it is equally applicable to Manoa): "Your coming, friends, revives me, for I learn / Now of my own experience . . . / How counterfeit a coin they are who 'friends' / Bear in their superscription (of the most / I would be understood). In prosperous days / They swarm, but in adverse withdraw their head, / Not to be found, though sought" (187–93). The Chorus and Manoa are the most loyal members of the minority in Dan and Israel that opposed the "governors and heads of tribes" (242). They are not, as has been charged, men who hold the "ordinary values of the world," men who betrayed Samson at Ramath-lechi, men indistinguishable from Philistines.[18] Those descriptions fit the Israelite "governors and heads" and the Israelites with what Samson calls "feeble hearts" (455).

Samson is Aristotle's man greater than we are; the visitors who are his enemies and the men who, like them, dishonor the law of nature are men less than we are. The visitors who desire to help Samson are men like us, or like the "us" of Milton's supposing, an audience whose fitness lies in its sympathy with Samson's cause, the establishment on earth of a civil and religious freedom ordained by God. Diverting attention by means of a kindly irony from Samson to the advocates of his cause, Milton takes a moment to remind the audience that those to whom God has given talents exist for the benefit of men no greater than ourselves, men to whom he has given only small change, and from whom he asks only that they should prove truepennies.

University of Regina

NOTES

1. For systematic typology see F. Michael Krouse, *Milton's Samson and the Christian Tradition* (Princeton, 1949), pp. 124–132, and Patrick Cullen, *The Infernal Triad: The Flesh, the World, and the Devil in Spenser and Milton* (Princeton, 1975), pp. 182–150, for incidental typological symbolism, see Anthony Low, *The Blaze of Noon: A Reading of "Samson Agonistes"* (New York, 1974), pp. 32, 56, 68. For Samson's rational victory, see Mary Ann Radzinowicz, *Towards "Samson Agonistes": The Growth of Milton's Mind* (Princeton, 1978), pp. 66, 348, 361–62. For the providential view of the crisis see G. A. Wilkes, "The Interpretation of *Samson Agonistes*," *Huntington Library Quarterly* XXVI (1962–63), 378; Mason Tung, "Samson Impatiens: A Reinterpretation of Milton's *Samson Agonistes*," *TSLL* IX (1968), 489; Balachandra Rajan, *The Lofty Rhyme: A Study of Milton's Major Poetry* (London, 1970), p. 142. For views of the close as wholly ironic, see Stanley Fish, "Question and Answer in *Samson Agonistes*," *Cricital Quarterly* XI (1969), 259; John Shawcross, "Irony as Tragic Effect: *Samson Agonistes* and the Tragedy of Hope," in *Calm of Mind*, ed. Joseph A. Wittreich, Jr. (Cleveland, 1971), pp. 295–96; Christopher Gross, "'His Uncontrollable Intent': Discovery as Action in *Samson Agonistes*," in *Milton Studies*, VII, ed. James D. Simmonds (Pittsburgh, 1975), pp. 49–50. For views of the close as partially ironic, see Joseph Summers, "The Movements of the Drama," in *The Lyric and Dramatic Milton*, ed. Joseph Summers (New York, 1965), pp. 173–74, and John Huntley, "A Reevaluation of the Chorus's Role in Milton's *Samson Agonistes*," *MP* LXIV (1966–67), 142–43. All quotations from Milton are taken from the modernized edition of Douglas Bush, *The Complete Poetical Works of John Milton* (Boston, 1965).

2. Summers, "Movements of the Drama," p. 173; Rajan makes a providential adaptation of the reading in *Lofty Rhyme*, p. 142.

3. Dennis Danielson, *Milton's Good God* (Cambridge, 1982), p. 64.

4. Arnold Stein, *Heroic Knowledge: An Interpretation of "Paradise Regained" and "Samson Agonistes"* (Minneapolis, 1957), p. 146.

5. Fish, "Question," 254; but Fish sees in the reversal Samson's decision to break free from the bondage of reason and the law.

6. See Danielson, *Good God*, pp. 58–91; but I doubt that Milton is dramatizing the doctrine of total depravity on which, Danielson demonstrates (pp. 70–75), Arminius agreed with the Calvinists.

7. Wilkes, "Interpretation," 375–76.

8. See Fish, "Question," 258. The argument of Irene Samuel, "*Samson Agonistes* as Tragedy," in *Calm of Mind*, ed. Wittreich, p. 252), is similar; but Fish makes a fideistic defense of Samson, while Samuel, a revisionist, condemns him.

9. Samuel, "Tragedy," p. 241; she is arguing that Samson's slaying of the Philistines is incompatible with Milton's belief that grace is denied to no one.

10. Samuel, "Tragedy," p. 251, argues, like Fish, that the officer could have been more imperious; Fish, "Question," 257, credits the officer with respect and solicitude. Assuming that Samson's guide at the temple is the boy of Judges, Fish argues that he is a sympathetic figure (259).

11. This reading is argued in my "The Schematic Design of the *Samson* Middle," in *Milton Studies*, XXII, ed. James D. Simmonds (Pittsburgh, 1986), pp. 233–54.

12. Low, *Blaze of Noon*, p. 32, adapts to Samson's praise a condemnatory typological argument by William Madsen, "From Shadowy Types to Truth," in *The Lyric and Dramatic Milton*, ed. Summers, p. 110.

13. Radzinowicz, *Towards "Samson,"* p. 62.

14. Fish, "Question," 259, believes the close ironic, and Samuel, "Tragedy," p. 250, believes the close horrific. Both elaborate Stein's attribution of barbaric hatred to the first Semichorus (*Heroic Knowledge*, p. 98). Samuel's concession, cited below, appears on page 247.

15. Huntley, "Reevaluation," 144, for example, dispraises Manoa's burial of Samson, while Helen Damico, "Duality and Dramatic Vision: A Structural Analysis of *Samson Agonistes*," in Milton Studies, XII, ed. James D. Simmonds (Pittsburgh, 1978), p. 108, a revisionist, finds evidence for the failure of Samson's mission in the effects of Manoa's tomb.

16. Shawcross cites Parker in "Irony," pp. 295–96, to belittle the Chorus; and cites Samuel in "Tragedy," p. 253, to belittle Samson.

17. Wilkes on marriage: "Interpretation," 369; on close: 378. Rajan on marriage: *Lofty Rhyme*, p. 135; on close: p. 131.

18. The charges are those of Stein, *Heroic Knowledge*, p. 193; Summers, "Movements," p. 164; and Gross, "'Uncontrollable Intent,'" 66–68.